Producing Places

A GUILFORD SERIES

Perspectives on Economic Change

Editors

Meric S. Gertler, *University of Toronto*   Peter Dicken, *University of Manchester*

Producing Places
RAY HUDSON

**Manufacturing Time: Global Competition
in the Watch Industry, 1795–2000**
AMY K. GLASMEIER

**The Regional World: Territorial Development
in a Global Economy**
MICHAEL STORPER

**Lean and Mean: Why Large Corporations Will Continue
to Dominate the Global Economy**
BENNETT HARRISON

Spaces of Globalization: Reasserting the Power of the Local
KEVIN R. COX, *Editor*

The Golden Age Illusion: Rethinking Postwar Capitalism
MICHAEL J. WEBBER and DAVID L. RIGBY

Work-*Place:* The Social Regulation of Labor Markets
JAMIE PECK

**Restructuring for Innovation: The Remaking of the U.S.
Semiconductor Industry**
DAVID P. ANGEL

**Trading Industries, Trading Regions: International Trade,
American Industry, and Regional Economic Development**
HELZI NOPONEN, JULIE GRAHAM, and ANN R. MARKUSEN, *Editors*

Producing Places

Ray Hudson

THE GUILFORD PRESS
New York   London

© 2001 The Guilford Press
A Division of Guilford Publications, Inc.
72 Spring Street, New York, NY 10012
www.guilford.com

Printed in the United States of America

This book is printed on acid-free paper.

Last digit is print number: 9 8 7 6 5 4 3 2 1

Library of Congress Cataloging-in-Publication Data

Hudson, Raymond.
  Producing places / by Ray Hudson.
    p.   cm. — (Perspectives on economic change)
  Includes bibliographical references and index.
  ISBN 1-57230-634-3 (pbk.)
  1. Production (Economic theory)   2. Marxian economics.
  3. Capitalism. I. Title. II. Series.
  HB241 .H83 2001
  338.5—dc21   00-066341

Preface

The seeds of the idea for this book date back to the late 1980s. I spent much of that decade finishing a research monograph on the relations between state policies and regional change in northeast England (Hudson, 1989a). For a variety of reasons (not least, length and production costs) I cut out a couple of planned theoretical review chapters, compressing discussion of those issues into a few pages in the Preface. One reviewer (I believe it was Gordon Clark) commented, not unreasonably, on the lack of a full theoretical review and statement of theoretical position. I decided to make amends by expanding what would have been in those two chapters into a book focused on how geographies of production relate to spatially uneven development within capitalism.

This volume builds upon the advances that Marxian political economy made during the 1970s and 1980s in comprehending the relationships between nature, place, space, and social relations in the organization of production and its geographies. Specifically, I aim to develop the most interesting insights further by drawing on various heterodox positions in the social sciences—such as evolutionary and institutional perspectives and regulationist approaches—that became prominent during the 1980s and even into the 1990s, thus helping to fill in some of the gaps and weaknesses in Marxian approaches. Ten years ago I sketched out a structure that largely remains intact in this book, but the contents within that structure have changed somewhat—a consequence of how radically both capitalist production and the geographies of capitalist economies have changed. It is no less interesting, of course, how economic geography and the social sciences have theorized about and sought to explain these changes.

Despite its obvious ambiguity, the title "Producing Places" captures two of the central themes that I want to explore here. First, it refers to those places in which production occurs (factories, offices, homes, and so on) and the ways in which these production sites fit into technical, social, and spatial divisions of labor between and within companies and other organizations. Second, it refers to the production of places defined by the intersection of the realms of use values and exchange values. In these places capital certainly seeks to produce profits via the exploitation of labor, but these are also places defined by the fact that people live their lives beyond their existence as the commodity labor-power, as socialized human beings with a variety of ties and attachments to other people and places. As such, places are always reproduced in precarious conditions, as the requirements of capital and people in their place can become dislocated. Consequently, the institutions and mechanisms enabling the reproduction of places and of production are a matter of some importance. In both cases—commodities and places—production involves the transformation of nature via human labor.

I initially made quite a bit of progress with the book, but then for a number of years writing ground to a halt, partly because of involvement in a number of collaborative research projects, mainly funded by the United Kingdom Economic and Social Research Council (ESRC), and involvement in the European Science Foundation's Regional and Urban Restructuring in Europe Program. These were extremely interesting in themselves and also provided ideas and materials that in due course became incorporated into this volume. But writing ceased mainly as a result of my becoming chairman of the Department of Geography at the University of Durham in England for five years. It was a great privilege to be chairman of such an outstanding department. However, it was also a very time-consuming commitment.

During those years I'd jot down ideas in notebooks, some derived from reading, others from talking to colleagues, participating in seminars and conferences, and so on. Some very good ideas also emerged from discussions with a succession of research students (most recently, Rich Bromiley, Jong Ho Lee, Tanya Gray, Lidia Greco, Per Lundquist, Mads Odgaard, Lei Shen, Amanda Smith, Delyse Springett, and John Thompson). Other sources of good ideas were the conversations about course projects with a succession of students who took a third-year "Geographies of Consumption and Production" option that I've taught with Mike Crang. Mike has proven to be a constant source of challenging and stimulating ideas over the period we've taught the course together. But for more than five years I did no serious writing on the book.

However, in 1997 I ceased to be chairman and then got an unpleasant surprise. I had been looking forward with growing anticipation to having time to write at length again, but when I finally got the time, I found that for several months I lost the knack of putting pen to paper (or fingers to keyboard), a problem I had never encountered before. I was on the verge of abandoning the project and will remain eternally grateful to Peter Dicken for persuading me not to do so. Over a couple of beers in Manchester one afternoon after an examiners' meeting, Peter told me (in slightly stronger terms than I recount here!) that packing it in would not be a sensible course of action and to stick with it. So I did and in 1998 got back into the swing of writing and finished the text. Subsequently, it has been revised in light of comments from Peter Dicken, Meric Gertler, and Peter Wissoker, to all of whom I am grateful for reading the full manuscript and making copious constructive comments that I found very helpful. Also, Ian Simmons kindly read a draft of Chapter 9, as I felt the need for guidance from an environmental expert in moving into what is still new territory for me. I am again very grateful to Ian for his help and advice.

While only one person's name appears on the front cover, a volume such as this is in many ways a collective project, as over the years ideas from conversations with others are appropriated and merged with your own, and—while published sources can be acknowledged—this sort of knowledge acquired via interaction and discussion is much more difficult to attribute and acknowledge. So, let me record my thanks to the following friends and colleagues: John Allen, Ash Amin, Huw Beynon, Angus Cameron, Kevin Cox, Mike Crang, Peter Dicken, Mick Dunford, Meric Gertler, Costis Hadjimichalis, Roger Lee, Gordon MacLeod, Anders Malmberg, Peter Maskell, Doreen Massey, Linda McDowell, Stan Metcalfe, Kevin Morgan, Martin Osterland, Joe Painter, Jamie Peck, Diane Perrons, Viggo Plum, David Sadler, Ian Simmons, Michael Storper, Mike Taylor, Nigel Thrift, Adam Tickell, Dina Vaiou, Paul Weaver, Sarah Whatmore, Allan Williams, and Peter Wissoker. In addition, I am very grateful to the Cartography Section of the University of Durham Department of Geography for converting my very rough sketches into clear diagrams and to Trudy Graham, who had the unenviable task of sorting out the manuscript. Finally, I want to acknowledge the support of the University of Durham via the award of a Sir Derman Christopherson Foundation Fellowship for 1997–1998, as this provided time for a sustained period of writing.

Finally, however, it is important to state that the usual disclaimers apply and that any remaining errors, faults, and omissions are solely my responsibility.

Contents

1. Prologue: Setting the Scene   1

    1.1.   Aims and Objectives   1

    1.2.   Defining Production and the Specificities of Capitalist Production   3

    1.3.   Five Basic Questions about Capitalist Production   4

    1.4.   Some Questions of Epistemology, Theory, and Method: Making the Case for a Marxian Point of Departure in Analyzing Production and Its Geographies   6

    1.5.   Summary and Conclusions   11

    1.6.   Notes   12

2. Placing Production in Its Theoretical Contexts   14

    2.1.   Introduction   14

    2.2.   Setting the Scene: Conceptualizing the Production Process within Capitalism via Some Basic Concepts from Marxian Political Economy   14

    2.3.   Varieties of Marxism and the Engagement between Economic Geography and Marxian Political Economy   26

    2.4.   Further Refining the Conception of Production as a Social Process   28

    2.5.   Concluding Comments: A Framework for Understanding Production and the Structure of the Remainder of This Volume   41

    2.6.   Notes   44

3. Capitalist Production, Societal Reproduction,   48
    and Capitalist States

    3.1. Introduction   48

    3.2. From a Theory of *the* Capitalist State and Toward a
          Theory of National States: Why Does the State Take
          the Form That It Does?   49

    3.3. National States, Economies, and Civil Societies   56

    3.4. National States and Social Regulation   59

    3.5. Crisis Tendencies, National State Regulation, and the
          Limits to Regulationist Approaches   61

    3.6. "Hollowing Out" and "Reorganization" of
          National States: From National State Regulation
          to More Complex Geographies of Regulation
          and Processes of Governance   68

    3.7. What Do National States Do to Ensure That
          Production Is Possible?   76

    3.8. Summary and Conclusions   91

    3.9. Notes   92

4. Recruiting Workers, Organizing Work   96

    4.1. Introduction   96

    4.2. Regulating Relationships between Capital and Labor:
          Collective Representation of the Interests of Capital
          and Labor "for Themselves"   97

    4.3. Competition in the Labor Market:
          Recruitment, Retention, and Resistance   107

    4.4. Organizing Work and the Labor Process   124

    4.5. Summary and Conclusions   140

    4.6. Notes   141

5. Company Connections: 143
    Competition and Cooperation, Part 1

    5.1. Introduction   143

    5.2. Competition within Existing Socio-Organizational
          and Technical Paradigms   144

5.3.   Competition via Creating New Technical
       and Organizational Paradigms of Production
       and New Products   147

5.4.   Competition via Market Creation and Marketing
       Innovation   162

5.5.   Market Structures, Competition, and the Processes
       of Globalization   166

5.6.   Competition via Learning and the Creation
       and Monopolization of Knowledge   169

5.7.   Summary and Conclusions   180

5.8.   Notes   181

6.   Company Connections: 186
     Competition and Cooperation, Part 2

6.1.   Introduction   186

6.2.   Make, Buy, or Network? Collaboration or Competition
       via the Market as Supply Strategies   187

6.3.   Boundaries of Firms and Networks: Closed and
       Bounded or Open and Discontinuous Spaces?   200

6.4.   Longer-Term Strategic Collaboration: Strategic
       Alliances and Joint Ventures   205

6.5.   Acquisitions and Mergers as Competitive
       Strategies   208

6.6.   Summary and Conclusions   213

6.7.   Notes   214

7.   Divisions of Labor: Cleavage Planes and Axes   217
     of Cooperation

7.1.   Introduction   217

7.2.   Organizing Workers, Dividing Workers: Trade Unions
       and the Institutions of Organized Labor   219

7.3.   Unity and Division between Groups of Workers:
       Dimensions of Simultaneous Unity and Division   224

7.4.   Summary and Conclusions   251

7.5.   Notes   252

8.   Production, Place, and Space   255

8.1.   Introduction: Place and Space   255

8.2.   Conceptualizing Places within the Spaces and
       Structures of Capitalism   256

8.3.   Producing Identities and Senses of and Attachments
       to Places   262

8.4.   Defending and (Re-)Presenting Places   268

8.5.   Reconciling the Tensions of Meaningful Place versus
       Profitable Space: State Policies, Social Cohesion, and
       Spatial Integration   272

8.6.   Varieties of Capitalist State Spatial Policies   276

8.7.   Summary and Conclusions   282

8.8.   Notes   283

9.   Materials Transformations: Production and Nature   286

9.1.   Introduction   286

9.2.   Production as a Process of Materials Transformation:
       Thermodynamics, the Laws of Conservation, and the
       Natural Limits to Production   287

9.3.   Production as a Process of Materials Transformation:
       The Materials Balance Principle, Industrial Metabolism,
       and the Social Limits to Thinking about Production
       in This Way   290

9.4.   Capitalist Relations of Production and the Production
       of Nature   294

9.5.   Capitalist Production as a Process of Deliberate
       Environmental Transformation   298

9.6.   Capitalist Production as a Process of Unintended
       Environmental Transformation and Pollution   303

9.7.   Sustainable Capitalist Production: But in What
       Sense Sustainable?   313

9.8.   Is Sustainable Production Possible within the Structural
       Limits Defined by Capitalist Social Relations?   321

9.9.   Summary and Conclusions   324

9.10. Notes   325

10. Postscript   330

10.1. Introduction   330

10.2. What Sort of Capitalist Economy, What Sort
of Geographies?   330

10.3. Challenges for the Future   334

10.4. The Final Frontier?   336

10.5. Note   338

References   339

Index   375

About the Author   386

1

Prologue
Setting the Scene

1.1. Aims and Objectives

The aims of this volume are twofold. First, it seeks to bring together and synthesize a wide range of materials about production in capitalist societies. It seeks to define production in general, to specify the key features of production that define it as specifically capitalist, and to explore the varieties of organizational forms that capitalist production and its geographies can take. It is important to emphasize from the outset that capital has always displayed considerable flexibility and ingenuity in seeking ways of organizing production profitably and places in which to do so. Second, this volume not only seeks to bring together this range of materials from a variety of social science disciplines but also to develop a particular perspective from which to understand production. This perspective is grounded and has its point of departure in Marxian political economy and recent developments therein. However, it then seeks further to elaborate how capitalist production is organized by drawing on work originating in a variety of other theoretical positions. These theoretical issues are discussed in greater detail in Chapter 2, but prior to that in the remainder of this chapter I discuss the definition of production, differing understandings of Marxian approaches, and some issues of epistemology, theory, and method in order to justify choosing one's starting point in Marxian political economy.

This emphasis upon the continuing salience of Marxian analysis may seem to some as deliberately—even unnecessarily—provocative. In an era of a "cultural turn" in human geography away from a concern with grand (and at times, any) theory and metanarrative and more generally of various "post-isms" (post-Fordism, post-structuralism, and so on) in the

1

social sciences, a return to Marxism may seem perverse. These various developments, after all, have at least in part been motivated by attempts to dismiss the Marxian tradition by interpreting it in a deterministic and totalizing fashion. It is for this reason that I want to make it clear at this stage why a Marxian[1] point of departure is necessary. Equally, I want to emphasize that I do not advocate deterministic and totalizing interpretations of Marx that claim to explain everything in capitalist societies from the basic concepts of capital. Indeed, there are many strands of the Marxian tradition, beginning with Marx himself, that seek explicitly to avoid such dangers, and yet this has often been willfully ignored by those who, for whatever reasons, wish to launch an assault on Marxism. But the gaps in Marxian analyses also provide reasons for exploring other approaches that can help fill in some of these lacunae, and some of the criticisms that have been made are helpful in identifying these and suggesting ways of filling them.

Marxian political economy nonetheless remains relevant, for it provides an insightful entry point and powerful analytic tools for understanding geographies of economies and production. Indeed, as capitalist social relationships have penetrated into new areas and become more firmly entrenched during the past three decades, it has become more rather than less relevant for understanding capitalist production. Thus, it is of utmost importance to stress that we live in a world in which capitalist social relations *are* dominant, the rationale for production *is* profit, class and class inequalities *do* remain, and that wealth distribution *does* matter. To make these points is not to argue that capitalism has no positive aspects or against a "cultural" inflection in political economy. Rather it is to remember that capitalism in an inherently uneven form of economic organization, marked by sharp inequalities of many sorts. Furthermore, while it can be cast in a variety of culturally and socially distinctive molds, there are definite limits that define these as varieties *of* capitalism and capitalist strategies for production and not as alternative *to* capitalism and capitalist production.

The approach that I seek to develop therefore begins with the recognition that capitalism is indeed with us and in varied forms. This approach encapsulates a particular way of understanding capitalist production and its geographies, with Marxian political economy as its point of departure. It does so on the grounds that this is essential in understanding the character of capitalist production.[2] This point of departure has three decisive advantages. First, it envisages the production process as simultaneously a labor process, a value-creating process, and a process of material transformations. Second, it facilitates the understanding of how production relations and exchange relations—in the "narrow" sense—relate to one another in the totality of the production process. Third, this point of departure permits analysis of how the production process relates to broader processes of social reproduction. As such, it considers how capitalist production relates to various noncapitalist forms and how the social, political, and institutional framework necessary for capitalist production to be possible is created.

Such an approach therefore builds upon work by geographers and other social scientists who began to engage with Marxian political economy during the 1970s. They did so in recognition of the limitations of the then dominant explanatory accounts, as part of a search for more powerful explanations of the structures and geographies of economies. I want to preserve the strengths that the rediscovery of Marxian approaches brought while seeking to address some of the ways in which they were problematic. This will involve two strategies to elaborate a framework that locates production within the context of relationships among the social, the natural, and the spatial. First, this framework entails consideration of various refinements that have occurred within Marxian political economy over the past two or so decades. Such changes have come about for two reasons. First, analysts recognized the limitations of existing Marxian formulations. Second, since capitalism is a shifting and slippery system, theory must be refined in response to such changes. However, in using Marxian concepts—as indeed those from any other theoretical framework—it is vital to ensure that they are used appropriately, that there is no attempt to overextend their application into inappropriate domains. In certain respects the framework therefore seeks to build upon Marxian analysis but also to go beyond it because there are conceptual gaps and lacunae within Marxian political economy. Consequently, and second, it involves consideration of other theoretical traditions in the social sciences that complement Marxian approaches and that can help elucidate the ways in which capitalist production can be made possible and in which it actually occurs. These other perspectives include evolutionary and institutional approaches in economics and sociology, theories of the state, regulation, and governance, and developments in modern social theory relating to such issues as agency, knowledge, and learning. The critical issues therefore relate to the ways in which Marxian analysis can be refined and deployed alongside complementary approaches within the social sciences, with the aim of offering a fuller understanding of processes of production and their geographies.

1.2. Defining Production and the Specificities of Capitalist Production

Production can be defined as the transformation, via human labor, of elements of the natural environment into products of use to people. These can be material products of varying complexity (a pair of shoes or a nuclear power station) or services (such as a haircut), recognizing that such services depend upon the availability of material products (for example, scissors to cut hair, a chair in which the customer can sit). Production thus involves different combinations of human labor, technologies, and tools and artifacts, as well as inputs directly from nature and the natural world. These mixes of inputs can be organized in different ways and vary among societies, times, and places.

Capitalist production is defined as a form of commodity production, with goods and services produced for the *purpose* of exchange, that is, for sale in markets. The totality of the capitalist production process extends from the appropriation of raw materials from nature to the consumption of produced commodities. For Marx, however, *the* transformative moment of crucial significance in the whole process is the moment of production itself, while recognizing that this moment is linked to all the others that constitute the totality of the process. For the moment of production is "the moment that allows capital to 'be' in the world at all" (Harvey, 1996, 94).

1.3. Five Basic Questions about Capitalist Production

Five basic questions may be asked about production: why does it take place, what is produced, how is production organized, where is production located, and how do the why, how, what, and where change over time? Within capitalist production "why" is unambiguous. The driving imperative is to create profits through producing commodities.[3] While limiting consideration to capitalist production, it is nevertheless necessary to consider the ways in which capitalist class relations of production relate to noncapitalist class relations. In addition we must inquire into the ways in which class relations relate to nonclass relations, such as those of ethnicity and gender. Not all production in capitalist societies is therefore directly shaped by the logic of production for exchange and profit. Capitalist economies thus may incorporate spaces of resistance to the logic of capital, built around a variety of social relationships.

"What" initially seems straightforward. At a given moment in time, companies produce different goods and services. The mix of products changes over time, however, reflecting product innovation and research and development (R&D) strategies, critical processes in the dynamism of production and competition between companies. As a result, understanding the "what" of production can become quite complicated. So too can understanding the "how" of production. There are different "models" of production through which the same commodity can be produced, encompassing different technologies and ways of organizing work. Not all commodities can be produced in all ways, however. There are both material and social limits to production. Changes in the "how" of production reflect, among other things, R&D in terms of process innovation. Changing ways of producing are not just a question of technical change in the narrow sense, however. They may also involve organizational innovation within workplaces and innovation in the institutional and regulatory forms through which production is made possible. Moreover, process innovation is often necessarily tied to product innovation, as new products require organizational and technical innovations. In both cases innovation is inextricably involved with issues of knowledge production, diffusion, and learning.

Sayer and Walker (1992, 112) give a sense of the resultant complexity of the totality of the production process:

> Production must be complemented by divisions of labour in the sphere of circulation . . . including distribution, communications and finance. Production systems in the full sense are thus much more than sequences of physical manipulation of materials; they are also sequences of research–development–manufacture, purchasing–manufacture–shipping, planning–financing–education, advertising–distribution–sales and the like, each of these involving feedback and interaction in a way that belies any simple notion of either sequential or parallel acts of labour.

"Where" production occurs seems a relatively more straightforward issue, centered on the construction of geographies of production and the ways in which companies seek to create and use spatial differentiation as part of competitive strategies. Recognizing a distinction between space and place introduces a greater complexity, however, focused on the ways in which (re)producing places created by socialized human beings with a wider agenda than simply profitable production relate to industrial (dis)investment. Various social groups may have radically different objectives in seeking to influence the production of space and places. As such, these are contested processes.

Moreover, what, how, when, and where are related. Where cannot be understood independently of what and how. Conversely, we cannot understand what and how without taking account of where. The spatial dimension is integral to decisions about production, not something to be taken into account only after what and how have been decided, and this must be reflected in the ways in which production is analyzed and theorized. There are, however, no simple and necessary one-to-one deterministic relations between where, what, and how. Rather, there is a range of possibilities, the realization of which depends upon the interplay between systemic processes, corporate strategies, and the specificities of places (Massey and Meegan, 1982). For example, there may be radical changes in what and how without altering where; there is no necessary change in the geography of production because of product and/or process innovation. Conversely, there may be radical changes in where without altering what or how: that is, a "spatial fix" to a new geography to preserve an "old" combination of products and methods of production. Then again, there may be radical shifts in what, how, and where simultaneously; or there may a switch to new sectors, either via organic growth or via acquisition and merger, accompanied (sunk costs permitting) by divestment from existing sectors of activity. This dynamism means that the objects of analysis are historical geographies rather than frozen geographies of production.

1.4. Some Questions of Epistemology, Theory, and Method: Making the Case for a Marxian Point of Departure in Analyzing Production and Its Geographies

The variety of possible outcomes that the organization and geographies of production can assume necessitates understanding why some possibilities are realized but not others, and why those that *are* realized exist in the particular ways that they do. Put another way, we need to comprehend the variety of possible relationships between form and process and construct an "adequate" conceptualization of the underlying social processes and of their relation to spatial differences and differences between places. What, however, defines "adequacy" in this regard? And how does the chosen point of departure—Marxian political economy—satisfy the two criteria, conceptual and explanatory "adequacy"?

Answering such questions is, admittedly, not a straightforward task. First, it is now generally accepted that we have entered an era of "epistemological relativism and methodological pluralism" (Gregory et al., 1994, 5), in which truth claims about knowledge, the validity of theories, and ways of generating valid knowledge are regarded with a degree of skepticism that was not typical of the earlier era (Clark and Wrigley, 1995, 207). Accepting the multiplicity of worlds and ways of world making does not invalidate the aim of creating theoretical frameworks, but it does indicate the need to be critically aware of the limits to theoretical claims. Methodological and conceptual pluralism is, however, "no bad thing" (Ward and Almas, 1997, 626). A continuing constructive dialogue between different perspectives, informed by a heightened sense of experimentation and critical self-appraisal, is clearly preferable to a continued search for a single new all-encompassing paradigm. While there are certainly dangers in an indiscriminate theoretical eclecticism (Fincher, 1983), a search for all-encompassing paradigms is doomed to failure. As Gregory (1994, 105) emphasizes, however, the issue is not to dispense with metanarratives (plural) but rather carefully to attend "to what it is they put in place and, equally, what it is they exclude." The point therefore is not to reject Marxism as a metanarrative but rather to be aware of the shortcomings and weaknesses within it and to seek to remedy them. Harvey (1996, 9), for instance, argues for "trying to re-build Marxian meta-theory in such as way as to incorporate an understanding of spatio-temporality (and socio-ecological issues) into its frame." There are evident dangers in seeking to read it as a totalizing system. There are, however, at least equal dangers in accepting critiques that seek to represent it in that way so as to be able to criticize and dismiss it. Since no single theoretical system can provide a complete and satisfactory set of answers, we must find ways of living—critically and creatively—with some degree of theoretical dissonance. Nevertheless, some theoretical approaches undoubtedly have greater explanatory power than others. Not all theories are equally useful. What criteria, then, should determine which theoretical perspective should be accorded priority?

Second, then, what defines an "adequate" theory? Drawing on ideas from critical realism, an adequate conceptualization needs to steer a path between the dangers of two fallacies: the ontic (the notion that the world determines our representations of it) and the epistemic (the notion that our cognitive lenses wholly determine how we see the world; Bhaskar, 1989). These fallacies specify what to avoid rather than what more positively is needed to achieve adequacy, however. In epistemological terms, critical realism argues that an adequate theory must reveal necessary causal relationships and mechanisms and recognize the existence of a variety of relatively autonomous causal structures (not just those of the social relations of capital: Sayer, 1984).[4] As such, an adequate theory cannot simply be mimetic, as these causal mechanisms and processes are real but not visible. Consequently, devising theory requires an active process of construction. By these criteria, Marxian political economy is an adequate theory for it offers a powerful description of the key causal processes and inner mechanisms of capitalist production and capital circulation, making cognitively visible the real, but otherwise invisible, social relations constituting capitalism.[5]

Within a critical realist perspective, the realization of causal powers is contingently dependent upon the ways in which these factors come together in spatially and temporally specific contexts; it thus depends upon the specific causal structures and local circumstances of each particular time-place. Such a position is broadly consistent with the conception of tendential laws within Marxian political economy, with empirically observed trends reflecting the relative weights of tendencies and countertendencies (some even located in noncapitalist social structures endowed with causal powers). Whether a particular set of causal powers is realized in empirically observable form (and if it is, the extent to which it is) depends upon the balance between such tendencies and countertendencies, both in the form of competing structures of causal powers and particular local circumstances. An important corollary of such a view of an adequate conceptualization is that the explanatory power of a theory is defined in terms of a description of causal structures and mechanisms. The criterion for judging the "goodness" of a theory is therefore the extent to which it aids interpretation and understanding of *process* rather than predictive power per se.[6]

Seen through the lens of critical realism, Marxian political economy provides a powerful point of departure for analyzing production and its geographies. It cannot, however, provide answers to all questions about production. There are three possible responses to this recognition of the limits of Marxian theories. One response is informed by a poststructuralist critique that there are no coherent sovereign individuals but only a world of difference and socially constituted identities (Barnes, 1998, 96). Consequently, it seeks to reject Marxian political economy on the grounds (among other things) of "essentialism," that is, it is seen to offer a totalizing account of capitalism and its geographies. However, as Thrift (1994a, 213–214) remarks, while nowadays Marx's work sometimes seems to be dangerously close to a totalizing system, many versions of Marxism after Marx have sought "to escape any taint of totality." Marx himself was at pains to insist that no discourse can totalize history (and, one can add, historical geographies).[7] Furthermore, descending into a poststructural world of difference raises serious difficulties of both explanation and politics. For example, there are great dangers in accepting poststructural views in which "anything goes" and that are "blind to the systemic imperatives of power and money in capitalist societies" (Harvey, 1996, 357–358).

A second response to recognizing the limits of Marxian theories accepts aspects of the poststructural critique but responds to it in ways that seek to retain a role for reformulated versions of key Marxian concepts. The ways are deeply problematic, however. A prominent example of this tendency is Gibson-Graham (1996, 1997). The essence of Gibson-Graham's critique is that economic geographers analyzing capitalist economies have focused attention solely upon the key social structural relations that define them *as* capitalist.[8] However, the Marxian concept of social formation precisely allows for a multiplicity of class and other social relations, but this seems to slip by unnoticed. Nevertheless, Gibson-Graham goes on to argue for an "anti-essentialist" but nonetheless Marxian redefinition of these concepts. One implication of this, however, is that she thereby denies that there are *any* necessary conditions or relations defining particular types of society.[9] In her eagerness to respond to poststructuralist critics and deconstruct and complicate basic Marxian concepts, she (no doubt inadvertently) loses her specific analytic cutting edge.[10]

A more helpful perspective, drawing on critical realism, acknowledges that there are necessary causal structures that define particular types of society but that societies encompass multiple causal structures, not all of which in this sense are necessary and not all of which are equally powerful. Moreover, in any case the causal powers of such structures can only be contingently realized in specific time-space contexts. Consequently, the causal powers inherent in the social relationships of capital may be preeminent and must be present in the sense that they define capitalist societies *as* capitalist. However, it does not follow that they have a determinate (let alone deterministic) influence on each and every occasion in shaping the geographies of capitalist economies. While wishing to avoid an interpretation of capitalist social relations as totalizing, it is equally important to recognize that there are broad social structural relations (of class, gender, and ethnicity, for example) that have determinate effects. This is "most especially" the case "if at the same time their multiplicity and contingency are recognized." Recognition of such broad structures "is not the same as the commitment to, or the adoption of, a metanarrative view of history. None of the structures . . . need to be assumed to have any inexorability in their unfolding . . . outcomes are always uncertain, history and geography have to be made" (Massey, 1995a, 303–304).

A third response therefore begins with a rejection of totalizing interpretations of Marxian approaches. Marxian political economy is seen as offering a valuable window onto the worlds of production and economies and their geographies and to provide a way of constructing a structured but nondeterministic and admittedly partial account of those worlds and their geographies. It specifies defining processes and key causal mechanisms but does not claim to grasp and account for all aspects of production in capitalist societies, let alone offer an overarching general and deterministic account of everything about those societies and their varied geographies. It reveals much, but by no means all, of the explanation for such geographies of production. It recognizes the limits to (existing) Marxian approaches but seeks to build upon their strengths and address these limitations, in two ways.

The first of these relates to developments and refinements within a Marxian framework. Given the marked changes in the character of capitalism over the past 150 or so years, it would be surprising if Marx's own analyses were able to deal with all of capitalism's contemporary complexities. Consequently, scholars working in and from a Marxian tradition have sought to accommodate such changes (for example, in the significance of meanings; Lash and Urry, 1994; Thrift, 1994a; Williams, 1989b). Building on this, we need to map a middle way between a too foundational and too authoritative modern Marxism and an after-Marxist critique "which, its important insights notwithstanding, has yet to create a coherent explanatory account of capitalism out of the ruins of that critique" (Castree, 1999, 154). The second strand involves gazing on production through other theoretical lenses, creating less abstract intermediate-level theoretical constructs relating to processes and mechanisms that help explain *how* production and its geographies are organized in varying ways. Such concepts need to be interposed *between* structural relations and value categories and empirically observable geographies of production. In these ways more powerful explanations of production and its varied organizational forms and geographies can be constructed.

The prioritizing of one theoretical framework over others cannot be defended simply within the terms of the theory itself or on grounds of the greater elegance or explanatory power of one theory relative to others, however. Justification of a theoretical position inevitably involves reference to the assumptions upon which the theory is founded and the values and norms in which it is grounded. Just as history and geography have to be made, so too do theories that seek to comprehend these processes have to be constructed. Theory making is a process of construction and as such is doubly contingent—both upon the predicament in which we find ourselves and upon the theoretical context in which we work. Constructing theory is a process of persuasion and argument both within and outside academia, and so one's choice of theoretical framework is to a degree always a political choice.

A theory of capitalist production that is "adequate" in relation to analytic and explanatory criteria must both reveal key causal mechanisms and processes and be sensitive to the specificities of time and space in the ways in which capitalist social relationships are constituted and reproduced. It is precisely the need to grasp this variability that necessitates going beyond a structural analysis of capital. It is necessary to understand the ways in which individual and collective agency is both enabled and constrained by structures and at the same time has the effect (sometimes intended, often not) of helping reproduce them. In this sense, this is a call for a version of "modest theory" (Thrift, 1996a, 30–47). He has called for the development of a "non-representational" version of "modest theory" that eschews claims to universal validity and that is grounded in an "ontological and epistemological stance [that] might be termed a kind of historicism, in that it stresses the historical and geographical variability of systems of social practices" (p. 33). In this Thrift lays heavy emphasis upon the importance of agency and has little to say about structure—indeed is deeply suspicious of admitting structure. In contrast, the approach advanced here seeks to retain a sense of structural determination (though not determinism) and to understand the ways in which the social structural relations of capital are reproduced via intentional and unintentional effects of actions. Furthermore, the version of theory for which I wish to argue is also a critical theory that has specific sociopolitical aims. Such a critical theory must revive a "certain kind of Marxism, but one neither so modern nor so post-Marxist that it is non-Marxist" (Castree, 1999, 154). It is a theory that seeks to represent the world in particular ways with a view to changing it in particular ways politically. By bringing critical concepts such as exploitation or value into view theoretically, the terms of political debate and the possibilities of public discussion may (but not necessarily will) be altered for the better. So too may the possibilities for progressive change in the organization of production and the economy, for these are not simply analytic issues but also moral, political, and normative ones. As Lovibond (1989, 22)[11] puts it, "If there can be no systematic political approach to questions of power, wealth and labour, how can there be any effective challenge to a social order which distributes its benefits and burdens in a systematically uneven way?"

1.5. Summary and Conclusions

In this chapter I have specified a definition of production, indicated what is specifically capitalist about capitalist production, and set out some broad questions about production and its organization and geographies for further investigation. Furthermore, and crucially, I have sought to justify grounding an analysis of production in Marxian political economy while acknowledging the limits to such a starting point and the need to transcend them. No single (meta)theory can satisfactorily deal with the range of issues posed by seeking to understand production (let alone the totality of economic and social life). Even so, despite living in an era of "epistemological relativism and methodological pluralism," it remains the case that some theories have more explanatory power than others. The criteria for theory that is "adequate" in explanatory terms were defined by reference to critical realism. In the next chapter, different theoretical approaches to the understanding of production and its geographies are considered at greater length, to help clarify the basic analytic building blocks to be used later in analyzing the organization and geographies of production.

1.6. Notes

1. Production can be conceptualized in various ways (Ricardian, Marxian, neoclassical, evolutionary, and institutional, for example), each distinguished by the questions it asks, the issues it seeks to investigate, and the methods and concepts that it deploys to do so.

2. There are various forms of political-economic organization (feudalism, capitalism, and state socialism, for example). The rationale for production varies among them. Consequently, it is necessary to distinguish what is specific about production within capitalism.

3. The rationale for production would clearly be different under the sway of other dominant social relationships—for example, satisfying needs or maximizing output.

4. For an analysis of the relationships between critical realism and Marxism, see Roberts (1999). The point is not that Marxism and critical realism are synonymous. In some respects the epistemological and ontological claims of Marxism differ from those of critical realism. However, in certain key respects Marxian methodology resonates with critical realism, and that is the point made here.

5. Revealing such mechanisms allows other questions to be raised, for example, about more progressive forms *of* capitalist production; second, beyond that, alternatives to capitalist production may be suggested by identifying the limits to capital and the social and natural limits to capitalist production in its current forms.

6. Although a "good" theory could certainly yield predictive insights in many circumstances, these should not be the criterion on which the theory should be judged. Moreover, failure to predict would not be a criterion for abandoning the theory.

7. The implication of Thrift's comments is, of course, that Marxism can be read as a totalizing discourse by those who—for whatever reason—wish to see it as that. Equally, it is not alone in its exposure to this danger.

8. As such, their critique is a perverse one. It ignores the extent to which economic geographers of a Marxian persuasion (among others) have acknowledged the significance of noncapitalist class relations and link between class and nonclass relations (including those of ethnicity, gender, and territory) in the constitution of the geographies of capitalist societies.

9. If the charge leveled by Gibson-Graham is that a focus upon capitalist class relations is misplaced because they are no longer dominant and defining, then clearly the object of analysis is no longer capitalist society (although it is unclear as to what it is that has replaced it). While I agree with the commendable wish for a more humane economy guided by different social relationships, simply wishing away the realities of capitalist power, material and discursive, is not a very helpful step toward attaining such a goal.

10. Revealingly, Gibson-Graham (1996, 5) admits to "constructing . . . [a Marxian] straw man [*sic*]" as a way of clarifying the distinctiveness of her own position. While she is by no means alone in caricaturing Marxism in order to at-

tack it, such an approach is less than helpful. Her position on class is further discussed in section 2.2 and on divisions within the working class in "Industry, Occupation, and Intraclass Differentiation" (in section 7.3).

11. Lovibond was in fact arguing that feminists should be wary of postmodern approaches that limit themselves to a concern with the veracity of "local truths" in a context of a social world marked by deep gender divisions, but the point has equal validity in relation to other forms of systematic inequality within capitalist societies.

2

Placing Production
in Its Theoretical Contexts

2.1. Introduction

The starting point for this chapter is the attempt by geographers in the 1950s and 1960s to try to explain and understand the spatial patterns of the economy, the structure of the space-economy. In so doing, they drew upon the orthodoxies of neoclassical economics. This approach was certainly an advance upon the economic geography of preceding decades, which had been preoccupied (like human geography in general) with description of spatial pattern. Nevertheless, it was based on an incomplete and unsatisfactory conception of the social processes that generated the spatial patterns of economic activities and soon led other geographers to search for more powerful explanations. This led economic geographers to explore Marxian political economy, bringing considerable advances in understanding but equally not without problems of its own. These limitations led to attempts to refine Marxian analysis to produce a more sophisticated historical-geographical materialism and also to the exploration of other, and complementary, theoretical traditions in the social sciences. These are explored in turn in this chapter.

2.2. Setting the Scene: Conceptualizing the Production Process within Capitalism via Some Basic Concepts from Marxian Political Economy

From Locational Analysis to Marxian Political Economy

After a period in which description was the primary focus of geographical scholarship, the 1950s saw a reawakening of interest in explanation and theorization within (among other things) economic geography. The rediscovery of economic location theories in the works of von Thunen, Weber, and Lösch led to a convergence of interests between some economic geographers and emergent regional scientists. This centered on a search for general explanatory statements about the spatial structure of the economy (Chisholm, 1962; Haggett, 1965; Isard, 1956). Refocusing concerns from description of the unique to explanation of more general classes of events and spatial patterns was a very important and radical break. On the other hand, the ways in which explanation was sought soon came to be seen as deeply problematic. At one level, this involved conflating explanation with prediction, that is, predictive accuracy became the measure of explanatory power. At another level, there were profound problems associated with an approach that sought to deduce equilibrium spatial patterns on the basis of restrictive assumptions about the natural environment, human knowledge, and the character of social processes.

The point of raising questions about the lack of realism in these assumptions is not simply to criticize location theories on that score. Rather, it is to emphasize that such assumptions were both a precondition for and a symptom of an impoverished and incomplete view of the social processes of the economy, of the economy understood *as* social process. Assumptions of static equilibrium deny the fact that economic processes are chronically in a state of dynamic disequilibrium, set on open-ended and unknown trajectories of change rather than inevitably and mechanistically circling around a point of static equilibrium. As such, they neglect the social construction, reproduction, and regulation of markets as institutions. Assumptions of perfect knowledge equally deny the fact that economic decisions are always made in a condition of ignorance. Assumptions of the environment as an isotropic plane ignore the grounding of the economy in nature and the chronically uneven character of economic development. They also reduce the significance of spatial differentiation to variations in transport (and sometimes other production) costs within a prior given space. The net result is that, while such approaches placed questions of explanation firmly back on the agenda of economic geographers, they did so in a way that was based upon unhelpful abstractions. Consequently, these resulted in inadequate theory, which failed to grasp the essential character of the key processes that produced geographies of economies.[1]

One response to the perceived problems of location theories was that of behavioral geographers. They developed their critique on the grounds that the behavioral assumptions upon which such theories were based were untenable in an economy that exists in real space and time (Pred, 1967). Behavioral geographers therefore argued the need to investigate what people actually did know, how they came to acquire this knowledge, and what locations they knew about, rather than assuming that they knew everything and about all locations of relevance to a particular type of behavior. Concepts such as "bounded rationality" (Simon, 1959) recognized that people could not in practice know everything while continuing to privilege individual actors and their knowledges.[2] Consequently, behavioral geographers began to conceptualize environmental knowledge in terms of "mental maps" or "cognitive maps" and, drawing on strands of psychology, to seek ways of measuring what people knew (Pocock and Hudson, 1978). Within the context of geographies of production, such approaches focused on the knowledge that key corporate decision makers possessed about alternative locations in an attempt to explain why economic activities were located in some places rather than in others. As a result, they yielded at best a partial and imperfect grasp of the relations between knowledge and production and its spatial organization. Such behavioral approaches typically amounted to little more than descriptive accounts of the locational strategies and behavior of particular firms.[3] Having set out to refine an explanatory approach, behavioral geographers unfortunately slipped into the descriptive trap that neoclassical location theories had set out to escape. As a result, the behavioral approach soon became marginalized. While often interesting in themselves, behavioral studies did little to address the explanatory weaknesses of location theories, but in abandoning them, economic geographers also pushed important questions of agency and action from the research agenda for a decade or so.[4]

The limitations of both location theories and behavioral critiques of them led economic geographers to search for more powerful conceptualizations of the processes that generated geographies of economies. In this, they established closer links with the social sciences. The social sciences themselves were undergoing significant changes in approach, however. Their established orthodoxies were increasingly seen as incapable of explaining the problematic character of capitalist development. As the long postwar boom spluttered to a halt, uneven development became more marked, and it became clear that poverty and inequality were again on the increase and that the limitations of the orthodox nostrums of the social sciences were becoming increasingly visible. Faced with this, the social sciences began to rediscover the Marxian heritage, as well as exploring other heterodox positions. In their search for more powerful explanations, economic geographers also began to engage with these strands of thought and in doing so became more involved in debates with other social scientists. Increasingly, they turned to Marxian political economy as a source of theoretical inspiration (Carney et al., 1977; Damette, 1980; Harvey, 1973, 1982; Läpple and van Hoogstraten, 1980; Smith, 1984). Marxian political economy offered powerful concepts of structure, of the social structural relations that defined particular types of societies (Harvey, 1982; Smith, 1984), and offered a powerful challenge to the spatial fetishism[5] (Carney et al., 1976) of locational analysis and spatial science. In the following sections, therefore, some basic concepts of Marxian political economy are briefly set out, as these are foundational concepts in terms of understanding capitalist production.[6]

Commodity Production, Values, and Modes of Production

In general, production involves transforming elements of the natural world into useful objects through the application of human labor. As production evolved historically, there was a gradual shift toward the creation of a social surplus beyond the needs of the immediate producers. This enabled the transition to systems of production for exchange, which provided crucial preconditions for the subsequent emergence of capitalist relations of production. First, the permanent production of a surplus and the development of a social division of labor provided the necessary economic conditions to allow (but not determine or guarantee) the emergence of social classes. Second, the development of money as a specific commodity to facilitate exchange was critical (Smith, 1984, 35–47) because the use of money as an individualized and exclusionary form of social power is a central feature of capitalism (Harvey, 1996, 236). Third, the transition to production for exchange necessarily involved the alienation of both consumer and producer from the product, and this had considerable significance in relation to the creation of markets and patterns of consumption and to the organization and control of the labor process. Not all production for exchange is capitalist, however. What then is specific about *capitalist* commodity production that distinguishes it from production in other types of society and from production for exchange in general?

One way to begin to answer this question is to draw upon a quite abstract conception of social and economic structure—the Marxian concept of mode of production. This seeks to catch the essence of particular types of economic organization, characterizing these in terms of specific combinations of forces of production (artifacts, machinery and "hard" technologies, tools—in short, the means of production) and social relations of production. In the capitalist mode of production *the* key defining social relationship is the class structural one between capital and wage labor. This is a dialectical and necessary[7] relationship because capital and labor are mutually defining; the existence of one presupposes the existence of the other. Capital needs to purchase labor-power in order to set production in motion since living labor is the only source of new value (surplus-value) created in production, while labor needs to sell its labor-power for a wage in order to survive and reproduce itself. What therefore is specific about the capitalist mode of production and distinguishes it from other forms of economic organization is that it is structured around the wage relation, with labor-power bought and sold in a market like any other commodity. The key point, however, is that labor-power is *not* like any other commodity—and in that recognition lies the key to understanding much else about the organization of production and geographies of economies (a point developed in the next section).

Commodities simultaneously possess attributes as use values and as exchange values. As materialized human labor, they have qualities that people find useful and, as such, use values. These use value characteristics of commodities reflect the concrete aspects of labor, the fact that labor is private and specific. At the same time, labor within capitalist relations of production is also abstract labor, universal, social, and general insofar as it defines the exchange values of commodities on world markets (Postone, 1996). Abstract labor is "a remarkable thing," simultaneously a social relationship, a measure of value, a determinate magnitude (socially necessary labor time), causally efficacious and invisible yet real (Castree, 1999, 149). In the capitalist mode of production the exchange value of a commodity is defined as the quantity of socially necessary labor time[8] required to produce it. Abstract labor and socially necessary labor time are therefore central to understanding the rationale of capitalist production, for the driving rationale of a capitalist economy is production for exchange and profitable sale through markets, that is, the production of exchange values.[9] Capitalist production is thus organized with the *purpose* of sale in markets.[10] Production therefore finds its rationale in, and is socially validated ex-post facto by, market exchange and the successful sale of goods and services.[11] This raises a key question, further discussed in succeeding sections, namely, how do qualitatively different use values become exchanged as quantitatively equivalent exchange values?

Capitalist Production, Accumulation, and the Circuit of Productive Industrial Capital

In the exchange sequence $C_1–M–C_2$ a given amount of money is used to purchase one commodity—for example, a pair of shoes—and the seller of the first commodity then uses that money to buy another and different commodity—say, a radio. Money therefore functions as a medium of exchange, allowing the quantitatively equal exchange of two qualitatively different commodities. Now consider a rather different sequence, $M–C–M'$ in which $M' > M$. Clearly, in this case money is not simply functioning as a medium of exchange. In fact, in this case money capital is being advanced to make more money, to make profits. This therefore raises a seminal question: where does this profit come from? It cannot, in a systematic and systemic sense, originate in the process of circulation—precisely because the exchange process involves the exchange of equivalents via market transactions carried out between formally free and equal agents. It can only originate, then, in the process of production itself and the way that this is structured within capitalist relations of production—hence Marx's emphasis on the centrality of this moment in the totality of the production process.[12]

Rather than being seen as a series a linear exchanges, however, capitalist production can more usefully be thought of as a continuous circuit, encompassing three analytically distinct yet integrally linked circuits: commodity capital, money capital, and productive industrial capital (see Figure 2.1).[13] The circuit of productive industrial capital provides key insights to understanding the creation of surplus-value, of profits, and the dynamism of geographies of capitalist production.[14] Capitalist production is simultaneously a labor process, producing material use values, and a valorization process, reproducing value and producing surplus value.

The circuit of productive industrial capital requires that capital be first laid out in money form to purchase the necessary means of production (tools, machinery, manufactured inputs, and raw materials)[15] and labor-power. Labor-power and the means of production are then brought together in the production process, under the supervision of the owners of capital or their managers and representatives. Two things happen in the moment of production. First, existing use values, in the form of raw materials, machinery, and manufactured components, suitably revalued according to their current cost of production, are transferred to new commodities. Second, surplus-value is created. This augmentation of value is possible precisely because labor-power is *the* unique commodity, for capital purchases not a fixed quantity of labor but rather the workers' capacity to work for a given period of time. During this time workers create commodities that embody more value than was contained in the money capital used to purchase their labor time. This difference in value is the surplus-value, the additional new value created in production, which is realized in money form as profits on the successful sale of the commodity, along with existing values transferred in the production process. Thus, the difference between the amount of money capital advanced at the start of the round of production and that realized at the end of it is equivalent to the difference in the value of commodities at the beginning and the end of the round. This is critical in understanding the rationale and dynamism of capitalist production. It also emphasizes that the totality of production involves more than simply the transformation of materials to produce goods or services. It also involves a myriad of other activities associated with transportation, distribution, and sale,[16] as well as the final consump-

(A)

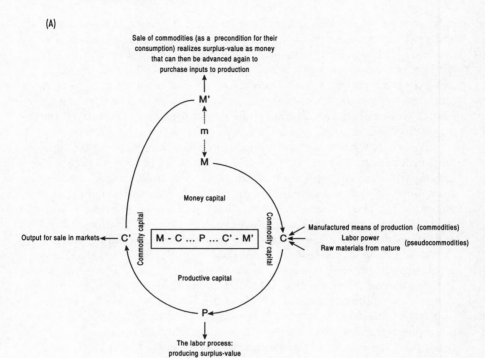

(B)

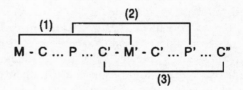

1 The circuit of money capital : M - C ... P ... C' - M'
2 The circuit of produce capital : P ... C' - M' - C' ... P'
3 The circuit of commodity capital : C' - M' - C' ... P' ... C'

FIGURE 2.1. Circuits of capital.

tion of goods and services and the meanings with which they are endowed, the identities that they help create and form.[17]

In summary, thinking of production in terms of the circuit of productive industrial capital foregrounds the fact that commodity production and consumption involve the creation and realization of value. Commodity production is therefore inherently geographical in a double sense. First, the material transformation of natural materials is predicated on relationships between people and nature, a social-natural dialectic. Second, commodity production and consumption involve the movement of commodities between various sites of production and consumption as they flow around the circuit of capital, a sociospatial dialectic. In this way, space and places are integral to the biography of commodities. The circuit of productive capital thus involves complex relationships between people, nature, places, and space in processes of value creation and realization.

Conceptualizing production as occurring in rounds, as successive journeys around the circuit of industrial capital, raises further interesting questions. In particular, what happens to the money equivalent of the newly produced surplus-value at the end of one journey around the circuit? This is of critical importance in understanding the processes of competitiveness, economic growth, and capital accumulation, both at the level of the individual firm and of capital in general. Two limit cases can be established. First, it could all be very conspicuously consumed on luxuries by the capitalist class. In this case the next round of production would begin with the advance of the same amount of capital as the previous one. This would define a situation of the simple reproduction of capital. Second, all of it could be used to increase the scale of production in a situation of expanded reproduction. This would correspond to the maximum possible rate of growth for that unit of capital or, if the whole of a capitalist economy were the object of analysis, then of that economy. In practice, expanded reproduction usually involves rather less than this maximum feasible amount of capital being advanced. The temporal fluctuations in this amount help define the cyclical variations of the "business cycle" around a longer-term secular growth trend of expanded accumulation.

The conditions necessary for sustainable expanded reproduction (economically as opposed to ecologically) are interesting and important. They also have different implications depending upon whether the focus is upon an individual company or capitalist production overall (Mattick, 1971). An individual company is subject to contradictory pressures. On the one hand, it wishes to minimize its own input costs. On the other hand, it wishes to maximize its sales and profits. Maximization of the latter depends, however, upon purchases by other companies (seeking to minimize their costs) and final consumers (whose wages may represent a significant proportion of other firms' costs of production). As such, a capitalist economy is reproduced via contradictory processes; it travels along an uncertain and crisis-prone trajectory. Marx made this abundantly clear in Volume 2 of *Capital* in setting out the conditions under which smooth long-term growth would be possible. In reality these are impossible conditions to meet, even in an economy conceptualized in very abstract terms as one of Departments 1 and 2 (that is, a two-sector economy, one sector producing the means of production, the other producing consumer goods). This knife-edge movement along a crisis-prone trajectory directs attention to three things: first, to competition between companies as the motor of industrial dynamism (considered more fully in Chapters 5 and 6); second, to the role of the state in managing this crisis-prone trajectory and in ensuring that capitalist production does not collapse under the weight of its internal contradictions (discussed in Chapter 3); and third, to the varied ways in which production is made possible within the confines of the social relations of capitalism (a recurrent theme in what follows).

Making the Transition to Less Abstract Concepts: From Values to Prices, Modes of Production to Social Formations

The concept of the capitalist mode of production is a high-level abstraction designed to reveal the essential defining relationship of a capitalist economy and not to describe social reality as experienced by people living in capitalist societies. The concept of social formation moves matters one step nearer to the experienced reality, as it denotes the ways in which capitalist and noncapitalist, class and nonclass, social relationships come together in a particular time-space context.[18] This creates conceptual space for different forms of capitalism, allowing that capitalist relations of production may be socially and culturally constituted in varying ways. Structural conditions and limits defining the parameters of capitalism and of capitalist production and its geographies are not, however, pre-given, "natural," and a product of unchangeable natural processes but are socially produced by human actions, discursive and material. People are not simply passive "bearers of structures" or, indeed, "bearers of discourse,"[19] but rather pursue their own projects and courses of action within particular institutional arrangements. Such actions have both intended and unintended consequences, however, and so variable relationships to structural reproduction. The ways in which such structural limits are socially (re)produced is therefore a pivotal issue. Consequently, this led to increased attention to the role of the state in capitalist societies in ensuring the reproduction of these relationships. For some, the state nonproblematically met the "needs of capital" so as to ensure societal reproduction. Such State Monopoly Capital formulations (Baran and Sweezy, 1968) were quickly seen to be too simplistic, however. Crisis theories focused upon the problems encountered by capitalist states in seeking to ensure the successful reproduction of crisis-prone capitalist economies and societies (Habermas, 1976; O'Connor, 1973; Offe, 1975a). Another strand of state theory sought to derive the existence of the state in a political sphere, formally separated from the economy, from the fundamental characteristics of the capitalist mode of production (Holloway and Picciotto, 1978). Subsequently, however, seeking to derive a theory of *the* capitalist state was revealed as a flawed project, and the focus shifted to constructing an historical geographical theory of capitalist *states*, cast at a somewhat lower level of abstraction.[20]

Another implication of shifting to a lower level of abstraction is a recognition that the two-class model of capital and labor was developed for particular purposes—specifically, to clarify the core class structural relationships that define the capitalist mode of production and the terrain on which the struggle over the future of that class structure is fought. A more differentiated conception of class is required in seeking to grapple with actual geographies of economies and production, however, one that recognizes the existence of "contradictory locations within class relations, mediated class locations, temporally structured class locations, objectively ambiguous class locations, dualistic class locations." This suggests "a picture of multiple possible coalitions of greater or lesser likelihood, stability and power contending over a variety of possible futures" (Wright, 1989, 348; see also Wright, 1978, 1985). The analytical consequence of acknowledging this variety is that concepts of class must be specified at appropriate levels of abstraction, given the task at hand. For an investigation of epochal changes in class structure the two-class model might well be ideal, but for investigating finer grained changes in geographies of production, divisions of labor, and class structures within capitalism a more nuanced conception is required. This needs to recognize (among other things) differentiation within the classes of capital (by sector, by branch of production within a sector, and by company within a branch of production) and labor (by industry and occupation, age, ethnicity, gender, and territory). At the level of abstraction of the capitalist mode of production, one can make plausible arguments that there is a certain kind of commonality of material interests, lived experiences, and capacities for collective action that are generated directly by the social relations of production as such. Such a coincidence may occur, but there is no necessary reason as to why it should—and in practice it usually will not.[21] Thus, when class is analyzed at a relatively concrete micro level, " there is no longer *necessarily* a simple coincidence of material interests, lived experience and collective capacity" (Wright, 1989, 295–296). This has implications for individual experiences, collective identities, and collective action.

In seeking to move to a lower level of abstraction in their analyses of

class, contemporary Marxist theorists have been "torn between two theoretical impulses" (Wright, 1989, 269). The first is to keep the concept of
class structure as simple as possible and then remedy the resultant explanatory deficiencies by introducing into the analysis a range of other explanatory principles. The second is to increase the complexity of the class
structural concept itself. These alternatives "place different bets on how
much explanatory work the concept of class structure itself should do."
The first strategy takes a "minimalist" position, seeing class structure as
at most shaping broad constraints on action and change. In contrast, the
second takes a "maximalist" position, seeing class structure as a potent
and systematic determinant of individual action and social development.
Neither approach is nonproblematic, however, and there is no reason
why they should be mutually exclusive. There may be advantage in seeking both to develop more complex conceptions of class and to acknowledge the relationships of class to other dimensions of social division and
identity such as ethnicity and gender. Harvey (1996, 359, original emphasis), for instance, defines class as "*situatedness or positionality in relation
to the processes of capital accumulation.*" As these processes are often
chaotic and disparate, operating at various spatio-temporal scales, individual positionality in relation to them can also be complicated and confused.

Others seek to accept aspects of poststructural critique and respond
to it in ways that reformulate the concept of class but do so in deeply
problematic ways (Gibson-Graham, 1996, 1997). Gibson-Graham (1997,
149) claims that economic geographers of a Marxian persuasion focus
only on landscapes of capitalist class relations, blind to the multiplicity of
other possible class relations.[22] In recognition of this "essentialist" view,
she argues for an "anti-essentialist" but nonetheless Marxian definition
of class as a social process involving the production, appropriation, and
distribution of surplus labor "*in whatever form*" (1997, 91, emphasis
added). As a result, for example, the household "is involved not only in
capitalist reproduction but in the reproduction of non-capitalist class processes" involving household members so that "[women's] class struggles
often take place in the household" (Gibson-Graham, 1996, 120–122).
Gibson-Graham concedes, however, that "to empty class of much of its
structural baggage [*sic*] and prune it down to one rather abstract process
concerning labour flows might seem rather reductive." While rejecting
the pejorative concept of "structural baggage," this is indeed "reductive,"
as defining class in this way robs the concept of analytic specificity. She
argues that her position allows the conditions of existence of *any* class
process to assume specific importance in the formation of class societies
and subjectivities without presuming their presence or role. In her eagerness to deconstruct and complicate Marx's two-class model, she (no

doubt inadvertently) loses sight of its specific analytic purpose and, more damagingly, the specificity of capitalist class relations. This is a clear case of throwing out the baby with the bath water.

Moving to a lower level of abstraction also involves recognizing that the routine performance of the social relationships of production and consumption and the day-to-day conduct and market transactions of a capitalist economy (such as declaring profits or paying wages) are conducted in prices, not values. Economic agents freely enter into market relations mediated by monetary prices. Money thus serves as both a medium of exchange and a measure of value, though one that does not equate to values defined in terms of socially necessary labour time. In much of *Capital* Marx proceeds for expository purposes as if money prices are perfectly correlated with the amounts of socially necessary labor time embodied in commodities. Given this (heroic) assumption, monetary exchange is equivalent to value exchange. In fact, this *never is* nor *can it be* the case, for while money is a representation of socially necessary labor time, money prices are always a slippery and unreliable representation of value (Harvey, 1996, 152). The discrepancies between supply and demand in markets result in commodities being exchanged at prices that diverge from their values. As production conditions diverge from the social and technical averages, the amounts of labor time embodied in commodities deviate from the socially necessary amount that defines the value of a commodity. Commodities thus contain varying amounts of labor time but are sold at the same market price, while money prices typically diverge from exchange values. As a result, there is a redistribution of value between sectors and companies via the processes of competition. This is also important in relation to the systemic dynamism of capitalist economies and their historical geographies of production and uneven development, and to processes of "creative destruction" as firms seek competitive advantage via innovation and revolutionizing the what and how of production.[23]

Marx gave no definitive solutions as to how value and price analyses should be related. Consequently, there has been much subsequent debate as to the "correct" way to connect these two levels of analysis. For some, the issue is how quantitatively to transform values to prices, reflected in the history of the "transformation problem" and more generally the issue of the validity of value analysis (Rankin, 1987; Roberts, 1987; Sheppard and Barnes, 1990; Steedman, 1977). Rather than seeking quantitatively to equate values to prices, a more constructive approach is to recognize the qualitative differences between them and that these are concepts of different theoretical status. Values and prices are indicative of the way in which capitalist social relationships unite a wide range of qualitatively different types of labor in the totality of the production process. Massey

(1995a, 307) trenchantly argues that the law of value is useful for thinking through the broad structures of the economy and for forming the "absolutely essential basis for some central concepts—exploitation for instance." Thus, value theory describes a specific set of social relationships in which exploitation is a process of extracting surplus labor that can only be understood in the context of the wider social forms constitutive of capitalism as a system of commodity production. Value theory therefore helps elucidate the social relationships specific to capitalism. However, attempts to use it as a basis for empirical economic calculation are misconceived and doomed to failure. Indeed, "the byzantine entanglements into which the 'law of value' has fallen make it . . . unusable in any empirical economic calculus" (Massey, 1995a, 307). It is therefore important not to confuse values and prices conceptually or seek to equate empirical data measured in prices with theoretical constructs defined in terms of values. The significance of value analysis lies in the way in which it focuses attention upon class relationships and the social structures that they help to define.[24]

2.3. Varieties of Marxism and the Engagement between Economic Geography and Marxian Political Economy

The Marxian tradition is rich and varied, encompassing a variety of approaches with different emphases and aspirations. As geographers began to discover this tradition,[25] they engaged selectively with its various strands. David Harvey was central to this voyage of discovery. His work and exploration of classical Marxian political economy was seminal in shaping the terms and terrain of engagement between Marxism and geography.[26] Indeed, part of the difficulties encountered in the subsequent engagement between economic geography and Marxian political economy during the 1970s can be traced to two issues that followed from this. First, Marxian political economy was more concerned with the temporalities rather than the spatialities of capitalism (though there were important exceptions, such as Mandel, 1963). Second, Harvey was primarily concerned with the relationships between the structural relationships of capital and geographies of capitalism. Harvey retained (and retains) a strong commitment to a scientific geography[27] and to constructing more powerful explanations of the structure of the space economy of capitalism than those offered by neoclassical location theories and spatial science (Harvey, 1973). Paradoxically, the combination of these two features led initially to limited and one-sided considerations of the links between social process and spatial form.

Some sought directly to deduce trends in the organization and geographies of production from the deep inner structural relationships of the capitalist mode of production (Läpple and van Hoogstraten, 1980).[28] Others went even further and sought to deduce forms of political action from the structures of capitalist relations of production (Carney, 1980). Such approaches thus echoed deterministic capital-logic and structuralist approaches that assumed people to be mere "bearers of structures," with no scope for human agency to alter trajectories of development that were to be revealed by the inexorable unraveling of structural relationships.[29] More sophisticated approaches recognized that structural analyses could define the limits to and constraints upon production organization and its geographies. Harvey (1982) remains the most elegant and thorough analytic statement of such an approach via his reworking of Marx's historical materialism into an historical-geographical materialism that sets out the necessity for territorially uneven development in relation to the structural limits to capital. Such approaches could not, however, specify how particular industrial trajectories or patterns of spatially uneven development would evolve within these limits, or indeed explain how (as opposed to why) these structural limits were reproduced. For example, while some cities and regions grow and others decline, explaining which grow and which decline is a matter for empirical investigation rather than deduction from immanent structural tendencies.[30] Moreover, structural conditions and limits are not pre-given and natural but are socially produced by human actions, intended and unintended. Consequently, the ways in which such structural limits are socially (re)produced within particular institutional arrangements have become focal issues. These processes of structural (re)production thus need to be problematized rather than taken for granted, especially as capital accumulation is an inherently crisis-prone process. This was recognized within Marxian political economy by the increasing attention given to the role of the state in keeping these crisis tendencies within "acceptable" limits.[31]

However, to begin to understand such issues more fully requires rather different and complementary approaches and levels of theoretical analysis to that of the law of value and the definition of class structural relations within the capitalist mode of production. In some ways, the "Afterword" to Harvey (1982) represents a critical acknowledgment of the limits to analyzing historical geographies of capitalism within such a framework. At the same time, it forms a bridge to other approaches that sought to explore more fully issues of the state and, more particularly, civil society and their links to trajectories of capitalist development and the mechanisms through which such geographies are produced by human action.

2.4. Further Refining the Conception of Production as a Social Process

One implication of recognizing the "limits to capital" is that theoretical concepts of more local relevance need to be developed at a less abstract level than that of the space of the capitalist mode of production as defined via value analysis. Such concepts must perforce have more limited and modest explanatory ambition and a more restricted domain of applicability. They must be interposed between the more abstract conceptions of value categories and structures and the empirically observable forms of production organization and its geographies. Such concepts focus upon individual and collective behaviors and their links to structures of social relationships within capitalism, recognizing that the latter permit a variety of developmental possibilities and trajectories, and bring the diversity of forms of capitalism and its institutions to center stage. Seeking to link the structural relations of capitalism with uneven development and geographies of economies also requires a more sophisticated and nuanced view of the relationships among society, space, and nature, for these are central to understanding the variety of forms that capitalism can take. These intermediate level concepts thus allow an explication of *how* the processes of capital accumulation proceed and of *how* capitalist social relationships are reproduced in spatially and temporally variable ways in order to make production possible. This in turn implies a greater concern for the meanings that various facets of social life have for people.[32]

Middle-level theoretical bridges can be built by drawing on concepts from modern social theory (Giddens, 1981, 1984) and from evolutionary and institutional approaches in the social sciences, especially economics and sociology (Hodgson, 1988; Metcalfe, 1998a), as well as from parts of anthropology and cognitive psychology (for example, see Amin, 1998). An evolutionary approach, for example, stresses the path dependent character of development and centers on two themes: how firms behave differently in similar contexts and how firms adapt to environmental change (Metcalfe and Calderini, 1997). Metcalfe (1998b, 2), in arguing against a view of evolutionary economics as grounded in biological analogy, emphasizes the links between evolutionary and institutional approaches and the institutional grounding and guiding of evolutionary market processes. He suggests that "patterns and rates of economic evolution are deeply conditioned by market institutions and the wider context in which these market institutions are embedded." While understanding of capitalist production can be enhanced by exploring the conceptual space between abstract conceptions of structures and empirically observable forms of behavior, understanding of institutional forms can equally be enhanced by relating them to the structural constraints that flow from their being embedded in capitalist forms of production.

This exploration of evolutionary and institutional approaches resonates with a strong theme in the ongoing debate about the emergence of a "new economic geography"—that there is a (re)recognition that the "economic" is culturally and socially grounded and embedded (Crang, 1997; Thrift, 1994b; Thrift and Olds, 1996). What we understand by "the economy" is culturally constituted (Albert, 1993). Thus, economic rationalities are culturally created, take diverse forms, and are territorially embedded, with distinctive geographies (Peet, 1997b). Culture has penetrated the economy with symbolic processes, including an important aesthetic component, permeating both consumption and production (Lash and Urry, 1994, 61). Culture must be seen as a product of social interaction rather than as some pre-given way of seeing the world. If economic practices are culturally embedded, this reflects ongoing and active social processes. It therefore is important to examine the processes by which cultures are actively produced and reproduced by social practices and institutions (Gertler, 1997, 51). As such, culturally embedded economic action should be seen as dependent upon collective understandings that shape economic strategies and goals.[33] Cultural embeddedness denotes the role of shared collective understandings in shaping economic strategies and goals, with culture providing scripts for applying different strategies to different classes of exchange (Zukin and di Maggio, 1990, 17).

There is much of value in seeking to problematize the economic in these ways. It is also important to emphasize, strongly, that a lot of what is claimed to be novel actually is not so new. Although the "cultural turn" in economics and economic geography may seem to some to be a radical shift, cultural analysis and an emphasis upon cultural specificity in economic and social relationships has a long history in Marxian political economy and strands of classical sociology. It can be traced back to Marx's analysis of commodity fetishism and reification and Durkheim's comments on the noncontractual elements of contracts (McDowell, 1994, 1997). The "cultural turn" can be seen as opening up conceptual space to recognize and accommodate different types of capitalism and capitalist production. It can also be seen as doing little more than to restate the point made by Marxian analysts in emphasizing that different social formations may exist within the structural limits of a given dominant mode of production or that they are the product of the articulations of different modes of production. Marxian analyses of capitalism precisely challenge competing representations that seek to deny this. Indeed, this is so central to Marxian political economy and its understanding of the historical geographies of capitalism that it is difficult to understand why it is seen as insensitive to cultural difference in this way (Lipietz, 1998). This is an important corrective to those views that seek competitively to counterpose political economy to cultural perspectives.

Agency, Structures, and Power Relationships

While agency, individual and collective, is important, individuals must be placed in their social context, avoiding both reducing them to mere "bearers of structures" and privileging the methodological individualism of neoclassical economics and behavioral geography. Structure is equally important, but it also has to be recognized that structures are socially (re)produced and that it is an illegitimate move to seek to read off or mechanistically deduce everything, including individual and collective actions and the geographies of economies, from such structures. The aim is to avoid collapsing agency into structure or structure into agency, in the process producing pale shadows of each.

Structures are both enabling and constraining as regards action and agency. As such, they influence human behavior while people reproduce structural limits and constraints via their behavior, albeit often unintentionally. For example, radical communist trade unionists may oppose the class relations of capitalism yet nevertheless help reproduce them via their everyday behavior of going to work, even if at the workplace they seek to disrupt production as a perceived way of furthering the immediate interests of those working there. Marx was very aware of the significance of human agency but insisted that people made their histories (and geographies) in circumstances not of their own choosing. As Anderson (1984, 34) notes, within Marxism there has been a "permanent oscillation" between those emphasizing the structural logic of the mode of production and those emphasizing the collective agency of human subjects as the main motors and explanatory principles of history (and, one might add, geography). A concern for the relationships between structures and agents was revived in geography following the discovery of Giddens's (1979, 1981, 1984) "theory of structuration." Structuration emphasizes the reciprocal relations between agency and structures—the "duality of structures." Giddens lays considerable stress upon individuals as agents but also recognizes institutions and other forms of social collectivities as possessing powers of agency.[34] He offers valuable insights in recognizing that agents are both shaped by and help shape structures, although the way in which he conceptualizes these links is problematic (Gregson, 1986; Thrift, 1996a). While seeking to reconnect agency and structure, Giddens does so in a way that problematizes both. As a result he has been criticized both for weakening the concept of structure and obfuscating that of agency. Rather than take the concepts of structures and agents and the links between them seriously, he tends to blur and weaken the distinction.

Others, working from feminist and poststructuralist perspectives, have emphasized the complexity and significance of agency vis-à-vis structure, deepening and transforming the concept of agency through notions of multiple identities. However, this is limited to concern with "the complexity of agency" or "the multiplicity of identity." As a result, the problem of adequately relating agency and structure remains since rationalized actions create through repetition the systemic logics of economic forms (Peet, 1997b, 37–38). Nonetheless, acknowledging the complexity of agency is important in helping bring recognition of dimensions of identity—and social division—such as ethnicity and gender.[35] This recognition of such nonclass dimensions emphasizes that the economy and processes of production involve more than simply the activities of white males and that this is central to comprehending their respective geographies.

In a further twist to this theme, other scholars claim that the problem of the structure–agency distinction has been abolished by the way that work in certain service occupations has been redefined to make the service or product indistinguishable from the person providing it. McDowell (1997, 121) argues:

> Workers with specific social attributes . . . are disciplined to produce an embodied performance that conforms to idealised notions of the appropriate "servicer." In this normalisation, the culture of organisations, in the sense of the explicit and implicit rules of conduct, has become increasingly important in inculcating the desirable embodied attributes of workers, as well as establishing the values and norms of organisational practices. . . . Here in the coincidence of embeddedness and embodiment the separation of structures from agents is overcome.

Much of what McDowell argues is valuable and helpful. What is problematic is her suggestion that the separation of agents and structures is a problem to be overcome by dissolving the one into the other, based on a weak sense of structure and a strong sense of agency. This circumvents the problem of specifying the ways in which agency and structure are dialectically related in such forms of work and represented in specific ways in certain circumstances to legitimate these new forms of heightened exploitation in the workplace. More positively, however, this emphasis upon embodied work can be seen as indicative of the way in which economic activities—of workers, managers, company directors and so on—are performed; of the economy as performative, constructed through and from these activities and performances (Thrift, 2000).

The concept of agency poses other problems, especially in terms of relationships between individuals and collectivities of various sorts. There are certainly dangers of reifying organizations, suggesting that they have powers independent of the people who constitute organizational activity. Organizational change is animated, resisted, or modified by the actions of organizational members. This again points to the performative character of production and other economic activities. Consequently, organizations must be seen as a terrain on which their members can mobilize. Corporate change therefore is interpreted, sometimes fought over and resisted, both by individuals and by groups of people who may have very different assumptions and agendas about what changes should take place and how they should occur and differential powers to pursue their aims (Halford and Savage, 1997, 110–111). Corporate strategy is often the strategy of an individual adopted collectively via negotiation, persuasion, or coercion (McGrath-Champ, 1999, 341). There is clearly a case, then, for not reifying companies, governments, and other organizations and arguing that organizations per se do not make decisions but that decisions are made by people who are their members. Such a position is reasonable to a point. Arguments to the effect that all that matters are individuals can, however, easily slide from a concern with individual psychology into a reductionist physiological argument that in the final analysis all behavior is to be explained via electrical brain activity. It is, therefore, important to remember that individuals exist as social beings whose patterns of thought and action are conditioned by the social relationships in which they are enmeshed.

There are, therefore, also dangers in ignoring or underestimating the influence of organizations over the behavior of their members. Organizational action is more than simply the sum of the actions of its members. Furthermore, the actions of these individuals cannot be understood outside of the organizational context and culture in which they occur. Firms, governments, and other organizations have a collective memory *beyond* that of any given individual or group of individuals. As such, organizations can be said to have cultures and histories that both shape and are shaped by the actions and understandings of their members, but the precise forms of these relationships are contingent and indeterminate.

However, this in turn raises the issue of how these relationships in practice hold together to create organizations that successfully reproduce themselves. Actor-network theorists argue their approach speaks to this question, offering a nondualistic perspective that focuses on how things are "stitched together" across divisions and distinctions. Actor-network theory seeks to connect the social and the material, in contrast to structuration theory, which neglects the material components of both action and structure and is seen by actor-network theorists to be overly dependent upon social interaction. Indeed, "activating networks of actors, and therefore agency, requires the mobilisation of all manner of things and this is probably where actor-network theory makes its most original contribution" (Thrift, 1996a, 26). Actor-network theory thus opens up but seeks to bridge a fresh divide between the social and the material[36] while seeking to bridge the divide between action and structure (Bosch and Juska, 1997). Consequently, actor-network theorists investigate the means by which associations come into existence and how the roles and functions of subjects and objects, human and nonhuman, are attributed and stabilized. Moreover, they acknowledge that there are distinct asymmetries in power between actors within networks. Actors organize associations or networks while intermediates are organized (Murdoch, 1997, 331). However, this distinction between the organizers and the organized is seen as coming at the end of the network construction process, which is shaped by the actors. The same person can, however, be an actor in one network, an intermediate in another. The "radical symmetry" that lies at the heart of actor-network theory thus stems from the belief that power and size are not immutable. Actor-network theorists seek to uncover how associations and networks are built and maintained. Thus, there is much that is attractive in actor-network theorizations.

There are also some major problems, however. Actor-network theory seems strangely indifferent to the differences among and between people and things. As Bassett (1999, 35) puts it, "can non-human entities be actors if they lack goals and intentions?" Despite its name, it in fact has little to say about why agency is exercised in the ways that it is or why structural limits exist in the forms that they do. Furthermore, while recognition of power inequalities is vital, these are seen as only arising *within* the structure of a given network. In actor-network theory, power is conceptualized as the outcome of the strength of associations between actors within a network; "understanding what sociologists generally call power means describing the ways in which actors are defined, associated and simultaneously obliged to remain faithful to their alliances" (Callon, 1986, 224, cited in Thrift, 1996a, 25). Power in this sense is always—and *only*—a shared capacity, a relational achievement, internal to the network. Murdoch (1995, 748, emphasis added) puts it like this:

> Those who are powerful are not those who "hold" power over others but those who are able to enrol, convince and enlist others into networks on terms which allow the initial actors to "represent" others. . . . The controlling actor grows by borrowing the force of others; it can inflate to a larger size. . . . *Power is, therefore, the composition of the network: if it lies anywhere it is the resources used to strengthen the bonds.*

There is thus no concept or theory of power outside the network, which raises problems in seeking to deal with the social sources of power and with the ability of some to control the position of others within a network.[37] Indeed, actor-network theory is characterised by a methodological agnosticism and as such slips from detailed descriptions of particular actor networks to quite abstract prescriptive methodological statements about how to analyze networks. It limits its ambition to providing a set of generalized tools for network analysis and eschews more robust "theoretical" prognoses. While helpful in describing relations *within* networks, it tends to fluctuate between minute description of the particular and rather abstract generalizations about the characteristics of all networks.

In particular, it has little to say about what forms of "stitching together" of networks are more probable than others, why this should be the case, and why those networks that do exist do so in the forms that they do. Indeed, it would seem to assume a priori that every network is unique and qualitatively distinctive. As such there is a danger of becoming obsessed with describing the unique at the expense of more general explanatory claims and statements.[38] Actor-network analysts therefore may simply describe networks of inequality and gloss over the reasons for inequality. In capitalist societies, for instance, agents (human and nonhuman) possess differential capacities to shape relationships. Moreover this differential power is systemically linked to their capacity to accumulate money (capital) and then use this as a source of power to force others to act as subordinate intermediaries.[39] Consequently actor-network theory may ignore the capacity of some actors to deploy the power of others, and in doing so limit their agency, and fail to seek the reasons for this. As a result, Murdoch and colleagues (1998, 15) conclude that it is "probably erroneous" to refer to it as a theory, as it is "somewhat under-theorised and, as a result, problematic as an approach for understanding agency-structure relationships."

Rediscovering the Significance of Motives, Knowledge, and Learning

Acknowledging that people are active and thinking subjects, but are not endowed with perfect knowledge, led to revived interest in knowledge and learning and uncovering the rationalities and motives that actually underlie and inform behavior. The basis of the behavioral geography critique of neoclassical location theories was recognition that people had imperfect knowledge and varying motivations, but this made little progress beyond descriptive studies of particular cases. More recent research in the cognitive and behavioral sciences emphasizes the ways in which different actor rationalities generate different forms of economic behavior. For example, substantive or scientific rationality leads to rule-bound behavior, procedural rationality favors behavior that seeks to adjust to the constraints imposed by the environment in which people operate, while recursive or reflexive rationality is linked to strategic behavior that seeks to shape that environment (Amin, 1998). The actions of economic actors depend, in part, upon the knowledge (both practical and theoretical) that they have acquired about the economy, how it operates, and about the anticipated effects of their actions. This in turn raises questions as to the ways in which "the economy" is discursively created and understood and the extent to which it is "knowable," both to such agents and to social scientists seeking to understand their behavior and the stories that they tell about it (Thrift, 1996b).

The rediscovery of the significance of what people actually know has focused attention on the links between knowledge and production, on learning firms and learning regions (Maskell et al., 1998). Learning and knowledge are also foregrounded via the recognition that organizations develop a "collective memory" and their own cultures of production, linked to an acknowledgment of the importance of modes of internal organization, competencies, and capabilities of firms (Foss, 1996; Richardson, 1972). Competencies express what a firm can do, core competencies what it can do more effectively than other firms (Prahalad and Hamal, 1990). Such core competencies and the knowledge and learning processes that underlie them define differences between firms. The development of unique firm-specific capabilities and competencies provides the grounding for corporate competitive strategies based upon dimensions such as quality, product differentiation, and product development rather than simply price and more effective forms of corporate organization. The firm can thus be thought of as an entity seeking to create and sustain competitive advantage via the cumulative development of a distinctive set of organizational (core) competencies (Liedtka, 1999). Such approaches emphasize the centrality of certain types of knowledge and competencies to competitive success and of the economy as dependent upon knowledge, learning (in various ways, such as by doing, by interacting, by imitating, and so on), adaptation, and evolution.

The emphasis upon learning within such approaches reflects the strong links that exist between them and strands of evolutionary economics and a view that economic development trajectories (corporate and territorial) may be strongly path-dependent (Nelson and Winter, 1982). There is no doubt that in one sense all production depends upon knowledge of various sorts; the more interesting questions concern the links between particular sorts of production and particular sorts of knowledge and learning process (Hudson, 1999a). Equally there are important limitations to the ways in which these questions have been framed and answered (Odgaard and Hudson, 1998). One way to begin to address some of these limitations is to recognize that learning is an interactive process (Lundvall, 1995). The emphasis upon interactive learning directs attention to the way in which production of new knowledge and learning necessarily involves action. The development of firm-specific competencies thus depends not just on knowledge but also the activities through which knowledge is produced and transmitted and more generally upon action by people involved in production. Firm-specific competencies are thus (re)produced through communities of practice within (but also to a degree beyond) the boundaries of the firm (Lave and Wenger, 1990). Within such communities people share tacit knowledge and through dialogue bring this to the surface and exchange ideas—that is, learn—about work practices and experiment with new ideas and practices (Hendry, 1996). Organizations can thus be conceptualized as hybrid groups of multiple and overlapping communities of practice (Brown and Duguid, 1998) in which learning is a matter of new meanings and emergent structures arising from common enterprise, experience, and sociability (Wenger, 1998). In short, communities of practice are grounded in learning-by-interacting.

Institutions, Instituted Behavior, and Social Regulation of the Economy

Conceptualizing the economy as culturally constituted foregrounds the importance of institutions, envisioning the economy as constituted via "instituted" processes.[40] As institutions are typically place-specific, this also involves taking seriously the territoriality of the economy, the organization of production, and the production of spatial scales. This institutional perspective draws heavily on the legacy of Polyani and the "old" institutional economists and upon economic sociology (Mulberg, 1995; Rutherford, 1994).[41] For Polyani (1957, 243–245) all economic processes are instituted processes. As a result, all economic structures are socially embedded in networks of interpersonal relations and so heavily influenced by the presence or absence of mutuality, cooperation, and trust (Dore, 1983; Granovetter, 1985). Embeddedness thereby denotes the contingent character of economic action with respect to cognition, culture, social structure, and political institutions (Zukin and di Maggio, 1990, 15). Thus, capitalism may be constituted in differing ways, and economic relationships may be grounded in, and dependent upon, a variety of noneconomic ones. "Traded inter-dependencies" may depend upon "untraded inter-dependencies," as relationships based upon particular conceptions of trust assume a critical importance in some types of economic transactions (Storper, 1995, 1997).

Conceptualizing economic processes as embedded in institutions leads, logically and historically, to recognition that the economy is regulated and governed in particular ways. There is a range of institutional forms, from formal institutions such as those of the state to the informal and tacit institutions of norms, habits, and routines, that shape the way in which production takes place and the economy is organized. Such varied institutions cohere to become appropriate institutional formations that provide a degree of stability in the face of uncertainty as well as constraints upon, or templates for, future economic developments (Hodgson, 1988, 1993). This resonates with the notion of the creation of distinctive "worlds of production" associated with particular ways of organizing the production process, a position that draws upon conventions theory (Salais and Storper, 1992). In a way reminiscent of Polyani's (1957) notion of instituted behavior, Storper (1997) defines conventions as practices, routines, agreements, and their associated informal and institutional forms that bind acts together through coherent and taken-for-granted mutual expectations. Conventions are sometimes manifested as formal institutions and rules, but often are not. As such, most conventions are a kind of halfway house between fully personalized and idiosyncratic relations and fully depersonalized easy-to-imitate relations (Storper, 1997, 38). Worlds of production are distinctive sets of practices that come together in particular ways as "bundles" or "packages," bound together via the glue of conventions and the mutual expectations and shared ways of understanding that they entail.[42] In some circumstances conventions can be economically advantageous, in others less so, producing a form of "conventional lock-in" that undermines competitive success. For example, Schoenberger (1994) explains the failure of U.S. companies to adapt particular restructuring strategies in terms of the ways in which managers' own interests and identities, and *their* sense of the corporation's interests and identities, were embedded in established institutionalized forms of organization. These acted as cognitive filters, effectively locking in companies to established ways of doing things and foreclosing options as to other ways of operating.[43]

Renewed recognition of the significance of institutions focused attention upon the regulatory role of the state (at the national but also the supranational and subnational scales: Jessop, 1994), but in a rather different way than in earlier Marxist perspectives.[44] Regulationist approaches seek to explain how the tensions inherent to capitalist production and capital accumulation can be held within tolerable limits as a result of state actions and policies. In particular, they focus upon how state policies can ensure a degree of correspondence between changes in production and consumption.[45] Beyond that, however, they have also highlighted the significance of mechanisms and institutions in civil society, as governance has increasingly replaced government as the focal point of analytic interest (Goodwin and Painter, 1996; Painter and Goodwin, 1995). Furthermore, different forms of regulatory and governance régimes may result in relations between structures and agents, and between the varying agents in the production process, being stitched together in different ways, taking varying forms as cultures of economies vary. Echoing the strands of the agency-structure debate, Gertler (1997, 57) stresses that the relationship between institutions and practices is "fundamentally dialectical" in nature, with practices having the potential to shape institutions over time. Taken-for-granted ways of thinking and behaving—which may variously be described as informal institutions or as conventions—can be a critical factor in establishing ideas and ways of doing things as unquestioned, unquestionable, and so hegemonic in the Gramscian sense. They may, however, be less a product of timeless cultural traits than of particular regulatory régimes and institutional forms. Gertler (55) suggests that traits and attitudes commonly understood as being part and parcel of inherited cultures of individual firms are produced and reproduced by day-to-day practices that are strongly conditioned by surrounding social institutions and regulatory régimes. Consequently, the very practices taken as signifiers of distinctive cultures are themselves influenced by institutions constituted outside the individual firm.

Reciprocal Relations between the Natural, the Social, and the Spatial

One of the problems of location theories is that they adopt a one-sided conception of relationships between social process and spatial pattern, deducing the latter from (an impoverished conception of) the former. While drawing upon more powerful conceptions of social process, some initial explorations of Marxian political economy in geography fell into the same trap in adopting a one-sided view of the links between spatial pattern and social process (as noted above). There was no recognition that spatial pattern not only could influence the ways in which those processes operate but also could have a formative role in the ways in which they were constituted in the first place. Relationships between the social and the spatial are reciprocal but indeterminate, however. Analysts place different emphases upon the strength and nature of these relationships. For Sayer (1984) they are limited to spatial form influencing how causal powers are realized. For Peck (1996) spatial difference plays a rather more active, though vaguely specified, role in shaping social relationships. For Massey (1995a) and Urry (1985) the character of social processes may itself be shaped by the way that they operate through time and space. Spatial forms are a product of social processes, while those forms in turn shape the ways in which processes are constituted and evolve. These latter stronger views as to the character of social-spatial relationships emphasize that space is socially produced, and so dynamic, rather than being a static container into which social relationships, including those of production, are poured. Indeed, social space is produced by the distanciated stretching of social relationships. Consequently, while the spatial patterning of the economy is an outcome of the social relationships of production, spatially uneven development and the characteristics of specific places help shape the particular form that these relationships take.

One consequence of seeing relationships between the social and spatial as reciprocal is that production, its organization and its geographies, must be viewed as contingent and, as such, contested. Particular forms and geographies of production organization result from struggles between capital and labor, between companies, and between groups of workers, with states implicated in such struggles both via their regulatory role and, on occasion, as participants. Different social classes and groups seek to shape the anatomy of production and the spaces and spatiality of capitalism to further their own interests. While this is a determinate set of struggles, it is not (pre)determined, as agency and structure combine in and through place to generate contingent outcomes. There is a considerable range of concrete socio-spatial practices and strategies through which the social relations of production can be realized and reproduced. Consequently, there is always a variety of potential resultant geographies (Cox, 1997, 183). The strategies of capital are undoubtedly of great significance in shaping the landscapes of capitalism, although the ways that they do so can vary greatly. Due weight must also be given to the significance of firms as organizational entities in the organization of production, rather than the latter being regarded as simply a response to the general requirements of capital. Production is organized by business enterprises operating within extremely complex dynamic networks of internalized and externalized transactional relationships of power and influence (Dicken and Thrift, 1992, 287). While there is considerable force to this argument, national states, trade unions and other labor organizations, and a variety of groups in civil societies may also influence the organization and geographies of production. While companies seek to shape space to meet their requirements for profitable production, other social forces seek to shape space in relation to differing and varying criteria, seeking to stretch other social relationships over space and form it in different ways. Organized labor can influence these landscapes in a variety of ways via its sociospatial practices, for example (Herod, 1995, 1997; Martin et al., 1994; Sadler and Thompson, 1999; Wills, 1998b).

Furthermore, people seek to create and reproduce meaningful places—understood as complex condensations of overlapping social relations in a particular envelope of time-space (Hudson, 1990)—in which to live and learn as well as work (Beynon and Hudson, 1993). The density, variety, and types of social relations that intersect there help define different types of place (village, town, city, and so on). The way in which place is conceptualized has also been problematized. The work of Massey in the 1970s and 1980s was seminal in convincing geographers of the need to conceptualize relations between social process and spatial forms as reciprocal and mutually constitutive. More recently, she and others have begun to develop more sophisticated conceptualizations of place. Places are seen as possibly discontinuous—open and with permeable boundaries—rather than as necessarily continuous—closed and with impermeable boundaries—although in practice it is unlikely that any place was ever completely closed. Places are seen to be complex, endowed with multiple and contested identities and meanings. As a result there are typically struggles to resolve which of these identities and meanings will or should become dominant. The extent to which places are spatially continuous or discontinuous, have permeable or impermeable boundaries, and have singular or multiple meanings and identities are recognized as issues for empirical investigation rather than a priori assumption (Allen et al., 1998).

In addition to recognizing reciprocal links between the social and the spatial, it is important to take account of relationships between the social and the natural (Smith, 1984). Some comments have already been made on these issues in the context of actor-network theory, but it is worth recalling Williams's (1983, 29) observation that nature is perhaps "the most complex word in the language," a consequence of the close involvement of people in nature. Paralleling the increased cross-disciplinary recognition given to the significance of spatial difference, relationships between people and their natural environments, the other prime historical concern of geographers, have also come to fore in a variety of other disciplines. Consequently, geography "has been displaced from its self-appointed position as guardian of the interdisciplinary frontier between the natural and the social sciences" (Bayliss-Smith and Owens, 1994, 139). Yet, in the same way as broader cross-disciplinary concern with the significance of spatial difference enriched understanding of links between society and space, so too has the broadened concern with connections between people and the natural environment enhanced understanding of those natural-social links. Within geography, this has helped rescue concerns for such relationships from "a somewhat disreputable past, tainted with the excesses of environmental determinism" (Bayliss-Smith and Owens, 1994, 113). One consequence of this cross-disciplinary reappraisal of social-natural relationships is that, from one of point of view, the natural is seen as socially constructed, and this can set limits upon forms of production organization and geographies.

In addition, however, production is acknowledged as unavoidably materially grounded in the natural world (the natural world is a source of raw materials and a repository for wastes, for example). The laws of thermodynamics, of the conservation of energy and matter, which govern chemical and physical transformations of materials, set definite limits on the production process. These laws also make it clear that production has unavoidable impacts upon nature and the natural world (Jackson, 1995). Production can therefore be thought of as encompassing both socioeconomically *and* socioecologically instituted processes. The precise ways in which this mediation between nature and society takes place are influenced by technological possibilities and structured by the dominant social relations of production. Relationships between the economy and the environment are thus shaped by the specific requirements of capitalist production for profits. This has myriad implications for the organization and geographies of production as well as, in the final analysis, the sustainability of the production process (M. J. Taylor, 1995). While knowledge of natural processes is itself socially constructed, there are natural limits to production that cannot be overcome.

There is, however, some ambiguity within Marx's views on the relationships between nature and production. At times, he showed an acute awareness of the adverse environmental consequences of production (Merchant, 1983). At other times, he tended to see the labor process as producing only its intended effects in transforming elements of nature into use values, with little recognition of its unintended side effects and by-products (M. O'Connor, 1994b, 57–58). Altvater (1993), however, argues that all of Marx's categories are of a "double-form," relating to both environmental and social process, although Marxists (Marx included) have routinely neglected the former. Consequently, Deléage (1994, 48) has suggested that capitalism ought to be thought of as a doubly exploitative system of production, with a parallel drawn between the hidden mechanisms by which surplus-value is formed and the hidden cost of things purloined from ecological systems. Consequently, he asks, "should the theoretical status of the concept of ecological cost not be ranked on a par with that of surplus-value?" Such issues are explored further in Chapter 9.

2.5. Concluding Comments: A Framework for Understanding Production and the Structure of the Reminder of This Volume

In this chapter several theoretical perspectives have been explored in terms of their utility in helping to understand the organization and geographies of capitalist production. While different perspectives are of varying value in this regard, none of them in and of itself can deal with the full range of issues to be explained. But, while acknowledging multiple possible methodologies and epistemologies, one must conclude that some theoretical positions have greater explanatory power and value than others (see section 1.4). For example, some are much more powerful in explaining why capitalist production is organized as it is while others have much more to say about how production is made possible and occurs in specific ways, times, and places. Consequently, various theoretical positions are of greater or lesser usefulness, depending upon the character of the issues to be explained and the types of questions to be answered. Understanding production and its geographies therefore requires developing an approach that combines different theoretical positions, taking advantage of their particular strengths while avoiding or at least minimizing their weaknesses.

How then should we think about the organization of production and its geographies within capitalist societies? How does this influence the structure of the remainder of this volume? The argument herein is that production can be analyzed from four interrelated perspectives that weave in and out of succeeding chapters, with greater prominence in some than in others. The first perspective emphasizes the ways in which production and processes related to it are governed and regulated as a necessary condition of their existence. It emphasizes that the conditions under which commodity production take place do not occur naturally. If they are not (re)produced socially, commodity production is impossible. For this reason they underpin the totality of the production process. These issues are discussed at length in Chapter 3. This discussion entails consideration of national (and supra- and subnational) states and of nonstate regulatory and governance mechanisms. It touches upon debates about globalization and the "hollowing out" of national states as well as specific policies relating to production.

The second perspective focuses on the ways in which companies, workers, and communities struggle to organize production and make its organizational models and geographies in ways that reflect their respective (often competing) aims, aspirations, and interests. In this way the social spaces in which economies and societies are constituted are produced as an integral part of the process of commodity production. While companies use space and spatial differentiation as part of their competitive strategies, workers and the residents of places affected by these corporate strategies seek to shape geographies of production to produce landscapes that favor their interests rather than those of capital. This second perspective thus sees production as a contested process, encompassing both competition between companies and between capital and labor.

These concerns are explored in Chapters 4 to 7. Chapter 4 deals with competition and cooperation between capital and labor. It focuses upon the ways in which labor markets are shaped so that labor is bought and sold in particular ways and upon the organization of the labor process once companies purchase labor-power. It thus views production as both a labor process and a value-creating process. There is a long tradition in political economy from Marx to Schumpeter and their respective followers of seeing competition between companies as central to the developmental dynamic of capitalism. Accordingly, Chapters 5 and 6 explore forms of corporate competition and cooperation between companies seeking to produce profitably, considering different dimensions and forms of competition, product, process, and organizational innovations, and the role of knowledge in competition. These chapters also explore markets, hierarchies, and networks as organizational forms and governance mechanisms. While the structural class of capital is divided, so too is that of labor. Thus, Chapter 7 analyzes divisions of labor and competition and cooperation between workers over the number and location of jobs and the terms and conditions of employment. It examines processes of labor market segmentation and divisions among workers along the cleavage planes of industry and occupation, types of jobs, gender, ethnicity, and the location of work, as well as the ways in which these are linked to forms of working class organization and trade union practices. It also considers the relationships between waged and unwaged work, especially in relation to the reproduction of labor-power.

The third perspective addresses the issue of how places are created, reproduced and, on occasion, destroyed as a necessary corollary of commodity production and the restructuring of production. Nonetheless, places have an existence beyond the social relations of capitalist production, grounded in local institutions, cultures, and life beyond the workplace. As such, there is a focus upon producing places in two senses. First, upon the places in which production occurs and the ways in which differences between places are deployed in strategies for and struggles over production. The emphasis thus is upon *producing* places, upon those diverse places in which goods and services in both commodified and noncommodified forms are produced. Second, there is an emphasis upon producing *places*, upon the production of places that are meaningful in various ways to people. It thus draws a distinction between capital's one-dimensional concern with profitable production spaces and peoples' concerns with meaningful places in which to live. While these concerns run through the preceding chapters in varying degrees, in Chapter 8 they become the prime focus of attention. Chapter 8 discusses the production of space and places, materially and discursively, recognizing that these are contested processes. It examines the role of the state in seeking to balance competing and contradictory claims. It also considers some aspects of consumption and identity formation related to people's senses of place. It emphasizes that class and other social struggles do not simply take place *in* and *over* space but actively shape that very space.

The final perspective centers on the ways in which the process of production is grounded in the natural environment, both drawing resources from it and discharging pollutants into it, and the fact that as a result there are natural limits to production. Put in slightly different terms, it explores how capitalist production is not but might be made sustainable economically, socially, and ecologically. Much of recent economic geography has paid but scant attention to the relationship between production and nature, so Chapter 9 focuses upon production as a process of materials transformation and upon relations between production, people, and the environment. It examines the social process of the transformation of elements of nature into socially useful products, grounded in the natural environment and having unintentional impacts on it (both as a result of production activities per se and through the impacts of consumption). It concludes by raising some normative and political questions about sustainable forms of production.

The final chapter reflects upon what has gone before and is organized around two sets of questions. The first is, What sort of capitalist economy and production system currently is dominant—for example, how accurate are claims that capitalism has become simply a post-industrial service economy? What does it mean to speak of a global economy? Second, how can the regulatory dilemmas posed by capitalist social relationships be tackled and the multiple contradictions of capitalist development be kept within tolerable limits?

2.6. Notes

1. It therefore follows that neoclassical accounts, predicated upon assumptions of certainty and static equilibrium, fall at the first hurdle in the theoretical stakes. They manifestly fail to meet the criteria of theoretical "adequacy" as set out in section 1.4. For discussion of the limits of neoclassical and technicist views of the economy based on analogies with the behavior of physical systems, see Barnes (1995).

2. Seeking to finesse the problems of assuming perfect knowledge via assumptions of bounded rationality thus fails adequately to address the problems of the undersocialized conception of the economy that is inherent to neoclassical approaches.

3. In the context of geographies of consumption and studies of consumer behavior, behavioral approaches typically sought to discover the knowledge that consumers possessed about the retailing environment and how they came to acquire such knowledge (Hudson, 1974).

4. Others sought to get around the problems of ignorance about individual knowledge and motives in a very different way. This involved adopting probabilistic macro-scale modeling procedures, which in due course became more rigor-

ously theorized via entropy-maximizing approaches that sought to predict the most probable distribution of activities and behaviors in space, subject to any known constraints (Wilson, 1970). These resulted in some circumstances in more accurate predictive models, but they pushed questions of explanation and understanding of social processes still further down the research agenda.

5. The analogy with the classical Marxian concept of commodity fetishism is deliberate.

6. Consequently, those familiar with the Marxian tradition may wish to pass directly to section 2.4. For those unfamiliar with Marxian ideas who wish to investigate them in more depth than they are presented here, Harvey (1982) remains an unrivaled account, although there is no substitute for Marx's own writings.

7. In a critical realist sense; see section 1.4.

8. That is, the amount of undifferentiated abstract labor needed under average social and technical conditions of production.

9. In contrast to—say—self-sufficiency, with each person or household producing all that (s)he or it needs, or to the maximization of physical output per se.

10. As opposed to the sale of some fortuitously produced surplus in an economy essentially devoted to subsistence production.

11. Rather than ex ante by state production planning or some other criterion.

12. See section 1.2.

13. Clearly such circuits have definite geographies, with different locations forming sites of production and exchange, linked by flows of capital in the form of money, commodities, and labor-power. Over time, the spatial reach of such circuits has increased, with the circuits of commodities, money, and productive capital successively becoming internationalized (Palloix, 1975, 1977).

14. Other approaches to understanding commodity production and circulation, such as commodity chain analysis (Gereffi, 1994, 1995), conceptualize flows as linear. In contrast, conceptualizing commodity production in terms of a circuit of value as well as in terms of the physical movement of commodities allows scope for nonlinearities and feedback mechanisms and a more complex and dynamic conceptualization of the total production process (see also Hartwick, 1998; Leslie and Reimer, 1999).

15. The appropriation of raw materials involves a different type of labor process to that of transformative industrial production; see below.

16. Harvey (1985) points out that the determination of socially necessary labor time is contingent upon the speed with which commodities can be distributed through time and across space, which is captured in the concept of "socially necessary turnover time."

17. Clearly a full analysis of the totality of the production process must encompass consumption. Production and consumption are linked rather than wholly separate categories (McDowell, 1994, 160). Companies consume commodities to produce other commodities; people as final consumers purchase commodities in the belief that they will be useful to them, materially and symbolically. Little attention is given here to the symbolic connotations of consumption and links between consumption and identity formation. This does not imply that they

are unimportant, simply that a line had to be drawn somewhere in terms of coverage (see Lee and Wills, 1997; Wrigley and Lowe, 1995).

18. Recognizing this, the concept of sociospatial formation perhaps better captures what is at issue here (cf. Thrift, 1996a).

19. Structuralist readings of Marx saw no scope for individual agency. People had no role beyond passively reproducing structures via their actions (Gregory, 1978). As the focus of attention in the social sciences switched from structures to discourses, it seemed at times as if people now had no role beyond the passive reproduction of discourses. Both significantly play down the role of human agency (see "Agency, Structures, and Power Relationships" in section 2.4).

20. These issues are more fully pursued in Chapter 3.

21. This is precisely the root of difficulties for trade unions seeking to organize workers collectively, issues discussed in Chapters 4 and 7.

22. The limitations of her views on this point are also discussed in section 1.4.

23. See Chapters 5 and 6.

24. It is also worth pointing out that as a consequence there are things that it cannot deal with: for example, many aspects of use values cannot be captured in value categories (see also Chapter 9).

25. I am conscious that this discussion focuses upon Anglo–North American geography. Within the discipline in other countries and cultures, rather different paths were followed (for example, see Carney et al., 1980). Equally, the terms of engagement varied among social science disciplines (Blackburn, 1972).

26. Had the initial point of contact been more with—say—Althusserian Marxism, with its emphasis upon the existence of contradictory structures within capitalism (Althusser, 1977), the subsequent trajectory of development might have been different. But it was not—which emphasizes the significance of human agency and contingency within as well as outside the academy. Subsequently, geographers (including Harvey himself) explored other strands within the Marxist tradition (Castree, 1999; Harvey, 1996).

27. Harvey (1969) was the key text that sought to provide an epistemological underpinning to geography as spatial science. It was also the pivotal moment in Harvey's turn to Marxism in recognition of the limits to orthodox positivist science.

28. Such approaches bore more than a passing resemblance to the deductive strategies of neoclassically inspired location theorists.

29. For a polemical critique of such positions, see Thompson (1978).

30. This is indicative of the limits to theory in this regard. Theoretical analysis can help define and explain the extent to which varied relationships between social processes and spatial forms are possible but revealing the extent to which they actually materialize is necessarily a question for empirical investigation.

31. See "Institutions, Instituted Behavior, and Social Regulation of the Economy" (section 2.4) and Chapter 3.

32. The production, circulation, and consumption of meanings within a circuit of symbolic exchanges has assumed an unprecedented significance within the contemporary capitalist economy (Thrift, 1994a, 215).

33. More radically, it can be claimed that no purely economic, social, or cultural relations are distinguishable. In contrast, each is already embedded within

the other (Halford and Savage, 1997, 109). This latter claim raises an awkward question, however, for if each is already embedded within the other, it may be difficult to distinguish them from one another—in which case, it is not at all clear what the cultural, economic, and social would denote.

34. He rejects the notion that classes can act as "collective agents," however. It is certainly possible, but not very helpful, to claim this. While capital and labor may not act for themselves as unified classes (bourgeoisie and working class) in pursuit of common interests, based on a shared understanding of their class interests and class structural position, this is no more than a recognition that the class structures of actually existing capitalist societies are much more complicated than the two-class abstraction that Marx used in unraveling the fundamental inner structural core relationships of capitalism (see section 2.3).

35. These are *relatively* neglected within historical materialism as a consequence of its insistent concern with the centrality of class relations.

36. Indeed it can be argued that in so doing actor-network theory challenges the established dichotomy of society–nature and seeks to replace this by new hybrid representations; the more limited issue of links between nature and production are considered in Chapter 9.

37. While all forms of social relations can be defined as actor networks, this still leaves unanswered the question of why some actor networks dominate over others.

38. Analogies with an earlier era in the history of geographical thought spring to mind here as geography sought to throw off its legacy of regional exceptionalism.

39. For example, capital can exert a structural power over labor, while some companies can exercise power over others by virtue of the resources they command (Allen, 1997).

40. Conversely, it explicitly denies the validity of conceptions of the economy and markets as naturally occurring, governed by natural processes.

41. "Old" institutional economics draws on two main strands of thought. One derives from Veblen and sees social norms, habits, and conventions as shaped by technology. The other derives from Commoner and sees conventions and norms as the outcome of a struggle. Rather than a coherent set of substantive theories, "old" institutionalism comprises diverse strands of thought united in opposition to neoclassical approaches.

42. While the fourfold typology of ideal-typical worlds of production advanced by Salais and Storper is useful for expository purposes, it fails to capture the nuances of production organization in its practical complexity. Nonetheless, the concept of worlds of production remains a valuable way of thinking about the organization of production.

43. Reciprocal links between human behavior and institutional forms are discussed in "Agency, Structures, and Power Relationships" in section 2.4.

44. There is debate as to the extent to which regulationist positions derive from Marxian ones; for example, see Boyer (1990).

45. See "Capitalist Production, Accumulation, and the Circuit of Productive Industrial Capital" and "Making the Transition to Less Abstract Concepts" (both in section 2.2).

3

Capitalist Production, Societal Reproduction, and Capitalist States

3.1. Introduction

The conditions under which capitalist production can be made possible do not occur naturally but need to be secured socially and politically. The state plays a key role in securing them. States are therefore intimately involved with production within capitalism—most obviously, when the state takes responsibility for organizing production via nationalization or other forms of public ownership. Such involvement runs counter to the "normal" private property ownership relations of capitalism, and it is important to understand why this happens and its implications for geographies of production. In addition states are also involved in the organization of production in other, and sometimes more subtle, ways: for example, providing education, health care, and housing for workers. Again provision may be removed from the "normal" sphere of market operations through direct state provision or influenced through legislation defining minimal housing standards or conditions of health and safety at work or the scope and content of industrial relations. This presumes that the state has secured its capacity to act in these ways, either via gaining general public consent that it is legitimate for it to do so or via coercive use of state power. In short, states are involved in the organization and geographies of production in diverse and historically geographically variable ways. The reasons for and the effects of this involvement need to be understood.

The state does not intervene in economy and society from a position that is somehow "outside" them. The institutions of the state apparatus are not simply involved in regulating economy and society, for state activity is necessarily involved in constituting economy and society and the ways in which they are structured and territorially organized. Recipro-cally, geographies of economies and societies influence the ways in which state policies are formulated and implemented. It is important to under-stand why the capitalist state takes the form that it does, constituted in a political sphere formally separate from the spheres of economy and civil society. Equally, it is important to comprehend the capacities, strategies, and functional, institutional, and territorial organization of the state and examine what it does, how it does it, and how it is organized so as to carry out its policy agenda. Consequently, understanding the tangled in-terrelationships among state, economy, and society must involve a combi-nation of structural and institutional approaches to political economy.

Despite the centrality of the state to the economy, there is a percepti-ble degree of uncertainty as how best to theorize and understand the state on the part of economists and economic geographers. Martin and Sunley (1997, 278) suggest that all mainstream schools of economics have prob-lems in coping with the role of the state, tending to treat it in a subsidiary and reductive way. Equally, they suggest that economic geographers have been remarkably reluctant to integrate the state into their theorizations and analyses of the space-economy. While there is certainly some truth in these claims, they are overstated. There are approaches to the state, both within the social sciences more generally and specifically within human geography, that provide at least promising starting points for understand-ing relationships between state actions and policies and geographies of economies. These are explored in the remainder of this chapter.

3.2. From a Theory of *the* Capitalist State and Toward a Theory of National States: Why Does the State Take the Form That It Does?

There are many competing theorizations of the state, and of relationships between state, economy, and society; and several ways of classifying these (see, for example, Clark and Dear, 1984; Held, 1983; O'Neill, 1997). Given the theoretical stance to analysis of the process of production out-lined in Chapter 2, state theories grounded in Marxian political economy (Jessop, 1982) and, more particularly, the German "state derivation" de-bate (Holloway and Picciotto, 1978) form the point of departure. This debate sought to relate the form of the state, and the formal separation of the political and economic spheres in capitalist societies, to the defining characteristics of capitalism, such as its specific property relations and so-cial relationships of production. Since the state is located at the level of the social formation rather than that of the capitalist mode of production, however, such an approach seeks to relate the state to relations of produc-tion, their varied conditions of existence, and their effects on other social relationships. It can, however, only be a point of departure in understanding the state, albeit a powerful one.[1]

Two conditions are necessary for the continued viability of capitalism: first, control or elimination of problems of capital accumulation and circulation that are inherent in decentralized processes of production, market exchange, and distribution; second, continual biological and social reproduction of a wage labor force that accepts (willingly or unwillingly) existing power structures, relationships of ownership and domination, and the political character of production and exchange relations. Crucially, however, neither condition is automatically realized within the confines of capitalist social relations; indeed, these are *structured* to lead precisely in the opposite direction. First, the accumulation process is inherently crisis-prone and does not automatically smoothly reproduce itself.[2] This is because it is grounded in competitive relations between social agents, since capital exists as competing units.[3] Second, the reproduction of a wage labor force providing labor-power as and when required and on terms defined, if not dictated, by capital is chronically challenged at both individual and collective levels within workplaces, local communities, and national territories.[4] Thus, the smooth operation of commodity production and exchange is constantly under threat from the contested basis of production and political conflicts among the classes of capital and labor over the distribution of social product (of the output produced), and the relative magnitude of wages, profits, and rents. In this sense, the need to regulate competitive relations between capital and labor, between companies, and between groups of workers *implies* the need for some systematic "mediating" agency that is relatively autonomous from these various class interests.

The "state derivation" debate sought systematically to derive the state as a "relatively autonomous" political form,[5] existing in a political sphere formally separate from that of the economy, from the character of capitalist relations of production and the category of capital.[6] As such, it is an attempt logically to derive the form of *the* capitalist state. The debate subsequently evolved to recognize the need to analyze the evolution of particular state forms historically (and by implication geographically). State derivation theorists increasingly emphasized the significance of the historical specificities of states within the general form of the capitalist state. There are several strands to the debate, but these can be condensed to two main approaches: those who sought to derive the necessity of the form of the state from relationships between capitals and those who sought to derive it from relations between capital and labor.

Deriving the necessity for the state from relationships between capitals is the "mainstream" approach (Holloway and Picciotto, 1978, 19), based on the premise that the existence of capital as competing units requires the existence of the state to ensure that the collective interest of capital-in-general is established. Capital and the state necessarily exist in formally separate economic and political spheres since the state must be capable of representing the interest of capital-in-general. This is because no individual capitalist can guarantee societal reproduction, and pursuit of the general interests of capital may of necessity involve policies that run counter to particular capitalist interests. State derivation theorists of this persuasion[7] assume that, within limits defined by the exigencies of capital accumulation, the state can identify and act to secure the general interests of capital. The competitive character of capitalist interests renders the notion of pursuing the general interest of capital problematic since state activity inevitably acts against some interests and hence is open to challenge and contestation. Nevertheless, while a considerable advance on State Monopoly Capital formulations, which nonproblematically fuse the interests of the state and monopoly capital (Jessop, 1982, 33–77), this approach is nevertheless open to criticism on four counts. First, it attributes power and knowledge to the state that it cannot possess. Insofar as the state is required to undertake a function that cannot be fulfilled by private capital, its ability to perform that function is presupposed, lending a strongly functionalist tone to the argument. Second, it has little to say about the state as a form of class domination; in particular, competitive capital-versus-labor relations are taken for granted. Third, it is fundamentally ahistorical. These points indicate the limits of form analysis as espoused by this strand of the state derivation approach. As Blanke and colleagues (1978, 110) put it:

> On this level of abstraction, we can only give a *general point of departure* for the development of "functions" of the reproductive process which must *take form* [original emphasis] in such a manner that they stand outside the system of privately organized social labour. The question of how this process actually occurs, of how it is translated into structure, institutions and process of the state, *can no longer be answered by form analysis* [emphasis added]. This question must be made the object of historical analysis.

In fact, one can add that this question also needs to be made the object of geographical analysis. Fourth, therefore, and of considerable importance to the argument here, this variant of the state derivation approach is fundamentally aspatial. It denies the historical geography of processes of (national) state formation. As such, it clearly points to the limits of *this* version of form analysis in going beyond deriving a theory of *the* capitalist state. It fails to illuminate the processes through which the mosaic of temporally and territorially bounded states emerges, and evolves as an integral part of the broader constitution of societies.

In contrast to this first strand, the second and more promising approach, particularly associated with Hirsch, focuses upon deriving the necessity for the form of the state from the character of capital-versus-labor relations, the exploitation of labor by capital, and the nature of the social relations of domination in capitalist societies. However, logically and historically, the establishment of capitalist production requires the abstraction and removal of relations of force from the immediate point and process of production, thereby constituting discrete "political" and "economic" spheres. The state is represented as a subtle, specific, and historically conditioned form of social relationship of exploitation and class coercion, rather than as a blunt instrument of class rule, "a discrete form that cannot be simply identified with the economic form, the realm of competition" (Holloway and Picciotto, 1978, 24).

For Hirsch the form of the state does not result from the necessity to institutionalize the general interests of capital. Indeed, the structural relationship of state to society renders pursuit of the general interests of capital by the state extremely problematic. The contradictions of capitalist society are reproduced *within* the state apparatus. As a result it is doubtful that the state can ever act adequately in the interest of capital in general. This is a crucial point, for it breaks the *logical* connection between the laws of motion of capital and the content of state activity. Once again, the limits of the state derivation approach are reached, for this suggests that the content of state activity is open to the influence of *other* social forces and groups (both class- and non-class-based) in addition to the interests of capital *and* that these other influences are historically and geographically variable. As such, they are to be revealed via careful theoretically informed empirical analysis rather than logical deduction. The state is certainly an institutional and organizational ensemble with its own powers and resources, but these are not equally available to all agents and social forces. There is a marked selectivity in who has privileged access to these powers. Nor, however, are these forces themselves fully constituted outside of the state; they are also partially formed and organized through state agencies and structures. The resources that the state can deploy, for example, render it an arena for social struggle. Understanding how struggles are resolved within it requires explicating linkages between agency and structure, taking into account the differential power and resources available to individuals and collectivities seeking to pursue their interests through the state. At the same time, the contours of this struggle are molded by the institutional and organizational forms of the state. Consequently, a nuanced and sophisticated understanding of the capitalist state must recognize that it is a social force in its own right. It does not *simply* reflect the dynamic of capital or the interests of particular social groups in civil society in its policy making and practices. Understanding how and why a particular state structure derives from and relates to a given capitalist social formation requires explaining exactly how the power relations of capitalism are constituted and translated into the institutions of the state apparatus.

There are some necessary relationships between capital and state, however. While the state does not represent the general interests of capital, its continued existence as a particular form of social relationship depends upon reproducing the social relations of capital and the successful continuation of the accumulation process. Once it has emerged *as* a capitalist state, in the final analysis such a state is necessarily committed to reproducing capitalist social relations. The state *is* not *and cannot be* "neutral" in its exercise of power. It is bound by its structural connections with capitalist property relations to secure conditions for accumulation and the reproduction of capitalist societies, on which its own reproduction depends. Consequently, the state's activities are bounded, constrained, and conditioned by this precondition to its own existence. While capital needs the state to secure conditions for accumulation, so states require successful accumulation to finance their own activities via siphoning off a share of the social product (as taxes on profits, rents, wages, and so on). Thus, capital and the capitalist state necessarily exist in relations of mutual but asymmetric dependence. Because of its form, separated from the immediate process of production, the state is essentially restricted to *reacting* to the outcomes of historically and geographically specific processes of private production and social reproduction. At the same time it is unavoidably bound up in establishing the conditions within and through which these processes can evolve. However, Hirsch perhaps takes too reactive a view of the state, reflecting the European context in which he developed his ideas. There is evidence of national states elsewhere adopting proactive strategies to increase private profitability rather than just reacting to the threat of falling profitability, but there is no doubting the value of his analysis of the state overall.

Thus, the activities, individual functions, and the institutional apparatuses of the state develop through mediated reactions to the vagaries of the contradictory processes of accumulation. For Hirsch, these contradictory tendencies are most emphatically expressed in the tendency for the rate of profit to fall. This, along with the countertendencies that it triggers, is consequently seen as central both to the trajectory of accumulation *and* to the development of the state. The tendency for the rate of profit to fall is thus not seen as some deterministic iron law of economics but as an expression of a social process of class struggle that is integral to capitalism and that generates the necessity constantly to reorganize capitalist relations of production—and, as one element of this, geographies of production.

Moreover, states are deeply implicated in mediating and regulating these processes of class struggle, and also in constituting the terrain on and through which these struggles take place. This is a problematic process that "can *only* proceed in a crisis-ridden manner" (Hirsch, 1978, 78, emphasis added). Thus, the trajectory of the process of accumulation and development of capitalist society decisively depends on whether and in what manner the necessary reorganization of the conditions of production and relations of exploitation succeeds. Since the state is necessarily embedded in crisis-ridden processes of societal reorganization, crisis tendencies are unavoidably embedded in the path of state activity and development. Hirsch's approach thus provides a framework for an historical and materialist analysis of the state. "Implicit in the very concept of 'form' is the idea that it is historically determined and developing. . . . It is hard to see how an adequate form analysis can be anything other than historical" (Holloway and Picciotto, 1978, 27). Indeed, Hirsch's analysis is at least implicitly historical-geographical.

While state activity and institutions evolve within limits set by the form of the capitalist state, that form itself is altered in the process of capitalist development. In this account, form analysis goes beyond explaining why the capitalist state exists in the form that is does to explore what the state does and how it does it, for it is through the processes of defining what and implementing how as it seeks to grapple with crisis management that the form of the state is altered over the longer term. The historical geography of the development of actual state functions and institutions is implicit in Hirsch's logical derivation of state form, rather than an adjunct to be added once the logical derivation has occurred. The social and the spatial are thus conceptualized as mutually constituting and determining. Consequently, "the investigation of state functions must be based upon the conceptual analysis of capitalist accumulation; . . . this is not a question of the logical deduction of abstract laws but of the conceptually informed understanding of an historical process" (Hirsch, 1978, 82). What the state does and how it seeks to do it will thus vary as an integral part of the combined and uneven historical geography of capitalist development.

The necessity to sensitize analyses of the state more fully to the exigencies of historical geographical processes is further emphasized by Gerstenberger (1978). She stresses the need to take account of the concrete course of class struggles in particular societies, of the fragmentation of capital into national capitals, and the associated organization of political power within the territorial shell of national states. Gerstenberger thus problematizes the issue of the extent to which we can speak of a theory of *the* capitalist state as opposed to a theory of territorially defined capitalist *states*. There is an ever present tension in analyses of the capitalist state. On the one hand, it is vital to acknowledge historical-geographical specificities in the ways in which states are constituted. Capitalist states have evolved over the long term, historically and geographically, on a national territorial basis that to a degree predates the rise of capitalism itself (Anderson, 1979). One implication of this is that modern capitalist states may well incorporate premodern legacies. On the other hand, the universalizing effects of the capitalist mode of production mean that a theory of *the* capitalist state is both possible and necessary. There is an unavoidable tension between the need for a general theory of "form" (the separation of the political and economic spheres) and for a theory of historically and territorially specific national states within the shifting limits of that form. While it is vital to acknowledge the significance of form, it is equally important not to reduce analysis of the state simply to derivation of its abstract form and slip into a capital-logic account of the state. The specificities of history and geography must be acknowledged in an adequate theorization of capitalist *states*.

Holloway and Picciotto summarize the contributions of the state derivation theorists in this way (1978, 30, original emphasis):

> The "form analysis" approach has not solved the problems of the Marxist theory of the state, but [it has] established the *essential prerequisite for an understanding of the state based in the dialectic of form and content of class struggle*. Form analysis alone is not enough, but just as long as the problem of form is ignored, an adequate approach to the state is just not possible.[8]

Far from assuring the functionality of state activity for capital, the formal separation of the political from the economic and civil society, and the resultant "relative autonomy" for the state, problematizes securing the conditions necessary for smooth accumulation. The "over-determination of state power" is central to understanding "the deeply problematic functionality of the state apparatus and state power" (Jessop, 1982, 227). The complexity and contradictory character of the conditions that make accumulation possible, and the range of potential trajectories of accumulation, ensure that there can be no simple identity between the (alleged) unified needs of capital and state activities and policies. The contradictory, complex, and multiply dimensional goals of the capitalist state can be defined as the protection, maintenance, and reproduction of capitalist society. They have to be translated into means through which these ends can be pursued through various state agencies and institutions via their operational objectives. While it is possible to make some general statements about relationships between forms and functions, there is no deterministic one-to-one relationship between them. These relationships must develop within determinate limits but are conjuncturally specific, contingent, and variable within them. It is, therefore, necessary to define which particular conditions must be satisfied to secure a given accumulation strategy, in a specific manner, time, and place.

3.3. National States, Economies, and Civil Societies

Whatever their differences, theorists of the capitalist state agree on the need to relate a theory of the state to a theory of society, on the premise that we cannot understand the form of the state, or the policies it pursues, outside of this context. Given the inherently uneven and contradictory character of societal development, the state exists in a complex environment, with intricate webs of relationships linking it to the society in which it is embedded and which it helps to constitute. One way of beginning to incorporate this complexity back into analyses of the state, therefore, is to conceptualize capitalist societies as consisting of a triad of economy, state, and civil society. The state is separate from the economy, with its autonomy (generally—there are exceptions, discussed below) grounded in the sphere of circulation (Urry, 1981, 30), and both are separate from the sphere of civil society. Economy, state, and society can thus be thought of as interlinked and mutually constitutive (see Figure 3.1) of the whole system.

"Civil society" refers to the realms of personal relations, family, relations of ethnicity, gender, and place, of interest groups defined in myriad ways other than those of class and economic interest. All seek to advance or protect their own cause, albeit on the basis of differential endowments of power and resources. Not all people in capitalist societies are capitalists, managers, or workers. But those that are, also are citizens with rights and obligations that are not coincident with their immediate economic interests. Nevertheless, all citizens are affected by the accumulation process insofar as this has implications for state revenues and redistributive policies and for issues such as pollution, environmental quality, and environmental risk. Political demands arising within the sphere of civil society can thus affect the how, what, and where of production. Speaking of citizens implicitly acknowledges the territoriality of national[9] states and the need for a theory of capitalist *states* that acknowledges these historical-geographical differences.

This conception of relationships between *national* state, economy, and society has two further important implications. First, it recognizes that national states influence a wide range of economic and social relationships, both inside and outside their territories. Moreover, the intra-

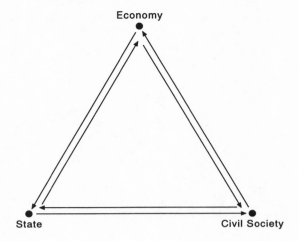

FIGURE 3.1. The triad of civil society, economy, and state.

national territorial organization of the national state is critical in terms of policy delivery and maintaining social cohesion and state legitimacy. Territorially defined national states have reciprocal relations to national economies and civil societies. However, the boundaries between state, economy, and civil society are not rigidly fixed but are shifting and permeable within and between these national territories (Urry, 1981). The national state has absolute authority over its territory, recognized as sovereign by other national states, with which it has a variety of linkages. As well as regulating these relationships, the national state must manage links (competitive and cooperative) with embryonic supranational states (such as the European Community) and extrastate organizations (such as multinational companies) (see Figure 3.2). The existence of national states as part of an international state system has important constraining effects. The trajectory of change of the world economy, and the position of a national economy within it, is both enabling and constraining. Political elites and governing politicians create their country's version of the dominant growth model within the constraints set by particular phases in the evolution of the world economy (Taylor, 1992, 41). While acknowledging the significance of these wider constraints, it is important to avoid a reductionist position, reducing national strategies to the effects of global swings of long waves.[10] It is necessary to explain *why* there are national specificities and why these take the forms that they do. National uniqueness as well as international interdependence is important in this regard. The territoriality of the political entity is paramount.

Second, this conception of relationships recognizes that the scope

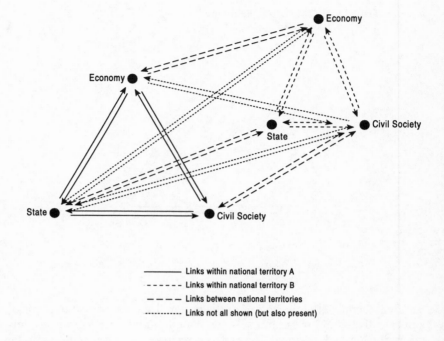

FIGURE 3.2. Relations between national civil societies, economies, and states.

and content of state policies is open to multiple sources of influence; there are many proximate causes, which mutually determine trajectories of state activity. States have to balance two sorts of demands in formulating and implementing their policies. First, they must ensure the smooth accumulation of capital in their national territory (with all that this implies for interstate competition over issues such as trade and investment). Second, they must continue to be seen to be acting legitimately, both to preserve the authority of the state and the hegemony of capitalist social relations. Seeking to satisfy these contradictory demands creates problems for the state in carrying out its own activities, displacing crisis tendencies from the economy and/or civil society into the operations of the state. They may then emerge as crises *of* state activity, translated into hard policy choices in which the prioritization of accumulation must prevail in a capitalist state. But if the state is exercising power with the objective "in the last instance" of reproducing capitalist social relations, this leaves open the question of *how* it seeks to do so. *How*, in other words, does it walk the tightrope between the competing demands of accumulation and legitimation?

3.4. National States and Social Regulation

The national state plays a—indeed, *the*—key role in social reproduction, although it is not the only national scale regulatory institution and mechanism; nor is the national the only territorial level of regulation. Moreover, reflecting the complex and multidimensional character of capitalist societies, and the variety of interests represented within them, the state is confronted with a demanding policy agenda. Internally, it seeks to balance competing claims over accumulation strategies and economic growth trajectories while also dealing with issues of equity and social justice in the distribution of the benefits and costs of growth. As capitalist societies have become more complex, the balance of issues on the agenda that the state sets for itself or has set for it by other social forces has changed.[11] There have also been significant changes in the ways in which states approach their roles of crisis avoidance and management in order to try to guarantee relatively long periods of economic prosperity and social stability. The state seeks to support a particular growth model and sustain a particular set of social and political bargains and compromises to allow this. The contrasts between the United Kingdom and the United States, West Germany, Sweden, and Japan during the 1980s provide a striking example of the different ways in which national state strategies can develop in the context of the same global economic and political environment (Lash and Urry, 1987).

A potentially promising approach to theorizing the state in these terms has been developed by the French Regulation School (Dunford, 1990). The significance of the national state in balancing increases in productivity and consumption within the national territory is perhaps the primary insight of the regulationists. They place particular emphasis upon the role of the state in equilibrating productivity increases with increases in consumption levels and patterns via its taxation and income redistribution policies.[12] Regulationists advocate an approach that privileges neither production nor reproduction but emphasizes the correspondence within a given mode of development between régimes of accumulation and modes of regulation necessary for social systemic stability. In this way they seek to escape "the functionalist dead end" of more traditional approaches to understanding the state (Mayer, 1992, 266). Regulationist approaches seek to negotiate the straits between "agentless structures and structureless agents" (Jenson, 1990), although they only partially succeed in doing so. Fully bridging the straits would involve conjoining regulation theory with discourse theory, in order to show how modes of regulation are discursively constituted. As Peet puts it (1997a, 40), "The dominant discourses of a time are the prime agencies in the cultural formation of economic rationalities. In such ways may discourse theory and regulation theory be conjoined."[13] Establishing a mode of regulation involves a "representational struggle" as to the most appropriate way of coupling consumption and production, emphasizing the political character of the mode of regulation (MacLeod and Jones, 1998).

A régime of accumulation refers to a relatively stable aggregate relationship between production and consumption. This temporal stability implies some correspondence between changes in consumption and the lifestyles and living conditions of waged workers and those in production—notably changing labor productivity. Mode of regulation refers to the regulatory mechanisms within the state and in civil society, the body of beliefs, habits, laws, and norms consistent with and supportive of a régime of accumulation and that, in fact, make it possible. As such, a mode of regulation is a set of mediations that contain the accumulation process within limits compatible with social cohesion within a given territorial formation (see Aglietta, 1999, 44). Not all combinations of régime of accumulation and mode of regulation are feasible, however. This insight directs attention to the complex relations—political practices, social norms, and cultural forms—that allow the dynamic and unstable capitalist system to function, at least for a period, in a relatively coherent and stable fashion. As a key element in this, the state seeks to ensure that national economic growth rates are both sufficient and sustainable, with the national territory appropriately located within the overall accumulation process. In this way the state can fund its own activities, avoid the dangers of fiscal crisis, and legitimate its policy stance. It also seeks to guarantee that changes in conditions of production and consumption are mutually consistent and compatible (via taxation and income redistribution policies, for example) and that the mode of regulation is itself successfully reproduced (for example, through educational and health policies).

Modes of regulation do not simply exist, preformed and awaiting discovery by national states, however. Conversely, national states are not "the prisoners of a fixed genetic code" (Weiss, 1997, 18), with no possibilities to adapt varied forms and modes of regulation. Indeed, experimentation with regulatory systems and projects is likely to be an ongoing process. The "problem" for the state is to "discover" or invent a mode of regulation appropriate to a particular macroeconomic growth model, a particular régime of accumulation. Modes of social regulation are formed within determinate limits through indeterminate political and social struggles, while the establishment of a stable coupling between an accumulation system and a mode of regulation is contingent, a chance discovery. An "appropriate" mode of regulation—which includes state policies as an integral component but is not reducible to them—enables the competing demands of accumulation, fiscal rectitude on the part of the state, and legitimation to be made temporarily compatible. Compatibility needs to be achieved on two levels. First, in terms of the different "political shells" within which state structures are situated, which are broadly divisible into democratic and nondemocratic, depending upon the extent to which state authority and power are secured by consensus and persuasion as opposed to coercion and the exercise of the state's legitimate monopoly of physical force and violence within the national territory.[14] Parliamentary democracy has long been regarded as the "best possible shell" for capitalism because it provides a powerful ideological buttress to the structure of capitalist social relationships (Jessop, 1978), although it is not the only feasible one (Tickell and Peck, 1995). Other democratic forms of representation include clientilism, corporatism, and pluralism, and these are not necessarily mutually exclusive within any given society. There are sufficient examples of nondemocratic political systems to illustrate the point that democracy is not necessarily associated with capitalism. These include the totalitarian German fascist state (Neumann, 1944), the apartheid state of South Africa, the dictatorial régimes of southern Europe (Poulantzas, 1975), and the "strong states" of southeast Asia (Wade, 1990; Woo Cumings, 1999). All of these had and in some respects still have direct impacts on production organization and labor control within and beyond the workplace. Second, within any particular "political shell," compatible combinations of growth models and forms of economic organization and modes of regulation must be discovered. There are, for example, national variations around the canonical generic Fordist régime of accumulation, with differences in both the dominant growth model and mode of regulation (Lash and Urry, 1987). The coexistence of these national variants was permitted by the international monetary system, which left scope for national autonomy in selecting the mode of regulation (Aglietta, 1999, 60). In the context of debates about a putative transition from Fordism to post-Fordism, a number of differing ways have been identified in which relations between capital and labor, between companies, and between companies, labor, and states can be feasibly configured (Dunford, 1991; Leborgne and Lipietz, 1991).[15]

3.5. Crisis Tendencies, National State Regulation, and the Limits to Regulationist Approaches

State involvement in economy and society does not abolish crisis tendencies but internalizes them within the state and its mode of operation. This is particularly so with the transition from a liberal to an interventionist mode of state operation (Habermas, 1976; Offe, 1975a, 1975b, 1976, 1984). A liberal mode of state involvement sets the parameters within which the law of value operates within a particular state territory and through which the variably (in)visible hand of the market functions as a resource allocation mechanism. An interventionist mode of state involvement goes beyond this with policies that reveal the visible hand of the state and supplement or replace rather than merely facilitate market mechanisms, for example, via nationalizing key sectors of industry or assuming responsibility for educational and health care provision. While the proximate motives for this major qualitative extension of state activities vary, in the final analysis it is because they are no longer (sufficiently) profitable to attract private capital. Nonetheless, they are seen as goods and services that "have" to be provided, for economic, political or social reasons, as the boundary between private and public sector provision is redrawn (Hudson, 1986a). Defined in this way, all national states in the advanced capitalist world are now, to varying degrees, interventionist. The issue is the extent and forms of involvement, the political projects and strategies that inform this, and the degree to which there are similarities and differences between national states in this regard.

The fact that the state assumes responsibility for provision of vital goods and services does not, however, abolish the economic crisis tendency that initially necessitated this extension of state involvement. Production of these goods and services does not become economically nonproblematic simply by virtue of being taken over by the state. As a result, the underlying crisis can, in the fullness of time, emerge in different forms, either within the operations of the state or within civil society. Three forms of such crises are of relevance here. Rationality crises arise because there are competing pressures seeking to shape state action: for example, those of efficiency versus equity. As a result, there can be, and often are, unintended effects as well as—or instead of—intended outcomes. Often these unintended effects are overtly spatial in their manifestations. While a mode of regulation must be capable of containing the spatial contradictions of an economic growth model, regulatory mechanisms often have unintended spatially differentiating effects, in part because regulatory processes interact contingently with existing patterns of uneven development and historically prior uses of space. Legitimation crises may emerge, or at least be threatened, because of this chronic gap between actual and intended outcomes. In some circumstances this can even lead to a challenge to the authority of the state itself, and so to the dominant pattern of social relationships represented through that state—as, for example, in Italy in the early 1990s. Or it may generate tensions that challenge the territorial integrity of the national state.[16] This leads the state to seek strategies to reassert the legitimacy of its actions and maintain the unity of its territory.

The generalized direct involvement of the state in the domains of other institutions and associations, such as political parties, trade unions, and corporations, and in the processes through which economic and social interests are represented to government renders state activity unavoidably problematic and crisis-prone for other reasons (Offe, 1984). Social turbulence and political resistance (for example, to rising taxation levels or fears of rising inflation) are continuously, chronically, and routinely internalized within the state apparatus. This is part and parcel of its ongoing attempts to manage and distribute resources in ways that satisfy prevailing notions of social justice and moral rectitude as well as the achievement of economic growth (O'Neill, 1997, 296). These too constitute threats to capital accumulation and state legitimacy. Conflict and tension are normal, as groups with different and competitive logics seek to influence the course of, or be included in the domain of, state actions. The state is neither an arbiter nor a regulator nor an uncritical supporter of capitalism, but it is "enmeshed"—and *unavoidably* so—in its contradictions (Held, 1989, 71). For "the social processes necessary for the reproduction of labour, private ownership and commodity exchange . . . are regulated and sustained by *permanent* political intervention" (Offe, 1976, 413, original emphasis).[17]

There may be yet another complication, however. In some circumstances the state may have to deal with internalized economic contradictions more directly if these reemerge as a fiscal crisis of and for the state itself. O'Neill (1997, 299) suggests that when the state accepts the position of an ex-post facto income distributor, it will "always" suffer fiscal crisis during downturns in the economic cycle, when there are increased distributional demands and falling revenues.[18] As a result, the successful performance of state functions simultaneously is impossible for any extended length of time. Resolving fiscal crises is perhaps the most difficult operation in crisis avoidance and management but one that must be attempted; otherwise, there is a risk that burgeoning state borrowing or public expenditure could trigger a much more generalized economic crisis. One response in such circumstances is to redefine the extent and form of state activity and reduce the resources needed to sustain it. This is not without danger, not least that of triggering a legitimation crisis. However, the immediate political dangers of a legitimation crisis are less serious than those of a generalized crisis of accumulation, although a profound and persistent legitimation crisis would almost certainly undermine accumulation. Not least, successful accumulation is critical for sustenance of the state's own interests. The boundaries between state and market, between public and private sectors, may nevertheless need to be redrawn to reduce the scope of state involvement in economic and social life. Decommodifying the production of goods and services under conditions of parliamentary democratic representation and bureaucratic policy making constantly acts to subvert the logic of the market (Jessop et al., 1988,

160). Consequently, it can generate counterpressures to redraw the public-versus-private sector divide, pulling in the boundaries of state involvement. This leads to recommodification of more of the production of goods and provision of services such as education and health, while introducing pseudoprofitability efficiency criteria into the remaining public sector industries and services and displacing other sorts of service provision back into the household. In summary, "the four centrally important strategies of restructuring of state services will be intensification, commodification, concentration and domestication" (Lash and Urry, 1994, 209).

Such moments of boundary redefinition between private and public sectors may or may not herald the transition to a new régime of accumulation and mode of regulation, may or may not mark significant turning points in developmental trajectories. Whether this actually has been the case can, of course, only be known after the fact and not before. The general implication is nevertheless clear: crises will appear in different forms, as the content, form, and style of state policies and politics varies. Theoretically, therefore, there is no expectation that the policies and political strategies characteristic of *any* feasible combination of régime of accumulation and mode of regulation will form a seamless web. Nor is there an expectation that any particular party political strategy would do so (Hudson, 1989b). One would, however, expect paradoxes and inconsistencies to be more apparent and visible in those moments of transition from an old to a new combination, in those periods of experimentation and seeking out new feasible combinations. Experimentation with regulatory projects is likely to be "particularly pronounced during the interstices of régimes of accumulation" (Peck, 1994, 168).

Paradoxically, and perversely, regulationist approaches have been hampered by a lack of theorization of the state. While they have the potential to provide a theoretical framework in which to understand relationships between state, economy, and society, "it is by no means a fully developed theoretical paradigm" (Mayer, 1992, 266). On the one hand, the way that the state sets about undertaking the practical tasks of "real regulation" (Clark, 1992) and the day-to-day management of the contradictory character of societal development within capitalism is largely unexplored. So too are other processes and institutions of governance. While regulationist approaches have thus opened up a rich conception of social regulation, encompassing both state and nonstate regulatory processes (Dunford, 1997; Theret, 1994), this has not been fully explored by them. On the other hand, the critical issue of the transition from one mode of regulation to another—and the processes of crisis management and resolution that this implies—is also left undiscussed, or assumed away. O'Neill (1997, 297) forcibly criticizes regulationist approaches on this count. They have too little to say about the crucial role of the state in moving societies from one period of stable economic conditions to another, "beyond describing them as intervals of crisis." Furthermore, regulationist approaches have little to say about crises and modes of crisis resolution. Accumulation crisis is depicted as a "singular, totalised event." The possibility of a multitude of unrelated economic events, in different cycles of growth and decline, at different spatial scales, and under different forms of governance is ignored. So too is the possibility of strategic economic restructuring driven by the state (as has been the case in southeast Asia since the 1960s).[19] There is an implicit denial that conflict and contradiction may be the normal course of events in the internal operations of state apparatuses. Rather, it is assumed that crises are resolved and a new stable combination of régime of accumulation and mode of regulation mysteriously emerges full-fledged and functioning. For other critics, conceptualizing regulation in terms of shifts between periods of stability is seen as misguided. Such periods of stability, in contrast, are seen as unusually rare events in a world more appropriately understood as uneasily held together by a web of contradictory regulatory practices (Goodwin and Painter, 1996; Painter and Goodwin, 1995).

O'Neill sets out four criteria against which to judge the adequacy of a theory of the state. It should "say something" about the way the state functions; how it stabilizes and transforms régimes of accumulation; how it operates through geographic scales, not simply how it is constrained by scale; and how it is, and should be, involved with redistribution. Regulationist approaches fail to meet these criteria because of their idealization of the form and function of the contemporary state. However, there is an extensive corpus of theory that specifically addresses the ways in which form and function are produced, enabling several of the deficiencies of regulationist approaches to be remedied. Recognition that the content and scope of state activities and policies are subject to multiple sources of influence has important implications for the way in which the state seeks to resolve the competing claims of accumulation and legitimation. The task confronting the state is generally more complex than simply managing its relations to capital, for it must address a wider constituency, often against the background of a rapidly changing environment. The state seeks to restructure *itself* in response to perceptions about the changing external environment with which it has to deal and the problems of dealing with qualitatively different and complex problems simultaneously. Consequently, the state's attempts to grapple with the problems and geographies of production must be seen in this broader context and not in isolation. Offe (1975a, 135) provides a very important insight into this; the state, he wrote, organises certain activities and measures directed towards the *environment* and it adopts for *itself* a certain organisational procedure from which the production and implementation of policies emerge. Every time a state deals with a problem in its environment, it deals with a problem of itself, that is, its internal mode of operation.

O'Neill (1997, 299) echoes this. The state is forced to make a constant attempt to reconcile the contradictions inherent to its involvement in the economy and society by altering its own internal structures and modes of operation. The specificities of this "problem solving," the "internal structures and mode of operation" of the state, must be investigated, historically and empirically. State theory must give major consideration to the structure and behavior of the state's apparatus (Cerny, 1990). The state is made up of numerous institutions (departments of central government, local government, other state agencies, and so on), and the ways in which they relate to one another and function are constituted politically. There is conflict between state agencies and organizations in deciding the policy agenda and the scope and content of policies in response to problems of governance and regulation that confront them. Rather than be treated as a "black box," which generates policy outputs in response to pressures and support from the economy and society, the state must be opened up to reveal the variety of its constitutive institutions and the ways in which they interrelate. The internal forms of organization of the state as an institutional ensemble, and its capacity to reproduce itself as such, are critical to the ways in which it addresses the problems confronting it. Moreover, the state is not simply an arena for conflict among classes and groups in civil society, a passive setting in which such struggles are resolved. It also provides an organizational structure through which groups can pursue their own interests and that shapes the ways in which they do so. Different classes, class fractions, and other interest groups have variable access to the institutions of the state and differential opportunities to try to influence and shape the state policy agenda and priorities. Moreover, state agencies and organizations seek to pursue *their* own goals as well as responding to pressures from other social forces.

In practice, a national state is trying to attain qualitatively different objectives *simultaneously.* Thus a state, itself internally differentiated and heterogeneous, consisting of conflicting institutions, chronically faces a barrage of competing and largely incompatible priorities to which it must respond in the face of very specific sets of demands. Thus, it operates in an environment that is uncertain, contradictory, conflict-ridden, and prone to create situations in which it will be unable to satisfy all the demands made upon it and all the expectations that it may raise as to its capacity to solve problems. Cerny (1990) refers to the "overloaded state,"

increasingly unable to deal with the demands made upon it because of enhanced flows of money capital, commodities, and information in an increasingly open and global economy at the same time that its traditional
tools of national economic management are increasingly being found to
be wanting. Certainly the underlying class relations that structure state
form and shape state policy priorities set limits to the relations between
organizational structure and objectives, but they do not determine them,
logically or historically (Hirsch, 1978, 107; Therborn, 1980, 35). While
the relationships are determinate, there are no simple one-to-one relationships, and not all relationships are possible (or, put another way, not all
combinations of régimes of accumulation and modes of regulation are
feasible).

In summary, the state is engaged in an attempt at permanent crisis
management, since it cannot abolish the crisis tendencies inherent within
the capitalist mode of production but can only "internalize" them, at
least in part, and contain them for a time. The "ultimate goal" of the
state is the "pursuit of stability," that is, negating the potential political
implications of economic crises, and there have been important changes
in the ways states have approached this task. There was a change in advanced capitalist states from a liberal to an interventionist mode in the
post-1945 period. Rather than simply set legislative limits within which
markets could function, national states increasingly supplemented or even
replaced markets as resource allocation and distributive mechanisms. In
regulationist terms, this represented the discovery of a new mode of regulation, associated with a switch from an extensive to an intensive régime
of accumulation. However described, the net result was growing state involvement in more and more spheres of economic and social life over the
first three decades of the postwar period in much of the advanced capitalist world: in short, varied "corporatist" arrangements. This further
blurred the boundaries between economy, state, and civil society in those
cases.

However, as the last two decades of the twentieth century sharply
demonstrated, with the growing prominence of neoliberal state forms, extending state activity was neither inevitable nor irreversible, as the state
has pulled back and allowed more space for market allocation. The
boundaries as well as the content of state actions are products of political
struggles. This in turn has been associated with a shift in emphasis in
many national states from service provision and direct involvement in the
production of goods and services to an enabling and facilitating role.
Such states seek to support initiatives from within civil society to provide
new sources of employment and service provision in interstices from
which the state has retreated and which the private sector previously
found unattractive. The growth of state activities over the three decades

from the mid-1940s in the advanced capitalist states, penetrating further across the boundaries of both economy and civil society, and the subsequent retreat in many of these same societies can be interpreted as a recognition of the limits to national states' capacities to manage, let alone resolve, crises. As the extent of state activities grew, the state *itself* became more and more the locus of conflict, more and more a participant in conflict (often waged between its own departments and institutions). Pulling back the boundaries of its involvement subsequently became one way of "depoliticizing" the state's activities, returning steering mechanisms from the state to the market (though a market crucially shaped by state policies), and favoring accumulation practices that involve redistributing incomes to capital—an outcome central to neoliberal discourse. This approach also became critical to avoiding state fiscal crises. Conversely, there are lower limits below which state expenditure and involvement cannot fall (within a parliamentary democratic state, at least) if the legitimacy of the state is to be maintained and, more prosaically but no less importantly, if political parties are to win elections (see Figure 3.3).

3.6. "Hollowing Out" and "Reorganization" of National States: From National State Regulation to More Complex Geographies of Regulation and Processes of Governance

Regulationist approaches have tended to give methodological primacy to the national level. This is assumed to be the sole—or at least preeminent—site of state regulation. This claim has increasingly been seen to be unsustainable, theoretically and empirically. There is no necessary reason for regulation to be primarily or predominantly a national scale process, as spatial scales are constituted through political and social struggles and particular representational practices (Jones, 1998). As national growth models and national states policies slipped into crisis, undermined by new and growing forms of globalization, the silences of regulation and state theories about the reallocation of state powers upward, downward, and outward became increasingly problematic. Without denying the continuing significance of the national, the shifting architecture of state power and mechanisms of regulation and governance required acknowledgment. Recognizing this, Peck (1994, 155, emphasis added) makes an important observation:

> Because the social structures of accumulation and regulation are relatively autonomous, yet bound together in a necessary relation, the causal liabilities with which they are endowed will be realised in different ways in different places, dependent upon contingent circumstance.

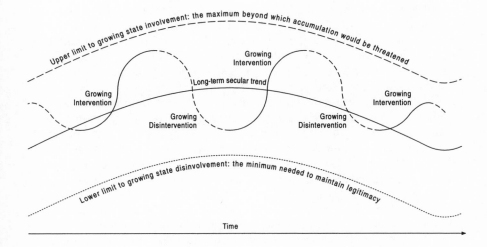

FIGURE 3.3. Limits to and variations in the extent of state involvement.

> One might expect, then, that the nature of the regulation–accumulation relationship *is qualitatively different at each geographical level.*

This suggests a distinctive multilevel geography to the ways in which accumulation and regulation are linked, involving qualitatively different and, to a degree, scale-dependent types of relationships.

Consideration of the extent to which regulation is carried out at other spatial scales is linked to debates about the "hollowing out" of national state activities (Jessop, 1994) and changes in the mode of operation of national states in response to pressures on the national state form "from above" and "from below" (Kolinsky, 1981). Pressures "from above" result from growing globalization of the economy and tendencies toward the transnationalization of political organization and the enhanced significance of regulatory bodies such as the International Monetary Fund (McGrew, 1997). These developments have been enabled by technological and organizational changes, which have been especially marked in markets for money capital. A combination of "securitization, deregulation and electronification" (Lash and Urry, 1994, 18–22) has facilitated radical transformation of these markets, with at least some product markets operating globally and on the basis of 24-hour-a-day trading. There certainly has been a resultant diminution in the capacity of many national states to control monetary and fiscal policy. Equally, however, the national remains critical in relation to money as a pivotal source of social power, for this depends upon its being a *privileged* means to control access to wealth. While money as a representation of value can and must circulate freely, as social power it depends upon some sort of territorial configuration and sociopolitical system (in short, a national state) that render that particular form of social power hegemonic rather than occasional and dispersed (Harvey, 1996, 235).

The relative denationalization of the world economy is thus a contradictory process. It has been linked to the power of private sector companies to create credit and a global credit system that is largely private and subject predominantly to market regulation (Altvater, 1990, 23; Strange, 1988, 30). These new global forms of credit in a debt and paper economy are beyond the control of national states but nevertheless exert great structural power over them (Leyshon and Thrift, 1992), reducing the powers of both national states and international bodies to steer national economies (Lash and Urry, 1994, 292). Moreover, finance and industry have both been internationalized but as relatively uncoordinated circuits of capital, further complicating the task of national states in managing and reproducing national economies, for in these circumstances money as a means of payment at best imperfectly represents value created through material processes.

This new set of circumstances emphasizes the inherently speculative character of transactions within such an economy. Credit represents a claim on surplus-value yet to be produced, and there is no necessary relationship between the national territories in which it is produced and those in which claims to it are made. However, only a fraction of financial product markets are organized and operate on a truly global basis, and even then in and through a very small number of nodes in the global economy (notably London, New York, and Tokyo; Sassen, 1991). Moreover, the creation of global markets has been actively authored by national states (Panitch, 1996), which continue to form key sites of regulation of such markets. Thus, "it is not a question of whether capital's internationalization *results* in the decline of the state, but rather how the state continues to *participate* in capital's internationalization in order to reproduce itself" (Yeung, 1998, 293).

Pressures "from below" are generated because of regionalist and nationalist movements within the boundaries of national states, informed by complex mixtures of cultural, economic and political motives.[20] For example, economically advanced regions seek increased autonomy in an attempt to reduce fiscal transfers to less successful regions (as in Catalonia in northeast Spain and the movement to establish "Padania" in northern Italy; Giordano, 1998; Schech, 1988). In contrast, economically disadvantaged regions seek greater autonomy precisely because central state regional policies have failed to improve their economic well-being (as in

Corsica and Scotland; Kofman, 1985; Smith and Brown, 1983). Such separatist pressures typically become most powerful when economic motives combine with a sense of political oppression of culturally "suppressed nations" (as in Quebec or in the Basque country in northern Spain; Anderson, 1995). As with the shift upward of regulatory powers, national states are not innocent and passive bystanders in these processes of territorial decentralization of power and/or responsibilities. For example, states may seek to preserve the integrity of their national territory by granting increased autonomy to cities and regions within their boundaries.

These twin pressures have reinforced tendencies to shift regulatory practices upward to the supranational level and downward to the regional level and so bring about qualitative changes in relationships between national, supranational, and subnational levels. It is, however, important not to overstate the extent of such changes. Supranational regulatory organizations are well established, and there is a long history of international regulation of global economic relationships by world organizations (Murphy, 1994). This suggests caution in conceptualizing the capitalist economy as *ever* one of sovereign political territories with impermeable national boundaries (cf. Ruggie, 1993).[21] However, there has been a significant expansion in the number of such organizations in the past fifty years (Zacher, 1992) and growing pressures to transfer power upward to the supranational level (for example, to the institutions of the European Union). As a result, a more complex architecture of political power and space has emerged. There has also been a long-established subnational territorial structure to state power in response to requirements of administrative efficiency and political legitimacy. Increasingly, however, there have also been pressures further to shift the power to shape policies for regions to the regional level (a decentralization of power to decide and resources to implement decisions rather than local and regional levels simply administering central government policies for these areas) and so produce a greater degree of correspondence between administrative spaces and locally meaningful places.

However, in many ways, "hollowing out" is a Eurocentric concept, developed in particular in relation to the recent experiences of western European states and shifting levels of state power between supranational EU, national, and regional levels. More generally, it is important to remember the legacies of (neo)imperialism and to situate debates about globalization and "hollowing out" in the context of new forms of combined and uneven development. Former colonial states generally embarked on postcolonial status with very little authority and power in key areas such as regulation of the economy. Consequently, they had very little to "hollow out." Moreover, their attempts to acquire effective powers are routinely undermined because of their position of structural subordination within the hierarchy of national states. Other states, notably the United States, have continued to maintain enormous structural power. Furthermore, such states (especially the United States), often in collaboration with multinational political organizations (such as the IMF, World Trade Organization, and World Bank) that they dominate, have promoted discourses and practices of globalization as a way of "hollowing out" other national states and reinforcing their dominant position.

The processes of state restructuring are, however, more complex than just "hollowing out." Jessop (1997) refers to the "reorganization" of the state, a triple process of denationalization (hollowing out), destatization of the political system and the internationalization of policy régimes. Thus, as well as shifting regulatory capacity up and down from the national level, there has been a shift in emphasis from government to governance, with enhanced significance placed upon the institutions of civil society. Regulatory capacities have been shifted "outward" to nonstate organizations, broadening the focus from issues of the state and regulation to those of social practices, civil society, and governance. A range of organizations and institutions within civil society has been incorporated into processes of governance, often with direct effects on the structuring of the economy and geographies of production (Dunford and Hudson, 1996). Furthermore, such formal institutions have increasingly become organized on a transnational basis, especially in relation to environmental issues that are widely acknowledged as global (for example, Friends of the Earth and Greenpeace have both evolved to become transnational organizations; Yearley, 1995b).

In summary, the reorganization of the national state involves moving regulatory capacities both upward and downward within state structures and outward from the state into the institutions of civil societies. The "hollowed out" metaphor is a partial account of a shift in, rather than a diminution of, the role of the national state, with complex new relationships emerging between and within different institutions at different scales.[22] The concept of reorganization is broader but does not denote the demise of national entities but rather the emergence of new and more complicated structures of regulation involving complex links between the national, supranational, and subnational. Moreover, while relationships between accumulation and regulation are constituted differently at each level, there are also variations *within* levels. The variety of national capitalisms finds a parallel in the variety of state capacities and strategies, and these are likely to become more rather than less pronounced (Weiss, 1997, 16). The growing emphasis on governance as opposed to regulation is recognition of the increasing importance—or perhaps more accurately is increasing recognition of the importance—of the institutions of civil society in securing the conditions under which successful production is possible. It acknowledges the social constitution of the economy, the embedding of the economy in cultural and political traditions and arrangements.[23]

Contrary to the claims of some advocates of both globalization and regionalism, national state regulatory and institutional arrangements continue to remain significant, despite the transfer upward of some state powers and competencies and the upgraded importance of regionally specific institutional and social arrangements. These national entities continue to influence geographies of economies and of production. Globalization of political and economic processes is partly a product of national decisions to change geographies of regulatory régimes, to agree on common objectives and implement common regulations and standards (Hirst and Thompson, 1995, 426). Indeed, the emergence of supranational regulatory and governance institutions in response to increasingly globalized economic transactions may in the long run further reinforce rather than diminish the importance of the national state (Cerny, 1990).[24] While there may be tendencies toward reorganization that weaken the capacities of national states, there may also be countertendencies that reemphasise the significance of national political entities. Some continue to see the national state as an important locus of accumulation, with national institutions continuing to structure economic space much as before (Wade, 1990).[25] While there has been a diminution in national state capacity to control monetary and fiscal policy in many states, they nonetheless retain considerable power and authority in other policy domains. The process of unbundling territoriality has gone further in the EU than elsewhere (Ruggie, 1993), but national states in Europe are neither dying nor retiring to the sidelines, convinced that they have, at most, merely shifted functions (Mann, 1993). Globalization of the economy is leading "neither to the disappearance of nations nor a minimalist state" (Aglietta, 1999, 64), and so reports of "the exaggerated death of the nation-state" (Anderson, 1995) should be treated with appropriate skepticism. Others argue that the national level remains decisive in the governance and regulation of economy and society, in innovation and technology transfer (Lundvall, 1992), in environmental policy (Hudson and Weaver, 1997), and in education, training, and the labor market (Peck, 1994). Indeed, Gertler (1997) suggests that what are commonly seen as differences in regional culture are more accurately understood as strongly shaped by differing national industrial policies and regulatory régimes—a point of immense significance, theoretically and practically. The mix and balance of forms of national state involvement and policy making have qualitatively and significantly changed, but the claim of "neo-medievalists" that the national state has largely been rendered redundant is seriously wide of the mark (Anderson, 1996). Rather than the regional replacing the national, the context in which devolved regional governments operate is strongly conditioned by national state decisions. Regional initiatives are most efficacious when there is effective integration between national and regional level policies and actions.[26] The critical issue is not the replacement of the national by the global and/or local but the character of the national state, the type of regulatory régime that it maintains, and the form of capitalist economy that it seeks to encourage.

Significant changes in the forms and balance of regulatory relationships among the global, national, and regional levels have led to corresponding alterations in the national mode of regulation. While in some important respects the administrative and policy making powers of the national state have declined and its role as an economic manager is lessening,[27] it nonetheless remains the supreme source of legitimacy and delegator of authority "up" and "down" (Hirst and Thompson, 1996). This suggests a thinner and more procedural national state, with its concerns in the economic domain limited to market regulation. It lacks real capacity to influence the economic domain, as it is "simply one class of powers and political agencies in a complex system of power from world to local levels" (Weiss, 1997, 16–17). Significantly, however, Weiss adds that it is doubtful whether this "basic state" hypothesis fits even the EU experience, "which appears to inform so much of this kind of reasoning." It certainly sits uneasily with evidence of other forms of national state regulatory régimes outside western Europe. The national state is therefore not so powerless in the economic domain as the "basic state" proposition implies. However, processes of globalization require different forms of state policy and activity, focused on developing the specific and unique place-bound socioinstitutional assets that enable national states (and their constituent cities and regions) to locate themselves favorably in a competitive global economy. There are therefore strong grounds for believing that national states will continue to have a central role in the processes of policy innovation, formation, and implementation. The question is, what sort of policies and what sort of national state are most appropriate in particular contexts?

One consequence of the retreat of the national state is a growing emphasis upon exploring forms of regulation beyond the market facilitating of the liberal and the market replacing of the interventionist, which in varying ways rely upon network conceptions of state activity and capacities. The national state has a pivotal facilitating role in encouraging and steering progressive policy networks—though the notion of "progressive" cannot be divorced from the goals of policy. For Weiss, the alternative is the catalytic state. This emergent state form is reconstituting its power at the center of alliances formed both within and outside the state. Catalytic states thus seek to achieve their goals by assuming a dominant role in co-alitions of national states, transnational institutions, and private sector groups rather than by relying on their own resources. The most important partnerships are those between government and business. These processes of coalition formation are "gambits for building rather than shedding state capacity" (Weiss, 1997, 24–27). This capacity building focuses upon increasing corporate competitiveness, excluding the concerns of organized labor and groups in civil society except insofar as these are seen to coincide with those of dominant private sector interests. For others, the emphasis is upon the enabling state, creating partnerships between state agencies and social partners, with a broader policy agenda encompassing social inclusion and not simply private sector interests (Amin, 1998). There has been a change in the mode of operation *of* national states. Rather than directly (or indirectly) providing goods and services on a decommodified basis *for* people, the state is now more concerned to provide an enabling and facilitating environment. This allows social partners to provide goods and services *for themselves* with state assistance and support. Such forms of self-help are partly a response to the void left by the retreat of the interventionist state, partly a response to new and previously unmet (and unarticulated) social needs. This shift in the character of state policy is informed by a view that more sophisticated nonprice forms of economic competitiveness necessarily depend upon cooperative social relationships within cohesive and inclusive societies.[28] However, the transition from an interventionist to a catalytic or an enabling mode of state activity does not mean that national states cease to have an interventionist role, any more than the transition from liberal to interventionist state ended national state involvement in the construction and regulation of markets.

The proponents of neoliberalism and a thin and procedural national state presiding over a competitive society of asocial, atomized individuals certainly present a particular view of the new relations between states and global markets. They do so precisely because they see no alternative to the forces of irresistible globalization. For example, for Ohmae (1995, 11) the national state is a "nostalgic fiction." However, they play down the extent to which strong states may be active facilitators and perpetrators rather than passive victims of the processes of "globalization" (Weiss, 1997, 20). Others emphasize the continuing significance of the national state as a site of resistance, both to the specifics of globalization and to the more general dominance of unfettered market forces. They emphasize the continuing possibilities for a strong state to act directly in pursuit of an egalitarian and inclusive society (Boyer and Drache, 1995). The transition to new forms of national state activity does acknowledge, however, that the mix and balance of forms of involvement and policy making have qualitatively and significantly been altered. Moreover, this shift is necessary because of increasingly interlinked national markets within a strongly internationalizing economy and the constraints of a formally democratic political system. O'Neill (1997, 298, emphasis added) makes the point as follows:

> Increasingly open and integrated national markets do not so much threaten or undermine the operation or effectiveness of state apparatuses as *require* them to undergo qualitative change. *Critically, this qualitative shift is not optional* for the continuation of successful accumulation processes and, *in the absence of oppression*, for the production and distributional outcomes that maintain legitimacy.

3.7. What Do National States Do to Ensure That Production Is Possible?

National states are involved with the regulation and governance of production in a variety of ways, set within the context of the generalized engagement between state, economy, and society in the constitution of capitalism. They seek to secure conditions of production that are not and cannot be produced through the laws of the market, so that capital has required access to labor-power, nature, and the infrastructure of built environments (J. O'Connor, 1994). They can be thought of pursuing a threefold hierarchy of operational objectives (Clark and Dear, 1984, 43, drawing on J. O'Connor, 1973). This rank ordering implies both priorities and contingencies in state actions. The preeminent objective is to secure social consensus upon, or in other ways guarantee acceptance of, the prevailing social contract—"the rules of the game"—by all groups in society. This *must* be given primacy, for two reasons. First, it provides order, stability, and security via generalized acceptance of state-defined rules of socially (il)legitimate activities. Second, *only* when these relations are set in place can production and exchange occur with any degree of predictability. Thus, social consensus or compliance—however achieved—is crucial in securing the conditions of production and reproduction as social activities. The next objective is to secure the conditions of production by regulating social investment and consumption to ensure the reproduction of a labor force, access to required natural resources and natural environments, and the provision of necessary infrastructure in the built environment. Attaining these objectives allows the state to guarantee—or at least appear to try to guarantee—the material survival of all social classes and groups and in this way its own survival. The third objective is to secure social integration by ensuring the welfare of all groups, especially subordinate classes and social groups (for example, ethnic minorities). This goal is pursued via taxation, income redistribution, and welfare programs, and is predicated upon the first two objectives being successfully attained.

The pursuit of these three objectives is inherently problematic, however. Consequently, national states are deeply involved in conflicting, contradictory, and spatio-temporally variable ways in regulating and governing production. J. O'Connor (1994, 166) emphasizes that "there is hardly any state activity or budgetary item that does not concern itself in different ways with one or more of the conditions of production." Furthermore, state policies help structure the choices available to firms (Mytelka, 1993, 60). Such policies may be conceptualized in a variety of ways, depending upon their effects of production, circulation, and exchange (Jessop, 1982, 233–241; O'Neill, 1997). A particular national state is not necessarily involved in all the forms of activity outlined below at any given point in time, and the ways in which a state pursues these objectives also varies as circumstances change. These varied activities can be thought of as falling into one of two broad types: setting framework conditions and more direct engagements with the organization of production and social reproduction.

Setting Framework Conditions

Constructing an Appropriate Architecture of Political Relations between the National, Supranational, and Subnational

While the "hollowing out" and "reorganization" theses suggest changes in the mode of national state regulation, national states continue to occupy a pivotal position in constructing political-economic framework conditions at three territorial levels: the international, the national, and the intranational. As well as influencing investment, output, and the location of activities within their territories via national economic policies, national states also seek to regulate interstate and intrastate economic relations. They pursue the first goal by international agreements over issues such as the movement of people and the circulation of capital in its various forms. They seek to attain the second objective via decisions about the distribution of political power and resources within their national territory.

At the international level the national state regulates affairs between itself and other national states (and "multinational" political and economic organizations), and, as suggested above, its capacity to form alliances with other national states and international organizations may be becoming more important as the economy becomes increasingly internationalized—perhaps globalized. There is undoubtedly a marked absence of effective global regulatory mechanisms. Organizations such as the International Monetary Fund (IMF) have limited powers and depend for them upon national states. As Lipietz (1986) emphasizes, the international division of labor does not exist as some deus ex machina but is the product of national state strategies, prevailing power bloc interests within national states, and asymmetrical power relations between national states. National states still largely set the political frameworks through which international flows of capital, commodities, and labor occur. There are clear links between changing international frameworks for trade, negotiated between national states, and changing international geographies of production and trade. For example, in 1948 international tariffs on traded commodities averaged 48%. Successive rounds of negotiations within the framework of the General Agreement on Trade and Tariffs (GATT) reduced their level to 5% by the end of the 1980s, enabling production to be located more in response to global differences in production costs. This change thus facilitated the emergence of a new international division of labor.[29] The transition from an old to a new international division of labor also critically depended upon the 1944 Bretton Woods agreement to fix exchange rates between national currencies. Money as a medium of exchange developed in the form of national currencies. National states issued national currencies so that international trade depended upon a recognized and accepted system of equating these currencies. The resultant stability of the financial system made it possible to invest offshore to minimize production costs at prices which could be fairly easily predicted (Swyngedouw, 1992, 57).[30] The ending of the Bretton Woods agreement in the early 1970s, and a switch to a new form of regulation of the global financial system and the transition to a system of floating exchange rates (Leyshon and Tickell, 1994), led to corresponding changes in international geographies of production. Global corporations have since sought to locate a production filière *within* a stable currency zone, cloning filières between zones to try to eliminate the unpredictability and risks of currency variations on production costs and profits. In the process they reagglomerated production on a macroregional rather than national basis.[31]

Decisions must be taken about the distribution of state power and resources within national states as between central, regional, and local government and the appropriate territorial bases for this. Changes in the character of accumulation can create pressures for a territorial restructuring of the state, for example, in terms of pressures for local government reform to give "greater efficiency" in service delivery (Hudson and Plum, 1986). This can directly impact on choice of product and location of production, but pressures for territorial restructuring of the state can take more complex forms. Determining the "best" territorial framework to facilitate state control over a spatially extensive and/or socially heterogeneous jurisdiction, and help ensure the legitimacy of state activities, can be a tricky task, especially if national state boundaries encompass or cut across distinctive "nations." The inhabitants of such nations may challenge the legitimacy of the national state and the territorial basis of the mode of regulation, and seek greater autonomy or independence. This may be done democratically and peacefully or violently, and especially in the latter case can have very direct impacts on geographies of production (for example, many parts of the Third World are "no go" areas for industrial capital). In turn, a national state may restructure its own territorial and functional mode of operation to contain such threats and preserve the territorial integrity of the state. The regional decentralization of the Spanish state in the post-Franco era (Fernández Rodríguez, 1985) and the establishment in the United Kingdom of the Scottish and Welsh Development Agencies in the mid-1970s and the Welsh Assembly and Scottish Parliament in the 1990s (Hudson and Williams, 1995) illustrate the point. Such changes can alter the competitive position of areas, and, in turn, geographies of production as regions with devolved powers are better able to compete for mobile investment projects.[32]

Establishing the Legal Frameworks for Markets: Constructing the Architecture of Supply

States face a key political choice as to whether to seek directly or indirectly to regulate economic activities. The former involves setting minimum performance standards, minimum health and safety at work or environmental standards, maximum emission levels, or prohibiting certain forms of action because of their potentially deleterious effects upon people or nature. The latter involves creating markets within which allocative decisions are taken. The boundary between direct state regulation and market mechanisms is a shifting one, but the market remains—and must remain—crucial to capitalist production. At some times issues may be dealt with via "real regulation," at others via constructing markets in particular ways for specific purposes (as, for example, with the emergence of markets for international trading permits in pollution in the 1990s).

The "architecture of supply"—that is, the structure of markets—is indispensable to capitalist production (Zysman, 1993, 107). Moreover, it must be socially and politically constructed and regulated.[33] The importance of this point cannot be overemphasized. There clearly needs to be a legal framework (dealing with capital movement, competition, environmental pollution, mergers, trade unions, and health and safety at work) within which commodity, labor, land, and money markets can operate. However, this legislative framework must respect the asymmetries in power relations that the class relations of capitalism presuppose (Dunford, 1988, 53–54). Such frameworks and markets can be constructed and regulated in different ways. At some points in time, for example, national states oppose mergers as anticompetitive, at others they encourage them to produce globally competitive "national champions" (Storey and Johnson, 1987). The issue is not, however, one of state intervention *in* markets, because the state is always involved in the constitution and formation *of* markets. Without states there would be no markets, and the salient questions concern the nature, purpose, and consequence of particular forms of state action. National states typically seek to define markets that coincide with the boundaries of their national territory or, in the case of former imperial powers, their empires. But often, and arguably increasingly more often, national states are involved in cooperation with other states to shape these markets on a wider spatial scale. These continue to be largely determined at the national level and internationally by agreement between national states, although, especially in the European Union, there is a growing tendency to settle these issues at the supranational level (Amin, 1992; Sadler, 1992).

Such systems of market regulation shape the organization and action of firms, while a market is in turn partly shaped by the rules that enable and limit the actions of firms and other organizations within it. These rules may be formal or informal but must be regularly reaffirmed by collective agreements among key groups, firms, and government institutions. In Japan, for example, since the 1920s state policies have sought to regulate markets so as to promote cartel-regulated competition and the mergers that this presupposes, facilitating cooperation among competitors on prices, output, and investment plans. Such policies seek to avoid the dangers of ruinous cutthroat competition while ensuring industrial dynamism. In this sense, markets are "planned," and governments there strive continuously to reconstitute them as a part of strategic industrial policy. Although new cartel formation became illegal after 1947 (with the enactment of a U.S.-style legislation), "flexible administration" of, and subsequent revision to, the antitrust laws rendered them largely irrelevant. The effects of regulation on markets are not always those intended, however. Antitrust legislation in the United States intended to promote competition by penalizing loose combinations of firms gave incentives to merger activity and the consolidation of activities within the firm (Best, 1990, 104, 168–176).

Shaping markets can be a key element in strategic industrial policies, and some of the many ways in which states can do this are discussed below. The critical point is that such policies are "strategic" precisely because they seek actively to shape markets rather than simply respond to them, to affect the forms that competition takes to enhance economic performance via promoting Schumpeterian, market-disturbing competition and collective entrepreneurial firms.[34] Such policies are increasingly pursued at the national level but also at the supranational level, for example, in the European Union via such initiatives as the European Strategic Programme for Research and Development in Technology (ESPRIT; Mytelka, 1993). Strategic industrial policies seek to go beyond attempts to influence individual firms (important though these were and are) by specific policy actions that shape market conditions confronting all firms in a sector (the "selection environment," to use the terminology of evolutionary economics). This implies that states need to shape markets in ways that promote cooperation as well as competition in order to ensure competitive success. There can be several strands to such strategic industrial policies: strong antitrust procompetition policies, whether formal or informal; creating, preserving or buttressing interfirm networks; ensuring the primacy of strategic corporate policies; a sectoral or universal, rather than firm-specific, focus; and, finally, maintaining an appropriate balance between competition and cooperation. The last aspect is seen as of particular significance in relation to market-shaping policies. As Best puts it (1990, 19, emphasis added):

> That a healthy industrial sector depends upon combining competition with co-operation has far-reaching implications for public policy. It suggests that the task of industrial policy is . . . to administer the paradox:[35] co-operation alone can ensure that commitments are made to the long-term infrastructural development of a sector; competition alone can ensure that business enterprises remain innovative and responsive to new challenges and opportunities.

Consequently, firms are constrained by the rules of markets, but markets are themselves shaped by the formal or informal rules that enable and proscribe the actions of firms within them. Such rules are socially constructed through agreements among key actors and institutions. "In this, markets are planned" (Best, 1990, 167, emphasis added)— suggesting that the dichotomy of "market" and "plan" fails to grasp key features of the social construction of markets. Furthermore, they may be "planned" to change in particular ways, and in this sense markets may be thought of as processes. Japanese industrial policy, for example, has sought to promote internationally competitive businesses in markets that are continuously reconstituted by strategically aware competitors. The role of the state has been instrumental in underpinning the exceptional success of Japanese manufacturing firms in world markets: "the strength of individual firms could not be isolated from the direct and indirect steps taken by government and other agencies to assist manufacturing industries" (Garrahan and Stewart, 1992, 13).

Markets for information and knowledge are a critical sphere of "strategic" market-shaping activity. Assuming that knowledge can be converted from a tacit to a codifiable form, or is from the outset created in codifiable form, establishing intellectual property rights requires a market for knowledge. In turn, this requires creating patents and copyrights. Patent and copyright laws refer to rights to a prototype that can be reproduced. In patent law that prototype is a material object; in copyright law it is an intellectual object or idea. As knowledge becomes increasingly central to the contemporary economy, issues of copyright have assumed greater significance, both in terms of the growing role of knowledge in material production and the increasing importance of the production of cognitive and symbolic products. The diversity of national régimes of intellectual property rights is linked to variations in models of innovation and legal and administrative arrangements governing commercial exploitation of intellectual property. "The viability of national régimes (that is, their ability to reconcile both protection and diffusion, and thus to assume the role of the general co-ordination of the innovative activities) is dependent upon their ability to fit with specific innovations" (Foray, 1993, 94). Thus, national states have a key role in the formation and regulation of markets for knowledge. This in turn influences and shapes corporate strategies for innovation, learning, and knowledge production. States establish the conditions for such markets to operate, and while information and knowledge have always been important in capitalist production, the increased emphasis upon knowledge and "knowledgeable production" has heightened their significance. There are, however, strict limits to the extent to which knowledge can be commodified (Athreye, 1998). These vary among sectors depending upon the nature of the product and production process. Consequently, markets for knowledge will be sectorally specific, and limited to sectors in which there is technological convergence because of the emergence of generic technologies.[36]

The most problematic—and vital—of all markets for a capitalist state to regulate is, however, the labor market. The act of labor coming into being as active wage labor is largely unrelated to calculations about its subsequent saleability on the labor market, to the availability of labor-power appearing for sale on the market (Polyani, 1957). Labor in this sense is a "fictive commodity." Unlike genuine commodities, it is not produced for sale. Consequently, incorporating labor into the labor market is a—maybe *the*—key regulatory problem. Offe and Lenhardt (1984, 93) assert that this "was not and is not possible without state policies." States are involved in educational and socialization processes that influence "willingness to participate" in the labor market and in defining which social groups may legitimately not participate in the labor market, a boundary that is constantly shifting as conditions in the economy change. For example, the minimum and maximum ages of labor force participation can be varied in response to demographic and economic changes. State housing policies can also have an important influence of labor market conditions (Allen and Hamnett, 1991). National states can also influence and shape labor markets via bilateral and multilateral agreements about migrations, often in collaboration with private sector companies. For example, there was a major influx of temporary migrant workers to the Federal Republic of Germany between 1961 and 1973, orchestrated by the Federal government and private sector employers. The government reached bilateral agreements with its counterparts in several countries, including Greece, Portugal, Spain, Turkey, and Yugoslavia, but individual employers and Employers' Federations within Germany had considerable scope for autonomy in recruitment practices within these framework agreements. Similar schemes linked other northwest European countries as destinations with southern European, north African, and west African countries (the latter often former colonies of the former) in managing and regulating labor migration flows (Hudson and Lewis, 1985, 19–23). This led to the proportion of migrant workers in their national labor markets rising significantly. State policies toward permanent immigration and emigration and temporary labor migration can therefore decisively influence labor market structures and the balance of supply and demand in these markets.

Clearly, state policies are not the only regulatory mechanisms shaping labor markets and firms' behavior in them,[37] but they are nonetheless important, often decisively so. Consider, for example, the contrast between neoliberal regulatory frameworks of labor market regulation and the German system of regulating labor relations based upon the principle of codetermination (Gertler, 1997). German workers, both directly through works-based works councils and indirectly through national trade unions, have a significant and institutionalized role in many aspects of decision making in the firm. Furthermore, because of labor's institutionalized power, there are serious curbs on employers' ability to dismiss or lay off workers. The labor market regulatory system is structured to encourage stable long-term employment relations and the active use of firms' internal labor markets to manage personnel needs. Furthermore, the strong degree of centralization in wage determination at the national level, and the convergence of wages between unionized and nonunionized workplaces, minimizes the effects of interfirm wage competition. In sharp contrast, neoliberal Anglo-American regulatory régimes generate much less long-term security of employment, as firms have greater recourse to extensive use of hire-and-fire tactics, leading to higher labor turnover rates. There are generally lower unionization rates, especially in the United States, allowing greater interfirm variation in wages and working conditions. Employers are encouraged to view labor costs as one of the chief dimensions of interfirm competition. More recently, however, there is evidence of the German regulatory régime moving closer to Anglo-American norms.[38] Under pressure from employment losses in Germany attributable to companies switching production abroad to cheaper locations such as eastern Europe and parts of the United States, German trade unions have become more accommodating to corporate demands. Major companies now often deal directly with local labor representatives at the plant level over issues of work organization and working time, bypassing the central national organizations of the unions (Bowley, 1998).

State Provision of Goods and Services: Direct Engagement with Issues of Production Organization and Societal Reproduction

Public sector production exemplifies an "interventionist" mode of state involvement. It occurs in two distinctive ways. The first is the public sector provision of certain industries de novo or the nationalization of formerly privately owned ones. Often postcolonial states seeking to industrialize have seen no option to the state's establishing key industries (such as steel; Hudson and Sadler, 1989) regarded as vital to their industrialization strategy but unattractive to, or beyond the capacities of, private capital. Often such "infant industries" have been protected behind tariff walls. In the advanced capitalist states, industries have been nationalized, or otherwise taken over by national states, because they produce outputs needed for private sector production elsewhere in the national economy but in themselves do not offer the prospect of (enough) profits to induce private capital investment in them. In other cases, there are more complicated reasons for nationalizations that go beyond the narrowly economic; for example, because of national security or defense concerns. In both cases, national governments can seek to use such industries as instruments of regional development policies. In general, these varied forms of public ownership, and their modes of operation, have marked effects, both intended and unintended, on geographies of production. Indeed, such involvement *inevitably* has implications for geographies of employment, production, and service provision, with differentiated and differentiating effects within national territories. Some regions and localities successfully lobby for investment (or against disinvestment) by public sector industries; others as a consequence are unsuccessful. The "losers" may object, in strong terms.[39] Even if protest is contained within more normal democratic channels and procedures, deindustrialization as a result of public sector industries' policies can generate pressures for new state policies to repair the spatially concentrated damage and maintain the legitimacy of the state. Typically, these involve new (or old) forms of "liberal" mode policies, which are discussed below.

As well as intervening directly in the production of material commodities, national states also engage directly with issues of social reproduction. These policies seek to address the welfare of all social groups within a national society rather than just the sectional welfare of capital. They are informed by the necessity to persuade all citizens of the legitimacy of the social structure, its rules and norms, especially if they occupy disadvantaged and subordinate positions within it. Moreover, because such state policies are aimed at a wider target constituency, they generally have more homogeneous spatial impacts (as compared to those of public sector mining and manufacturing industries), although by no means equally impacting in the same ways on all areas. Health, education, and welfare policies are of particular relevance. Their main objective is to guarantee the successful reproduction of both labor-power and the nonwage working population (of the chronically sick and disabled, the unemployed, mothers and children, and pensioners), vital to sustaining normative claims about social justice and a civilized society. It is important to emphasize this point—and avoid the dangers of functionalist interpretations of such policies as simply a response to "the needs of capital." The emergence of this type of policy reflects political and social struggles within the arena of the state and the aspirations of various social classes and groups.

Clearly, the state's expanding involvement in these activities provided a powerful stimulus to growth of public sector employment. The provision of such services through the state also enhanced the capacity for the social regulation and control of marginalized groups. Insofar as such groups are housed in public sector (social) housing and/or are the residents of deindustrialized localities, there is often a strong spatial dimension to such policies. This spatiality serves to highlight the ambivalence as to whether this constitutes integration or exclusion, as such housing areas are often spatially separated from those of other social classes and groups. State provision of such services also has a powerful ideological effect, for, by situating social pathology at the level of the individual, group, or community, it results in state regulation penetrating deep into the fabric of the social relations of civil society, even to the levels of the family and the individual.

The rise to dominance of neoliberal modes of regulation over much of the capitalist world in the 1980s and 1990s reversed the imperatives of preceding decades to extend the reach of state involvement in the direct provision of goods and services. This raises important theoretical and practical questions, given that there clearly were once pressing reasons to extend the scope of public sector provision. From one point of view, the tendency to privatize can be understood in the context of *limits* to the policies of the interventionist state and the transposition of potential rationality and legitimation crises into a potential fiscal crisis for the state. One response to this, rich in wider ideological connotations, was to rein in the boundaries of state involvement through privatization. This, together with the preprivatization restructuring required to make privatization possible by making industries again profitable to the private sector, has had great impacts on geographies of production. Exactly *where* it is affected depends very much on decisions as to *what* to privatize and on the preexisting geographies of these industries. Privatization has also led to often great social and locationally concentrated costs and so has at times been fiercely contested.[40]

Privatization can also take other—and not necessarily new—forms, however. There is a well-established pattern in many countries of the state contracting with other agencies for the production and distribution of goods and services. Public procurement policies, and the criteria on which they are based, have become matters of considerable concern, given the recent neoliberal turn in state policies. The activities of the state as purchaser can be critical to the continuation and success of production within the national territory. For example, the international competitiveness of French firms producing "high-tech" products such as digital processors, nuclear reactors, and large complex aircraft is strongly dependent upon the purchasing patterns of the French state (Storper, 1993, 143). Such purchasing policies can effectively restrict permissible suppliers to those located within the national territory of a state, and so powerfully influence geographies of production. The interaction of the policies of government and large firms has created a particular geography in "high-tech" employment in France, with "technopoles" of growth based on "high-tech" industries (notably aerospace and electronics) dependent upon the defense spending and purchasing patterns of the national state (Beckouche, 1991). There has been a long tradition of state provision of welfare and social services via funding private sector contractors in several European countries (Borzaga and Santuari, 1998). In others this is a more recent tendency, associated with the retreat of the state and processes of "hollowing out." Within different national frameworks and models of intervention, there appears to be a growing use of a "contract style" of administration and service supply, separating finance from service provision. Thus, the growth of the "contracting out" of state activities—the emergence in the United Kingdom and elsewhere of compulsory competitive tendering, for instance (Reimer, 1999)—is an expansion of existing forms of public provision rather than an innovation. These trends represent an extension of a well-established approach whereby the state contracts with private sector agencies for the production and distribution of goods and services. One consequence of this, however, may be the fracturing of national uniformity of provision associated with Keynesian welfarism and enhanced intranational variations in regulatory environments and service provision (Martin and Sunley, 1997, 286), in turn influencing the location of other economic activities.

There is though again a twist in the tale, and in the tail, for the growth of contracting out has increasingly been used to import pseudo-profitability "efficiency criteria" into the remaining public sector industries and services. The previously existing *qualitative* differences in the operating criteria of private and public sectors are being eroded in many areas. Equally, though, there may be limits—some economic, some social and political—to the privatization tendency. Two examples from the United Kingdom illustrate the point. First, the National Health Service is proving resistant to further inroads of privatization for social and political reasons and concerns about a potential legitimation crisis. Second, much of the nuclear power industry had to be retained within the public sector, as it proved to be economically unprivatizable. In both cases, the economic crisis tendency encompassed in these diverse forms of activity remains internalized within the U.K. state. More generally, these varied forms of public ownership, the modes of operation of nationalized industries, and denationalizations can all have marked effects on geographies of production (Dunford, 1988, 59–60; Hudson, 1986a, 1986b, 1989c).

State Indirect Involvement: Influencing the Volume, Form, and Location of Private Sector Investment

This form of state activity represents a "liberal" mode of state involvement. Historically, it generally preceded public sector provision of goods and services by the national state,[41] but in turn the impacts of such interventionist policies can generate fresh demands for this older form of involvement. Three aspects are of particular relevance here. The first, the macroeconomic framework—monetary and fiscal policies on the one hand, industrial and technology policies on the other—shapes the economic environment and influences companies' (dis)investment decisions. National demand management policies seek to influence levels of aggregate demand and so output, investment, and employment via varying levels and compositions of public expenditure, taxation, prices and incomes policies, and interest rate and credit control policies. More specific policies (such as those for housing and transport) aim to influence the level and composition of demand in particular spheres of socioeconomic life. Such significant interventions in the sphere of circulation influence national competitiveness and the relative attractiveness of the national territory to private capital.

Alternatively, national states seek to influence patterns of production via supply-side policies. As Weiss (1997, 18) remarks, "The East Asian experience has shown [that] there is much more to governing the economy than macro-economic policy." In part this "much more" encompasses market-shaping activities (discussed above). It also includes a wider range of policies intended to influence the supply side of the economy. For example, such policies may be "strategic," seeking to encourage the development of generic technologies or technological innovation in particular sectors. In part, the relative emphasis upon different mixes of demand and supply-side policies reflects the economic climate prevailing at particular conjunctures in time and space. For example, Weiss (19, original emphasis) puts the point as follows in relation to national state policy responses to growing international economic integration:

> It is not the state as such that is enfeebled by economic integration. If anything, it is the efficacy of particular *policy instruments* which is in question—in particular, *macro-economic* adjustment strategies which focus almost exclusively on fiscal and monetary policies. . . . But the very opposite is the case with *industrial*—read also technology—policy. In so far as industry itself is constantly changing, "industry policy" must of necessity be creative. . . . *The very capacity for industrial policy is one that requires the state to constantly adapt its tools and tasks.*

The emphasis upon the state adapting its own procedures, priorities, and structures to changes in the environment in which it is entangled echoes Offe (see above). The lack of consensus as to the most "appropriate" mix of demand- and supply-side policies is therefore only to be expected. Perceptions of the optimal mix are shaped by the economic environment confronting the state and the balance of class and other social forces seeking to influence the content and priorities of policy. Policy choices reflect political priorities and the balance of social forces within a country. From one point of view, these disputes are a political expression of the relative weight of different fractions of capital and labor in influencing policy formation. For example, the Keynesianism versus monetarism debates of the 1980s brought such choices and disputes into sharp focus. Keynesianism favored "big" capital and trade unions in production industries, while monetarism favored financial and money capital and workers in financial sectors. The fiscal crisis tendencies engendered by Keynesian demand management policies were threatening to undermine the legitimacy of national states and the viability of the accumulation process within their national territories. However, the deflationary consequences of monetarism threatened accumulation while growing poverty and income inequalities raised questions about the legitimacy of such a policy stance in a modern civilized society. Whatever interpretation is put upon it, the choice of policies clearly influences the attractions of the national territory to capital, both as a location for capitalist production and/or as a market.

The second strand of such policies relates to infrastructure investment. States have a long history of involvement in infrastructure investment and the provision of general conditions of production, necessary use values either not included in the direct process of production and/or used collectively. These again can fulfill one of two broad roles, either facilitating the circulation of commodities (for example, via investment in various forms of transport infrastructure) or augmenting the forces of production (for example, via investment in irrigation or power schemes). For various reasons related to the scale of capital investment, the pace of turnover of fixed capital, and the probable rate of return, such investments are usually unattractive to the private sector. There is also another dimension to such investment. At one level, such conditions need to be provided nationally to attract or retain private sector investment in competition with other national state territories. But selective infrastructure investment within the national territory can be and has been used as one instrument in regional and urban planning strategies. As such, it can be one element in intranational as well as international competition for investment and employment, with a powerful influence on geographies of production at various spatial scales.

Grants and loans directly given to private sector companies are a third form of intervention in the sphere of circulation through which states seek to influence the what, how, and where of production. Such policies can influence geographies of employment and production in the short term but can also have longer-term effects on both sectoral and spatial development trajectories, especially in industries manufacturing complex, large, and technologically sophisticated products. This can be exemplified by Mowery's (1993, 52, emphasis added) comments about the effects of state support on the development of new commercial aircraft, specifically the European Airbus:

> Commercial aircraft is an industry in which public intervention has lasting competitive effects. The very high fixed costs, long product lives, steep learning curves and significant economies of scope associated with aircraft "families" mean that the effects of technological or commercial success in one generation . . . may persist in other generations of the product. *Public subsidies for the introduction of new commercial aircraft thus may have lasting competitive effects that are stronger and more pervasive in this industry than almost any other.*

More generally, numerous criteria are used in deciding which companies get grants and loans, but basically these relate to the development of new products or sectors, sectoral restructuring (for a specific industry), or spatial restructuring (as part of regional or urban policies). Aspatial policies can have significant spatially differentiating effects. The implementation of explicitly spatial policies is based on the premise that spatially uneven development has become a "policy problem"—although one might legitimately inquire, a problem for whom?[42]

How Do States Secure Authority to Act?

Answering this question focuses attention upon the means that a state uses to secure implementation of its chosen policies. Broadly speaking, it can seek to do so peacefully and democratically via persuasion or violently and undemocratically via coercion and physical force. Its capacity to project its cognitive representation of the national interest is critical. The state's ability to command considerable resources for purposes of communication, information dissemination, and representation to convey *its* version of events has been and continues to be of obvious significance. Historically, this has been of tremendous importance in constructing national identities and in persuading people to adhere to them. Anderson (1982) referred to this as the construction of "imagined communities"— that sense of common territorial identity shared by the residents of a national state who will never meet on a face-to-face basis—that first became possible on the basis of "print capitalism." Equally, it has always been a contested process of identity formation, with a variety of groups challenging this, often on the basis of regionalist or nationalist identities On occasion, this protest can spill over beyond democratic channels. State influence over communications channels can also impact on processes shaping geographies of production in other ways. For example, the government's portrayal of the 1984–1985 miners' strike in the United Kingdom and the way in which pictures on the television news were always from the perspective of the police had a decisive impact upon public understanding of the strike and the issues that it raised (Beynon, 1985). It can also have a direct bearing on the shaping of geographies of production in other ways, such as place marketing.[43]

Capitalist states usually are formally democratic, with disputes settled nonviolently via due process of law in courts of justice, but not all such states are democratically constituted. Even in those that are, repression and violence can have a strong effect upon geographies of production, especially because of the state's monopoly of the legitimate use of violence via the police and armed forces. Three examples, at different spatial scales, illustrate the point. First, from the days of empire onward, military intervention abroad by major capitalist states has been used to secure spaces for production and trade. This was central to the formation of the old international division of labor. However, it persisted into the transition to a postcolonial new international division of labor, as the involvement of the United States in Vietnam in the 1960s and 1970s and the United Nations and the United States in the Gulf War in the 1990s illustrates. As J. O'Connor (1994, 166) put it: "[President] Bush's war in the Persian Gulf is only the latest and most dramatic example of the role of the military in capitalist societies." The subsequent involvement of the United States and NATO in the Balkans in the second half of the 1990s provided further graphic and tragic evidence of such continuing military involvement to secure the geopolitical spaces of capitalism and neoimperialism (Gowan, 1999; Hudson, 2000; Mann, 1999). Second, "strong states," in the last analysis underwritten by the use of physical force, can secure "stable" conditions in which capitalist production can flourish, as in the "Little Tigers" of southeast Asia (that is, Hong Kong, Singapore, Taiwan, and South Korea). In the past, examples such as the South African apartheid state, the totalitarian fascist German state, and the dictatorships of southern Europe all reinforced the point that national states can resort to physical force, repression, and violence to ensure the continuation of production. Such régimes may also be attractive to multinational companies because of the resultant labor market conditions, especially in states on the periphery of the global economy (Fitzsimmons et al., 1994, 209). Third, within formally democratic states, military force and police violence may also be used to break strikes. The tactics used by the state in 1984–1985 in the United Kingdom to ensure the defeat of striking coal miners or in 1979–1980 in Lorraine to ensure the defeat of striking steelworkers powerfully exemplify this point. Clearly, in a mature parliamentary democracy this route to enforcing state power is both unusual and potentially risky, insofar as it *may* lead to questioning of the state's authority to act in such ways and will not automatically bring popular consent for following such a course of action. It may require careful preparation to defuse any potential threat of a challenge to the legitimacy of the state acting in this way (Beynon, 1985).

3.8. Summary and Conclusions

There are close and necessary relationships between state policies and the organization and location of production. Understanding these poses considerable theoretical challenges. This chapter has reviewed various theorizations of the capitalist state, beginning with those that sought to derive the form of *the* capitalist state from the category of capital and its essentially contradictory character. As the state derivation debate evolved, it became clear that what was required was a theory of capitalist states that acknowledged their historical-geographical specificities as national states.

Equally, the chronically crisis-prone character of state activity increasingly became a focus of attention as crisis tendencies were absorbed from economy and society into the state rather than being abolished by state activity, in due course emerging as crises of the state itself. The regulation school addressed the question of how the unavoidably crisis prone path of capitalist development can be held within acceptable limits for relatively long periods of time and stable development. It however initially privileged the national state as the mechanism and national scale as the site of regulation. Subsequently, greater attention was given to other spatial scales and to nonstate governance mechanisms within complex multilevel systems of governance and regulation. Integrating elements of state theories with regulationist perspectives allows a fuller and more nuanced understanding of capitalist states, their policies, and the limits to them.

Specific consideration was given to the relationship between state policies and the organization and geographies of production. This involved examining a range of forms of state activity that directly and indirectly bear upon these issues and upon the ways in which states maintain their authority and legitimacy to act in these ways. This is critical in allowing them politically to establish the conditions within which profitable production is possible.

3.9. Notes

1. Jessop (1982, 221) sets out five criteria against which the adequacy of a Marxist theorization of the state may be judged and a further four guidelines for constructing such a theory. O'Neill (1997, 293) specifies a different set of criteria, discussed below. The nature of the criteria cannot be divorced from the way in which theory is conceptualized.

2. See "Capitalist Production, Accumulation, and the Circuit of Productive Industrial Capacity" in section 2.2.

3. A point developed in Chapter 5.

4. See Chapter 4.

5. This degree of relative autonomy is periodically reduced by the contradictions of capitalist development.

6. The state derivation debate was in part a reaction to theorists of the state, such as Habermas, Offe, and Poulantzas, who, following Gramsci, were seen to assume that the political was a pre-given autonomous object of analysis. For Poulantzas (1975, 1978), the state acted in the interests of capital because of constraints imposed on its mode and scope of operations by wider structures of social and economic power. This essentially structuralist view of the state drew on Althusser's reading of Marx. Poulantzas was responding to Miliband (1969), who argued that the state acted as the instrument of the ruling class in response to class interests located, constituted, and organized outside of the state system, in the economy or civil society. Miliband and Poulantzas offer one-sided accounts of the

state. Instrumentalist accounts allocate primacy to the voluntaristic agency of social forces at the expense of their structural conditions. Structuralist accounts assert the primacy of social structures over individual or collective agency. However, in some respects at least there was a fusion of concerns between concerns of theorists such as Offe and those of state derivationists such as Hirsch (see below).

7. Such as Altvater and Blanke, Jürgens and Kastendiek.

8. In making this point, Holloway and Picciotto create conceptual space in which to consider the effects of noncapitalist class relations and of nonclass relationships upon the content of state policies and the ways in which social relationships are variously constituted over time and space.

9. The reference to national state rather than nation-state is deliberate. The difference between the two terms is not merely semantic. Nation-state refers to the nationalist ideal of a perfect correspondence between the distribution of a culturally homogeneous nation with the bounded territory of a state. In reality, national states typically include peoples from a variety of nations while national state boundaries may divide a nation. As a result, national states have sought to convert their sovereign territory from space to place (Taylor, 1999) and create a sense of shared national identity among the "imagined community" (Anderson, 1982) of citizens resident within their borders. Differences between cultural groups resident in distinct regions within national states have often had important impacts on state policies.

10. For a consideration of Kondratiev and long waves of capitalist development, see Mandel (1975) and Marshall (1986).

11. Consider the way that ecological issues have assumed greater prominence in the priorities of many capitalist states; see Chapter 9.

12. There is in fact a variety of emphases within regulationist approaches, and this is one reason why it is more appropriate to refer to a Regulation School rather than a regulation theory (see Brenner and Glick, 1991). The version drawn on here owes most to Lipietz and others of the Parisian variant of regulationist approaches (Lipietz, 1986; MacLeod, 1997).

13. Jessop more generally (1990, 205) argues that "theoretically what is needed is a synthesis of regulation, state theoretical and discourse analysis concepts." While attempting such a synthesis here is out of the question, the argument is developed in line with Jessop's views.

14. Jessop (1982, 233) refers to these as, respectively, "normal" and "exceptional" régimes.

15. It is worth emphasizing, however, that formulations of a dichotomous progression from Fordism to post-Fordism are theoretically misconceived and practically and politically dangerous (Hudson, 1989a; Sayer, 1989).

16. These are discussed more fully in the next section; see also Chapter 8.

17. This suggests that in the last instance it is not the economic but the political that is determinant, since Offe insists that there is no possibility of the economy existing on a "pre-political substratum."

18. Such crisis tendencies will be even more marked during the downswings of long waves and the troughs before the turning point upward to the upswing of a new wave.

19. O'Neill seems to attribute several of the shortcomings that he sees in regulationist approaches as resulting from "a heavy reliance on the observations

of the UK experience." While this may be a fair comment in relation to the influential work of Jessop and his collaborators, it also reveals a particular reading of regulation theory by O'Neill. Moreover, events in 1999, such as the economic crisis in south Korea, revealed the contradictory character of and limits to national state strategies for economic restructuring in southeast Asia.

20. Such tendencies were not visible to the same extent in all capitalist states. In the United Kingdom in the 1980s, for example, there were strong centralizing tendencies at the national level that sit uneasily with the canonical model of "hollowing out" (Hudson and Williams, 1995).

21. Issues relating to the conceptualizing of space are discussed further in Chapter 8.

22. There are those who seem to interpret "hollowing out" more in terms of a paralysis of the national state, however (Thrift, 1989).

23. See "Institutions, Instituted Behavior, and Social Regulation of the Economy" in section 2.4.

24. For example, only massive national state funding by the major G7 capitalist states of their banking systems prevented the U.S. stock market's crash in October 1987 from becoming a generalized global slump.

25. The relative emphasis placed upon the continuing autonomy of the national, and upon the policy spheres in which the national state remains important, is influenced by the states under consideration. Thus (at least until the events following the failure of financial institutions were in late 1997) analysts examining east Asian states stressed the continuing and largely unchanging significance of the national, whereas those considering the national state in western Europe placed more emphasis upon "hollowing out" and shifting regulatory capacities "up" and "down."

26. See "Varieties of Capitalist State Spatial Policies" (Chapter 8).

27. Chesnais (1993, 12–13) suggests that only Germany, Japan, and the United States are not suffering from such a "loss of economic and political sovereignty."

28. These issues are discussed more fully in Chapters 5, 6, and 8.

29. Although it was not the only factor; see section 5.2.

30. Although manufacturing investment outside core, higher labor cost countries of the world economy is limited. In 1967, 69% of the world stock of Foreign Direct Investment (FDI) was located in the United States, United Kingdom, Canada, and Germany; by 1990 this had risen to 80% (Weiss, 1997, 211).

31. It is also worth noting that the creation of floating exchange rates created the opportunity for major transnational companies to engage in currency speculation, often as a more profitable activity than their "core" activities in the production of goods and services. This in itself helped destabilize currency markets.

32. These issues are discussed more fully in Chapter 8.

33. The denial of naturally occurring markets is a defining characteristic of institutional economics and the "new" economic geography (see Chapter 2), challenging the neoclassical view of the market as natural and self-regulating. In this it echoes a central tenet of Marxian political economy.

34. These forms of competition are discussed in Chapter 5.

35. There are echoes here of Offe's notion that state policies are enmeshed in a situation in which the necessary is impossible, the impossible necessary; see section 3.5.

36. These issues are more fully discussed in section 5.5.

37. For example, the impacts of family and community are discussed in Chapters 7 and 8.

38. By the latter part of the 1990s the same point could be made about Japan.

39. See section 8.4.

40. See section 8.4.

41. Although there has often been provision of such goods and services at the municipal level by local governments.

42. For a fuller discussion of these issues, see sections 8.5 and 8.6.

43. See sections 8.4 and 8.6.

4

Recruiting Workers, Organizing Work

4.1. Introduction

This chapter explores relations between capital and labor in the labor market and at the point of production and the ways in which they are governed and regulated. Capital needs "free labor" available to sell its labor-power, labor needs capital to purchase that labor-power so that it can live and reproduce itself, physiologically and socially. Relationships between employers and employees are complex, simultaneously involving competition and cooperation. Given the structural asymmetry in the capital-versus-labor relation, in the power possessed by these structurally defined classes of economic agent in the production process, the underlying relationship is antagonistic. However, the relational definition of capital and labor presupposes a degree of necessary cooperation between them, however grudgingly this is given in particular times and places by either or both of them. Just *how* competition and cooperation are socially constructed in historically-geographically variable forms is a critical issue. The institutional forms and processes through which the interests of employers and employees are constructed and represented are of central importance to the constitution of these relationships. Labor markets are a fortiori not naturally markets but must be socially produced as such.[1] The idea of a self-regulating labor market is a fiction because labor itself is a "fictitious" commodity: it is not produced for sale, it cannot be stored, it cannot be separated from its owner, "it is only another name for human activity which goes with life itself" (Peck, 1994, 149). The production and reproduction of labor are intrinsically social processes. It follows that the labor market must be socially regulated.

Recognition of the necessarily social constitution of labor markets foregrounds the significance of institutional forms of collective organization of both capital and labor in regulating competition and cooperation between them.[2] Such institutional forms are required to ensure their re-production and to counter or contain the potentially self-destructive dy-namic of market systems (Polyani, 1957, 243–250). Equally, the repro-duction of labor markets and availability of labor-power on them necessarily involve unwaged work in households and processes of gover-nance in civil society detached from the immediate labor market con-cerns.[3] This results in a degree of institutional indeterminacy and spatio-temporal variations in the ways in which labor markets become regulated and governed. Spatial scale and differentiation are central to processes of labor market regulation. These processes vary between national states, re-gions, localities, and workplaces, but local institutions—broadly de-fined—play a key role in labor market reproduction within a complex ar-ray of regulatory processes and mechanisms. Furthermore, firms must choose what and how to produce and where to locate production. This choice is reciprocally related to labor market conditions and to policies such as to "hire and fire," recruitment and retention, the capacity to con-trol the labor process and the organization of labor at the point of pro-duction and in the workplace.

The remainder of this chapter therefore examines the implications of simultaneously competitive and cooperative relationships between capital and labor via three broad themes: first, the processes of regulation and governance through which the interests of capital and labor are repre-sented and that make production possible; second, the sale and purchase of labor-power by formally free and equal agents in the labor market; and third, the subsequent deployment of labor-power in the act and process of production.

4.2. Regulating Relationships between Capital and Labor: Collective Representation of the Interests of Capital and Labor "for Themselves"

Employers and employees deploy a variety of strategies and tactics in or-ganizing and representing their collective interests in a dialectic of compe-tition and cooperation between capital and labor. Capital routinely seeks to organize to articulate its interests, both "in general"[4] and in relation to particular sectoral or corporate interests. There is a long history of orga-nizations that represent particular fractions of capital on different territo-rial bases. For example, in the United Kingdom the Confederation of Brit-ish Industry represents the interests of "big" capital, Chambers of Commerce those of smaller and more locally based companies. There are also sectorally specific institutions (for example, the Engineering Em-ployers Federation or the Chemical Industries Association). These organizations can themselves often be in competition—for example, in seeking to influence state policy agendas to favor the particular interests of their members. Such organizations often seek to negotiate over wages and working conditions with workers or their representative organizations such as trade unions in particular sectors or industries to reach sectoral and national agreements on wages and working conditions linked to nationally defined regulatory frameworks and limits. Indeed, while there has been considerable emphasis in recent years upon individualization of labor contracts, companies need to be able to deal with workers on a collective basis.

Capital can be thought of as trying to "disorganize" labor. One way of doing this is by segmenting the labor market, dividing workers from one another on a variety of dimensions (including industry, occupation, age, ethnicity, gender, and location) to create optimal conditions for profitable production. Rather than seeking simply to "disorganize," however, capital may instead seek to organize it in particular ways. So, for example, companies may encourage "sweetheart" unions or sanitized and compliant company unions or nonunion company councils—there are a variety of options available to them. Often these involve the selective cooperation of sections of labor. The point at issue is not a binary choice between accepting or rejecting collective organization but rather the ways in which varying forms of such organization facilitate different methods of control of work and the labor process. The ways in which companies seek to (dis)organize labor depend on their choice of production strategy. Conversely, labor seeks to "organize" (usually but not exclusively by forming trade unions) to improve the terms and conditions on which labor-power is bought and sold on the market—for example, by securing better wages, better and safer working conditions, and shorter working hours. However, labor organizing in these ways simultaneously involves groups of workers distancing themselves from, and often directly competing with, other groups of workers.[5] Competition between capital and labor, and labor's stance within this competitive struggle, is shaped by expectations and norms relating to prevailing forms of work organization.

The organization of labor, and the representation of labor interests by trade unions, is thus critically important in the labor market. Martin and colleagues (1994, 70–71) suggest that in order to understand the formation of collective labor identities it is necessary to address three sets of issues: the fundamental significance of the economic context; the importance of tradition and culture; and the activities of formal institutions and political parties. In addition, there is a fourth set of issues: the informal institutions grounded in the routines of everyday life in the *work*place and work*place*. Trade unions must be conceptualized in terms of cultural and political as well as economic relations. They are perhaps the key formal institution through which the interests of labor are promoted in the labor market, although at the same time they often become involved in controlling and disciplining workers within the workplace. This paradoxical position reflects the inherent ambiguity of their relationships to capital. Trade unions accept the legitimacy of unequal power relations between capital and labor while simultaneously seeking to maximize the benefits to workers within this constraint via challenging the rights of capital to purchase and deploy labor-power on its own terms. They are ambiguous organizations and unavoidably so, with these ambiguities integral in their "very nature" (Moody, 1997, 54). On the one hand, they are poised to fight capital in defense of labor. On the other hand, at the top level, they attempt to hold the lines of defense through long-term stable bargaining arrangements, a rudimentary type of social partnership. In addition, trade unions often seek to forge alliances with capital at a variety of spatial scales. Such alliances further add to the ambivalence of their position.

There are various forms of trade union organization, related to the types of work and working conditions experienced by workers in different industries, companies, times, and places and to their members' identities *as* workers (Hyman, 1998). The trade unionism of skilled workers is typically different from that of unskilled workers, for example. Craft and skilled workers have more control over their pace of work and the ways in which work is controlled and organized. Consequently, their trade unions have more room for maneuver in negotiations and are able to deploy a range of often quite subtle negotiating arguments. Trade unions representing unskilled workers—for example, assembly workers in car factories—have much less room for maneuver in negotiation since their members either do or do not do the job, with minimal control over the pace and organization of their work. Consequently, such unions are more likely to resort to industrial action, strikes, and the picket line in an attempt to further their interests (Beynon, 1984, 187–188). The character of trade unions and the tactics that they deploy may also reflect the type of work that their members perform. For example, public sector hospital workers involved in "caring" occupations may be unwilling to engage in strike action because of the impact that this would have on those in their care. The attitude of employers toward trade unions and regulation of the labor process can also significantly shape the form and content of trade unions' strategies. For example, in the 1920s and 1930s companies such as Ford and General Motors were implacably opposed to trade unions whereas a company such as Imperial Chemicals Industries (ICI) deliberately constructed cooperative and compliant forms of company unionism. The aim was to avoid damaging industrial disputes and incorporate trade unions into day-to-day regulation of the labor process and production (Beynon et al., 1994, 40–49).

The formation of trade unions and their geographies of organizational and representational spaces was and is the result of struggle, often bitter and bloody, on the part of workers to improve their lot and defend the gains they made. This began in the historical heartlands of industrial capitalism in the United Kingdom and subsequently spread to countries in continental Europe such as France and Germany and to the United States. Prior to, and then subsequently alongside, the formal constitution of trade unions, workers used a variety of informal means of collective action to further their interests (Thompson, 1969). Employers typically sought to oppose the creation of trade unions, via both state legislation and seeking to coerce and intimidate workers in a variety of ways. In this they were often helped by their control over workers' access to housing and local shops, especially in monoindustrial places (Beynon and Austrin, 1993; Corbin, 1981; Hudson, 1993). Often they imported nonunion labor to break strikes (and in many parts of the world still do). Some employers such as the Ford Motor Company took their opposition to trade unions to considerable and institutionalized lengths, creating private police forces to suppress trade unions, for example.

Establishing trade unions was therefore an historical struggle with a definite geography, in terms both of the places in which it occurred and the geographical scales at which unions were seeking to represent workers' interests. The subsequent growth of trade unionism has been a very uneven process, varying with types of worker, companies, types of industry, and locationally (Jonas, 1996). The struggle to establish trade unions, and union rights, continues in much of the Third World and, in at least some senses, remains ongoing in the First World. The recent imposition of legislative restrictions on the scope of trade union activities in countries such as the United Kingdom and declines in trade union membership throughout much of the advanced capitalist world demonstrate this. For example, trade union membership fell between 1985 and 1995 in seventy-two countries, especially the former state socialist countries, as membership ceased to be compulsory. At the same time, membership rose in twenty other countries, including Chile, the Philippines, South Africa, South Korea, Spain, and Thailand. For a variety of reasons political and economic changes there created spaces for trade union growth. In only fourteen of these ninety-two countries did union density exceed 50%, however (International Labour Organisation, 1997).

The construction of trade unions and representation of workers' interests are uneven processes, at once uniting some workers while simultaneously dividing them from others. The historical geography of trade unionism has had a critical formative effect upon unions' tactics and strategies, the legacies of which in many ways are still present. Trade unions typically developed from a plant or local level to a national basis; in some instances industry-specific unions developed, in others more "general" unions. Over time, the national level increasingly became the territorial basis on which trade union institutions were built, especially in the corporatist "Fordist" era of national regulation in which unions played an important role in national wage bargaining. In effect, in the countries of advanced capitalism they struck a deal that enabled them to wield considerable bargaining power over wages, terms and conditions of employment, and "grievances" in exchange for ceding control of the labor process to management. Trade union influence was most pronounced in large industrial companies and plants. In contrast, many small firms and much of the services sector remained largely nonunionized.

However, there were national variations around the canonical Fordist model, with different national models of industrial relations and institutional practice within the framework of Fordism in the advanced capitalist states (Boyer, 1990; Burawoy, 1985; Esping Anderson, 1990; Lash and Urry, 1987). This both allowed for and reflected national differences in the regulatory involvement of trade unions. In the Federal Republic of Germany, for instance, they had a more prominent role in shaping policies for education and technological change than they did in the United Kingdom or the United States. This was a legacy of the "guild ethos" of German production (Lash and Urry, 1994, 82) and the importance attached to apprenticeships and practical training there.[6] Furthermore, there were very different sets of relationships in more peripheral capitalist countries, often linked to the presence there of dictatorial and nondemocratic political régimes. Consequently, the position of organized labor was (and often still is) much weaker and the terms and conditions of work much worse from the point of view of workers.

The "Fordist" era nonetheless marked the high point of national trade union influence in the territories of advanced capitalism. The growing strength of the trades union movement, and increasing shop-floor militancy in periods of intensified industrial unrest such as the "hot autumns" of the late 1960s in turn helped precipitate a series of changes in the technical-spatial organization of production. These undermined the bases of trade union power at the shop-floor level and influence in national regulation; for the 1960s saw the archetypally mass collective worker in big factories in tight urban labor markets challenging managers' "right to manage" and control over the labor process and to increase line speeds unilaterally. Increasingly Taylorist mass production was threatened by a militant mass collective worker, with "wildcat" strikes disrupting profitable production. Such challenges to trades union officials from militant shop-floor workers further emphasize the contradictory position of unions as convenors sought to maintain order and discipline in production in the face of "unofficial" strike action (Beynon, 1984). As a result, there were pressing imperatives on trade unions to reorganize their structures and practices as well as upon the managers of capital to reorganize work and production to restore control and profitability.[7]

The growing power of the militant mass collective worker led companies to reassess their production strategies—initially via a series of spatial fixes—to try to preserve Taylorist mass production by outflanking militant workers. This served to divide workers within companies and sectors on a territorial basis, first intranationally, then internationally. The emergence of a new international division of labor is often interpreted as a response to massive labor cost differentials (Fröbel et al., 1980). However, it is important not to overestimate the significance of labor cost differentials, as the involvement of national states in creating stable conditions for profitable production was of much greater significance (Gordon, 1988).[8] Whatever the precise proximate causes, the resultant changes in turn allowed companies more room to maneuver in imposing in situ restructuring strategies in their remaining plants in the industrial heartlands, further reducing employment and union membership and influence. Trade unions' attempts to restore unity via "combines" and international agreements met with little success in the face of companies' ability to divide and rule via relocation and capital flight. The position of unions was further challenged by a growing tendency toward globalization, casting further doubt upon the salience of "the national" as a basis for effective trade union organization (Cox, 1997).

Even so, there are limits to companies' ability to undermine trade unions by restructuring the how and where of production. Production relocation does not automatically translate into the erosion of trade unions' capacities. The international expansion and integration of capitalist social relations "does not necessarily undermine working class political organization. The political effects of economic changes cannot be so easily determined" (Wills, 1997, 6). Globalization processes may have made workers' organization and resistance more difficult and problematic, but the nature and character of their resistance to corporate attempts to change ways of working and labor market conditions continues to influence the unfolding of political-economic processes and outcomes. For example, workers may build up community support in localities in which they retain influence over production strategies. This can restrict companies' capacity to play one plant off against another, despite moves to plant-level bargaining (Jonas, 1997). In cases in which resistance is ineffective, it may *seem* that global forces are irresistible, but other trade union strategies *might* have been successful (Vanderbush, 1997). "Traditional" trade union strategies and forms of organization were further called into question by the increasing adoption of new production concepts such as those of high-volume production and the growing decentralization of production to both small firms and smaller workplaces. Increasing reliance on outsourcing and subcontracting as a systemic element of production strategies further divided workers from one another. Sectoral changes in the economy—especially the growing importance of traditionally little-unionized service sectors[9]—posed further growing challenges to established forms of trade union organization and representation.

In summary, with the triumph of the global market and hypermobile capital scouring the globe in search of cheap labor and other factors of production, a consensus of sorts has emerged according to which workers are scripted as powerless, unable to defend their jobs, communities, and localities. Wills (1997, 5) strongly contests this view that such changes automatically weaken organized labor, arguing that with respect to Europe "it is not clear that capital is as footloose as some pundits suggest. . . . The majority of investment is still attracted to locations where social costs are relatively high." For example, semiconductor production was relocated in response to low wages in parts of the Third World for only a short time in the 1960s and early 1970s. Moreover, this locational strategy was only adopted by merchant (that is, mass) integrated circuit producers in the United States. Since then the dominant pattern of investment has been via interpenetration of the United States, European Union, and Japanese economies in the form of factories incorporating increasingly capital-intensive, often automated, production processes. Moreover, there are considerable sunk costs associated with major fixed capital investments. This may mean that companies are limited in their spatial restructuring strategies because of spatially specific sunk costs and the "embeddedness" of local production systems (de Lamarlière, 1991).

Even accepting these qualifications, however, many trade unions have clearly been weakened by changes in corporate policy and production approaches. Many workers are worse off because of the resultant labor market changes, stranded in marginal, precarious jobs (and with many in no job at all). Equally, however, as part of the same processes of change, other workers seemed to be more secure and to be better-off. Thus, the new labor recruitment, retention and work organization, and remuneration practices—such as performance-related pay or individually tailored contracts for some within internal company labor markets—have led to "winners" as well as "losers." Key "core workers," for example, are frequently materially better-off. Trade unions have often been involved in establishing such new employment régimes. In agreeing to one-union deals—since the alternative is often a no-union deal, with works councils (works councils are discussion forums within a company involving managers and workers, but the latter take part as individuals and not trade union representatives)—trade unions have acknowledged the weakness of their position and the extent to which they have been outflanked by labor market and organizational change. Companies have actively sought to undermine the solidarity of workers at the plant and industry level that characterized mass production. They have done so via innovations in management techniques (notably those associated with human resource management) that seek to forge company-based identities and that pinpoint workers who fail to conform to the performance standards specified by the company (Yates, 1998, 139). Consequently, the only realistic position in the "after-Fordist" economy is seen to be for trade unions to work collaboratively with companies and not in antagonism to them. Workers and their employers have shared interests in this world of "new realism" in trade unions' attitudes and neopaternalism in employment practices. Thus, growing and deepening labor market segmentation and divisions within workforces are in part a product of some trade unions seeking to (re)gain members by participating in the introduction of new forms of work and production.

While the shift to new forms of "flexible" production has certainly challenged established modes of trade union operation, it has also—so some argue—opened up fresh possibilities for unions in three respects. First, it offers opportunities to challenge the imperatives of capital in novel ways and to shift the focus of trade union activities beyond the immediate concerns of the workplace to those of the surrounding locality and community. For example, new flexibly networked just-in-time production models are very vulnerable to any stoppage in production and therefore offer considerable potential bargaining power to workers. The possibilities for realizing this potential depend heavily upon broader labor market conditions and coexisting national and local variations in modes of labor market regulation and union organization, however. For this reason companies introducing such approaches to production carefully select labor markets in which there is "green labor"[10] and/or high unemployment. There are, then, both possibilities for labor and the problems of organizing effectively to realize them (Cox, 1997, 180–181):

> The way in which many firms . . . are, in effect, locked into . . . locations by the difficulties of re-constituting their web of exchange relations and their other forms of transaction elsewhere suggests that workers may enjoy some leverage over wage and work conditions. This does not mean to say that this will be exercised collectively. Rather it may be through more individualised forms, as in the case of internal labour markets. But even less skilled workers can share in the flow of value through the social relations of a local economy, to the extent, that is, that they organise. . . . The difficulties . . . may be less the invulnerability of employers to workers claims and more the problems that unions have in organising . . . dispersed workforces.

Cox goes on to add that these difficulties are not necessarily insuperable. However, while the contours and vulnerabilities of international production chains may be well enough known in labor circles, very few unions actually act on this basis (Moody, 1997, 57)

Second, others see new opportunities for transnational trade union organization as the scale of regulation and representation of workers' interests shifts upward. Corporate acquisition and merger activities create fresh possibilities for closer transnational union links (Wills, 1998a, 3–8). Organizations such as the International Confederation of Free Trades Unions (ICFTU) and the International Trade Secretariats (ITS) have become more effective in recent years. There is a movement toward super-concentration and/or "translocalisation" of some elements of labor relations (Herod, 1997, 186). There is, therefore, growing evidence of cross-border worker organization and cooperation and implementation of cross-border internationally imposed labor and workplace standards, although such global regulation remains embryonic. For example, while implementation of ILO Code of Labor standards prevents the most extreme forms of exploitation and cutthroat competition and establishes a process by which wages and working conditions could gradually be improved (Jordan, 1997), there continue to be very considerable differences in labor market conditions between countries. With the creation of the EU's Social Chapter and European Works Councils initiatives, developments in the EU have received particular attention. There is some evidence of growing collaboration between trade unions across national boundaries within the EU. For example, the General, Municipal and Boilermakers Union (GMB) in the United Kingdom and IG Chemie in Germany have concluded an agreement to give joint membership to their two million members. This can be seen as an important step toward developing a transnational labor movement, although "the hopes of some trades unionists for the development of pan-European collective bargaining are surely premature" (Hodge and Howe, 1999, 182). Even so, there are different views as to the potential of new institutions such as European Works Councils: some see them as potentially progressive (Rogers and Streeck, 1995), others see them as a little more than an empty token gesture toward labor (Amin and Tomaney, 1995a, 31). Moreover, it is recognized that such a development may simply shift the spatial scales of division up a level, with the danger of a trade union "Fortress Europe," perhaps buttressing the privileged position of a European labor aristocracy and dividing it from workers elsewhere as a result.

In one sense, such international organizations can be thought of as "imagined communities" of trade unionists, extending the imagined community from the national to the international level (cf. Anderson, 1982), although there are real barriers to the realization of this imagination and its translation into practice. Not least, this is because people who become wage workers enter that relationship with a myriad of preexisting differences and identities, linked to ethnicity and gender for example, that they continue to keep. Consequently, while they share a commonality of interest as wage workers, they do so bearing a variety of other identities that potentially divide them.[11] These differences pose real barriers to unity. Wills (1997, 12) is under no illusions about the significance of these barriers. She stresses that the history of efforts to foster labor internationalism indicates that solidarity between workers is difficult to achieve. The fortunes of the First, Second, and Third Internationals, the ITS, the ICFTU, and the World Federation of Trades Unions (WFTU) highlight the difficulties of overcoming national political and economic differences. Trade unions remain national organizations, and "they think and act nationally, despite acknowledging the importance of the international scale" (Wills, 1998a, 3). Insofar as workers do struggle against the worst impacts of globalization, that struggle is largely conducted on and through a *national* terrain (Moody, 1997, 57):

> Most of the struggle against the structure and effects of globalisation necessarily occurs on a national plane. That is, after all, where workers live, work, and fight. That is also the lesson of the first round of mass strikes [in the 1990s] and even more the localised struggles against the global régime of capital. The most basic feature of an effective internationalisation of capital of this period is the ability of the working class to mount opposition to the entire agenda of transnational capital and its politicians in their own "back yard." For this agenda too is ultimately carried out at the national level.

Third, there are those who see scope for trade unions to take on a broader role than simply employment issues and plant and industrial politics. This can also be seen as recognition of the point that workers as class individuals or collectivities in capitalism are also always individuals or groups with other nonclass attributes and identities. Social movement unionism envisages a labor movement with constituencies spreading far beyond the workplace and with demands that include broad social and economic change. Trade unions are no longer seen as "an aristocracy of labour, but as a social movement fighting to preserve communities" (Moody, 1997, 60; cf. Beynon, 1985). Social movement unionism implies (Moody, 1997, 58–59)

> an active strategic orientation that uses the strongest of society's oppressed and exploited, generally organised workers to mobilise those who are less able to sustain self-mobilisation: the poor, the unemployed, the casualised workers, the neighbourhood organisations. Social movement unionism means transforming the union into a vehicle

through which its members can not only address their bargaining demands but actively lead the fight for everything that affects working people in their communities and in the country.

Social movement unionism of this type thus presumes the acceptance of commonality-in-difference rather than a subordination of differences to one privileged domain of commonality—wage labor. Such unionism would have its own distinctive geographies that sought progressively to relate struggles at the national and community levels (though it is less clear what this might mean internationally). Trade unions can in any case provide wider range of services to members, and many are already doing so. They can seek to combat falling membership by greater community involvement in issues such as training and employment provision (as for example the Iron and Steel Trades Confederation sought to do in the United Kingdom from 1997 on). In some places trade unions have long had such an embedded role in the local society and community—in Emilia Romagna or Piemonte, Italy (Locke, 1990), for example, where this involvement has been seen as a crucial condition of regional economic success.[12]

4.3. Competition in the Labor Market: Recruitment, Retention, and Resistance

The Price of Labor-Power and Methods of Wage Determination

Given that labor markets have come into existence, competition between capital and labor is essentially a struggle over the terms and conditions on which labor-power is bought and sold. There is an ongoing struggle over the price of labor-power and the terms and conditions of wage determination and work. There is a broad distinction between work organized on a piecework basis, on a measured-time basis, usually by the hour or day, and on the basis of remuneration involving some combination of measured time and productivity. There are broad variations among industries and places in the balance of these approaches to wage determination. In countries on the periphery of global capitalism and in urban areas within more central parts of the capitalist world, homeworking is typically associated with piecework in a range of consumer goods industries (Leontidou, 1993; Portes et al., 1988). Furthermore, within industries such as clothing in which production occurs within factories, piecework remains a common method of wage determination in the core areas as well as in the peripheries of the capitalist economy (Greco, 2000). In contrast, work in other industries in specifically designated workplaces such as factories and offices is typically remunerated on a measured-time basis, albeit often with a productivity element of wage determination. The forms of such productivity payments can vary, however. For example, in the nineteenth century in northeast England and similar regions, labor relations in industries such as chemicals, coal, and steel were constructed around paternalist principles, and wage determination was based on a system of sliding scales. As such, wages varied with the strength of demand for companies' products (Hudson, 1989a).

Moreover, within a given sector a range of methods of wage determination can coexist at a particular point in time. For example, while most auto producers in the United States paid by the piece in the early twentieth century, Ford from the outset introduced measured-day work at its Highland Park factory with the $5 day. Ford set out its opposition to piecework as follows (cited in Beynon, 1984, 26):

> We do not have piece work. Some of the men are paid by the day and some are paid by the hour, but in practically every case there is a required standard output below which a man is not expected to fall. Were it otherwise, neither the workman nor ourselves would know whether or not wages were being earned. There must be a fixed day's work before a real wage can be paid. Watchmen are paid for presence. Workmen are paid for work.

Some fifty years later in the U.K. auto industry there was an equally complicated mixture of methods of wage determination, a complex variety of piecework, hourly, and daily wage rates that varied both by plant and company (Beynon, 1984, 46–47). More recently there has been a tendency to introduce a greater element of performance-related pay alongside basic hourly or daily rates in a wide range of industries in both manufacturing and services in the advanced capitalist world, linked to new and more individualized ways of organizing work and assessing performance. Increasingly, wage levels have become linked to either collective (via team working) or individual worker's productivity. Thus, the determination of the wage entails a basic element related to time and a productivity-based element related to output, performance, and/or corporate profitability, defined at the individual, workplace, or company level. Thus, while the long-term historical trend has perhaps been for measured-time work to become more prevalent, piecework and its legacies have by no means disappeared.

There are enormous differences in the price at which labor is available in spatially distinct labor markets. In clothing and textiles, for example, wage costs vary from around 50 cents (U.S.) per hour in China to $25 (U.S.) in Germany (Townsend, 1997, 48). While capital may seek the sort of labor-power that it wants at the lowest possible price, this does not necessarily mean the cheapest labor in terms of absolute levels of wages. Not all companies want only—or indeed any—of the absolutely cheapest labor; not least, it will usually be the least skilled and of no use for many sorts of work. Wage cost differentials are chiefly of significance insofar as companies are pursuing strategies of weak competition based around minimization of wage costs. Strong competitive strategies of necessity are based upon upgrading product quality and the sophistication of production technologies, and so they require different types of labor, more skilled and nominally more expensive to hire, often found within labor markets structured and regulated in particular ways. In circumstances in which wages are removed from competition, unions are strong, centralized bargaining systems ensure a high prevailing wage rate, and layoffs are discouraged by labor market institutions, "firms naturally turn to others means of competition—especially the technological capabilities or qualitative aspects of their products" (Gertler, 1997, 54). Even so, such companies are not insensitive to labor costs. In the final analysis, however, companies are concerned about unit production costs, not nominal wages per se, and in maximizing labor productivity in relation to wages—though labor productivity is only one measure of efficiency in production.[13]

Ensuring the Recruitment of Workers with the Desired and Required Characteristics

Whatever their competitive strategy[14] companies never want just one type of labor; production is too complex a process, even in the smallest firm, to make this a feasible strategy. Rather, they want various types of workers and so seek to recruit a workforce with a mix of skills and qualification levels, performance qualities and capacities. The precise mix that companies seek varies with production processes, and so they typically develop specific recruitment strategies for different segments of the labor market.

Activities requiring highly skilled labor typically exhibit little spatial mobility, tied to labor markets that can reproduce the skilled labor (whether managerial or technical) that they need. Indeed, if there are labor shortages, these are addressed via migration and the mobility of appropriately qualified labor in spatially extensive labor markets. Often companies have considerable "sunk costs" as a consequence of developing labor markets in particular ways and embedding themselves in them. This acts as a strong deterrent to relocation. For example, Dicken and colleagues (1994, 40) emphasize that high-level functions (headquarters offices, R&D) of transnational corporations "remain strongly concentrated geographically, primarily in the firm's home country or region, precisely because they are so deeply embedded locally." The availability of particular types of skilled labor-power, typically in complex metropolitan labor markets within these countries and regions, is a critical element in this deep local embedding.

In contrast, other activities, in which labor costs form a large share of total production costs, are much less tied to particular labor markets. Wages account on average for some 25% of production costs in clothing and textiles, for example, so that the location of production is sensitive to variations in the availability of cheap labor (Burt, 1995). Activities and functions simply requiring large masses of labor that is (socially defined) as unskilled and therefore cheap may be able to switch locations in search of it with little penalty. Geographies of production thus become spatially recast at varying scales (intraurban, intranational, international) as companies seek out locations in which such labor can be found in abundance. However, while some activities that are very sensitive to labor costs can be readily relocated to facilitate the recruitment of cheap labor, others cannot, and the extent to which they can vary location in response to labor cost variations is circumscribed. In these instances companies must find other ways of cutting labor costs. For example, despite high levels of capital investment, labor costs remain very significant in retailing in the advanced capitalist world, but the extent to which companies can relocate in search of cheaper labor is severely circumscribed because they need to be near to customers. In these circumstances, they seek other routes to cut labor costs, although the range of options open to them depends upon labor market conditions and regulatory régimes.

Second, therefore, companies may seek to substitute part-time for full-time workers. For example, following labor market deregulation in the 1980s, multiple retailing chains in the United Kingdom increasingly employed part-time workers as companies sought to match employee levels over the day and week to fluctuations in consumer demand and thereby to control labor costs. This was a response to intensive competition and pressure on margins, particularly in food stores that were part of national or international chains. This has also been associated with changes in the character of work. The expansion of part-time work "is closely associated with the charge of de-skilling; self-service retailing has reduced the specialisation required previously in a shop assistant's job and has reduced the bulk of tasks within larger stores to shelf-filling or till operation" (Townsend, 1997, 165). The growth of part-time work is not simply or solely a tactic to control labor costs in de-skilled and low-wage service sector activities, however. There is, for example, evidence from North America and the United Kingdom of major corporations agreeing to senior management staff and highly skilled workers, predominantly married women with children aged under ten years, shifting to part-time contracts and working from home. This is seen as a way of retaining key staff, in whom companies have made considerable investments in training and who have company-specific competencies and knowledge in occupations such as software development, human resources management, and finance, in which such qualified labor is scarce (Cane, 1999).

Third, companies can vary the proportion of permanent, temporary, and casual workers. Subject to regulatory limitations, they may replace permanent with temporary or casual workers as a further tactic to control or cut labor costs. This has occurred in a variety of service sector activities in which the level of labor demand fluctuates markedly over time and in which there is considerable demand for large amounts of unskilled labor (such as contract cleaning or simple office work, as well as retailing). Halford and Savage (1997, 112) point to the increased use of casual and part-time female clerical staff in the banking sector in the United Kingdom, both in regional service centers and in High Street branches. In these circumstances, employers seek to cut labor costs via new forms of functional and numerical flexibility to match labor supply more closely to demand. Moreover, they may not simply exploit the existent marginalized workers, but in some cases, as with temporary recruitment agencies, they actively and deliberately help to create labor market conditions that make such recruitment strategies possible (Peck and Theodore, 1997). In similar fashion, companies may use homeworking to restructure local labor markets and open up a new source of labor supply in relatively underutilized market segments, typically involving female labor, as well as homeworking constituting a strategy for enhanced labor control (Peck, 1989).

Moreover, employers are often concerned with more than simply technical skills. Across a whole range of activities companies are increasingly interested in the personal appearance, attitudes, and social attributes and skills, such as flexibility and malleability, of workers, in their commitment to the company and (non)involvement in trade union activities. The extent to which, and ways in which, this is significant again vary with the choice of the production model, both in manufacturing and services. In many financial and technical service sector occupations know-how and "knowing how to go on" are critical. The key to success is combining "soft skills" with "hard technologies" to deliver a particular service. As such, the location of employees with the requisite technical and social skills and personal attributes can be an important determinant of the location of such activities. Much of the recent emphasis upon personal attributes and characteristics of employees has been in relation to work in other parts of the service sector and in occupations in which there is also a strong emphasis on "knowing how to go on," appearance, and performance. For example, they are of increasing significance in personal service industries and in a variety of "front desk" operations. A concern with personal attributes is now far more general, however, as dealing face-to-face with people becomes a part of a greater range of jobs. Allen and colleagues (1998, 103–104) report the views of a male personnel director recruiting security guards in the City of London: "We recruit specifically for whatever assignment it is, and the calibre of the person has to reflect that, so they sometimes have to be personable and able to reflect that, and stand at reception and be well dressed, well presented."

More generally within the service sector, McDowell (1997, 121, emphasis added) argues that in many occupations in service-based economies, from fast food to fast money:

> the service or product has become inseparable from the process of providing it. *Workers with specific social attributes, from class and gender to weight and demeanour, are disciplined to produce an embodied performance that conforms to idealised notions of the appropriate service.* In this normalisation, the culture of organisations, in the sense of the explicit and implicit rules of conduct, has become increasingly important in inculcating the desirable embodied attributes of workers as well as establishing the values and norms of organisational practices.

Thus, in the service sector, the product—that is, the service that depends upon the copresence of its producer and consumer since it is simultaneously consumed and produced (Walker, 1985)—is often intimately connected to the identity and performance of the person providing the service. Although this has recently been emphasized in relation to some services, it has long been the case in relation to others. For example, in the United Kingdom, the organization and practice of banking have "always been tied into the embodied characteristics of gender, class, age and race, and to the notions of appropriate behaviour and style" (Halford and Savage, 1997, 116). As the nature of the product and service have changed, however, so too have the required and desired embodied characteristics. Thus, redefinition of products or product innovation unavoidably implies redefinition of the workforce, with consequent changes to workers' identities. Referring to the U.K. banking sector in the 1980s and 1990s, Halford and Savage (1997, 114) discuss the strategies of "Sellbank" and suggest that one of the goals of restructuring was to make bank branches less intimidating places. Furthermore:

> This cultural shift has clearly gendered concomitants, highlighting the "feminine" qualities of accessibility in place of the distant authoritarian image associated with the male bank manager. Sellbank has tried to put women in the bank in order to encourage people into the banking hall and increased sales of new services.

In fact, this recomposition of the workforce is not only strongly and selectively gendered but has strong ageist and ethnic dimensions. It is predom-

inantly physically attractive young white women that Sellbank (a pseud-
onym for a major High Street bank in the United Kingdom) seeks to
employ in its banking halls.[15]

Gender also features prominently among the desired criteria of employees in the "new" City of London, although the gendering of work is
here very different to that in the front offices of High Street banks. The
sorts of employees who are recruited by merchant banks (McDowell,
1997, 127, emphasis added)

> are distinguished *not only by the combination of class and gender char-
> acteristics but also by a further set of attributes that partly shape and
> partly are shaped by everyday performance in the workplace.* . . . Physi-
> cal appearance, weight and bodily hygiene, dress and style [are all seen
> as] a crucial part of an acceptable workplace persona.

The perception of desired gender characteristics was altered in the
1990s, however, at least in part in response to changing market conditions. As the "carnival atmosphere" of the 1980s gave way to a new aus-
terity in the 1990s (McDowell, 1997, 127, emphasis added),

> women began to report what might be termed a more feminised way of
> interacting, and certainly a style that women found more congenial, be-
> came more highly valued. Careful attention to the needs of the individ-
> ual client accounts and careful monitoring of them *brought women
> growing recognition and financial rewards.*

Workers must also increasingly conform to the highly prescribed, almost
theatrical, requirements of working in other service sector activities such
as fast food outlets, restaurants, or tourist and entertainment facilities.
This powerfully shapes recruitment and retention criteria and practices
(Crang, 1994; Marshall and Wood, 1995, 168; Urry, 1990). Typically
workers in such activities are chosen on the basis of their possessing appropriate sorts of cultural capital in terms of age, gender, bodily appearance, and interpersonal skills in interacting with customers. To a considerable extent, workers performatively interacting with customers *become
the product.* Examples such as these demonstrate clear relationships between changes in labor markets, recruitment criteria, and changes in
product markets for services.

Manufacturing companies can be equally selective about the characteristics of workers that they wish to employ, though often emphasizing
rather different personal attributes to those prioritized by service sector
companies in their recruitment criteria. Such selectivity of recruitment is
well established. The employment manager of the Ford Motor Company
in Detroit remarked in 1929 that "men of between thirty and fifty years

of age are best for automobile work. . . . After fifty most of them can't stand the pace" (Beynon, 1984, 28). Moreover, Ford wanted to recruit responsible married men with families, on the grounds that they would be less willing to risk loss of wages through strikes and other forms of industrial action. Beynon goes on (1984, 65) to describe the way in which Ford set about recruiting labor for its new car assembly plant at Halewood on Merseyside some thirty years later. Many managers and supervisors at Halewood had previously worked at Dagenham, a plant with a history of labor relations problems. Managers wanted "a good plant; one with good industrial relations" and so sought to avoid recruiting workers with experience in car production: "most of the labour was 'green' and recruited locally." As it turned out, managers failed to achieve their objectives: "We wanted to get a trouble-free plant, to get away from Dagenham and Dagenham ways. It didn't turn out like that though." While it may "not have turned out like that," the point to emphasize here is that managers had a deliberate recruitment strategy that was intended to produce the managerially desired results. In a way that revealed striking parallels with its recruitment strategies in Detroit three decades earlier, Ford sought to avoid union activists and to recruit young married men with mortgages and families.

With the introduction of variants of high-volume "lean" production, incorporating notions of "just-in-time," the imperatives for careful selection of workforces in the car plants of the 1980s and 1990s became even more powerful. While the criteria remained much the same, the selection procedures and screening processes became both more intense and more sophisticated. Manufacturing companies employ such procedures in selecting shop-floor production workers to try to ensure recruiting employees with the desired commitment to the company. As well as manual and dexterity tests, they have increasingly deployed a range of psychological and psychometric techniques and interviews involving existing workers and on occasion trade union officials to seek to identify potentially good "team workers" committed to the company, in recruiting production line workers. And, like Ford half a century earlier in Detroit, they often seek married men with young children and financial commitments, reasoning similarly to Ford that they would be less likely to chance losing wages through strikes and industrial action. For instance, at its automobile plant at Washington in northeast England Nissan has been extremely careful in selecting its workforce. It has predominantly recruited physically fit young married men, many already working for other companies, with no history of trade union activism and shown to have appropriate attitudes and commitment to the company through a series of in-depth psychological screening processes and tests (Hudson, 1995a). Others are equally selective about the type of women employees they seek to recruit. For example, clothing companies in northeast England prefer to recruit older married women with children and mortgages and no history of trade union activism (Greco, 2000). Companies thus often go to great lengths to ensure that "troublesome" trade union activists are kept from their workforces, especially in the wake of industrial disputes.

Such processes of "cleansing" workforces of active trade unionists are common in many parts of the world. Vanderbush (1997, 72, emphasis added) describes the outcome of a protracted dispute in Mexico between Volkswagen, aided and abetted by the Mexican state, and employees at its Pueblo factory. Following the labor board's finding that the strike was illegal and the union therefore nonexistent, VW fired all 1,420 of its workforce. "In the next couple of weeks, it rehired approximately 905 of the old workforce, *minus any known troublemakers.*" More generally, companies may use redundancies as a way of selectively recomposing their workforces, getting rid not only of trade union activists but also of other workers who in various ways are classified as undesirable. For example, redundancies may be used to shed workers whose performance and productivity levels fall below the average for a workplace, company, or industry. Such approaches can, however, often cause difficulties and be contested by workers precisely because they are selective and discriminatory, but whether they do so depends in part on local labor market conditions. On the other hand, the deployment of "last-in, first-out" approaches to retention, while administratively easier to operate since the criteria are publicly known, may lead to companies jettisoning more productive workers while retaining less productive ones (Greco, 2000).

Recruitment Mechanisms

Clearly, companies seek to recruit labor in different ways, varying recruitment strategies in the light of labor market conditions and their choice of "production model." In broad terms we can distinguish between two types of recruitment strategies. First, there is recruitment via personal ties and family-and-friends networks: essentially on the basis of "who you know" as well as "what you know" or what you can do. These informal interpersonal networks operate in a wide range of circumstances. Granovetter (1974) demonstrates the importance of the "weak ties" of personal contact networks to blue-collar manual workers in finding out about jobs in the United States; this was the most effective source of information for them. Hanson and Pratt (1992, 163–173) show how word-of-mouth communication was central to the labor recruitment practices of a range of companies in Worcester, Massachusetts, with almost 95% of companies using it. Leontidou (1993, 63) shows how extended families create intricate self-help networks that enable people to find employment in Greece, and similar networks are common over much of Mediterranean Europe, in places with a strong culture of clientilism. Companies such as Imperial Chemicals Industries on Teesside developed strategies based upon the recruitment of successive generations from the same families (Beynon et al., 1994). Similar approaches were developed by other companies in varied industries, especially where they dominated a particular spatially demarcated labor market. In coal mining villages and textile and steel towns, children often followed their parents into the same workplace. Recruitment via family networks can be a very effective means for employers to link external and internal labor markets in a way that ensures a relatively compliant workforce. In such cases, employment of additional family members depends upon *all* of them behaving appropriately.

Consequently, "know who" has often been—and currently remains—of critical importance in spatially isolated labor markets dominated by a single employer. Equally, it can be critical in complex urban labor markets in industries in which the "normal" form of employment is a sequence of contracts for different employers, for skilled and unskilled workers alike. In northeast England, craft workers in industries such as engineering and shipbuilding moved routinely between jobs and firms on a more or less uninterrupted series of contracts, with jobs allocated via informal contact networks based in working men's clubs, pubs, and trade union offices (Hudson, 1989b). More recently such practices have become transposed into newer industries such as offshore construction (Cumbers, 1991). In these cases being seen as a "good" worker is a critical precondition for recruitment.

Such recruitment criteria and practices are also decisive in very different segments of the labor market, such as banking. In the "old" ascriptive culture of banking "organisational positions were based on explicitly classed and gendered criteria [and] succession within the banking hierarchy was heavily managed by senior management. *Jobs were not advertised and promotions were not applied for*" (Halford and Savage, 1997, 112, emphasis added). Similarly, in high-level financial services in the "elitist and masculinist" environment of the "old" City of London, professionals were recruited "through personal networks, school and family ties, and an extreme gendered division of labor separated women from men." In the "new City" of the 1990s, there is less reliance upon the "traditional" recruitment criteria, but recruitment processes remain highly selective and dependent upon particular network relations (for example, recruiting from a small number of universities). As a result, there has been little evidence of significant ethnic or gender change, while "class composition remains solidly bourgeois" (McDowell, 1997, 123–128).

Despite the increasing availability of information through a variety of media, information derived from personal contact therefore remains of considerable significance in many contrasting segments of labor markets. In cultural industries recruitment is often through highly personalized contact networks. In the film industry, for example, information and personal contacts "are at a premium." Recruitment relations "are almost quasi-subcontracting relations in the labor market, as an art director will have one or two assistant art directors and production designers whom he/she likes to work with. Those in turn will have their networks of wardrobe and costume designers" (Lash and Urry, 1994, 115). Thus "know who" and the resultant interpersonal network relationships are critical to the way in which project teams are recruited and assembled. This is both a transaction-rich network of firms (Storper and Christopherson, 1987) and a transaction-rich network of individuals since many firms are self-employed people. In emergent "high-tech" sectors, characterized by burgeoning labor demand and considerable interfirm contacts because of networked production strategies, "know who" can also be critical in recruitment. In the 1980s in Silicon Valley, for example, almost 80% of engineers leaving companies there took their new job with another Silicon Valley company (Angel, 1989). While this had certain advantages for companies in diffusing knowledge and skills, it also posed problems of retaining key employees and safeguarding repositories of sensitive embodied knowledge. Such contact networks are, however, both inclusive and exclusive and as such can be advantageous to some workers but disadvantageous to others. For example, in Germany, German youths were able to utilize information and contact networks to secure access to apprenticeships and training places whereas Turkish youths, excluded from these networks, were consequently denied similar access (Lash and Urry, 1994, 189).

The second main recruitment strategy is via "impersonal" market mechanisms and public and private sector institutions. These can take many forms. At one extreme there were (and in some places still are) the casual recruitment practices of industries such as dock work, with men turning up at the gates to see if they could be taken on for the day. These are forms of recruitment strategies being reinvented in parts of the unskilled and de-skilled service sector of contemporary capitalism, often mediated by private sector employment and recruitment agencies. For example, recruitment practices have changed in the U.K. banking sector as work has been reorganized, internal labor markets have become more deeply segmented, and the composition and demand for labor has undergone alteration. Thus, "workforces have been segmented, especially by using tiered recruitment to allow specialisation of services and products, and there has been an increased use of casual and part-time female clerical staff" (Halford and Savage, 1997, 112).

The state has often become involved in facilitating recruitment via a range of organizations—featuring, for example, in the United Kingdom various parts of the Department of Employment and associated agencies such as the Training and Enterprise Councils. However, it is estimated that only around one third of all vacancies in the United Kingdom are registered with such state agencies. In the United States almost 45% of employers in Worcester, Massachusetts, reportedly used state employment agencies as a means of recruiting employees (Hanson and Pratt, 1992, 168). Employers also use a variety of other media (such as newspapers, television, specialist trade journals, or the Internet) to advertise jobs and recruit workers, putting potential workers in touch with potential employers. In Worcester, for example, over 90% of employers used newspaper advertisements, and almost 45% used private sector employment agencies as methods of recruitment. For many companies, however, such practices may be inappropriate or may simply constitute the first stage in the recruitment process, as they require more skilled workers and/or workers with particular personal and social characteristics, as well as technical skills. Recruiting these workers requires more targeted, selective, and company-specific approaches that in turn may depend upon particular and spatially specific labor market conditions (as discussed above).

Spatial Variations in Labor Market Conditions and Recruitment and Retention Strategies

Companies often adjust existing recruitment practices, working practices, and shift systems to reflect local labor market conditions, both favorable and unfavorable in terms of their concerns. They may alter working patterns to facilitate recruitment in tight labor markets and to ensure continuing production; conversely, in labor markets characterized by supply exceeding demand they may take the opportunity to restructure, shed labor, and alter working patterns to increase productivity and profitability. For example, companies may alter shift systems, introducing "twilight shifts" or shift systems synchronized with school hours to enable women with child-care responsibilities to work part-time in "tight" labor market conditions (Hudson, 1980). During the 1990s banks in the United Kingdom began to adjust their recruitment and retention strategies in the face of growing skill shortages in key "high-tech" areas, introducing new systems of homeworking to allow women with children to combine child care with paid work (Summers, 1998). There is also evidence of extensive homeworking in more mature, low-technology, and labor-intensive industries such as clothing, as companies respond to tight labor market conditions and/or exploit the existence of reserves of female labor available for work in but not outside the home residence (Hadjimichalis and Vaiou, 1990a, 1990b; Peck, 1996). As well as easing recruitment problems and lowering fixed capital investment costs, homeworking can increase capital's control over the labor process, but it can also exacerbate problems of control precisely because of the spatial separation of workers and managers.

Another response to difficulties of recruitment is to shift to more mechanized or automated production methods. During the 1980s, automobile and integrated circuit producers in Japan experimented with heavily automated methods of production in response to labor shortages in "full employment" labor markets (Hudson, 1994a; de Lamarlière, 1991). Fiat followed a similar strategy in the Mezzogiorno, not so much because of absolute labor shortages but rather because of the problems of recruiting workers who could be socialized into the disciplines of high-volume automobile production. It subsequently reverted to less automated strategies as labor market conditions became more favorable, problems of recruitment eased, and levels of demand for automobiles declined (Conti and Enrietti, 1995). A further option for employers is to alter recruitment practices so as to substitute part-time for full-time jobs, or temporary for permanent contracts in labor markets characterized by high unemployment, or alternatively increasingly casualize work and "Taylorize" contracts. In labor markets characterized by high unemployment companies may use initial temporary employment to "screen" workers prior to offering more permanent contracts (Beynon et al., 1994, 146–148).

Recruitment and (non)retention strategies may also to a degree be linked to firm size as well as local labor market conditions. Many small firms, especially those employing skilled artisanal workers and/or in which the owner actively works in the company, often pursue spatially specific and linked recruitment, retention, and labor control strategies. These form one element in their "traditional," or (neo)paternalistic, welfare approaches to labor that seek to connect workplace regulation with life outside the workplace. Recruitment and hiring practices of companies engendered a close network of ties between workplaces and residential areas within Worcester, Massachusetts, especially for routine production workers and for women. Intergenerational recruitment practices remained common even until the late 1980s, with companies often focusing their campaigns on specific neighborhoods within the metropolitan area. These practices have both shaped patterns of strong gender and occupational segregation within the workforce and have enhanced the dependence of local companies on the local labor market so that they are unwilling to relocate from it. This in turn reproduces the significance of "traditional" recruitment practices, which in turn were integral to reproduction of welfarist labor control strategies (Hanson and Pratt, 1992, 163–173). Such forms of paternalism are by no means confined to "traditional" industries or small firms. When Henry Ford established his revolutionary "Five Dollar Day" at his Highland Park factory in Detroit, greatly increasing wage rates for automobile production workers, the Ford Motor Company not only introduced stringent recruitment criteria but also an intrusive paternalism that reached far beyond the factory. The company[16] disapproved of the lifestyle of most of the immigrant families that settled in Detroit in search of work at Highland Park. A prerequisite for their becoming Ford workers was that they recognize "the folly of their ways." Some of the company's efforts to bring about this change of perspective were valuable (for example, in helping immigrants to learn English and become aware of the dangers of life in Detroit). However, "the paternalism which the whole programme expressed often degenerated into petty and heavy-handed interference into the private lives of vulnerable people" (Beynon, 1984, 22).

The recruitment practices of paternalism have become rather more subtle and sophisticated in the years since Ford was active in this way in Detroit. Firms in new high-tech sectors characterized by labor shortages may practice neopaternalist recruitment and retention strategies as a way of securing the labor-power they need in tight labor market conditions (Angel, 1994; Saxenian, 1984). In order to help secure the reproduction of conditions conducive to innovative production in labor markets with low unemployment rates and labor shortages in key occupations and skills, companies seek to minimize competition for such labor. As a corollary, they seek to retain key core employees, in part by emphasizing corporate commitment to place, with Silicon Valley as the command-and-control, research-and-development (R&D), and prototype production center within corporate global geographies of production. Companies have adopted neopaternalist labor practices, which encompass attempts to rebuild a sense of community and belonging among employees, despite evident and growing social polarization, not least because of the presence of substantial immigrant communities. Thus reconstituting a "sense of place" both at the level of companies and individual employees has become central to strategies for labor recruitment and retention, again emphasizing the importance of links beyond the immediate workplace.

Other companies basing their production strategies on unskilled or semiskilled labor can have different recruitment and retention policies since such workers require little training. Even so, there is no simple link between recruitment, retention, and production strategy. Ford used the circumstance of large numbers of people seeking employment as the basis for a selective and paternalist recruitment strategy. Other companies responded very differently. Ford's policies stood in stark contrast to those of other automobile producers in Detroit (and beyond) that were recruiting large number of laborers for routine Taylorist mass production. Detroit in the early years of the twentieth century had a reputation as a city of abundant and docile labor, a characteristic closely related to the concerted antiunion open shop policy of the Employers' Association of Detroit. Companies pursued aggressive "hire-and-fire" policies, often with rapid labor turnover, and paid low wages, confident in the knowledge that there was an abundance of laborers in search of work. Such policies in many ways came to be seen as generally representative of mass production industries in labor markets characterized by high unemployment.

The ability of employers to pursue such hire-and-fire policies, or alternatively to be very selective about whom to employ, was predicated upon high unemployment. In tighter labor markets, recruitment strategies and criteria were of necessity relaxed or else production was relocated to more favorable labor markets—as was increasingly the case from the 1960s onward. Having sought to continue pursuing rigorously selective recruitment policies even some fifty years after their origination, within a few years after the opening of its new Halewood factory on Merseyside in 1958, Ford was forced to relax substantially its stance on recruitment as the only way of securing labor. Some twenty years later still, electronics companies in the United States switched routine production to locations in southeast Asia such as the Export Processing Zones of Malaysia in search of largely female workers from rural areas to undertake Taylorized production tasks (Ong, 1987). Companies were able to ensure a rapid turnover of workforces composed of inexperienced workers because of the interplay of state regulation, local culture, and large reserves of female labor. Consequently, they were able to minimize (though not wholly eliminate) opposition and resistance to intensifying work practices that often led to deterioration in women's eyesight—in turn creating pressures to increase labor turnover.

Companies—both small firms deploying "flexible specialization" approaches and large ones using high-volume flexible production strategies—necessarily pursue selective recruitment and retention policies. Because forms of "lean" high-volume production typically incorporate principles of "just-in-time" production, predicated on minimal inventory levels, companies must carefully select workers to ensure smooth, trouble-free, and error-free production. Companies using competitive strategies based upon flexibility of production or quality of product seek to recruit workers on a longer-term basis, since the practical knowledge and skills that they acquire in the process of work become a key competitive asset to the company. Such strategies rely more heavily upon skilled labor, flatter and less hierarchical management structures, and relations of trust between managers and workers that are not easily or quickly produced. Consequently, in such cases there is more care in selection and more concern with retention of workers. Also, in such cases, companies cannot buy the company-specific skills they often want in the labor market but rather they must recruit workers who then must learn these skills and be socialized into the company's practices (Penrose, 1959). Equally important, companies ideally seek workers that are sufficiently committed to them that they are not prepared to engage in industrial action or disrupt production. In the "full employment" labor markets of postwar Japan, this degree of certainty was achieved via policies of "jobs for life" for core workers in the major companies. In return for their loyalty, workers were guaranteed security of employment—at worst, redeployment within the firm or the wider keiretsu of which it was a part if for some reason their jobs were made obsolescent. As competitive pressures have intensified, such a strategy has become increasingly difficult to pursue.[17]

In other labor markets, characterized by high levels of unemployment, companies (often the same companies) have been able to be much more selective in their recruitment policies. For example, in the 1980s PMA (which stands for positive mental attitude) established a carpet weaving factory at Hartlepool, a town in northeast England devastated by successive rounds of industrial closures in the engineering, shipbuilding, and steel industries (Beynon et al., 1994; Hudson, 1989a). It received 2,500 applications for just 24 advertised jobs (Boulding, 1988). A few miles further north, Nissan received over 10,000 applications in the mid-1980s when it advertised for an initial 240 production workers for its new factory on the fringes of Sunderland and Washington New Town. A few years later it advertised for a further 600 workers there and within six weeks had 33,000 applications in hand (Hudson, 1995c). Mazda had over 96,000 applications for 3,500 jobs when it opened its first plant in the United States (Fucini and Fucini, 1990). Under such labor market conditions, companies can indeed be very selective in their recruitment criteria and strategies.

Three further points need to be made about relationships between spatial variations in labor market conditions, strategies for recruitment and retention, and managerial control of the labor process and workers' resistance to this. The first is that capital is generally more mobile than labor. Because of the social nature of its production and reproduction, labor is the most "place-bound" of the factors of production (Beynon and Hudson, 1993). This is all the more true for women and others with family commitments that confine them to the home as the location of waged as well as unwaged domestic work (Peck, 1996). The production and reproduction of labor-power is dependent upon the supportive effects of social institutions (family structures, schools, recreational organizations, and the like) and, as a consequence, requires a substantial degree of stability. This results in a "fabric of 'communities' and 'cultures' woven into the landscape of labour" (Storper and Walker, 1983, 7).[18] People thus become committed to places. In contrast, if a company finds that labor market conditions in a particular location become disadvantageous and recruitment and retention problematic, it has the option of relocation to secure more favorable conditions (assuming for the moment that "other things are equal" so that, for instance, the existence of various sorts of "sunk costs" do not rule out this option). Conversely, it may in some circumstances be possible to re-create favorable recruitment conditions in situ via population immigration, or temporary labor migration (as, for example in Detroit during the early years of the twentieth century, the Federal Republic of Germany during the 1960s, and California during the 1980s and 1990s; King, 1993, 1995). A variant on this theme is "body shopping," the recruitment of specialized employees from other places on terms and conditions advantageous to the recruiting company. For example, information technology companies in the United States recruited Indian consultants to work in the United States at Indian wage rates plus a subsistence allowance (Mitter and Rowbotham, 1995).

The second point is that capital has come to exploit spatially differentiated labor markets in another sense, as labor market conditions may influence corporate choices as to the location of production. The growing size of corporations[19] has enabled companies to split up production processes, both functionally and spatially, while technological changes have allowed certain sorts of jobs to be de-skilled. As a result, companies can locate particular parts of the overall production process in locations that have "appropriate" labor market conditions, and in particular shift de-skilled work to areas characterized by large masses of people prepared to undertake such work, usually for lower wages. This is true of a wide range of activities, spanning the whole spectrum of manufacturing and services. This development is reflected in the extensive literature on spatial divisions of labor at various scales. Geographies of Taylorist mass production were thus recast over an increasingly extensive spatial reach, stretching the social relations of production over successively greater distances (Fröbel et al., 1980; Lipietz, 1987; Massey, 1995). Such spatial decentralization of production in search of appropriate labor market conditions can also be characteristic of newer high-volume production approaches (Hudson, 1994b; 1997) and form a central element of the "glocalisation" strategies of firms (van Tulder and Ruigrok, 1993, 24).

The third point that needs to be made, however, is that "things aren't always equal," and companies do encounter barriers to mobility because of considerable sunk costs. Sunk costs refer to those costs of a firm that are irrevocably committed to a particular use and so are not recoverable in the case of exit (Mata, 1991, 52). They can be categorized in a variety of ways (Clark and Wrigley, 1995, 1997). As sunk costs increase, barriers to exit in the form of tangible and intangible sunk costs make exit unattractive and costly, even when profits fall and, possibly, losses accrue (Chesnais, 1993, 180). Such costs also may be a significant barrier to entry. Sunk costs often relate to the embeddedness of production in place-specific labor market conditions. In these places particular sorts of labor are routinely reproduced and made available for recruitment via a range of customs, habits, and institutions (both formal and informal). Educational and training provision is acutely tuned to the needs of particular types of production. Such cultural-institutional environments characterize many of the most successful regional economies of the past two decades (Storper, 1997).

4.4. Organizing Work and the Labor Process

Spatial variations in labor market conditions, regulatory régimes, and governance mechanisms, and in the extent to which firms, factories, and other workplaces are embedded in the social relations of particular places are crucial determinants of geographies of production. Not least, they have an important influence on how workers practice "the politics of production" and "politics in production." It clearly is not enough for capital simply to recruit workers and purchase labor-power. It then has to deploy it in production to produce surplus-value. The ways in which it seeks to do so depend upon both choice of production strategy and labor market conditions. It is pointless for a capitalist enterprise to produce, say, shoes unless it can produce them *profitably*. Producing profits requires that work be organized in ways that vary depending on the goods or services being produced and the choice of techniques for producing these commodities. The collective and social character of production necessitates bringing workers together in specific time-places in order that production can be carried out. Such "coupling constraints" (Hagerstrand, 1975) are reflected in commuting flows, the time-space distanciation of relations between home and workplace. While there is scope for flexibility in the working day (for example in terms of its length and hours of starting and finishing) and for outsourcing of work (although this requires coordination of work between different workplaces), managerial control of the labor process necessitates bringing workers together in the workplace. As Sayer and Walker (1992, 120) put it: "The basic organising principle of the workplace is containment within a limited area. . . .

The workplace is a system of labour control." Time discipline crucially depends upon the creation of distinctive spaces of surveillance and control, but these may well be contested by workers. As a result, running through the workplace is a "frontier of control" around which managers and workers negotiate and struggle, sometimes violently, sometimes more subtly, for control over the labor process and work. In seeking to understand how companies attempt to organize work in ways that suit their purposes, a useful distinction can be drawn between the ways in which management itself is organized and the ways in which relations between managers and workers shape the organization of work at the point of production.[20]

Structures of Managerial Organization within Companies

Managerial strategies depend in part upon firm size, workplace size, and form of ownership. In small, one workplace companies, the owner is typically the manager and involved in the day-to-day production activities. Consequently, (s)he typically lacks time to attend to strategic managerial tasks. Often relationships between the owner/manager and workers are structured around paternalistic principles. The situation in the large workplace and firm is very different, however. Here there is a necessary division of labor between managers and managerial structures of varying degrees of complexity, designed, among other things, to facilitate the tasks of those seeking to organize work at the direct point of production and in general to ensure the successful reproduction of the firm. As large companies became increasingly large—but especially with the emergence of the mass-production manufacturing company during the early years of the twentieth century—the need for new forms of managerial structure and mechanisms of management and control became a pressing issue.

This became apparent with the emergence of the American system of manufacture in the mid-nineteenth century. This system was based upon new ways of organizing work at the point of production, shifting control of the factory from the craftsman to the manager. This in turn required the creation of impersonal bureaucratic management control methods, encompassing new middle management tasks and managerial structures. With the emergence of industrial corporations in the United States by the first two decades of the twentieth century, the dominant managerial form became a single managerial hierarchy. Coordination by such a hierarchy replaced coordination by the market as the means of seeking to manage a geographically scattered and diverse range of business and production activities within a single corporation (Best, 1990, 35–46). These vertically integrated systems were, however, unwieldy. The paradigmatic response to this challenge of devising new and more effective managerial structures was that of General Motors, under the influence of Alfred P. Sloan (Ghosal and Bartlett, 1997). This new multidivisional structure was based around two central guiding principles: first, decentralization within managerial structures to increase the number of employees who could exercise entrepreneurial judgment; second, new cost accounting systems to coordinate entrepreneurial initiatives and maintain overall corporate coherence. Best (1990, 67, emphasis added) summarizes the key features of this new managerial system:

> The system of financial control at GM [included] overhead and fixed costs in the calculation but *divisional managers were not held responsible for items they could not control.* At the same time, GM was a decentralised system in that responsibility and authority for operations were lodged with the divisional managers. *Thus the co-ordinated control of decentralised operations underlay an organisational form that could expand without loss of efficiency beyond anything imagined before. It also allowed for planned contraction in output.*

General Motors was transformed from near-bankruptcy in 1919 and within two years had developed enormously successful coordinated control of decentralized operations. This model was adopted in varying ways by other major multiproduct, multidivisional companies such as du Pont, International Business Machines (IBM), and Philips as they sought to discover a viable balance between centralization and decentralization of control, but the principles of vertical hierarchical management structures of control within the company remained dominant.

Faced with an increasingly uncertain economic environment from the early 1970s onward, companies began to seek new managerial structures better suited to the new environment. New production and communication technologies offered fresh possibilities for organizing production in ways that were more attuned to increasingly volatile market conditions and an enhanced emphasis upon product differentiation and market segmentation as competitive strategies.[21] The multidivisional model increasingly reached the limits of its capacity to deal with the complications and complexity of organizing production posed by technological progress and market instability. The "command and control" model that in one form or another had been dominant for most of the last century seemingly became obsolete, unable to respond rapidly enough to changes in market conditions (Pasternak and Viscio, 1998). More decentralized management structures appropriate to "flexible production" emerged to fill the resultant void. They emphasize that corporate success depends upon people, their collective and combined knowledge within a company, and the coherence with which different parts of the company are combined within looser, more decentralized, and fluid horizontal network structures of management. This in turn is creating demands for new managerial skills and "fast subjects" (Thrift, 2000), a qualitatively different type of manager.

This alternative conception is particularly associated with the approach developed by Percy Barnevik at Asea Brown Boveri (ABB). Whereas Alfred Sloan at General Motors emphasized strategy, structure, and systems, Barnevik emphasizes purpose, people, and processes. Dicken and colleagues (1994, 30) identify the "newly emerging organisational form" as "the complex global firm" that has as its "key diagnostic feature" an integrated network configuration and capacity to develop flexible coordinating processes both inside and outside the firm. As of yet, such models of corporate organization remain more an aspiration (for some) than a reality. There is ongoing debate about the extent to which such new managerial structures are being created and over the extent to which they are decentralized and radically different from those preceding them. Nonetheless, the canonical ABB model has been modified in various ways by other companies, but with an emphasis on decentralization and loose horizontal relationships rather than rigid vertically hierarchical ones within intracompany management structures. Ultimately, such "deep integration" models of corporate organization would involve completely cloned organizational structures in affiliated and subsidiary companies, with the entire functional range of corporate activities present in each company, subsidiary, and territory (United Nations, 1993).

Organizing and Controlling Work at the Point of Production

The ways in which owners and/or managers of capital may seek to organize work so as to ensure profitable production can initially be considered at quite a high level of abstraction in terms of labor time and value via the organization of the working day (see Figure 4.1). The focus here is upon the "classic" Marxian transformative labor process of capitalist manufacturing (Braverman, 1974), other forms of the labor process being considered briefly below. Assuming that the level of the wage is constant in real terms, *analytically* separate ways of increasing the rate of surplus-value within such a labor process can be identified (Aglietta, 1979, 49–52; Palloix, 1976, 49–51). These imply different forms of conflict and cooperation between capital and labor, or, less abstractly, workers and managers. They therefore also imply different choices for companies as to methods of production and organization of the labor process in different times and places. Whatever the choice, however, it has been argued that the extent to which the material nature of both instruments of labor and raw materials impose limits on transformative processes is not acknowl-

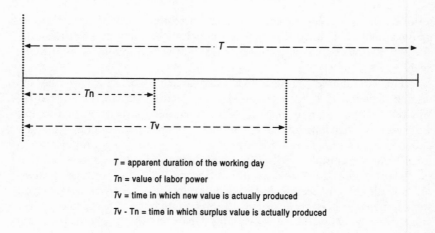

T = apparent duration of the working day

Tn = value of labor power

Tv = time in which new value is actually produced

Tv - Tn = time in which surplus value is actually produced

FIGURE 4.1. The organization of the working day.

edged sufficiently within accounts of the labor process (Benton, 1989, 71).

Increasing the rate of surplus-value creation requires increasing the difference between T_v (the time in which new value is produced) and T_n (the socially necessary time needed to reproduce labor). This can be achieved in one of three analytically distinct ways (Dunford, 1988, 20–22). The first involves increasing the production of absolute surplus-value, holding the value of labor-power, T_n, constant and increasing the length of the working day, T. This may be on a permanent and secular basis or on a temporary and cyclical basis—via overtime, for example. This is certainly an "old" strategy but one that remains commonplace in the contemporary world of capitalist production. Second, it may be achieved by increasing the production of absolute surplus-value through intensification of the labor process to reduce the time that the worker is "idle" and so increase the time in which new value is actually produced, T_v. The "porosity" of the production process arises for two reasons. On the one hand, it arises because of insufficient coordination and control of operations (for example, reflecting the time lost in setting up production runs or moving materials and parts around the factory). On the other hand, it arises because workers need periods of rest, as they cannot sustain the pace of work continuously. Seeking to reduce "porosity" involves a reorganization of methods of work to reduce "idle time" and/or intensified surveillance and supervision of existing working methods so that less time is spent "unproductively." For example, managers may change work organization to enable workers to operate a number of machines simultaneously. This clearly implies a greater degree of direct control over the work process by capital and its managers. At the start of the "industrial revolution" this was initially achieved by bringing workers together in factories, establishing a collective work rhythm. Later, with an increasing technical division of labor fragmenting work into specialized and predefined limited tasks, it was achieved by growing mechanization and then automation so that the pace of work became increasingly determined by machines *for* workers rather than *by* workers. More recently, there has been an emphasis on redesigning production processes so that workers become less "machine minders" and more "problem solvers," supervising a number of machines and ensuring that they function smoothly. This allows a discrete increase in labor productivity that is not necessarily or simply based on speeding up the pace of work or upon organizational innovation.

The third strategy involves increasing the production of relative surplus-value, that is, holding T_v constant while reducing T_n. The shift from strategies of absolute to relative surplus-value production has typically been a consequence of state regulation. In the United Kingdom, for example, during the nineteenth century factory hours legislation was crucial in preventing continuous extensions of the working day and in shifting the emphasis to the production of relative surplus-value. At a systemic level, and still assuming constant real wages, reducing the value of labor-power requires increases in labor productivity in the wage goods sector (Marx's Department 2 of production) or in those parts of Department 1 that produce the means of production for Department 2. While no new value is produced, rising labor productivity leads to increased output and reduces the unit value of wage goods. Consequently, the value of labor-power is reduced, and the rate of surplus-value creation is increased. For individual firms, increases in the rate of surplus-value creation may be achieved fortuitously via temporarily discovering new and cheaper sources of supply of goods and services. For individual firms, however, the most important systematic way of pursuing the goal of enhanced production of relative surplus-value is via the introduction of new methods of production and/or principles of work organization. This seeks to increase labor productivity and the value of output produced by a worker in a given period of time. This often involves restructuring the skill composition of the workforce, reducing both the average skill and wage levels. Increasing productivity in these ways is also central to the process of competition between companies.[22] This approach to the organization of the working day—and more generally of the labor process—is a general one. The three strategies are analytically distinct ones, and in practice companies will use more than one of them simultaneously, though in varying combinations at different times and places. Attempts to introduce such changes and reorganize the labor process are not unproblematic, however; they are often contested by labor. In response, companies may search for a "spatial fix" via relocation to find more favorable labor market conditions for pursuing a particular approach to production.

There are also different "production models" between which companies can and must choose, although such choices are the outcome of complex and not always well-understood processes.[23] The choice of the production model has implications for the organization of work and control of the labor process, for the balance between competition and cooperation between employer and employee in the regulation of the labor process, and for the way in which the "frontier of control" is constructed and regulated. These implications are reflected in, but go beyond, the immediate issue of organizing the working day and social relations within the workplace, however. Leborgne and Lipietz (1991) identify neo-Taylorist, Californian, and Kalmarian (referring to work practices at Volvo's automobile plant at Kalmar, Sweden) forms of work organization and labor contracts in a way that points strongly to the territoriality of particular bargains between capital and labor. This resonates with concepts of "cultures of production" or "factory régimes" (Burawoy, 1979, 1985; Warde, 1989), as managers seek not only to organize work in workplaces but to construct relations between those *work*places and the surrounding work*places* (Peck, 1996) in varying ways in different time-places.

One such model of production is based around craftwork, typically in small firms, requiring specific forms of work organization and labor control. A distinguishing feature of craftwork is that the worker necessarily has a high degree of control over the labor process and pace of work while worktime cycles are relatively long, perhaps several hours or even days. There has been a long-term tendency for capital to seek to replace skilled craft workers with less skilled labor, for reasons that are clearly identified by Best (1990, 42, emphasis added) in describing metal products manufacture in Birmingham, England, during the middle of the nineteenth century:

> Birmingham arms manufacturers were organised by handicraft methods utilising highly skilled labor. Firms could produce hundreds of product types and shift product lines altogether. Catalogues with over 500 different types and sizes of steam engines, for example, were common. . . . When the demand for guns declined, such firms could shift to shoe buckles or brass buttons. Thus these firms were extremely flexible *but within the limits of handicraft manufacturing methods.*

Despite strong tendencies to restructure work so as to replace skilled craft workers with unskilled workers, craftwork remains of critical importance in some activities and sectors. Within the Parisian haute couture industry, for instance, the more highly skilled workers, such as cutters, are "gens de métier (craftspersons with a strong craft identity): their work rules are their own." As such, "their labour processes are not be rationalised or codified by any outside force, *including their employers*" (Storper, 1993, 443, emphasis added). Employers recognize that they necessarily depend upon the knowledge and skills of craft workers—knowledge and skills that cannot be disembodied and transferred to machines. Consequently, they cannot control craft workers in the same way that they seek to control and discipline unskilled workers. The labor process must be controlled in ways that rely more upon cooperation (or responsible autonomy; Friedman, 1977) than coercion. As a result, craft trade unions typically operate in a very different way than those of unskilled workers, for example (as noted above).

Moreover, recently there has been a resurgent emphasis upon the knowledge and skills of craft workers as a key determinant of the success of some industrial districts and of new models of corporate competitiveness. Workers in the knowledge-intensive activities of high-tech industries such as electronics carry out their tasks at speeds determined more by their own inclinations and motivation, a consequence of flatter managerial hierarchies and control strategies based upon "responsible autonomy" rather than close supervision. This can, however, be a route to very high levels of exploitation, as workers work very long hours (far beyond those to which they are formally contracted). They are driven to do so by a mixture of commitment to the company and personal pride in and satisfaction from performing their job as well as they can (Massey et al., 1992). Furthermore, as knowledge more generally has come to be of growing importance to the economy, there has been an expansion of "creative" occupations involved with producing and transmitting knowledge in its various forms. Perhaps prototypically, some 75% of the labor force in software companies is composed of professional-managerial and technical staff, and this level is now being reached in new semiconductor firms in the United States.[24] Consequently, there has been an expansion of "reflexive" jobs characterized by long job cycles, ranging from days to weeks in the case of engineers and technicians, to months or years in the case of advertising executives (Lash and Urry, 1994, 57, 99). This expansion of occupations concerned with producing and disseminating knowledge is closely linked to the increasing significance of product differentiation, product innovation, and product quality in corporate competitive strategies. When competition is based less on price than on the technical and qualitative aspects of products, worker involvement becomes a key factor in the firm's success (Gertler, 1997, 54).

There has often been a link between such "responsible autonomy" strategies and paternalism as a process of governance within firms. Paternalistic approaches seek to develop alliances between companies and their workers so that workers identify their interests with those of their company. While many small firms, both in manufacturing and services, deploy deeply paternalistic practices in managing work and the labor process, paternalism is by no means confined to small firms. Hanson and Pratt (1992), for example, reveal the origins and legacies of paternalism and welfarist labor control strategies in Worcester, Massachusetts. Large manufacturing companies such as Ford (see above) and Imperial Chemicals Industries (Beynon et al., 1994; Nichols and Beynon, 1977) have developed paternalistic approaches to labor relations at different times and places, often deeply tinged with authoritarianism. Paternalism has also been prominent in banking and financial services (Halford and Savage, 1997). Such paternalistic practices were perhaps most prominently visible in the financial service nexus of the City of London, controlled by a tight group defined by education (and socialization) at particular public schools and Oxbridge, and appropriate accents and tailors (McDowell, 1997). There is, however, evidence that even these are changing because of the demands of new methods of working and the social relationships of production (Allen et al., 1998, 92).

Taylorist mass production constitutes another model of production, requiring a very different approach to disciplining workers and organizing work and the labor process. Although the archetypical Taylorist workplace has come to be seen as the mass production automobile plant, it is important not to equate Taylorism with either big firms or manufacturing. The origins of Taylorism and mass production lie in the emergence of the American system of manufacture specifically as a way of wresting control over the production process from craft workers. The defining feature of the American system was the use of specialist machines to produce interchangeable parts. The idea of interchangeability meant breaking down products into their simplest parts, designing a specialist machine capable of producing each piece, and inspecting each part with a custom-designed set of gauges. Consequently, "interchangeability meant that parts could be machine processed and assembled *by workers who had not been apprenticed in the craft tradition*" (Best, 1990, 32, emphasis added). This was a key development in manufacturing, with profound implications for workers and the organization of work. It clearly prefigured Taylorism, but the full implications of this development for deepening the technical division of labor and the organization of the labor process were not developed until Taylor's work on scientific management and Ford's revolutionary mass production automobile plant with its mechanized assembly lines.

Mass production is based around selling low-cost standardized products in large homogeneous markets. When initially introduced into automobile production by Ford, it led to dramatic increases in labor productivity. The labor time needed to produce a model-T Ford fell from 12 hours and 8 minutes in October 1913 to 1 hour and 30 minutes six months later (Pine, 1993, 16). Mass production thus conferred great competitive advantage but required workers to be organized and to work in specific ways, based on a separation of mental from manual work, extreme specialization of tasks, and a deep technical division of labor within the workplace. Workers typically perform simple, repetitive de-skilled tasks with very short job-task cycles (often defined in seconds) on the production line. The moving line delivers materials to them at speeds determined by management. Increases in labor productivity were achieved via increasing the line speed in accordance with managerial decisions. As such, workers (who were sometimes increasingly alienated) perform repetitive routine tasks on an uninterrupted basis at a pace dictated by the speed of the line. Shift systems allow for the maximum utilization of machines. There are well-known problems associated with Taylorist mass production that are a consequence of both labor and product market changes (Sayer and Walker, 1992, 167–169). The initial challenges to Taylorism arose due to increasing resistance by workers in the "full employment" conditions of the core urban and regional labor markets that emerged in the advanced capitalist countries during the 1960s. There was increasing resistance to the speed-up and intensification of work, which erupted in a range of industrial disputes and official and unofficial "wildcat" strikes that disrupted production. Later, more fundamental challenges were posed by the emergence of more volatile market conditions.

Some commentators have proclaimed the demise of mass production in many branches of manufacturing, but Taylorism is far from dead. Indeed, there has been an expansion of both "downgraded manufacturing" and "downgraded services" (Sassen, 1991) as the principles of Taylorism have been extended to encompass more occupations and locations. On the one hand, Taylorist manufacturing has been preserved by switching production to locations with labor market conditions that allow its defining practices to be introduced and re-produced as parts of new intranational and international divisions of labor. Many of the new maquiladora factories on the Mexican side of the U.S.–Mexican border have been relocated from the United States precisely because they involve labor-intensive assembly operations. Relocation provides labor market conditions that enable companies to continue to use mass production methods and despotic employment practices akin to "bloody Taylor-isation" (Lipietz, 1986). On the other hand, Taylorist principles have increasingly been introduced into large swathes of routine service sector activities. For example, the McDonalds chain of restaurants and drive-ins epitomizes a trend in the fast-food sector toward mass production of standardized meals and for carefully scripting standardized forms of work that prescribe precisely what employees are to do and say. The aim is to make the production and delivery of a given meal identical in all McDonalds restaurants (Leidner, 1993). Such a process of Taylorization is also marked in service sector activities that involve processing large amounts of data and/or paper or dealing with customer inquiries (Mc-Crae, 1997), leading some commentators to refer to the "industrialisation of whitecollar work" (Taylor, 1995). Indeed, in white-collar industries such as advertising the labor process was "regularised and Taylorized" from the early part of the twentieth century (Lash and Urry, 1994, 139). Increasingly, however, more skilled white-collar professions, such as computer programming, are being relocated to countries with abundant low-wage skilled labor, such as India (Lakka, 1994).

Such forms of work organization in parts of the service sector often also involve reworking and extending Taylorist principles. A prominent feature of work organization in the service sector in recent years has been an increased "contractualization" of employment, with people employed on different contractual terms in respect to hours, benefits, and entitlements. The generalization of employment insecurity thus becomes a regularized feature of working life. While often described as "flexibility it is therefore perhaps more accurate to refer to this 'individualisation' of employment relations as a form of Taylorism" (Allen and Henry, 1997, 185). This new Taylorization of employment relations reflects the temporal limitation, legal (non)protection, and contractual pluralization of the employment of labor (Beck, 1992, 147). Thus, the growth of contingent and (sub)contract employment represents the further widening and deepening of the social and technical divisions of labor as specialization secures, for employers, more efficient and possibly cheaper ways of doing things.

Another model of production centers around new forms of high-volume "lean" production, which seek to combine the positive aspects of both mass and craft production and so require rather different approaches to the organization of work. In contrast to the command-and-control culture of Taylorism, such forms of production seek to manage the labor process via employee commitment to and involvement in the job each one does via a range of human resource management practices (Wills, 1998a, 15–16).[25] This can be illustrated by reference to just-in-time production strategies. Strictly speaking, "just-in-time" refers to a way of organizing the immediate manufacturing process and buyer–supplier relations between firms (Sayer, 1986; Sayer and Walker, 1992,

130), but these principles have become incorporated into a variety of approaches to high-volume (but not mass) production. Just-in-time is predicated upon a particular pattern of capital-versus-labor relations, and it crucially depends upon guaranteed smooth and trouble-free production along the entire supply chain. Sayer and Walker (1992, 176, emphasis added), in a way that emphasizes its lineage as a system of mass production, describe just-in-time as

> *a system of mass production* consisting of a highly integrated series of small-lot production processes. Further, JIT is a learning system which generates economies by . . . reducing the amounts of machinery, materials or labour which are at any time inactive. . . . Economies do not follow simply from major technological developments, nor from the simple speed-up of individual tasks, *but from a different way of organising the labour process*, coupled with piecemeal changes to machinery.

Companies pursue greater flexibility in the allocation of workers' time on the line, the scheduling of overtime, and reorganization of shifts to ensure that factories and machines produce goods for as many hours of each day and week as is possible within regulatory limits. In this sense it represents a more profound realization of the principles of mass production. Often this has been associated with reductions in workforces. Moreover, the pursuit of such flexibility is by no means confined to manufacturing industry. For instance, Lash and Urry (1994, 124) argue that in the television industry in the United Kingdom flexibility "has been in large part an exercise in multi-tasking, labour shedding and general cost cutting." Detailed information on the performance of individual workers is central to this "different" way of organizing production. Combined with management innovations, it enhances managerial control over the labor process and over individual workers. In this way, companies seek to intensify the labor process and pace of work and to cut the turnover time of fixed capital.

The introduction of just-in-time as a "different way of organising the labour process" cannot, however, be understood outside of the context of the emergence of just-in-time in Japan in the 1950s, for the "Japanese" model of industrial relations is not some timeless cultural characteristic of Japanese society. On the contrary, it emerged from bitter class struggle, a series of strikes culminating in the 1953 lockout at Nissan, which resulted in the defeat of vigorously militant left-wing trade unions. In the aftermath of this, it proved relatively easy to socialize workers within company unions into the emergent dominant managerial conception of production, aided by promises of employment for life in deeply segmented labor markets characterized by underemployment or unemployment for many. One result of this was a sharp contrast in the employment conditions of the relatively privileged workers of "big" companies and those of workers in smaller companies situated further down the production chain. The former, a sort of labor aristocracy, obtained relatively secure employment in exchange for an intensification of the labor process and functional flexibility, while many of the latter were often seasonally or temporarily employed on a casual basis.

Consequently, companies in the United States or Europe seeking to introduce just-in-time into existing factories, or moving factories to other locations in areas with a long industrial history, have typically encountered problems. Companies seeking to introduce just-in-time practices there have typically sought out locations with "green labor"—relative to the particular industry in which they are operating, with either no trade union representation or single union deals with compliant and non-adversarial unions. Consider the locational strategies of the Japanese car companies in the United Kingdom. Honda, Nissan, and Toyota have established assembly plants in different English regions, but always in locations without a previous history of making automobiles (Hudson, 1995a). Clearly, just-in-time requires a very specific sort of micro-regulatory régime within workplaces in order for it to function as a profitable form of production organization. This in turn requires a particular type of macroeconomic environment to encourage the emergence of labor market conditions within which such workplace régimes can be constructed. Macroscale changes can therefore undermine the stability of the microscale regulatory régimes within the company and the workplace. This was graphically illustrated during the 1990s by companies in Japan being, first, forced to trim the notion of "a job for life," then to actually make workers redundant. Under these circumstances, even against a background of high unemployment, it may be increasingly difficult to guarantee the smooth pattern of industrial relations upon which just-in-time depends.

The introduction of just-in-time principles also has implications for the organization of work beyond the immediate point of production, in retailing establishments and distribution points. Adjusting production schedules to short-term fluctuations in consumer demand—in clothing and food factories, for example—depended upon the introduction of real-time electronic links from the point of sale to the factory. This required a restructuring of employment—already under way as part of a broader cost-cutting strategy in retailing—which involved the increasing conversion of skilled sales staff to de-skilled checkout operators. This in turn was linked to the growing predominance of part-time employment in retailing. Thus, the introduction of just-in-time has employment implications throughout the production filière, but this involves combining "new" and "old" ways of organizing work rather than the former systematically replacing the latter.

Supporters of just-in-time argue that—in contrast to Taylorist mass production—it provides a working environment that empowers workers and engages them creatively in the process of production. It does so via more varied and skilled work with longer job-task cycle times, built around themes such as flexibility, responsibility, teamwork, and quality. This in turn requires a constant restructuring of workplace spatial layouts, as well as workplace time schedules, as shop-floor workers adjust the microgeography of production to create a more personalized workplace in response to the changing flow of just-in-time orders (Lash and Urry, 1994, 56). Similar claims are made more generally by advocates of new methods of human resource management and "high-performance" manufacturing. Systems of "high-performance" work organization in manufacturing, based upon the generalized introduction of new computing and IT technologies, are seen to mobilize all workers in problem-solving and quality improvement teams, requiring them to gather, process, and act upon information. This has led to a renewed emphasis upon training, security of employment, and the introduction of incentive pay schemes to improve the commitment and trust of a more valued workforce. It both produces better quality and more highly remunerated and satisfying jobs for workers and enhanced competitiveness and profits for companies. The effectiveness of individual employees is enhanced by giving them more discretion in carrying out their jobs, and collective effectiveness is enhanced by creating new opportunities for organizational learning through employee participation. It is claimed that there is little evidence of any "dark side" to these systems of work organization (Economic Policy Institute, 2000).[26]

Critics suggest that—both in Japan and as exported and implemented elsewhere—just-in-time is a disempowering régime that intensifies the pace of work and is characterized by new and more subtle methods of control, exploitation, and surveillance, intensification of the labor process, and increased stress on workers (Okamura and Kawahito, 1990). New methods of production and human resource management associated with "high-performance" manufacturing elsewhere share similar characteristics. A supervisor at Nissan's factory near Sunderland in northeast England commented that in interviewing potential shop-floor workers: "We lay it on the line that it's hard work, that they probably haven't ever worked as hard before" (reported in Tighe, 1998). The reorganization of work into teams and the ergonomic reorganization of workplaces to encourage the smoother flow of production provide the physical basis for companies to encourage a set of internal workplace social relations defined around notions of customer and supplier (Yates, 1998, 127–137). Consequently, workers relate to one another as "suppliers" further up the line or as "customers" further down the line. No longer is it a question of "them" and "us" inasmuch as "we" are also part of "them," with consequent implications for workers' identities and sense of solidarity (Hudson, 1997). Cloaked in an ideology of teamwork and collective effort, it represents a system of labor control that individualizes work norms and remuneration systems while legitimating this in terms of group work and collective effort. The culture of teamwork and competitiveness replaces direct supervision with peer pressure to ensure that workers continue to work as required. By the 1990s "it had become impossible to believe the promises of the human resource management, team concept, total quality, or whatever name the new ways of working were known by. The new workplace, whether in the private or public sector, was worse, not better, in most cases" (Moody, 1997, 55). Best (1990, 150–151, original emphasis) makes an acute observation in relation to the debates about teamwork and the organization of the labor process:

> The integration of thinking and doing has a crucial implication for managerial hierarchy and power relations within the firm. Thinking and planning *by* workers required horizontal information flows across functional boundaries; thinking by management and planning *of* workers' activities by management require vertical information flows coordinated by middle management. Thus the relations of teamwork are superimposed on relations of hierarchy. But teamwork demands relations of trust between managers and workers that are antithetical to the top-down power relations between manager and worker that are built into the scientific management paradigm.

At the same time that Taylorist principles are being increasingly introduced and reworked in large swathes of the services sector (as noted above), there are claims that other new sorts of employment are emerging—or at least becoming more prevalent—in services. These jobs are seen as characterized by a greater degree of worker autonomy, empowerment, and responsibility (to a degree analogous to new forms of manufacturing employment). Sometimes it would seem that what is involved is less the emergence of new forms of employment and more a reinterpretation of the characteristics of well-established jobs. Fashion retailing is hardly a new activity, for example, but McRobbie (1997, 87) has recently argued that aspects of performance and presentation involved in the work of selling are both specific to that activity, integral to the job, and tied to the appearance of the person performing the work. Work in a variety of service occupations associated with tourism and leisure is also seen to involve embodied performances requiring a range of personal and social as well as technical skills that provides satisfying work for those that carry it out. Even poorly paid workers in restaurants have a considerable degree of autonomy in organizing their work activities. Indeed, much of their work consists of socializing with customers who are also often friends

(Marshall, 1986). As a result, much of their work revolves around interpersonal interaction and coproduction of services. The work of waiting in restaurants does not simply involve low skills and all-embracing managerial control. It also involves skilled performative displays to customers, the workplace becoming a stage on which particular types of performance involving a mix of emotional, manual, and mental labor are played out, creating a particular atmosphere that staff must work to sustain (Crang, 1994). Such dialogic coproduction involves the development of fine classificatory distinctions between service consumers and producers associated with increasing individualization of consumption, especially among the new middle classes (Bourdieu, 1984).

In such services the labor process necessarily involves ceding considerable responsible autonomy from managers to workers since part of the delivery of the service involves interpersonal interaction between a copresent customer and supplier. Nonetheless, such work remains poorly paid (not least because wages can constitute up to 75% of total costs in highly competitive sectors) and often precarious. Moreover, insofar as workers become the product, they become involved in a particular form of self-exploitation. Furthermore, insofar as such work necessarily depends upon the appearance and personal attributes of the worker, it may be linked to age and stage in life cycle and as such be limited in its duration for any one individual. As McRobbie (1997, 87) puts it, fashion retail workers' "self-image must surely be undercut by the reality of knowing that in a few years time, possibly with children to support, it is unlikely that they would hold onto the job of decorating the shopfloor at Donna Karan." It may well be the case that what is involved here is in fact a reinterpretation of the character of old service sector occupations rather than the emergence of new and qualitatively different ones.

Service occupations and service sector labor processes do not therefore always sit easily within the "classic" Marxian conceptualization of the labor process of transformative manufacturing industry. Indeed, similar points can be made in respect to the labor process in agriculture and mining. In these the focus is, respectively, upon maintaining or enhancing the conditions in which natural processes operate or in appropriating elements from nature rather than transformation within a manufacturing process.[27] As Benton (1989, 69, original emphasis) puts it, within the "classical" Marxian framework for analysis of the labor process, "Labour processes whose intentional structure emphasises the dependence of labour on non-manipulable conditions and subjects in which labour adapts to its conditions, sustains, regulates or appropriates its subjects, as distinct from transforming them, are given *no independent conceptual specification*."

This is not to deny the validity of the Marxian framework but rather to point to the need to extend and refine it to encompass a wider range of labor processes organized within capitalist social relations of production. Such "eco-regulatory" labor processes and labor processes of "appropriation" often of necessity cede considerable autonomy to workers, weakening effective managerial control. This was perhaps to be expected—indeed, to be unavoidable—in activities such as underground mining, in which there was a considerable separation of workers from managers, which led the latter to strive to restructure the labor process to approximate more closely the effective working rules of the transformative factory production line.[28] More generally, it helps to explain why management strategies in a wide range of nonmanufacturing activities have often sought to reorganize such work so as to conform more closely to the characteristics and organizational forms of the transformative manufacturing labor process.

4.5. Summary and Conclusions

Within the limits defined by regulatory systems, companies and workers routinely struggle over the extent, terms, and conditions of employment. Workers form trade unions to seek to further their interests, while companies often form alliances to seek to further *their* interests. This struggle is conducted on a territorially varied regulatory terrain that defines both possibilities and problems for both companies and workers but in circumstances in which there is a powerful structural asymmetry in the powers of capital and labor. Companies seek to recruit different types of labor, with different combinations of technical skills, social skills, and personal attributes, in varying ways and via varying mechanisms, and on different terms and conditions, depending upon their chosen production strategy and prevailing labor market conditions. They vary recruitment strategies depending upon the types of labor that they require and whether they are seeking to preserve existing models of production or to move to new ways of producing. The combination of labor market conditions and mode of regulation of labor at the point of production becomes crucial in shaping labor recruitment strategies. Recruitment strategies and the mix of workers recruited, (non)retention strategies, and the choice of production strategy and production model are interrelated.

Ways of organizing work and the labor process vary with the nature of the product, choice of production strategy, and the extent to which firms are dependent upon retaining skilled and knowledgeable workers, often with company-specific knowledge and skills. What is at issue is not only the quantitative division of the working day between productive and nonproductive (in relation to producing surplus-value) time and but also qualitative issues associated with the working environment, the culture, and the social relations of production. While *analytically* distinct strategies for organizing work and the labor process can be specified, in practice companies use more than one of them simultaneously, though in varying combinations at different times and in different places. Capital's attempts to introduce changes to working practices and ways of organizing the labor process are not unproblematic, however; they are often contested by labor. Not least, this is because the restructuring of work and working practices implies changes to workers' identities and the ways in which they relate to other workers. The fact that workers contest the restructuring of production and work is an important reason why companies may search for a "spatial fix" via relocation. This in turn however can lead to localized job losses and in turn may be vigorously contested by those who may lose their jobs.

Notes

1. See "Establishing Legal Frameworks for Markets" in section 3.7.

2. Divisions and competition between companies and between groups of workers are considered in the next three chapters.

3. This is also considered more fully in Chapter 6.

4. Recognizing the inherent difficulties that such a project involves; see section 3.2.

5. See section 7.3.

6. Moreover, even during the Fordist era marked subnational divisions continued to characterize the organizational geography of trade unions; see section 7.2.

7. See Chapter 5.

8. See also Chapter 3.

9. It is important to note that the definition of the service sector and "services" is far from unproblematic, and that this has had implications both for academic analysis and trade union practice. This is discussed more fully in later chapters.

10. That is, workers with no previous history of working in a given industry or, alternatively, no history of the social relations of capitalist industrial production in any form.

11. See section 7.3.

12. These issues are discussed more fully in section 8.6.

13. Conceptualizing and measuring efficiency depends upon the way in which production is envisaged within different "cultures of production." Best (1990, 148–149, original emphasis) makes the point as follows: "*Operational* throughput efficiency, the indicator of success for mass production, is measured in terms of productivity per labor or machine input hour. *Process* throughput efficiency is the ratio of the time a product is being transformed in the production

system. Process efficiency has led to a new set of success indicators. One is work in progress (WIP) turn: the ratio of WIP to annual sales."

14. Issues of competitive strategy are discussed more fully in Chapters 5 and 6.

15. Such divisions between workers are discussed further in section 7.3.

16. Interestingly, the Ford Motor Company established its own sociology department as the vehicle through which its paternalistic policies of labor recruitment and control were primarily pursued ideologically, along with a de facto private police force that provided physical force and violence when needed.

17. This was highlighted in 1999 when Nissan announced a major redundancy program that resulted in layoffs in its Japanese factories.

18. See also Chapter 8.

19. This is in part a result of process of centralization of capital via acquisitions, takeovers and mergers, which are discussed in section 6.5.

20. Clearly this dichotomy fails to reflect the complexity of the processes through which work is organized and labor processes are controlled, but as an analytic division it represents a useful starting point. Within the categories of "manager" and "worker" there are important variations in power, autonomy, and control.

21. See sections 5.3, 5.4, and 5.5.

22. Since innovations (process, product, and organizational) tend to diffuse within a sector, or in the case of generic technologies across sectors the competitive advantage that companies achieve via increasing relative surplus-value production in these ways tends to be temporary; see section 5.3.

23. Labor market conditions are not the *only* variable affecting choice of production model, for ultimately the selection of a particular model depends upon perceived profitability. That said, there is no simplistic or deterministic economistic process at work here, but rather a more subtle and nuanced process of selection. See Chapter 5.

24. In part, however, this increase is due to the outsourcing of fabrication as part of a continuously redefined sociospatial division of labor (Sklair, 1990).

25. Although often represented as new, such approaches share much in common with what Friedman (1977) termed "responsible autonomy" managerial strategies.

26. Such systems of work organization have become increasingly common within manufacturing in the United States. Between 1987 and 1995 the proportion of workers employed in self-managed teams rose from 28% to 68% in the clothing, medical electronics, and imaging, and steel industries in the United States (Economic Policy Institute, 2000).

27. The implications of this are discussed more fully in Chapter 9.

28. For example, in the deep mines of the British coal industry managers in the nationalized industry sought to introduce more automated methods of production (the MINOS system) that would enhance managerial control of the process of mining coal (see Winterton, 1985).

5

Company Connections
Competition and Cooperation, Part 1

5.1. Introduction

A central insight of Marxian political economy is that competition between companies is central to the developmental dynamic of capitalist production, providing the impetus for revolutionizing the "how" and "what" of production. Such competition pivots around the production and distribution of profits. Companies compete over a range of issues in pursuit of profits—for market share or control of new growth products and sectors, for example. They therefore compete in various ways—for example, via product price and quality. Others have subsequently taken up these ideas. While several dimensions to intercorporate competition can be identified, Schumpeter (1961, 60) famously summarized these in terms of a distinction between adaptive forms of competitive strategy that take given constraints as binding and creative strategies that do not. This dichotomy has been echoed within recent approaches in economic geography under rubrics such as "weak" and "strong" competition (Storper and Walker, 1989) or "structure dependent" and "structure focused domains of competition" (Clark, 1992). These distinctions (setting aside semantic differences in the terms used to describe them) are important in denoting qualitatively different forms of intercapitalist competition. Whereas "weak" strategies revolve around price competition within a given technological-organizational paradigm, "strong" strategies are based upon quality, product differentiation, and product innovation. As such, "strong" strategies crucially depend, among other things, upon the intrafirm development of specific capabilities and competencies that allow companies to develop particular—even unique—segments of markets and production.[1]

These distinctions between types of strategies are, however, analytic—a company can pursue several types of strategy simultaneously. There is abundant evidence that in practice corporate decision making cuts across this analytic distinction (Sabel and Zeitlin, 1997). In terms of the dynamics of historical geographies of production and which firms survive longer-term, however, the development of successful Schumpeterian "creative" strategies is critical. Schumpeter saw "market disturbing activity" as lying at the heart of competitive strategy, raising questions as to *how* markets are to be "disturbed" and how methods of "disturbance" vary among companies, sectors, times, and places. This is closely echoed in concepts of "strong" or "structure focused" strategies. This chapter explores these issues of diverse forms and dimensions of competition and the ways in which differences between places and spaces are implicated in them. While some attention is given to the relationships between collaboration and competition, consideration of collaborative strategies is largely reserved for the next chapter.

5.2. Competition within Existing Socio-Organizational and Technical Paradigms

"Weak" forms of competition revolve around companies seeking reductions in production costs within the parameters of an existing technological paradigm, within which all firms producing a particular product operate.[2] Such competition can occur in many domains. It can, for example, involve price cutting via discovering cheaper sources of varied factor inputs. This form of competition thus emphasizes the importance of "know where."[3] Cheaper sources of inputs to production are typically—though not necessarily—found in more distant locations. This enhanced "distanciation" (Giddens, 1984) of the social relations of production is made possible by technological improvements and resultant falling costs of communications and transport, often allied to shifts in state policies. It is reflected in new patterns of commodity movements, trade, and geographies of production. For example, changes in U.K. national state policies, the growth of international coal markets, and improved bulk transportation of coal enabled the British Steel Corporation to switch to importing coking coals. This led to new geographies of the coal trade, linking its Teesside works in northeast England with a range of locations and, as a result, coking coal collieries in nearby County Durham closed, as their market disappeared (Beynon et al., 1991).

However, the most visible and well-publicized direct impacts on geographies of production have resulted from firms using knowledge of the location of cheaper and more malleable labor to seek "spatial fixes" via relocating production to enhance or preserve competitiveness. Thus, companies compete by seeking out "better" labor market conditions, both intranationally (Lipietz, 1980; Massey, 1995a) and internationally (Fröbel et al., 1980). There are numerous well-documented cases of multinational companies exploiting differences in wage rates and other labor market conditions in organizing production, both in terms of their intracompany geographies and subcontracting strategies. For example, Nike pioneered a shifting international division of labor in athletic shoes production that relies largely on subcontractors in a hierarchically nested set of offshore production locations. Shoe assembly remains a highly labor-intensive operation, sensitive to variations in wage rates (Donoghue and Barff, 1990; Schoenberger, 1998). If local costs become too high, a given location may be either upgraded in its tasks so that its costs are not out of line or abandoned in favor of a less expensive locale. This strategy has been imitated by most of Nike's competitors. Companies in labor-intensive sectors *become* multinational, exploiting variations in labor market conditions as a necessary condition to their survival. For example, until 1990 Dewhirst (one of Marks and Spencer's main suppliers) produced clothing only in the United Kingdom. It opened its first factory outside the United Kingdom in Malaysia in 1990. In the latter half of the 1990s it opened further plants in Indonesia and Morocco, locations in which labor costs were a fraction of those in the United Kingdom, closing factories there as a result. By the end of the 1990s only one-third of its labor force remained in the United Kingdom (Blackwell and Voyle, 2000).

This reshaping of corporate geographies of production requires manufacturing companies to have sophisticated systems for monitoring spatial variations in wage costs and adjusting production strategies in light of this knowledge (Kehoe, 1992; Marsh, 1997).[4] Often subcontracting in manufacturing involves widespread use of informal work in peripheral locations in the global economy. Hadjimichalis and Vaiou (1996, 4) refer to the growth of "what may be called 'bloody informalisation' due to extremely exploitative conditions including child labour from the age of four."[5] Such labor market differences are also helping shape a new international division of labor in service sector occupations such as those involved in electronic data processing (Pearson and Mitter, 1994; P. Taylor, 1995).[6] It is important, however, not to overstate the significance of labor cost differences in the construction of new international divisions of labor. Reliance upon low wages in newly industrializing countries is a very sectorally and temporally specific form of intercapitalist competition (Berry, 1989; Gordon, 1988). Nevertheless, such labor cost differences can set the scene for restructuring labor relations and working conditions in situ under the threat of relocating (Beynon et al., 1994; Hudson,

1989a; Marsh, 1997) unless labor agrees to such changes, as well as to the transfer of production to more favorable locations.

Companies may openly seek to set factories against one another, playing upon and exploiting the immobility of labor and people's ties to place. The threat of relocation can, in these circumstances, be as effective in meeting corporate goals as actually relocating. Beynon (1984, 52–53) describes the situation as experienced by workers at Ford's Dagenham plant in southeast England in the mid-1960s:

> The full meaning of multinational production began to make itself apparent in the PTA [Paint, Trim, Assembly] at that time. The company owned another assembly plant in Cologne [in the Federal Republic of Germany] manned mainly by Spanish and Turkish workers whose immigrant status made them extremely vulnerable. The sack [that is, dismissal] could mean deportation. The "Cologne Yardstick" was increasingly applied to the Dagenham PTA plant in the 1960s. Supervisors were frequently taken to the Cologne plant to compare the way the job was run in the two plants.

Some thirty years later, workers at Osram's Augsburg factory in southern Germany agreed to move to more flexible shift systems. They did so knowing that the company was considering moving to Bari, in southern Italy, which would cut labor costs by 40% (Marsh, 1997). However, Osram did not relocate there, illustrating that variables other than wage costs were relevant, including plant flexibility, labor productivity, the technical content of the work, and closeness to markets. There is therefore no simple deterministic relationship between de-skilling and relocation of production. Activities may remain "in situ," as work is de-skilled, without the threat of relocation or competition from another plant. For example, printing has certainly been de-skilled via technological change, as typographic skills have been rendered redundant and printers reduced to button pushers. Even so, a considerable amount of printing—especially small-batch job printing for small businesses, or of local newspapers—remains constrained by the necessity for physical proximity to markets (Cox, 1997, 180). Similarly, many service industries remain close to markets despite an efflorescence of new job categories that require little skill in the way of training but that are highly market-oriented. These include the armies of cleaners in the downtown and city center offices and hotels and the rapidly expanding corps of private security guards and parking garage attendants.

In summary, specific forms of capital-versus-labor relations are a strategic element in intercorporate competitive strategies. Companies use them to preserve or enhance competitiveness vis-à-vis competitors working within the same technological paradigm and others deploying more advanced technologies and/or bringing new products to the market.

5.3. Competition via Creating New Technical and Organizational Paradigms of Production and New Products

Whereas the emphasis in "weak" competition is upon allocative efficiency within a static equilibrium economy, the emphasis in "strong competition" is on dynamic disequilibrium. This latter view of competition has its roots in the concerns of classical political economists. It is, however, perhaps most closely associated with Schumpeter and other evolutionary economists and concepts such as "creative destruction" and the associated redrawing of historical geographies of production as companies strive to create sustainable long-term competitive advantages. For example, global competition forced semiconductor producers in Silicon Valley to prioritize strategies of strong competition over those of weak competition. It became increasingly important to integrate innovation and production more closely since the dynamic of this industry has been driven by innovation rather than the search for cheaper labor (Jonas, 1997, 17).

Strategies of strong competition revolve around chronic and deliberate disturbance of capitalist markets, the constant revolutionizing of the what and how of production via innovation in products, processes, and forms of production organization, and the redefining the socio-organizational and technological paradigms of production. This constant pressure for innovation is often seen as a progressive aspect of capitalist production, generating a constant flow of new products and processes of production. Moreover, relationships between different types of innovation may vary within different models of production. The simultaneous development of product and processes is a well-established feature of the system of mass production. Even so, as products move through their life cycle, the appropriate processes of production are altered. Within mass customization, however, the importance of any individual product decreases "because there are so many of them. Processes become decoupled from products and now outlast individual products—some of which are developed and sold only once—and can outlast the entire product life cycles. It is *process life cycle* that has become more important" (Pine, 1993, 215, original emphasis). Others suggest that variations in regulatory régimes can shape the trajectories of innovation. For example, different national regulatory régimes for intellectual property rights can encourage some innovations while discouraging others. Conversely, the viability of such régimes depends upon their compatibility with particular forms of innovation (Foray, 1993).[7]

Organizational Innovation

Companies seek to increase productivity via organizational innovation, discovering new ways of producing more efficiently via "better" use of labor and other resources. These are changes that involve discovering new ways of working more efficiently *within* existing technological paradigms. Organizational innovations therefore directly impact upon regulation of the labor process and the organization of work at different points along the production filière. Initially within industrial capitalism such innovations revolved around bringing production into factories; since then, various approaches have been developed to increase the efficiency of production within given technological paradigms. The pressure to design productive organizations—more specifically, those that can integrate thinking and doing and recombine mental and manual work—is increasing because "Schumpeterian competition is turning into time competition" (Best, 1990, 14). Whereas mass production focused upon one form of time competition, namely, economies of time in throughput, newer forms of production emphasize the importance of process time, the time required for materials to be processed. Japanese firms have organized plants to reduce process time from days to hours and raise productivity without increasing the speed of work or machines (Stalk, 1988). For example, Toyota developed the concept of multimachining based upon machines arranged in U-shapes with a group of machines overseen by a single worker. This permitted a discrete increase in labor productivity based on organizational innovation rather than intensification of the pace of work of the individual worker.

In addition to utilizing organizational innovation at the immediate point of production, companies seek to compete via organizational innovation in methods of management. For example, during the 1920s General Motors was transformed by the introduction of new managerial methods and structures.[8] In the contemporary globalizing economy large companies are devising new "hybrid" organizational structures to cope with the complex challenges posed by increasingly fluid and dynamic markets. In such an environment large firms, seeking to build their "strategic architecture" on carefully selected core competencies, tend to develop a dual organizational structure that emphasizes, first of all, an integrated network structure to manage core competencies. This assumes intense exchanges of all forms of knowledge between the component elements of the firm to enhance their ability to exploit local externalities and contribute to the construction of sustainable collective knowledge.[9] Decisions concerning core competency activities are detached from regular and ongoing decision-making mechanisms based on transaction costs. Long-term commitments based on sunk costs are required to assure the learning capabilities of these core components. The smooth functioning of the whole network of core competencies requires specific governance mechanisms to ensure the effective circulation of knowledge within it. Second, such firms need a classical hierarchical managerial structure to manage their noncore competency activities, which form the majority of their activities. This hierarchical structure is needed for two reasons. First, managing the company as a whole via the mechanisms used to govern core competency structures would be prohibitively expensive. Second, noncore activities satisfy the current allocation of resources for the firm and as such principally require regulation of basic flows of codified information between noncore components. The decision as to whether to retain these activities within the firm depends upon "traditional" transactional cost criteria. The "major fault line" between core and noncore activities is that the former are vital for the firm, and the decision to sustain them "is disconnected from any current make or buy decisions" (Amin and Cohendet, 1997, 13). However, the boundary between core and noncore is fluid and shifting, for these activities are relationally defined. Indeed, it may be more helpful to think of a shifting continuum of activities rather than a dichotomy between "core" and "noncore." A corollary of this is that the boundaries of the firm are also fluid and dynamic as the make or buy decision fluctuates and the boundary is redefined or as acquisition and merger or divestment and demerger redefine the anatomy of the firm and the boundaries of core competencies.[10]

Organizational innovation is an ongoing process. The emergence of the "virtual firm" may signal a significant change in corporate organization. This brings together members of existing companies to execute a specific task quickly and efficiently—effectively a process of "mass customization of the enterprise" linked to the emergence of "agile manufacturing enterprises," with "the ability to form virtual companies routinely." Pine (1993, 258–260) elaborates on this concept:

> Virtual enterprises are cross-functional and multi-company teams brought together solely to accomplish a specific task; then, once the market opportunity fades, the team is disbanded so that the enterprise can re-apply its capabilities and resources to the next task through the next virtual enterprise. Tasks can range from providing a total solution to meet the wants and needs of one individual consumer to developing a new product or service that itself can be mass-customised for thousands or millions of consumers, to creating new processes that can provide their own dynamic flows of goods and services.

This new and project-based organizational form renders the boundaries of the firm, in the conventional sense, virtually irrelevant. The key element becomes the networks of linkages within and across the boundaries of the firm. Moreover, "virtual enterprises" simultaneously contain and combine different existing approaches to production. There are examples of companies that already come close to meeting the specifications of such a virtual enterprise (Pine, 1993, 262–263):

A special attraction to companies (and indeed to national governments formulating strategic industrial policy, as in Japan over the past fifty or so years) of seeking to ground competitive advantage and success in organizational innovation and structure is that organization is a nonmarketable input. Once established, it is difficult, time-consuming, and expensive for competitors to emulate or match. Companies seek competitive advantage via organizational innovation precisely because it is embedded in company-specific knowledge and skills that rivals cannot buy in the market or easily imitate. It is not amenable to diffusion in the same way as, say, technical knowledge about a new production process. This sort of competitive advantage, embedded in the institutions of the firm and the expressed and latent knowledge of those who work for it, may allow a company to maintain a long-term competitive edge over its rivals. This is very much the basis of competitive success for a range of "learning" companies—from the major corporations of Japan to the small and medium-sized enterprises of the Third Italy or Jutland in western Denmark.[11] There may, however, be limits to the extent to which organizational innovation can be sufficient to guarantee competitiveness. For example, significant differences in labor or other input costs may offset superior organization in sectors producing mature products.

Process Innovation and New Technological Paradigms of Production

Process innovation denotes technologically new ways of making existing products. Consequently, there is a critical link between process innovation, fixed capital investment, and technological change. Different methods of production involve varying combinations of dead and living labor (that is, different technical compositions of capital)[12] as well as differing ways of organizing the labor process and relationships between production and the natural world. In part, companies generate new production processes and ways of organizing production because on occasion new products require such changes. For example, many product innovations in financial services have been possible only because of changes in production processes enabled by developments in communications and information technologies (Sassen, 1991, 5). In some cases, organizational innovations have been necessary to ensure that such technologies, often culturally emblematic of the modern world, be economically viable (Lash and Urry, 1994, 253). There are, however, more generally applicable and strong systemic competitive pressures to find "new" ways of producing "old" commodities. An important analytic distinction can be drawn between incremental process improvements within an existing technical-organizational paradigm and the shift to a new paradigm. Once this latter shift occurs, companies can compete via choosing between models of production for a given product.

Companies seek to revolutionize production processes in order to steal a competitive head start on their rivals. Process innovations can be particularly important in mature industries such as chemicals, coal, and steel.[13] Thus, industries often represented as "old" and "smokestack" experience radical changes in process technologies via the deployment of "high technology" production processes. This "hunt for technological rents" (Mandel, 1975) enables "surplus" profits to be made. Process innovations permit the labor time needed in production to be reduced below the existing socially necessary amount. This is significant because producers who use the "new" technology can then sell at below average prices, increasing market share while collecting above average profits on each unit of the commodity sold. Such a strategy is risky, however. There is no guarantee that it will work; it may not and the company could fail. On the other hand, if it succeeds, its rivals may fail. If it does succeed, it retains this competitive edge until the "new" technology diffuses to other producers and becomes generalized, establishing new productivity norms for that commodity (or sector). Thus, the new productivity norm reduces the required amount of socially necessary labor time. This in turn triggers a fresh round of R&D in search of another technological advance and competitive advantage. In this way the process of constantly revolutionizing production technologies proceeds, and competition becomes the motor of accumulation.

This conception of the dynamics of process innovation is specific to certain sorts of production approaches and market conditions, however: essentially mass production of standardized commodities sold in mass markets. In other models of production, process innovation has a differing significance. Decoupling product and process technologies in flexible forms of high volume production has further enhanced the importance of process innovation to competitive strategy, with significant implications for the ways in which companies deploying these production approaches seek to compete. Such companies are investing in general-purpose processes that are more flexible, responsive, and easily reused across products and product families. They have longer process life cycles relative to the products they create, thereby providing a stable base for the dynamic supply of products and services. Thus, "once developed process change is evolutionary and often developed for its *potential* applicability to a broad range of future products. *Therefore businesses no longer need to be defined by their products but can be defined by their processes*" (Pine, 1993, 216–217, emphasis added). Consequently, companies seek to move from mass-customizing products and services on the basis of flexible process technologies to the "mass customization of process uniquely suited to their new market opportunities" (Pine, 1993, 256). There are, however, limits to the decoupling of product and process innovation within these new high-volume approaches to "agile production." For example, Pine (1993, 241–253) identifies several sources of such limitations: radical new product and process innovations that homogenize markets via creating new dominant designs (homogenizing consumer demand, for example, via a reaction to accelerating product obsolescence); information overload, as consumers are overwhelmed by information on a burgeoning range of products; minimum times for development cycles; and minimum life cycles for products and services. Such limits would tend to reestablish different relationships between product and process innovation strongly reminiscent of those characterizing mass production.

Process innovations can have direct implications for where production occurs as well as for how production is organized. Conversely, spatial variations in labor market conditions can shape which sorts of process technologies and competitive strategies are deployed in particular locations. These locational implications arise for two reasons. First, companies using "old" technologies and/or organizational forms may become bankrupt; they may selectively close some plants; or they may relocate production to places in which labor market (or other) conditions permit the "old" technology to be competitive with the "new" one. Second, companies using the "new" technology may need to find fresh locations in which it can be profitably deployed. For instance, this could be in areas in which labor that is "green"[14] in the context of producing those commodities *in these new ways* is available. Such labor will lack knowledge and experience of *existing* "norms of production" for these commodities and thus will accept the conditions associated with the "new" technology more readily. Conversely, in other circumstances the importance of knowledgeable labor can tie production to particular places as these develop the endogenous capacity to generate new processes (and products) that ensure a competitive edge in the market. Such "technology districts" are places in which economic growth occurs on the basis of in situ "product-based technological learning" (Storper, 1993).

Once two or more ways of producing the same commodity exist, companies face difficult decisions about how and where to produce, which may also be linked to the choice of what to produce within a given product sector.[15] For example, in clothing the high fashion industries of the Paris region include two basic segments. First, "true haute couture," where the product is made in batches of less than ten and the production process is truly artisanal (St. Laurent, for example, has less than fifty in-house couturiers). Second, the much larger brand-name ready-to-wear market (that is, moderately expensive clothes produced in small to medium-sized batches, on a strictly seasonal basis). These branded ready-to-wear (*prêt-a-porter*) garments cannot be competitively produced in-house. Consequently, a hybrid production system has evolved that is "a kind of half-way house between high fashion and the competitive sweatshop system found in the United States" (and in many other places), with considerable decentralization of production to peripheral regions within France (Storper, 1993, 442). Elsewhere clothing manufacturers mass-produce clothing, often with direct links to major retailing chains (Crewe and Davenport, 1992), locating production in diverse areas with abundant cheap female labor. These include inner-city areas and peripheral regions in core capitalist countries: for example, the sweatshops of core metropolitan regions such as Los Angeles and New York (Sassen, 1991); peripheral regions (such as northeast England) in core countries (Hudson, 1989a); and varied locations in semiperipheral countries (such as inner Thessaloniki and peripheral regions of eastern Macedonia and Thrace in Greece; Hadjimichalis and Vaiou, 1996); and parts of the Third World (Elson and Pearson, 1981; Portes et al., 1988).

The most significant process innovations have undoubtedly been linked with the emergence of mass production. The essential innovative feature of mass production is its focus upon economies of time rather than scale of production per se—that is, increased scale has been a result, rather than a cause, of increased throughput. Mass production generated economies of operation and lower unit production costs by accelerating the passage of materials through a workplace rather than by increasing the workplace's size (Chandler, 1977, 257). The emergence of the then new American system of manufacture in the nineteenth century was based upon incorporating new specialized machines to produce interchangeable parts, significantly increasing labor productivity. Production was still organized around ensembles of machines, however. Consequently, increasing scale of production required adding identical sets of machines rather than accelerating the pace of production. The critical innovation in the latter part of the nineteenth century was the replacement of functional machines with the sequential layout of the flow-line, arranging machines in the order of machining operations. Flow-line arrangements explicitly revealed the different time cycles of each stage in a production sequence, with bottlenecks emerging at machines with longer time cycles. Enhancing time economies on any one machine immediately creates excess capacity for that machine and/or bottlenecks at the next machine in the flow-line sequence. By reducing the time cycle of the machine with the longest cycle, engineers could speed up the whole line, but removing a bottleneck at one point simply transposed it elsewhere. Seeking to achieve a balanced flow implied one of three things: running a machine below its potential capacity; adding machines at the bottleneck; or reducing the time cycle of the slowest machine. By the 1880s flow-line methods had been refined to produce continuous flow processes. Functionally distinct machines were linked into a single complex, with materials input at one end and processed products output at the other. Initially developed in refining and distilling industries utilizing gas and liquid materials, continuous flow-line technologies were subsequently introduced into industries such as bulk chemicals and metals production, with continuing refinements of production technologies via ongoing process innovation. These resulted in significant territorial agglomeration of production because of economies of scale and interprocess and interfirm linkages and flows of materials (Hudson, 1983, 1994a).

The adaptation of flow-line methods for use in mass production of consumer goods, involving the assembly of large numbers of often complex components, following Ford's path-breaking innovations in automobile production, was of crucial importance. This dramatically reduced the labor time needed to produce automobiles.[16] A corollary was an equally dramatic reduction in price. Thus, mass production paved the way for, and simultaneously necessitated the rise of, mass consumption, creating pressures for further organizational and process innovation. Designing complex integrated machines capable of exploiting economies of time by incorporating flow-line principles became a challenge for production engineers in other consumer goods industries as diverse as "white goods" and clothing. These process innovations generated new sources of market instability as the high fixed-cost structures of mass production altered the dynamics of market adjustment. Scale economies (like "technological rents") present companies with a strategic opportunity to reduce prices and increase production, provided that increased sales volumes more than offset lower unit prices. Seeking to enhance market share in static or declining markets inevitably reduces the market share of rival companies, however. This could destabilize existing mechanisms for regulating market prices, possibly leading to "ruinous competition." In recognition of this, there are strong systemic pressures for firms to find ways of controlling or bypassing markets as regulatory mechanisms in sectors and product segments in which mass production is prominent.[17]

In due course, mass production reached its limits in the core territories of the capitalist economies in which it first became established. In response, companies sought spatially to extend mass markets and further standardize consumer tastes. The limits of this response were soon reached, however. The methods and practices by which mass production achieved success (a focus on operational efficiency, on Taylorist control of the labor process, on breakthrough innovations, on selling low-cost standardized products in large homogeneous markets) increasingly became a barrier rather than a route to competitiveness. Each focus carried with it a number of detrimental effects that undermined mass production from within (Pine, 1993, 100). An initial response was (implicitly) to deny that the problems originated "from within" and to seek to contain the inherent contradictions via "spatial fixes" (Harvey, 1982), first intranationally and then internationally, to sustain mass production.[18] Another, sometimes linked, neo-Fordist (Palloix, 1976) response was to increase automation within mass production factories (for example, by introducing robots into parts of automobile production lines). Neo-Fordism can be defined as "automatic control or automation. . . . The basis of the entire system is thus the ability *to construct machines that control their own operations*" (Aglietta, 1979, 123, original emphasis). As such, it can be seen as a further attempt to perfect flow-line principles within mass production.[19]

Companies also began to seek systemic alternatives to mass production, however. In part this depended upon technological innovations, allowing the use of "very flexible machine systems in manufacture" to cut setup times and accelerate materials flows (Schamp, 1991, 162). These changes impacted upon the ways in which individual companies and workplaces organize production. Moreover, "through changes in the technical foundations of accumulation, there has been a reorganisation of the industrial economy as a whole. New principles are at work and are re-shaping it" (Coriat, 1991, 134). While Coriat was particularly concerned with the impact of programmable machines, the point he makes has a more general validity. Redefining economies of time and distinctions between productive and unproductive time and operational and process efficiency is central to the competitiveness of these new methods of production (Best, 1990, 147–148). Operational efficiency measures the success of mass production, process efficiency that of methods of flexible high volume production. Operational efficiency is defined in relation to productive time, the time during which materials are being transformed by machining operations, for example, in terms of labor productivity. Process efficiency is defined in relation both to productive and unproductive time (the time materials spend in inventory or other nonoperational activities such as handling, transporting in the workplace, inspecting, reworking or recording), measuring the total time a product is being transformed via variables such as work-in-progress (WIP) turns.[20] These newer approaches to flexible high-volume production therefore conceive of economies of time and production efficiency in a way different from mass production, for "over and above the capacity to reconcile high productivity and product diversity, it is 'dynamic flexibility' and adaptation to the uncertainties associated with movements in demand that are becoming strategic factors. . . . The integrated management of time is becoming the strategic factor in the search for competitive advantage" (Veltz, 1991, 198).

In one sense any process innovation necessarily involves organizational innovation and changes in management practices to ensure efficient production incorporating the fresh possibilities offered by new hardware and "hard" technologies. For example, Toyota introduced "automatic machines" and a new configuration of machines on the factory floor, enabling one worker to manage several machines. For Toyota, automation meant creating machines with a built-in capacity to stop before defective products were produced. Automated machinery revolutionized the organization of production in several ways. First, it liberated machine operators from constant attention to a single machine. Second, machines shut themselves down every time an abnormality occurred, focusing worker and management energy on detecting these problems and developing a solution. Increasingly the task of the workers shifted from mere operators of a single machine to maintaining machines and seeking modifications so that machines would not shut down. *"Thus workers became problem solvers as opposed to merely machine minders"* (Best, 1990, 154, emphasis added).

More generally, new methods of flexible high-volume production involve bringing together four basic innovations (Pine, 1993, 50): first, just-in-time delivery and processing of materials and components to eliminate process flaws and reduce inventory carrying costs; second, reduced setup and changeover times, directly lowering batch sizes and the costs of variety; third, compressed cycle times throughout all processes in the value chain, eliminating waste, increasing flexibility and responsiveness while decreasing costs; and fourth, producing upon receipt of an order instead of a forecast, lowering inventory costs and other costs such as writeoffs of unsalable products. This may involve the use of computer-assisted design and manufacturing technologies that simultaneously offer economies of scale and scope, reducing unit production costs as the variety of products increases by expanding the overall volume of production. It may, however, simply involve changing the ways that workers work with existing technologies. The systematic exploitation of economies of scope—whether via implementation of design changes (range of product) or flexibility of product mix—is a "key way in which the hegemony of the canonical Fordist model is broken" (Coriat, 1991). While each of these four elements involves technical process innovations, it is their combination into new ways of producing via organizational innovation and innovative methods of managing the production process that confers competitive advantage.

However, flexible high-volume production methods require particular combinations of labor and product markets in order to be profitable. Consequently, in a variety of product markets companies face a choice between Taylorist mass production and newer forms of more flexible high-volume production. Coriat (1991, 150) stresses that in situations in which output is increasing "everything" depends on the relative importance of the economies of scale and of scope for specific products. Once the former are large and greater than the latter, "it will be more efficient to produce in two specific plants in longer runs the two joint products formerly made with a flexible technology." The relative importance of economies of scope and scale thus determines whether flexible specialization or dynamic flexibility becomes the dominant organizational model. Moreover, these new forms of flexible production do not necessarily rule out the survival of earlier forms of mass production:

> Diverse strategies are . . . possible on the basis of the implementation of complex principles governing the externalisation of functions, industrial subcontracting, and co-operation and partnership, in addition to or in conjunction with different modes of implementation of flexible and/or classical mass production.

As a result, such new organizational developments are creating more varied landscapes than those of the 1950s and 1960s (Veltz, 1991, 194). Nonetheless, there may well be strong continuities between the past and present landscapes (Martinelli and Schoenberger, 1991, 119). Mariti (1993, 193), however, suggests a need for caution in assessments of the extent of landscape variability, as empirical evidence suggests that economies of scope are "somewhat limited" in the field of production, mainly influencing selling and marketing. Current developments in manufacturing flexibility made possible by computer integrated manufacture (CIM), however, "seem to provide a technological solution to flexibility problems." These techniques in general require substantial, often specifically dedicated, investments. Because of them, larger businesses can quickly change products on the assembly line and fill different market segments or niches and at lower cost than small specialized firms. Thus, "flexible manufacturing techniques *could* act to negate some of the advantages of small firm flexibility and reduce its scope. With reference to Japan there is, however, some support for the idea that CIM may in fact be restricted to single applications . . . to solve specific production problems." Mariti is careful to speak only of the possible implementation of CIM in manufacturing, and in practice the limits to CIM alluded to are by no means restricted to Japan (Hudson, 1994b, 1997; Hudson and Schamp, 1995a, 1995b).

In general, companies deploy a mixture of production approaches, dependent upon labor and product market conditions (Hudson and Schamp, 1995b). Small-batch production of specialized and sophisticated products is based on short production runs and long job cycles. Indeed, major items of equipment and the means of production and transport (for example, power stations, generators) have always been produced on this basis, and complex commodities (for example, large jet airliners and ships) have never been mass produced but rather built to order.[21] It would however be erroneous to suppose that flexible production centered around economies of scope has become dominant and that mass production has disappeared. Mass production remains prominent, not least in "high-tech" sectors typically seen as characterized by rapid product and process innovation. As computer manufacturers have increasingly sought to compete via more customized products, "the search for scale effects has been displaced from computers to standardised components, particularly the semi-conductor components" (Delapierre and Zimmerman, 1993, 77–78). The continuing importance of mass production in large, often vertically integrated, companies and large factories is strongly at variance with suggestions that "leading-edge" sectors are dominated by small firms and vertical disintegration of production. The development of new areas of growth in electronics "provides little support for models of flexible specialisation" or for the view that a new order has been established in which vertical disintegration and market relations are increasingly predominant (Dunford, 1991, 78). In the United States, electronics companies typically seek to introduce Taylorist mass production of standardized products. The "conventions of the system" effectively encourage invention and innovation but then privilege the efficiencies of mass production (Storper, 1993, 449).

The rise of vertically integrated Japanese semiconductor producers to a position of global domination in merchant (mass) semiconductor markets during the 1980s exemplifies the reasons for the persistence of mass production in new "high-tech" sectors. Their rise coincided with some important changes within the global industry, ultimately driven by the pursuit of profits via deployment of new technology. Semiconductor production was becoming more capital-intensive. Packing the maximum amount of circuitry into a state-of-the-art chip required increasingly expensive manufacturing equipment and machinery. The capital costs of a fabrication line for leading-edge chips rose from about 15% of total fabrication costs in the mid-1970s to about half the costs by the mid-1980s and over 60% by the early 1990s. Much of this equipment was highly specialized, with little or no scrap value outside of the semiconductor business. Due to the rapidity of technological change, it had a relatively short economic life span. "Investments in semi-conductor manufacturing therefore were often difficult to liquidate for more than a fraction of their acquisition cost. Such investment took on the character of a sunk cost. The increasing share of such sunk costs in total manufacturing costs made entry to and exit from the industry more expensive and difficult" (Flamm, 1993, 66–70).

In summary, these factors combined to create considerable pressures for dedicated mass production of successive generations of chips within large vertically integrated companies. The changing character of the product because of technological innovation is of particular importance for the choice of the production model. Previously, when only relatively small numbers of circuit elements could fit within a single integrated circuit, manufacturers developed "standard" chips that produced general "generic" functions that could then be combined into more complex proprietary systems. Once entire systems could be integrated into a single chip, it was no longer competitive to assemble standard building blocks into more complex systems, as the costs of wiring and testing became prohibitive. However, continuous mass production requires particular labor market conditions to allow companies to produce on a 24-hour-per-day, seven-day-per-week basis in order to minimize the turnover time of fixed capital (Kehoe, 1992).[22]

Product Innovation

Whereas process innovation involves firms in competition for shares of existing markets, product innovation aims to create new markets in which companies can be sole and monopolistic producers. Given the pace of technological change, "performance superiority will be brief," however—hence the emphasis on continuous product innovation as a route to competitive advantage (Mitchell, 1998). The scale of product innovation is truly staggering. For example, from 1980 to 1993 the number of new products introduced in supermarkets in the United States grew at an average annual compounded rate of 14%. More than 17,000 appeared on store shelves in 1993, a pace of product innovation linked to the increasing customization of commodities (Wernick et al., 1997, 148). Product innovation can thus relate to enhancement of "existing," often seemingly mundane, products. Such innovation can also involve creating qualitatively different products within the same market segment as companies strive for a competitive edge by further segmenting mature markets (Griffith, 1998).[23] Incremental innovation is increasingly important in allowing changes in response to consumer demand in more differentiated markets (Nooteboom, 1999). Such product differentiation and market segmentation encompass both manufactured goods and services. For example, product innovation in holidays has involved a switch from an "old" tourism based around packaging and standardization to a "new" tourism that encompasses segmentation, flexibility, and customization (Poon, 1989). Creating totally new products is of the greatest significance, however, and involves the construction of new markets rather than a "zero sum game" as to the allocation of shares of a given market. It therefore has a potentially much greater transformative impact on the geographies of production and trajectories of economic growth. New products need to open up new markets if they are to succeed within the parameters of capitalist production and allow individual companies to increase their mass of realized surplus-value. Capital displays great ingenuity in creating new products. For example, people's growing anxieties as to their identities in a period of fierce time-space compression led to the (re)invention of tradition as a sphere of commodity production and consumption (Harvey, 1996, 246). There are, however, no guarantees of success, as product innovation is risky (Mitchell, 1998).

The systemic tendency of capitalist production to generate new products in turn raises further issues. The first relates to the ways in which companies develop new products and the relationship *between* research and development. In Taylorist mass production there is a linear sequential model of R&D creating "breakthrough" product innovations, then producing them in long runs of standardized products. In more flexible systems of high-volume production the processes of product innovation and development are structured differently. In particular, there are three distinctive organizational features: "self-organizing" development teams; overlapping development phases, replacing a segmented with a shared division of labor; and a commitment to continuous learning. Changing the form of product innovation from the mass production linear R&D model to new flexible forms of production—at the limit, producing batch sizes of one in deeply fragmented markets—severely circumscribes the utility of the concept of the product life cycle. Competitive success depends upon being the first to identify an emerging market, a segmenting market, or a change in consumer requirements in a previously unchanging market. Success depends upon minimizing product development and product changeover times, not upon being the lowest-cost (or highest-throughput) producer. In California, for example, small and medium-sized enterprises (SMEs) manufacturing "high-tech" products are involved in an intensely competitive "race to the market," as many of them are seeking to make the same product innovations. This "race" is the principal axis of competition for these small firms—not price competition. Moreover, such pressures for accelerating product innovation are increasing. This is linked to increasing volatility and ephemerality in fashions and tastes as product life cycles for many commodities become increasingly brief, even transitory, as when the commodity is a performance or spectacle (Harvey, 1989).

The growing emphasis on networked approaches to production organization has also influenced product innovation and has led to a reappraisal of the linear R&D model, in two spheres. First, the emergence of new forms of network relationships between firms is influencing the organization of product innovation. "Quasi-vertical disintegration" can help facilitate coordinated design and investment. As a result, the product development process, from planning and conceptualization through designing and engineering to manufacturing, is more reflexive, consisting of overlapping and recursive rather than discrete linear stages (Sayer and Walker, 1992, 218). Second, incorporating network concepts into the internal organizational structures of firms as well as the structuring of interfirm relations, has also influenced processes of product development by highlighting the importance of information flows and interaction within and between all sections of a company.[24]

Nevertheless, human creativity remains central to product innovation, however this process is organized and whatever model of production is deployed. Consequently, there may well be tensions and complex relations between certain sorts of processes and product innovations. Not least, there are limitations to innovation and product flexibility within automated production systems and computer integrated manufacturing. The product flexibility of such systems depends upon modeling the part or product within the computer system. As such, product flexibility is confined to the range of possibilities programmed into the controlling computers, and this becomes critical to product innovation. Thus, firms committed to developing highly automated production strategies and "unmanned factories" still depend upon people somewhere for innovative capacity. This raises important questions about creativity and the creation of new knowledge—as opposed to the diffusion of existing knowledge and learning by others seeking to "catch up."[25]

The second issue concerns where new products are produced—in "new" or "old" firms, in "new" or "old" industrial spaces, in previously unindustrialized areas or in areas with an industrial history and tradition—and the factors influencing this locational choice. In some circumstances there is a close relationship between product innovation and new firm formation in particular locations. In certain respects, the volatility and ephemerality of products is enhancing the significance of particular places as centers of product innovation. Industrial districts, producing a range of commodities, have often been centers of product innovation, based on intense linkages and sharing of knowledge between firms and other institutions. For example, product innovations in banking and financial services have become closely linked to London, New York, and Tokyo, centers of innovation, interpretation, and interaction (Amin and Thrift, 1992; Sassen, 1991). In the late twentieth century new industrial spaces of California, new firm formation is closely tied to product innovation in the information technology and computing industries (Storper 1993, 446). New product-pioneering firms are spun off from existing ones, deepening both horizontal and vertical divisions of labor and the transactional tissue of the local industrial complex. Cox (1997, 179) notes the importance that analysts such as Storper have placed upon spatial proximity between the producers and users of new technologies in product innovation and development. He points out that at another stage in the development of new products, their actual launching on the market, spatial concentration again becomes important because frequent personal communication and rapid decision making are crucially necessary at that stage (Pryke and Lee, 1995). There are echoes here of an older notion of product innovations diffusing down the settlement hierarchy, from the largest to successively smaller cities and towns. The greater density of population in metropolitan areas, along with the greater receptivity of at least some of their residents to more radical change, makes them the most promising locations in which to launch new products (Brown, 1975). The third issue of how demands are created for new products is explored in the next section.

5.4. Competition via Market Creation and Marketing Innovation

Best (1990, 14, emphasis added) argues that firms can succeed by identifying and *"responding to"* changes in markets or consumer preferences. "Responding to" changing demands means being the first to supply consumers with a newly designed product, highlighting the significance of minimizing product development cycles. As such, Best perhaps overestimates the extent to which firms simply respond to exogenously given changes in market demands rather than actively seeking to change consumer tastes and cultivate preferences for new products via advertising as part of Schumpeterian "market disturbing" competitive strategies. Because consumers possess imperfect knowledge, they are susceptible to influence via advertising (Mort, 1997).

Advertising has a venerable history, but it is only quite recently that it has been more than a marginal influence on patterns of sales and production (Williams, (1980, 177–186). The great bulk of products manufactured during the early stages of the factory system were sold without extensive advertising. The formation of modern advertising has to be traced to the emergence of new forms of monopoly capitalism around the end of the nineteenth and beginning of the twentieth century. The development of modern advertising—or, put another way, product and process innovation in advertising—was one element in corporate strategies to create, organize, and where possible control markets, especially for mass-produced consumer goods. Mass production necessitated mass consumption, and this in turn required a certain homogenization of consumer tastes for final products. This entailed radical changes in the organization of advertising itself, both in terms of advertising media and via more conscious and serious attention to the "psychology of advertising." Thus, the period between 1880 and 1930 saw the "full development of an organised system of commercial information and persuasion, as part of the modern distributive system in conditions of large-scale capitalism." Indeed, modern capitalism could not function without advertising, which offered mass-produced visions of individualism (Ewen, 1976). It is impossible fully to grasp the significance of advertising "without realising that the material object being sold is never enough: this indeed is the crucial cultural quality of its modern forms." Thus, commodities, even the most mundane necessities of daily life, must be imbued with symbolic qualities and culturally endowed meanings. Commodities thereby meet both the functional and symbolic interests of the consumer (Williams, 1980, 185, original emphasis):

> We have a cultural pattern in which the objects are not enough but must be validated, if only in fantasy, by association with personal and social meanings. . . . The short description of the pattern we have is *magic*: a highly organised and professional system of magical inducements and satisfactions, functionally very similar to magical systems in simpler societies, but rather strangely co-existent with a highly developed scientific technology.

The competitive pressures of contemporary capitalism have stimulated further refinements to "the magic system," with heightened importance attached to culturally endowed and symbolic meanings of commodities and the identities that people (in part) form through consuming them. People's identities have been "welded to the consumption of goods" (Ewen, 1988, 60), linked to further product and process innovations in the form of advertisements (Lash and Urry, 1994, 140–141). One corollary of the enhanced significance of cultural capital and the meanings of things has been a deepening social division of labor that incorporates a complex and sophisticated advertising sector in addition to advertising divisions within companies. The growing significance of advertising and marketing has generated "white-collar" jobs, heavily concentrated in major urban areas, in—or subcontracted from—manufacturing firms

(Perrons, 1992). Advertising knowledge and skills have become critical resources and marketable commodities. Moreover, in strong opposition to those who argue the case for "consumer sovereignty," Williams (1980, 193) emphasizes that "in economic terms, the fantasy operates to project the production decisions of the major corporations as 'your' choice, the consumer's selection of priorities, methods and style." Or, as McDowell (1994, 160) puts it: the production, advertising, and marketing of goods is a crucial part of their consumption, "as anyone who wears Levis knows!" This highlights the ways in which companies seek to imbue commodities with particular meanings via advertising and marketing strategies.[26]

Although Warde (1994) argues that there is a strong tendency to exaggerate the significance of establishing self-identity via consumption, others have emphasized the increased significance of advertising for contemporary capitalism in creating consumer demand via appeals to consumer individuality and identity (Lury, 1996). Jameson (1988, 84), for example, argues that there is now an absolute preeminence of the commodity form. The logic of the commodity has reached its apotheosis. This is based upon a heterogeneous market that thrives on difference and incommensurability, fueled by the cut and thrust of "symbolic rivalry, of the needs of self-construction through acquisition (mostly in commodity form) of distinction and difference, of the search for approval through lifestyle and symbolic membership." This elaboration of commodification has been made possible by the development of the mass media, especially television. Advertising and design companies, in conjunction with the mass media, have produced an enormous machine for generating a desire for commodities—a greatly enhanced "magic system"—via more powerful, sophisticated, and persuasive processes of sign production. Such production via the advertising industry is a necessary condition *for* exchange relations and the circulation of capital, the dominant driving process.[27]

Some argue that such a perspective tends to overemphasize the power that advertisers, allied to retailers, can exert over consumers (Jackson, 1993). Advertising is rarely the sole or even most important source of prepurchase knowledge about the existence or qualities of particular commodities, "seldom the single stimulator of wants and desires" (Pred, 1996, 13). It is certainly the case that "consumers do not *straightforwardly* draw upon meanings prescribed by retailers and advertisers, but rather that commodity meanings are often contested and re-worked by consumers" (Leslie and Reimer, 1999, 433, emphasis added). While producers "create a series of texts," these are "read by different audiences according to their own social conditions and lived cultures" (Jackson and Taylor, 1995, 365).[28] While the process may not be straightforward, advertising undoubtedly can exert enormous influence in mediating and shaping the changing relationship between the sign values of commodities, their symbolic meanings, and their material content and form (Fine and Leopold, 1993, 28). One can, however, go too far in celebrating consumer autonomy, reflexivity, and resistance. Not least, companies continue to realize surplus-value via the successful sale of commodities, suggesting that advertising strategies have considerable efficacy in relation to reproducing capital on an expanded scale. While Jameson may underestimate the capacity of consumers to challenge or even subvert the commodification strategies of capital (Thrift, 1994a, 222), it is more difficult to challenge claims as to the creation of demand via advertising and marketing strategies.

There is therefore a decisive difference between firms in "structure dependent domains of competition" that react to market conditions as exogenously given and firms in "structure focused domains" that actively create demand and shape markets (Clark, 1992). Unlike the representative small firm, the strategies of representative large management-controlled corporations are not dependent on market structure (Clark and Wrigley, 1995, 207). These latter have the resources and market position to formulate and implement strategies aimed at changing the long-term configuration of the market via product development and advertising. While capacity to shape markets should not be conflated with firm size, it is important to differentiate between firms that respond strategically *to* market turbulence and those that, by being first-movers in their industry, strategically *create* market turbulence for their competitors (Pine, 1993, 135). Reducing product life cycles, fragmenting demand, and creating demands for new products can yield powerful advantages for those causing these changes and problems for those forced to react to them.

The power to shape demand, to create and disturb markets, has become an increasingly important part of competitive strategy as product life cycles shorten and/or markets become increasingly fragmented and segmented and/or the boundaries between goods and services become increasingly blurred. The fusion of goods and services, redefining what constitutes the product, and the consequent mutation of markets are "without doubt" the most significant aspect of the "new economics of production." Rather than, say, a car being thought of as simply a material product, it "is conceived from the outset as a set of services provided to the user; in addition it is sold with various services that make it a service good" (Hudson and Schamp, 1995b; Veltz, 1991, 199). This, among other things, strongly challenges conventional accounts that seek to differentiate between services and manufacturing or to identify a "post-industrial" economy.[29]

Corporate (lack of) capacity to create and shape demand and markets is thus crucial to competitive strategy. Some firms can only react to exogenously given market changes. Their focus is essentially short-term, reactive, and adaptive. Other firms generate these changes and deliberately introduce market instability as part of *their* longer-term strategies for competitive success, often allied to product, process, or organizational innovation and the shaping of demand within a "strong" competitive strategy. The way in which leading companies in a sector (re)structure product markets thus becomes critical. Lagging companies can only delay and not permanently forestall the factors that cause markets to change: "Companies that recognize this will not so much manipulate the market to regain stability as much as revel in its uncertainly to gain significant advantage over competitors" (Pine, 1993, 61). Recognition of the significance of different types of corporate responses is important, although Pine (like Best; see above) understates the extent to which companies create market turbulence rather than simply "revel" in exogenously produced uncertainty resulting from rapidly and unpredictably changing consumer preferences in markets shaped by "consumer sovereignty."

5.5. Market Structures, Competition, and the Processes of Globalization

The processes of globalization generate coexisting pressures to both homogenize and differentiate product markets via advertising. On the one hand, there are pressures toward market segmentation. In higher-income countries there is more scope to play upon the symbolic aspects of products; the same point could be made with respect to higher-income social groups irrespective of location. This suggests that companies will develop strategies to segment markets socially and spatially and will develop different advertising and sales strategies dependent upon the characteristics of consumers and places. For example, in clothing the mass market has undergone a process of fragmentation in terms of both consumption patterns and retailers' attempted manipulation of these. This has led to the growing importance of strategies aimed at tapping precise segments of the consumer market and hopefully building up allegiances to one store (Crewe and Davenport, 1992, 186). Storper (1993) attributes the growth in the branded ready-to-wear (*prêt-a-porter*) clothing market in France to the rise of new social groups, especially the urban professional classes, and the resultant new forms of social distinction in fashion. High fashion in the strict sense has been replaced by widely marketed but nonetheless not mass-produced garments. More generally, there has been a clear relationship between the rise of "flexible specialization," the production of commodities for niche markets, the expansion of certain types of private sector services, and the regressive redistribution of disposable income to the middle classes in the core capitalist countries. This further concentration of purchasing power in already affluent social groups was central to neoliberal political projects in the 1980s (Currie, 1993).[30]

On the other hand, there continue to be pressures globally to homogenize consumer tastes for final products (for example, to allow the continuing realization of scale economies). This is an important pressure toward globalization (Mariti, 1993). Many argue that market structures have changed decisively as one dimension of the processes of globalization, as companies seek to shape markets within a global economy. In a wide range of industries and product groups, the world market is shared by, at most, ten to twelve firms (Organization for Economic Cooperation and Development, 1992). In these circumstances leading firms have considerable scope to create market conditions via a variety of regulatory and governance mechanisms—for example, by market sharing and price setting—rather than simply respond to them, thereby avoiding the worst excesses of "ruinous competition." Such behavior is not, however, new. Best (1990, 50–72) notes how capitalists in the United States responded to the threat of "ruinous competition" in the late nineteenth and early twentieth century by, among other things, seeking to control product markets and to coordinate supply and demand at profit-making levels. They sought to do so in one of three ways: via dominant firm regulation, interfirm cooperation and cartel formation, or government regulation. The owners of the Great Northern Coalfield in northeast England effectively controlled markets via the Vend, a market-sharing arrangement, during the eighteenth century (Sweezy, 1938), while cartels were central to the organization of the interwar economies of Germany and Japan (Best, 1990). More generally, markets are of necessity routinely governed and regulated in varied ways.[31]

Global oligopoly has become the most significant type of supply-side structure, coupled with important changes in the marketing strategies of multinational enterprises (Chesnais, 1993, 12–13). It is now the dominant form of supply structure in most R&D intensive or "high-technology" industries as well as in many "scale-intensive" manufacturing industries in which scale economies remain pivotal. Moreover, new forms of flexible high-volume production have reinforced the significance of oligopoly, since the firms involved in such production evolve in a world of oligopolistic competition. Their capacity and cost strategies *reconstitute the principle of barriers-to-entry—and oligopolistic rents—which characterize large scale production*" (Coriat, 1991, 155, emphasis added). The oligopolistic character of markets was further reinforced—given an "irreversible character" (Chesnais, 1993, 17)—by the entry of the Japanese keiretsu onto the global stage in the late 1970s. While seeking to extend their global reach, the keiretsu also developed sophisticated systems of excluding foreign companies from much of the Japanese economy by denying them acquisition of any Japanese company that could serve as a market entry point or enable them to control any distribution system. By keeping tight control of distribution systems in Japan, the keiretsu could charge market prices significantly above those of their competitors in western Europe and North America. The resultant superprofits could then be used to take risks and support new technologies that were unprofitable in the short run but were seen as significant to long-term strategic corporate goals (Lie and Santucci, 1993).

More generally, within the constraint that prices must allow for a return on capital invested in the form of profits, pricing policy reflects corporate goals and the time span over which companies consider profitability. In circumstances of serious overproduction, perhaps coupled with technologically obsolete production methods, companies may adopt predatory pricing structures via the phenomenon of "dumping" goods. There is a well-documented history of such dumping practices in the steel industry in Europe, for example (see Hudson and Sadler, 1989). There may be important differences in pricing policy guided by varying strategic objectives. Companies use average cost pricing in situations of rapid technological advances in which they anticipate falling marginal costs because of scale economies and learning effects (for example, in the electronics industry) and in which their concerns are directed at long-term profitability and reasonable market share (Lie and Santucci, 1993). Conversely, in circumstances in which there is an emphasis upon short-term profitability and a rapid turnover time for the capital invested, prices are set in relation to actual costs, typically on a cost-plus basis. While the former approach is often thought of as representative of major Japanese firms, the latter is typically seen as characterizing Anglo-American companies (reflecting different cultures of capitalism).[32]

While competition is often much more complex than simply setting appropriate prices, embracing issues such as product quality, reliability, and after-sales service, it is important not to underestimate the continuing salience of price competition. The benefits of low prices arising from economies of scale and other cost advantages of mass production are enduring features of production (Pine, 1993, 50). Companies that can produce at lower costs and prices have a distinct competitive advantage. They will however be more successful if they can retain low prices while providing the variety that their customers demand. Put slightly differently, other things being equal, price competition remains very significant—and in some circumstances lower prices may well take precedence over higher quality (for example, because of income constraints on consumers). On the other hand, as the feedback loops from customers to suppliers become reinforced, niche markets become smaller and the logical limit to this process is the customization of individual commodities, analogous to the outputs of craft production, the significance of price as a dimension of competition is diminished. While this may be the *logical* conclusion, it is certainly not a practically *feasible* conclusion. There are two main reasons as to why this is so. First, because of technological constraints, mass customization seems most feasible in product segments in which new information or telecommunications technologies are central to the provision of goods and services (Pine, 1993, 155). Second, because of income constraints on consumers that both limit the extent to which markets can be fragmented into myriad niches and generate pressures toward consolidation and homogenization of consumer demand (Pine, 1993, 241–253). Consequently, many products will continue to be produced on a mass or batch, as opposed to individually customized, basis, and price will remain a critical dimension of competition in many markets.

The unprecedented variety of choices available to companies in terms of combinations of marketing and production strategies can be illustrated with reference to the ways in which they can respond to market saturation in sectors dominated by mass production. For example, in the most advanced capitalist countries markets for many "white" consumer goods had reached saturation levels by the 1960s and 1970s. Companies wishing to grow in saturated markets can adapt one or more of several approaches, some of which are explicitly spatial (Pine, 1993, 64): they can invade foreign markets with current products; create alternative uses for current products, to "break through a natural saturation limit"; create extended products for alternative use; increase the rate of innovation to decrease the life of existing products and speed up product replacement times; or meet customer needs more closely by increasing the amount of variety or product customization, to gain a larger share of new or replacement sales. The first two, perhaps three, of these options allow firms to retain mass-production strategies—and to these one could add relocating production to cheaper production sites to reduce prices and increase market share.[33] The last two, perhaps three, of these options involve moving toward different methods of more flexible high-volume production, although the geographies of production associated with such a shift are contingent. Moreover, each of these options implies different strategies in terms of marketing and the creation of markets.

5.6. Competition via Learning and the Creation and Monopolization of Knowledge

Innovations depend upon learning, the production and dissemination of knowledge. Recently the significance of knowledge and learning in the contemporary organization of production and the performance of individual firms within the economy has been increasingly emphasized (Giddens, 1990; Strange, 1988). Knowledge is seen as the most strategic resource and the capability to learn as the most important process within the contemporary capitalist "learning economy" (Lundvall, 1995). Information increasingly forms outputs from as well as inputs to production. However, knowledge and learning have always been central to economic performance and commodity production. Knowledge has always been embodied in goods and services. The key issue is therefore the *new* ways in which knowledge is important in production.

Some years ago Penrose (1959) developed a theory of the firm that revolved around notions of learning. She defines the firm as a bounded administrative unit, involving teamwork among individuals in order for it to function. Since everything cannot happen at once, it takes time for people to learn and for teamwork to develop.[34] Similarly, the boundaries of the firm can only be extended with time. The idea of the "learning firm" is therefore not new, but it too has recently experienced a revival. There are, however, several strands to the learning literature, emphasizing different aspects and ways of learning: learning-by-doing (Arrow, 1962); learning-by-using (Rosenberg, 1982); and learning-by-searching (Boulding, 1985; Johnson, 1992). Such ideas of learning explicitly or implicitly are central to evolutionary and institutional approaches that emphasize the centrality of knowledge to behavior. For example, the idea of learning-by-doing underpins that of firms as communities of practice.[35] Perhaps the most influential, however, has been learning-by-interacting (Lundvall, 1992). It focuses upon companies learning about and adapting to "best practice" via networked interaction with other firms and institutions as the route to competitiveness in circumstances of rapid technological change and uncertainty. Learning thus involves more that simply transactions of information within markets or hierarchies, in turn raising questions about the extent to which such networks are sectorally or territorially constituted (and, if so, at which spatial scale; see below). It is acknowledged to be strongly path-dependent, although significant breakthroughs often involve shifting onto new, rather than further along existing, paths.

Another important distinction can be drawn between single-loop and double-loop learning, especially as this relates to incremental and radical innovations (of product, process and organizational form). Single-loop learning involves the exploitation of possibilities within the boundaries of existing production paradigms, while double-loop learning is a means of exploring alternatives to those paradigms (Levinthal, 1996). As such, single-loop learning involves incremental change within a given production paradigm rather than redefinition of that paradigm. Learning can thus entail a form of inertia via cognitive lock-in, thereby threatening competitiveness. Double-loop learning reflects the increased grounding of production in discursive knowledge. Knowledge based on reflexivity operates via a double hermeneutic in which the norms, rules, and resources of the production process are constantly called into question (Lash and Urry, 1994, 160–161). Thus, production involves complex processes of learning. Double-loop learning entails radical transformative change and, as such, involves an "unlearning" process, as learners discard obsolete and misleading knowledge. Such an "unlearning" capacity may be critical to corporate survival in uncertain and volatile environments. Conversely, for leading-edge firms, the ability to create "market-disturbing" strategies based around radical change and double-loop learning can be a source of considerable competitive advantage.

Learning thus both presupposes and produces knowledge, and some sorts of learning require forgetting what is already known. However, knowledge is heterogeneous. It exists in varied forms. There is, in particular, a critical qualitative difference between information and tacit knowledge, and this can be related to different forms of transmission mechanisms and corporate governance structures (see Table 5.1). Information is codifiable (and so commodifiable and tradeable) knowledge that can be transmitted mechanically or electronically (for example, as bits along the fiber optic cables of a computer network). In principle it can become

TABLE 5.1. Types of Knowledge and Modes of Learning

Modes of learning	Types of knowledge	
	Tacit	Codified
Internal	• Learning in doing and experiential learning • Communities of practice • On-the-job training • Need for local action	• In-house R&D • Intrafirm training programs • Coordination between R&D and workforces
External	• Largely learning localized tacit knowledge • Face-to-face contact and informal exchanges by acquaintances • Importance of the localized learning milieu	• Organizational embodiment of external explicit knowledge • Interfirm alliances and joint ventures • Importance of a firm's absorptive capacity • Need for a mode of coordination between participating firms

Source: Based on Lee (2001).

ubiquitously available. Tacit knowledge in the form of know-how, skills, and competencies cannot be so codified and ubiquified. "Experiential, practical or 'tacit' knowledge may be embedded in skills, routines, practices or teamwork" (Polyani, 1967, 127). As such, tacit knowledge "is inseparable from the collective work practices from which it comes"[36] and "some tacit knowledge is always required in order to use new codified knowledge" (Foray, 1993, 87).[37] Foray thus emphasizes the asymmetric relationship between qualitatively different types of knowledge. Acknowledging that knowledge is "tacit" problematizes its communication and transmission to others who lack access to the unwritten codes of meaning in which such knowledge is embedded and upon which its meaning depends.[38] Such tacit knowledge may indeed be unique to particular individuals rather than collective in character—in which case communication is, for even greater reason, problematic—but it often *is* collective rather than simply individual, locally produced, and often place-specific. Know-how thus cannot be divorced from its individual, social, and territorial contexts; as such, it is at best only partially commodifiable. It can only be purchased, if at all, via the labor market as embodied knowledge and not in the form of patents, turnkey plant, or other forms of "hard" technology. In certain circumstances mobility within the labor market can be a crucial mechanism of knowledge diffusion. For example, the labor market of Silicon Valley "serves as a conduit for the rapid dispersal of knowledge and skills among Silicon Valley firms" (Angel, 1989, 108). Recognition of these uncodifiable aspects of learning and knowledge creation is important, signifying that these processes are qualitatively different from the simple transfer of codifiable knowledge as information. Such tacit knowledge and learning capacity is often seen as *the* key competitive corporate and territorial asset.

For knowledge to be commodified it must exist in an alienated form. Much of the debate about knowledge versus information and codified versus tacit knowledge "is actually about the possibility of, and difficulties with, such alienation in the case of technological knowledge" (Athreye, 1998, 14). For knowledge to become information and markets in technological knowledge to emerge, it must become commodified and exchangeable. It must be produced by a firm not for its own use (as a use value) but to sell to another to deploy in its production process (as an exchange value). Technological convergence is necessary in creating the "unique conditions" under which specialized markets for selling knowledge-embodied products can emerge (Athreye, 1998, 13–28). Furthermore, technological convergence goes hand in hand with the emergence of new generic technologies. As industries share similar technological bases, "technological knowledge can be freed from its particular context and sold in specialised ways." Such convergence also makes possible a second condition necessary for the emergence of specialized knowledge markets: that is, the existence of recurring and reasonably frequent transactions. Industries based upon specific and nongeneric technologies do not develop such markets, and production remains grounded in firm- or industry-specific technologies and tacit knowledges. Athreye stresses that the emergence of markets in technological knowledge is historically (and one can add, geographically) specific, confined to periods of technological convergence. Even so, their existence does not guarantee equality of access to information traded in them. There may, for example, be considerable barriers to acquisition and entry to such markets as a result of cost.

Renewed emphasis on the generalized significance of knowledge in production problematizes the distinction between "product" and "process" innovations. It challenges the validity of the "linear" Taylorist R&D model and of the routinization of R&D within large firms as dominating knowledge production. This organizational model remains appropriate and powerful in some circumstances but in others can incorporate crucial weaknesses, especially given rapid shifts in product markets, for there are no necessary feedback loops from users of and customers for innovations to those within the firm charged with responsibility for producing them. Consequently, new products may not be attuned to consumer tastes and may fail in the marketplace. As Cornish (1995, 34) puts it, "Continuous learning on the part of both producer and consumer leads to the dynamic process of perpetual innovation that, in successful firms, results in growth." Conversely, opportunities for new products may be missed. Furthermore, the growing significance of the symbolic meanings attached to consumption, especially in circumstances in which the commodity is an event or spectacle (Harvey, 1989), places an even greater premium on knowledge of consumer tastes and the ability to shape them via advertising.

In these circumstances, knowledge creation and innovation must become pervasive processes throughout the firm. The ideal is to emulate the (originally Japanese) process of "kaizen," continuous improvement through interactive learning and problem solving (Sadler, 1997), generated by an actively committed and engaged workforce dedicated to enhancing corporate performance.[39] The emphasis is upon creating dense flows of knowledge and information, horizontally and vertically within and between the functional divisions of a company, while sensitizing those involved within the company to voices from outside its boundaries. The aim is to create and support "communities of practice" within the company and build a "seamless innovation process," bringing together everyone involved in product development, from those who have the initial idea to those who finally take it to the marketplace. Creation of multidisciplinary and cross-departmental "concept teams" with responsibility for product development is seen as a way of sharply reducing the socially necessary labor time taken to bring new products to market. Increasingly these are organized as "globally distributed teams" which "meet" via video conferencing and other forms of electronic technology. This reliance on distanciated social relationships of intellectual production, rather than face-to-face meetings, reflects increasing pressures on managerial time and resources but can also create problems in transmitting tacit forms of knowledge as these teams seek to work together on very tight deadlines (Miller et al., 1996). While these globally distributed teams are not quite "virtual organizations" or "virtual corporations" (Pine, 1993), they do represent a significant change in the organization of intracompany processes of knowledge creation and innovation.[40]

Because social systems evolve nonlinearly (Amin and Hausner, 1997), revolutionary innovations may be produced in unexpected ways via interactive processes that involve synthesizing different types of knowledge rather than by privileging the scientific knowledge of the R&D laboratory over other knowledges. Indeed, the production of such general and abstract formal knowledge depends in part upon other sorts of knowledge, tacit skills, and capabilities (Arora and Gamborella, 1994, 528), but "firms cannot be content just with understanding problems in abstract terms. In order to come up with specific new products or processes, they have to deal with the complexity and idiosyncratic aspects of applying knowledge to concrete problems, a process which relies heavily on tacit abilities and trial-and-error." This requires acknowledging the legitimacy and "voice" of different types of knowledge (not least as radical innovations often challenge the dominant "logic" within an industry) and enhancing corporate competitiveness by producing higher-quality products more flexibly. It necessitates closer integration of R&D with other sections within companies, with far-reaching implications for their internal organization and operation. Such tendencies are observable in both small flexibly specialized firms and units and in new forms of high volume production.[41] In its most pronounced and knowledge-intensive form, production becomes very much a "design process" and an "R&D process"; production becomes R&D and the production system operates as an expert system (Lash and Urry, 1994, 96). Growing emphasis on the significance of learning and knowledge creation in new forms of production organization links in with propositions about emergent forms of more rewarding, satisfying, and engaging work, reuniting the manual and the mental.[42] Even at the high point of Fordism, however, much manual work was performed by knowledgeable craft workers (Pollert, 1988). Innovation and learning are now nonetheless seen as creative processes that must be suffused throughout the entire workforce, capturing the knowledge of *all* workers to increase productivity and enhance the quality of both product and work in a knowledge-based economy (Florida, 1995). Flexible production is both innovation-intensive and knowledge-intensive. "Specialised product requires flexible process, requires innovatory process, requires knowledge-intensive process" (Lash and Urry, 1994, 121).

Know-how historically was, and in large measure still is, typically a kind of knowledge developed within, and then kept within, the confines of a firm. Such knowledge defines its core capabilities and competencies (Penrose, 1959). As such it is an asset that companies seek to keep from their competitors, imposing an economic limit on the extent to which companies are prepared to share at least some sorts of knowledge. Nevertheless, the growing complexity of the knowledge base upon which the economy depends is increasing the social division of labor in knowledge production, resulting in growing numbers and varied forms of collaborative long-term relationships between firms. Consequently, know-*who* is of growing importance in the production of know-how (Lundvall and Johnson, 1994). Enhanced emphasis on knowledge and learning therefore links with claims about new forms of relations between companies, based on cooperation, trust, and sharing knowledge for mutual benefit.[43] Emphasizing networks has foregrounded the significance of territory and proximity. Proximity may be critical in innovation and learning, especially in situations of rapid and radical technological change (Lundvall, 1988, 355, emphasis added):

> When the technology is complex and ever changing a short (geographical and cultural) distance *might* be important for the competitiveness of both producers and users. Here the information codes must be flexible and complex, and a common cultural background *might* be important in order to establish tacit codes of conduct and to facilitate the decoding of the complex messages exchanged. . . . When the technology changes rapidly and radically . . . *the need for proximity in terms of geography and culture becomes even more important.* A new technological paradigm will imply that established norms and standards become obsolete and that old codes of information cannot transmit the characteristics of innovative activities. In the absence of generally accepted standards and codes able to transmit information, face-to-face contacts and a common cultural background *might* become of decisive importance for information exchange.

Subsequently, the importance of spatial proximity to corporate innovation, learning, and competitive success has been increasingly emphasized. Lundvall (1992) stresses the significance of national innovation systems and shared language and culture, as well as formal legislative frameworks, in shaping trajectories of innovation and learning.[44] Others privilege the local or regional over the national in the production of knowledge and learning,[45] heavily influenced by the "rediscovery" of industrial districts in the Third Italy (Bagnasco, 1977). The major strength of such districts is an institutional capacity continuously to learn, adjust, and improve in economic performance. The ideal of a dynamic industrial district is networking without hierarchy. The notion of a community of producers, in which a single firm is at the apex of a captive hierarchy, is replaced with that of intersecting networks with multiple apexes in which no single firm is permanently at the head of any hierarchy. This "protean" feature of a dynamic industrial district enhances learning capacity. Supplier firms with multiple relations to firms in other sectors are exposed to new ideas (Best, 1990, 234–237). The merits of complex networks of territorially agglomerated small firms are stressed as the main—perhaps the only—route to learning.

However, the conditions for social learning and development of the division of labor cannot be reduced to some ideal type of network composed of vertically and horizontally disintegrated small firms. They may be within-plant and within-firm as much as they are between plant and between firm. The occurrence of "extremely dynamic firms, like Boeing, Cummins or Pilkington dominating local economies with little local synergy is exemplary" in this regard (Cox, 1997, 179). Furthermore, in some circumstances linked processes of interfirm and intrafirm learning may be decisive. For example, complex processes of interactions between and within firms of varying sizes characterize the Italian case, often seen as the archetypical example of the advantages of small firms linked into industrial districts. Thus, the Italian model "very effectively illustrates the mechanisms by which channels of accumulation of tacit or non-tacit codified knowledge develop and shows how virtuous circles are established between these channels and the processes of formation of industrial know-how in advanced mid-sized and large companies or in integrated networks of firms (industrial districts)" (Garonna, 1998, 228).

Others have sought further to develop these ideas of regionally based learning via concepts such as "technology district" or "regional world of production" (Storper, 1992, 1993), "learning region" (Morgan, 1995), or "regional innovation system" (Braczisch et al., 1998), which do not *necessarily* privilege networks of small firms. Storper (1993, 434–435; emphasis added) insists that user–producer interactions

> involve the difficult and not easily objectifiable process of interpretation. . . . The whole transaction structure may be subject to redefinition as new types of products and new firms enter the structure and as

whole new sub-nodes, channels and codes of transactions are defined. *Where rapid learning is taking place, the transactional structure is likely to involve constant negotiation, re-negotiation and dependence upon achieving common re-interpretation of new evidence and opportunities. . . .* Rules, institutions and practices of key collective agents enable local technological learning.

Technologically dynamic production systems consist of clusters of firms linked into an intricate social division of labor—both horizontal and vertical in nature—*at the regional level* (Storper, 1993, 450). These production systems continually redefine best (product and process) practices for their respective markets. Territorially bounded conventions grounded in a shared culture make product-based technological learning possible and define the basis of external economies within them (Storper, 1992, 86–90).[46] Thus, this particular type of corporate learning is seen as territorially grounded, collective, and socially governed and regulated.

There has therefore been growing acknowledgment of the significance of noneconomic relationships in underpinning regional economic success and regionally based learning systems. Emphasis is placed on territorially embedded shared values, meanings, and understandings, and tacit knowledge and the institutional structures through which it is produced. This is registered in concepts such as "institutional thickness" (Amin and Thrift, 1994) and "social capital" (Putnam, 1993) but perhaps most powerfully in the idea of "regions as a nexus of untraded interdependencies." As Storper (1995, 210, emphasis added) puts it, "the region is a key, *necessary* element in the 'supply architecture' for learning and innovation." Emphasizing "untraded interdependencies" or "relational assets" foregrounds the necessary territoriality of critical elements of nonmarket relations and tacit knowledge. This decisively shifts the focus from firm to territory as the key institutional form in the knowledge-based competitive struggle, to a collective and territorialized definition of competitive advantage that emphasizes the cultural and social underpinnings of economic success.

Regional institutional formations that allow regions to adjust to, indeed anticipate and shape, changing market demands are seen as pivotal. Innovation and knowledge creation are conceptualized as interactive processes, shaped by a varied repertoire of institutional routines and social conventions. This creates links between companies, the (local) state, and institutions in civil society as well as intercorporate collaborative links as the basis of regional competitive advantage. In a world in which codified knowledge is becoming increasingly ubiquitously available, uncodified knowledge rooted in relations of proximity becomes critical in deriving competitive advantage. Thus, *"as long as institutional sclerosis can be avoided,*" the relational assets of regions constitute a prime, and unique, source of success in a globalizing political economy "owing to their inimitability" (Amin and Cohendet, 1997, 4, emphasis added). The specific caveat "as long as institutional sclerosis can be avoided" is a crucial one, however. More generally, it is important to be aware of the limits to such an approach and emphasis.

Rather than privilege territorial over corporate knowledge production and learning (or vice versa), the *relationships between* these two institutional bases of learning must be explored. Equally, there is no a priori reason to privilege any particular spatial scale or size of firm, irrespective of time and place. Regional and locality-based learning and knowledge production systems can be of great significance (Larsson and Malmberg, 1999; Maskell and Malmberg, 1995, 1999; Maskell et al., 1998), especially if innovation systems are constituted sectorally—and at least potentially globally—rather than nationally (Metcalfe, 1996). The sectoral constitution of innovation systems across national boundaries emphasizes the significance of the place-specifically local within the global and of the links between corporate learning and territorially embedded knowledge. Globalized forms of corporate organization are predicated upon integrating fragmented products of local learning to further corporate interests. This may involve disembedding them from the contexts in which they were initially produced, and perhaps therefore finding ways of converting tacit knowledge into codifiable information.[47] Global corporations are developing organizational forms to repatriate the varied results of different localized learning experiences and integrating them within a collective body of knowledge to serve strategic corporate interests in increasingly international markets. There are powerful pressures on companies to source key inputs to production on a worldwide basis, notably in the form of scientific and technological advances made in foreign countries (Chesnais, 1993, 14–15). Securing access to locally produced knowledge is therefore also a process of intercorporate competition, involving complex relationships between knowledge production and acquisition and competition and cooperation between various territorial and corporate interests.

Competitive success depends upon how companies combine different types of knowledge and learning strategies rather than on a choice between types of knowledge (tacit and codified) or the strength of ties among firms and business networks. The critical factor is the corporate ability "to *evolve in order to adapt*" (Amin and Cohendet, 1997, 6, original emphasis) or anticipate and shape evolving internal and external environments. This primarily depends upon organizational structure and a culture of strategic management and coordination. Such success in complex environments depends upon governance cultures that facilitate the generation of variety and mixtures of competencies rather than privileging one type of knowledge over another. This emphasizes the interaction between knowledge and managerial strategy and corporate governance structures. Major firms, especially those that are developing global strategies, are developing dual organizational structures,[48] dealing with qualitatively different types of function and requiring qualitatively different types of knowledge and learning mechanisms.

Moreover, there are definite geographies associated with these forms of knowledge and organizational structures. The network structure for core competencies allows the firm to benefit from "decentralized specialization" by coupling islands of localized knowledge, each exhibiting strong advantages deriving from local externalities. Within this structure, the firm functions as a real processor of knowledge. The production and circulation of knowledge between different islands is critical for enhancing the efficiency of each component island as well as that of the firm as a whole. The hierarchical structure for regulation of noncore activities is premised upon a more traditional conception of the firm as a processor of information, focused on efficiency of distribution of codified knowledge. This dual organizational structure requires a dual governance structure: one set of governance mechanisms for producing, circulating, and distributing knowledge relating to core competencies and another for transactions related to other activities. The central problem for the firm is the coupling between the two sets of mechanisms and their successful reproduction in the day-to-day practices and transactions of the firm, its workers, and the communities of practice that they form within and across the firm.[49]

The strategic key to sustained competitive success is identifying and assembling appropriate core competencies. This presumes mastery of diverse learning processes—know-what; know-how; know-why; know-who; and the ability to integrate fragmented pieces of localized learning. Effectively exploiting the advantages of strong localized learning depends upon the firm's successfully managing the circulation of knowledge among its core locations. This necessitates the effective circulation of codified knowledge through new information systems and the efficient circulation of any kind of knowledge through the development and control of all modes of knowledge conversion within the knowledge creating company (Nonaka and Takeuchi, 1995).[50] The globalized firm therefore must direct learning in the desired direction while ensuring the repatriation of different local experiences to the collective body of knowledge. For example, globalized chemical and pharmaceutical companies and agribusinesses accumulate competencies to shape their selection environment and to negotiate collaborative agreements that give access to new knowledge. In their learning processes, the development of corporate capacities for exploiting new technology is based as much on their ability to appropriate exogenous knowledge as on their own R&D (Walsh and Galimberti, 1993, 187–188). Difficulties arise, however, when key technical knowledge required for application is not built into equipment or machines but is intertwined with nontransferable local knowledge (Zysman, 1993, 109). Possible corporate responses to this problem include developing technology in-house (hierarchies), buying on the open market (markets), and teaming up with others (joint ventures and networks). Globalized firms must select and integrate fragmented core competencies that resulted from the wave of mergers, acquisitions, and joint ventures made since the early 1980s,[51] which led to the emergence within firms of local islands of knowledge spread all over the world (Amin and Cohendet,1997, 8).

While there has been considerable advance in the sophistication of analyses of learning processes, the decisive issue of the processes of the "*creation*" of knowledge remains largely unexplored. There are important differences between "learning to adapt" to best-practice standards set by others and "creating" knowledge, that is, "learning to produce new knowledge" that redefines best practice. The processes of *producing* new knowledge, knowledge that comes into existence for the first time, are not dealt with directly in learning approaches because of their grounding in associationist, stimulus-response conceptions of learning and their concern with outcome rather than process (Odgaard and Hudson, 1998). This represents a major problem with the learning approach *on its own terms*. Equally, there are crucial qualitative differences between strategies that seek actively to redefine the market and wider economic environment rather than adapt to such changes, whether on the basis of anticipation of them or reaction to them once they have happened. There are advantages to being a "first mover" in an industry rather than being an outsider contemplating entry into it. Being in the industry allows for the accumulation of knowledge that cannot be found on the outside, "which tends to reinforce prior choices" (Clark and Wrigley, 1995, 212). This reinforcement points to the advantages of "besting out" via innovation but also emphasizes that path-dependency is strongly built into development trajectories.

5.7. Summary and Conclusions

Competition between companies is central to the organization of production within capitalism, and in this chapter some of the main dimensions and forms of intercorporate competition have been considered. While cost and price are important, they are not necessarily the only—or even the most important—dimensions of competition. From the very inception of industrial capitalism companies have engaged in a search for new forms and methods of competition as they seek to advantage themselves vis-à-vis their rivals. Crucially, this ongoing search has not simply involved attempts to find lower cost production solutions within existing technical-organizational paradigms but, more importantly, has encompassed a search for new products and production paradigms. Such "strong" forms of competition involve (product, process, and organizational) innovation and processes of market creation and market disturbance. This in turn is central to the constant dynamic to revolutionize the what, how, and where of capitalist production. This has not resulted in a simple linear sequence of one form of competition succeeding another but rather in capitalist production being constituted via a complex mosaic of competitive strategies, varying by product, sector, time, and place. At the same time, however, intercorporate competition has often also involved strong elements of intercorporate collaboration, and it is to the consideration of these that the next chapter turns.

5.8. Notes

1. See "Rediscovering the Significance of Motives, Knowledge, and Learning" in section 2.4.

2. These forms of weak competition echo neoclassical economists' views as to the *only* form of competition, predicated upon assumptions of static equilibrium and perfect knowledge. Such views of competition are integral to the locational models of Lösch, Weber, and their adherents.

3. Discussed further in section 5.6.

4. LSI Logic closed a "state-of-the-art" semiconductor factory in Braunschweig, Germany. The advantages of "local" manufacturing in Europe were outweighed by, among other things, lower wage costs elsewhere ($20 per hour in Germany, $15 in the United States, and $2.80 in Hong Kong). As a result, it was more profitable to produce outside the European Union and serve that market via imports, despite a 14% tariff and increased transport costs (Kehoe, 1992). Osram regularly monitors labor costs in different countries. Its labor costs per worker in 1997 were 50 times greater in Germany than in China (Marsh, 1997).

5. See also "Divided by Territory" in section 7.3.

6. In software engineering labor costs account for over 40% of total costs. In North America, Europe, and Japan computer programmers are paid around $4,000 per month, but only $500 to $800 per month in India. Consequently, many companies subcontract computer programming tasks there (P. Taylor, 1995). Alternatively, such skilled workers may become low-cost temporary mi-

grants to the First World; see "Spatial Variations in Labor Market Conditions and Recruitment and Retention Strategies" in section 4.3.

7. See also "Establishing Legal Frameworks for Markets" in section 3.7.

8. These are discussed in "Structures of Managerial Organization within Companies" in section 4.4.

9. The cognitive aspects of this are discussed more fully in section 5.6.

10. See sections 6.2 and 6.5, respectively.

11. Discussed in section 5.6.

12. There is no simple relationship between changes to technical and organic compositions of capital. For example, increasingly technologically sophisticated methods of production may be predicated upon a fall in the value of fixed capital.

13. The introduction of basic oxygen steel-making technology reduced the socially necessary labor time need to convert iron to steel from 8 hours to 45 minutes (Hudson and Sadler, 1989). The invention by ICI of the steam reforming process for ammonia production reduced the number of workers per shift from 63 to 7 (Hudson, 1983). The introduction of mechanized and partially automated heavy-duty faces into collieries in the United Kingdom was intended to lower labor inputs and increase managerial control of the labor process (Winterton, 1985). The widespread introduction of computer control and IT technologies into a range of manufacturing industries in the United States (steel, instruments, electrical and nonelectrical engineering, and paper and publishing), as well as services such as finance, insurance, and health care, was central to sustained high annual rates of productivity growth of almost 6% in the late 1980s and 1990s (Economic Policy Institute, 2000).

14. See Note 14, Chapter 4.

15. Choice of production method may not be straightforward. Approaches may be adopted simply because "they become fashionable in management cultures, because they protect the interests of powerful groups within an organisation, or because managers find it hard to see beyond established social norms and practices" (Halford and Savage, 1997, 109). Furthermore, "like all social interactions, economic decisions are *as much* affected by tradition, historical precedent, class and gender interests and other social factors as by considerations of efficiency and profit" (McDowell 1997, 119, emphasis added). While one might query "as much," the broader point about the complex overdetermination of such "economic decisions" is valid.

16. See "Organizing and Controlling Work at the Point of Production" in section 4.4.

17. These are discussed in sections 5.4 and 5.5; see also Chapter 3.

18. See section 5.2.

19. Such processes of automation involve people, as wage laborers, become little more than extensions of machines; compare Haraway's (1991) theses on cyborgs.

20. In fact, Ford achieved high WIP turns on model-T lines by producing only one model. Toyota devised a system of flexible high-volume production that allowed dramatic reductions in WIP turns, with every doubling of WIP increasing labor productivity by 38% (Best, 1990, 148). By the late 1970s Toyota's WIP

turns exceeded 300, while most western European and North American companies were below 10. Such gaps have subsequently narrowed as western companies
sought to imitate "Japanese" production methods, but they have not disappeared.
By the early 1990s Toyota was offering five-day delivery of custom-ordered automobiles in Japan.

21. Thus, to equate small-batch with "post-Fordist" production, as Lash
and Urry (1994, 94) do, is erroneous.

22. For example, LSI Logic closed a "state-of-the-art" semiconductor factory in Braunschweig in Germany because of, among other things, the superior
productivity of its factories in the United States and southeast Asia, operating 21
eight-hour shifts per week, compared to 10 in Germany. See also Chapter 4.

23. For example, Gillette acquired a market share in excess of 70% in
North America and western Europe via a strategy of ongoing innovation, bringing a major new product (or "system") to market every nine years since the early
1970s. Even so, product innovation for something as simple as a razor can be a
slow process. Gillette took almost thirty years to develop a three-blade razor. The
new product required changes in the production process, significantly increasing
"continuous" movement of the assembly line and reducing production costs
(Griffith, 1998). Its latest premium razor sells at significantly higher prices than
its previous "top of the range" model.

24. See section 5.6.

25. These are explored more fully in section 5.6.

26. Gillette's Mach3 razor is an interesting recent example of how companies seek to use advertising to create markets for new products. Describing it as
the "stealth bomber of the shaving world," John Darman, vice president of male
shaving at Gillette, proclaims on a promotional video that "Aerodynamics and
shaving are two technologies that have impacted the lives of men for nearly half a
century. Now they come together for the first time" (cited in Willman, 1998).
This clearly appeals to a particular construction of masculinity in an attempt to
create a market for the new product via advertisements that show a square-jawed
fighter pilot breaking through the sound barrier three times "before enjoying the
mother of all shaves" (Willman, 1998).

27. In contrast, Featherstone (1991, 66–67), argues that in the contemporary (postmodern) phase of cultural production, the sign value of things has come
to dominate exchange relations and consumer culture.

28. They continue: "Moreover, the 'circuit' does not stop there, continuing
through successive rounds of production and consumption as consumers 'second
guess' advertisers' intentions and advertisers try to anticipate consumers' reactions."

29. These issues are taken up again in Chapter 10.

30. The provision of personal services via servants and paid domestic labor
and niche production of luxury goods for the very affluent both predates, and
also has always been a part of, industrial capitalism.

31. See Chapter 3.

32. Although by the end of the 1990s such behavioral differences were
seemingly narrowing.

33. See the discussion in section 5.2.

34. As Penrose puts it (1959, 53): "Experience . . . develops an increasing knowledge of the possibilities for action and the ways in which action can be taken by the firm. This increase in knowledge not only causes the productive opportunity of a firm to change but also contributes to the 'uniqueness' of the opportunity of each individual firm."

35. See "Institutions, Instituted Behavior, and Social Regulation of the Economy" in section 2.4.

36. That is, it is embedded in communities of practice.

37. Penrose also stressed the crucial significance of "tacit" knowledge in creating competitive assets. Consequently, not all goods and services can have a price and be exchanged in markets. Their value to a firm depends upon experience, teamwork, and accumulated knowledge within a firm. This has "far reaching effects," undermining the neoclassical assumption of homogeneous inputs to production processes and making explicit that inputs to production processes are heterogeneous and firm specific (Best, 1990, 132).

38. There may be a danger of "tacit knowledge" thereby being invoked as an unknowable residual explanatory variable, in a way analogous to neoclassical growth theorists' treatment of technical change (Hudson, 1999).

39. From the perspective of shop-floor workers however, kaizen often appears to be a very different process. As a Mazda worker in the United States put it: "They were going to kaizen out this and kaizen out that. The more they talked, the more it sounded like the whole thing was just a way to squeeze more work out of every worker, with a good old fashioned dose of paternalism thrown in to keep everybody happy" (cited in Fucini and Fucini, 1990, 87).

40. See also Chapter 4.

41. See "Process Innovation and New Technological Paradigms of Production" in section 5.3.

42. See "Organizing and Controlling Work at the Point of Production" in section 4.4.

43. See sections 6.2 and 6.4.

44. See also Chapter 3.

45. Gertler (1997) emphasizes the importance of "proximity," both "culturally" and "spatially," in innovation at the regional level, especially in situations in which technological development crosses a boundary from an "old" to a "new" paradigm. However, he argues that what is often represented as "regional culture" is more appropriately understood as a consequence of differences in national regulatory systems.

46. See "Institutions, Instituted Behavior, and Social Regulation of the Economy" in section 2.4.

47. Alternatively, it may simply involve big firms acquiring smaller ones as a way of gaining access to such knowledge; see section 6.5.

48. See "Organizational Innovation" in section 5.3.

49. Howells (1993, 222) makes a similar point in identifying two strategies, global switching and global focusing, that "appear to be emerging amongst key corporate players of international switching under the pressures of 'time space compression.' "

50. Dicken and colleagues (1994, 30) identify a key diagnostic feature of the "newly emerging organisational form" of the "complex global firm" as an "integrated network configuration and . . . capacity to develop flexible co-ordinating processes," both inside and outside the firm.

51. These varied forms of competitive and cooperative interfirm relations are explored more fully in the next chapter.

6

Company Connections
Competition and Cooperation, Part II

6.1. Introduction

The previous chapter focused on various dimensions and forms of competition between companies but only hinted at ways in which competition could involve *cooperation* between companies. Cooperation implies that key capabilities and competencies may in certain respects at least cross firm boundaries, problematizing the definition of the firm as a productive unit. Cooperation between companies as part of "weak" competitive strategies in fact extends back to the roots of industrial capitalism (for example, over market sharing; Sweezy, 1938). Such forms of cooperation were designed to regulate price competition and ensure markets that were orderly and more predictable for companies operating in them. So, while competitive relationships are pivotal, there is a long history of companies inventing strategies to ensure that competition is not "ruinous" and acknowledging that by cooperating with some rivals they can compete more effectively against others. Such cooperative partnerships have typically taken the form of regional or national alliances (often legitimating the creation of oligopolies, as in the regional or national interest), not least because markets and regulatory spaces have been territorially defined.

Cooperation between firms is not confined to market sharing and price regulation, however. It is also found in relation to forms of "strong" competition, for example, sharing R&D costs for new products or sharing technological and other skills. Such cooperative groupings typically are made up of firms that come together within various sorts of network relationships for a specific purpose while in other respects remaining competitive. Recently there have been suggestions that in some key sectors such cooperation has become more important as a route to competitive success. Processes of globalization and the reconstruction of economic relations on the global scale, allied to the rising costs of R&D and product innovation, make it impossible for even the largest firms to command the full range of technologies necessary for these activities. Moreover, new forms of corporate organization are emerging as companies respond to the pressures of globalization, the latest expression of what Penrose referred to as "the restless firm." For example, Lung (1992, 70; emphasis added) argues that globalization does not imply homogenization of the world car market. On the contrary, commercial success requires a clear perception of the preferences of the targeted clientele. This results in

> a tension between the requirements to operate on a global scale and the local requirements which the firm must handle. *This tension imposes new rules on the competitive game, which now associate competition and co-operation, and results in the elaboration of strategies of regional integration and inter-regional co-ordination.* It is in this way that the transregional firm emerges.

This raises critical questions as to whether the firm or network is the unit of competition.

This chapter explores these issues of competition via cooperation. It considers different types of cooperation and collaboration, the often complex links between them, the varied forms through which collaborative relationships are governed and regulated (from market relations to strategic alliances, acquisitions, and mergers), and the ways in which differences between places and spaces are implicated in processes of competitive collaboration.

6.2. Make, Buy, or Network? Collaboration or Competition via the Market as Supply Strategies

The tensions between competition and cooperation require a political strategy orchestrated by the state to enable capitalist conditions of production to be reproduced.[1] Within these framework conditions, broadly speaking, companies have three analytically distinct choices in terms of securing supplies of required inputs to their production processes: to produce in-house; to secure inputs via arms-length market relationships; or to enter into network relationships based on longer-term collaboration with and commitments to other companies. Such longer-term collaborations can take varied forms and extend over differing time periods. In practice companies blend in-house supply, arm's-length transactions based on price and quality, and "embedded" relations grounded in networks of loyalty, reciprocity and trust in constructing their competitive strategies (Uzzi, 1996, 1997). Companies combine different forms of transactions since each offers specific and complementary advantages within a dynamic environment of unequal power relations. Nonetheless, there are advantages in recognizing the analytic distinctions.

The first option is to rely upon intracompany capabilities and competencies and provide production inputs within the company, coordinated by its internal management hierarchy. In general, such an approach is adopted in circumstances in which interfirm transaction costs would be high or in which transactions would occur in an environment of considerable uncertainty. Intrafirm provision is seen as cheaper and/or more certain. Such an approach may lead to greater vertical integration in the organization of the firm, and indeed first emerged with the growth of big business and giant corporations in the United States as coordination by managerial hierarchy replaced coordination by the market. Vertical integration focuses on product competencies (Pine, 1993, 229). As a consequence, there may be strong arguments for retaining production within the boundaries of the firm. For example, particular tasks may be too exacting and specialized to be given to subcontractors; they may well also involve firm-specific knowledge that must be protected from competitors.[2] Vertically integrated production within the boundaries of a company may entail producing components at differing locations within an intracorporate geography of production, depending on the relative weights attached to economies of scale and scope. In such cases, however, irrespective of their dispersed geographies, production and utilization of inputs remains within the internal corporate control hierarchy. Despite recent evidence of and emphasis upon growth in external sourcing, such forms of intrafirm organization and provision of inputs are certainly not a thing of the past, subjects of industrial archaeology. There are strong tendencies toward vertical integration and coordination by managerial hierarchy in "leading-edge" sectors such as semiconductor production (Flamm, 1993) and the production of computer software (Coe, 1997). Furthermore, the tendency to blur boundaries between material products and services is also leading companies to increase vertical integration by extending activities both upstream and downstream in the supply chain—for example, in steel (Hudson, 1994c) and automobiles (Hudson and Schamp, 1995a). As Dicken and colleagues (1994, 30) point out, however, forms of intrafirm organization of production no longer necessarily conform to simple ideas of vertically integrated "hierarchy" but may have become more complex within the boundaries of the firm.

The alternative to supply from within the company is to source inputs from other companies—and no company of any significance has been wholly vertically integrated and met all of its needs internally. A second option therefore is to source via market relations, specifying the technical and performance criteria to be met by supplier companies, which then bid for orders on the basis of price. Often outsourcing in this way is an overt element in strategies to cut production costs. It is often the strategy adopted for supplying components and parts embodying little specific knowledge, especially those produced via labor-intensive processes that can be sourced from low labor cost locations (Rainnie, 1993; Schamp, 1991). It is commonly deployed as a strategy for supplying relatively simple commodities for final consumption, such as mass-produced shoes or clothing (Crewe and Davenport, 1992). The decision to supply via market transactions is not simply determined by production technologies or the character of commodities, however. Local labor market conditions may also be important is shaping choice of production methods and sourcing strategy. Manzagol (1991, 214–215) analyzes the growth of the "high-tech" defense-related complex of Phoenix, Arizona, and emphasizes that mass production and weak labor market segmentation led to a very different sociotechnical combination from that in Orange County or Silicon Valley in California. Because of the absence of unions, large firms had no incentive to subcontract work to low-wage secondary labor market firms, as they did in California. Such subcontracting can take many forms: for example, shoe production in Athens involves both "putting out," subcontracting work to smaller companies and homeworkers, and "splitting in," with external subcontractors bringing their workers into the factory to work on the contracting company's machinery (Hadjimichalis and Vaiou, 1996, 7).

Market-regulated supply relationships between customers and suppliers are relatively distant and noninterventionist. Regulating interfirm relationships in this way is central to just-in-case mass production. It is often associated with structuring supply chains in such a way that smaller and weaker firms are confined to market niches that are unattractive to larger and more powerful firms and on terms that favor the interests of the latter over the former. More generally, pricing policies and modes of price formation reflect and shape relations between companies, both as suppliers and customers. Forms of pricing and price formation strategy depend, in part, on the character of commodities, markets, and links between customer and suppliers: for instance, administered "cost-plus" prices were central to the Fordist mode of regulation (Leborgne and Lipietz, 1988; 1991). Cost-plus pricing was, and in many instances still is, endemic in defense-related industries (Smith, 1988).

The "make" or "buy" dichotomy as conceptualized in some versions of transactions cost theory (Williamson, 1975) and represented in these first two options has been subject to various criticisms, however. Such a conceptualization focuses the choices facing the firm upon the relative costs at the margin of "internalizing" and "externalizing" in an environment of partial knowledge and bounded rationality. As such, it is essentially a static viewpoint.[3] Dicken and Thrift (1992, 285, original emphasis) comment acerbically that this categorization of complex and varied organizational frameworks into firms (hierarchies) and markets "is a truly *disabling dichotomy*." Recognition of these limitations led to a search for a more sophisticated understanding of the ways in which firms meet their requirements for inputs and to consideration of more dynamic and collaborative approaches to interfirm relationships. These relational contracting approaches constitute the third option in supply strategies. The choice facing the firm is therefore not simply to make or buy, but to make, buy, or collaborate via relational contracting to provide necessary inputs.[4]

These forms of relational contracting occupy a "middle ground" between the "tight dualism" of firms and markets (Sayer and Walker, 1992). Confronted with a dynamic environment, companies face tricky choices, much more complex than a choice between existing alternatives in a given context of markets and firms. Often, what is required to produce, innovate, and compete in a dynamic capitalist system simply does not exist and must be created. Capitalists therefore build an organizational framework at the same time that they produce commodities, "and one way in which they do this is by probing outwards, forming alliances and networks with other firms." This emphasizes the need to produce appropriate organizational structures[5] and offers a more sophisticated view of the range of ways in which companies seek to assure their needs for inputs, acknowledging that relational contracting still involves sourcing via market transactions. Thus, "to say that collaboration and networks lie 'between' markets and hierarchies is to miss the point: they are over, under, and around markets and firms" (Sayer and Walker, 1992, 140). Equally, however, to regard such collaborative approaches as a "middle ground" between firm and market rather than as a qualitatively different way of ensuring the supply of required inputs is perhaps to miss an equally important point and underplay the significance of the variety of relational contracting approaches. Indeed, Sayer and Walker (1992, 128–129) hint at this in commenting that once the tight dualism of market and firm is forced open, the "middle ground" of relational contracting turns out to be an arena "so vast . . . that the void in the initial dualism cannot be patched over."

Relational contracting thus involves ongoing relations of exchange, interaction, and mutual development between two or more firms. It is most likely to develop in situations in which one company relies on another for parts, components or services embodying considerable skill and requiring trust in sharing knowledge and key competencies (Schamp, 1991). Such systemic sub-contracting is not new. In industries such as shipbuilding sub-contracting developed from an early stage as an integral part of production strategies. However, in other industries such as computers, telecommunications, and other "high-tech" electronic equipment, it has increasingly become adapted as an integral part of corporate production strategies in recent years (Hudson, 1989a).[6] Often subcontracting was and still is part of a cost cutting strategy or a response to short-term fluctuations in demand. However, the new customer–supplier relationships also involve longer-term closer relationships *"based upon a high level of mutual trust*; they are deeply socially, as well as economically, embedded. As such, they offer much greater potential for firms of all sizes to engage in integrated network activities" (Dicken et al., 1994, 39; emphasis added). Dicken and colleagues (1994) go on to elaborate on the implications of "trust" for the structuring of supply networks, pointing out that *"a corollary of such close, deeper relationships is that the supplier population becomes increasingly differentiated.* Many major firms now operate an upper tier of suppliers that is closely integrated at all stages of the production process, from design to final production." Equally, there may be limits to the circumstances in which such customer–supplier strategies are successful and circumstances in which production within the firm remains the optimal strategy.

The most direct, formal, and limited type of relational contract is that between two firms (Coe, 1997). Relational contracts often involve more complex configurations of several, or many, firms, linking them into coherent networks, the specific form of which depends upon the particular tasks that they are charged to perform. Such loosely entwined networks can incorporate a variety of forms of cooperative and competitive relationships, varying from the relatively closed (for example, Japanese keiretsu) to much more open-system networks. They can, nonetheless, be split into two broad groupings: first, relatively egalitarian horizontal associational networks such as those found in parts of the Third Italy, for example (Asheim, 1996; Scott, 1988); second, vertically differentiated hierarchical subcontracting networks incorporating differential degrees of power and influence between constituent firms (Dicken and Thrift, 1992, 285–286). Vertically disintegrated flexible production is quite compatible with hierarchical and exploitative relations among firms. The production system can be fragmented, but control can in principle remain quite concentrated (Martinelli and Schoenberger, 1991, 120).[7] Consequently, some forms of network relationship, such as "vertical near integration" (Leborgne and Lipietz, 1991, 38–39), resemble hierarchical relationships between firms while formal vertical disintegration may be "complemented by strong, but highly stratified, vertical organisation" (Sayer and

Walker, 1992, 218). This highlights the ways in which invoking "trust" as a key—or even sole—organizational principle in such networks may be problematic, not least because trust itself is a problematic concept (Lane and Reinhard, 1988; Sztompka, 1999; see also below).

Network relationships are thus constituted in varied and often complex ways, with different degrees of closure, with different structures of power relationships within them, and with varying degrees of legal formality and informality. Decisive power can be located at a range of locations within the network, depending upon the character of the commodity it produces and upon the cultures of production in interfirm relations.[8] In agriculture, for example, food quality concerns have become a major dimension of retail competition and innovation. Major food retailers have been the prime movers in pushing these down the supply chain in an attempt to ensure that methods of production comply more closely with the expressed preferences of consumers (Murdoch et al., 1998). As a result, major food retailers in core capitalist states dictate the what, how and when of production of a range of crops both in First and Third World countries (Cook and Crang, 1996). Often retailers are simultaneously seeking to shape consumer preferences via advertising strategies so that these correspond more closely with the food on the shelves of their supermarkets.[9] Franchising represents a similar sort of arrangement extending in the opposite direction along the supply chain. McDonalds, for example, lays down stringent specifications as to how its franchisees should cook and prepare hamburgers. In manufacturing, automobile assembly companies specify precisely the quality standards and delivery schedules to which their components suppliers must conform (Hudson, 1994b).

Production typically involves a variety of companies, each manufacturing components or parts or supplying necessary services required to create the final product. These are linked to one another and to companies manufacturing the final product in specific ways, within a social division of labor. The precise configuration of these links depends upon the overall structure of the production system for that industry. For example, the creation and reproduction of just-in-time procurement systems within a broader system of production clearly reflects and requires a particular conception and practice of cooperative relations between firms. It requires precise relationships between the companies linked into the production chain. Meeting the required rigorous demands for quality and delivery schedules could not be assured via market regulation and price competition between suppliers. Still less could requirements for suppliers to take on a greater share of R&D and product development costs, in exchange for long-term but never unconditional contracts. A strong element of trust and mutual interdependence is central to the success of such network relationships.

Major manufacturing companies, and increasingly a select few first-tier suppliers, function as "system integrators," assembling components produced by others into subassemblies and final products—echoing a long-established and well-developed model of organization in "one off" or small-batch production of capital goods (Vaughan, 1996). While a few upper-tier suppliers (often major multinationals) may enjoy relationships based upon trust, however, further down the pyramid of the supply chain regulation via price competition remains the order of the day. The *relatively* flat nature of networks (as compared with hierarchical structures) and their *relatively* collaborative character (as compared with arms-length market transactions) do not, therefore, eliminate significant differential power relations within networks. Not all parts of a network are equal (Dicken et al., 1994, 32). Indeed, price reductions have typically been a requirement of the renewal of contracts, with productivity gains resulting from cooperative R&D and more generally kaizen, or continuous quality improvement, passed on to the final product manufacturers.

Within the canonical examples of the Japanese automobile and other consumer goods industries, interfirm relationships are structured within the framework of the keiretsu, the relatively closed networks of capital that dominate Japan's economy. This resulted in a much smaller proportion of "in-house" production of components in Japan, as these were sourced from within keiretsu networks. This gave—or more accurately *seemed* to give (Williams et al., 1987)—much higher labour productivity and a sharp competitive edge to producers of goods for final consumption markets but simultaneously could conceal weaknesses within supplier companies, protected within the structure of the network.[10] At the same time, major assembly companies dealt with a much smaller number of first-tier suppliers, enabling them to reduce and focus managerial time and resources. As competitive pressures have grown in increasingly international markets, so too have pressures on non-Japanese producers to restructure their production methods by adopting just-in-time protocols or by seeking alternative ways to increase productivity and cut production costs. As a result, supplier companies have been increasingly subject to rigorous screening and selection procedures by their customers to ensure that the customer-specified criteria will be satisfied (Hudson, 1994b). This has often posed problems, however. The institutional and social contexts in which they have sought to do so have posed barriers to the smooth transformation of intercompany relationships to the form that just-in-time presupposes. Nevertheless, the resultant impacts of such pressures are clearly visible in the automobile industry, in which the component supply chain in both the United States but, more particularly, Europe has been radically restructured (Hudson, 1995a; Sadler and Amin, 1995; Womack et al., 1990).[11]

Just-in-time principles have been extended into bulk continuous-flow industries such as chemicals and steel.[12] These no longer simply produce undifferentiated basic commodities in great volume (Hudson, 1994c).[13] On the other hand, in certain circumstances there may be limits to the extent to which just-in-time can be introduced or sustained as a way of organizing relationships between companies.

As market conditions change, for example, companies may become increasingly resistant to just-in-time deliveries. In the 1990s Japanese petrochemical companies, organizing through the petrochemicals industry association, collectively ceased just-in-time deliveries as small-batch production proved increasingly uneconomic. On the other hand, it is debatable whether just-in-time interfirm relations can be similarly curtailed in other industries and places. The Japanese petrochemical producers are parts of powerful keiretsu (such as Kawasaki, Mitsubishi, Mitsui, and Sumitomo). They have the power and resources to impose fundamental changes in logistics practices. Other suppliers in Japan (as elsewhere), often small family-owned businesses delivering to large automotive or electronics groups, are less able to impose such changes.[14] In Europe, however, automobile component suppliers are often powerful companies (Sadler, 1997) and may be more able to influence the form of supply relations, although *their* room for maneuver may in turn be constrained by fierce competition between assembly companies.

The extent to which just-in-time structures supply relationships between manufacturing companies is therefore a contingent matter that depends, among other things, upon power relations between companies, macroeconomic conditions, and microeconomic and technical conditions of production within workplaces. The pressures of just-in-time can also change the balance of power between different types of companies and lead to a redefinition of the tasks that companies undertake within the totality of the production process. In a variety of industries wholesalers are extending their influence both upstream and downstream, typically in response to the impacts of just-in-time production and market fragmentation, leading to demands for greater flexibility in production. In industries ranging from computers to steel production, wholesalers are extending their activities into production (for example, via customizing products to customers' demands) and, as a consequence, into retail distribution (Hudson, 1994c). Equally, just-in-time manufacturing allows greater flexibility in the output of mass production industries in response to greater consumer selectivity. The retailer–manufacturer link becomes crucial in shaping just-in-time production, especially in mass consumption industries such as processed foods, clothing, or various sorts of electrical "white goods" (see Figure 6.1). In such industries there can be daily—even hourly—variations in the patterns of demand that can be directly relayed to the production line from electronic points of sale (EPOS) in shops via electronic data interchange (EDI). This has promoted an intensification of the existing tendencies in the relationships between such retail and manufacturing companies (Doel, 1996; Foord et al., 1996; Hughes, 1996; Marsden and Wrigley, 1996).

Another variant of changes within the network structure involves increasing further the power of major retailers within the supply chain. Market domination by major retailers as customers of production companies can decisively influence the ways in which interfirm relationships are structured within the framework of just-in-time. For example, the degree of market domination enjoyed by major clothing retailers in the United Kingdom allows them to dictate prices to manufacturers, imposing increasingly stringent quality, design, and delivery demands and pass-

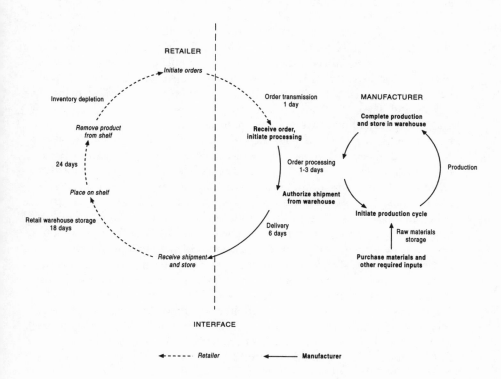

FIGURE 6.1. Linkages between manufacturers and retailers.

ing the costs of holding additional inventory on to suppliers. Major retailers can thus secure just-in-time supply at the expense of increased stocks held by producers, a sort of "pseudo-just-in-time" similar to that which has emerged in parts of the automobile production system (Hudson and Schamp, 1995b). A convergence between previously distinctive "close control" and "arms-length" control strategies of regulating relations between retailers and manufacturers has resulted in the development of a new hybrid form, "a single pyramidal model." The pyramid is hierarchical in structure, made up of the dominant retailer along with multiple tiers of suppliers. It is predicated upon the establishment of a first tier of preferred suppliers, but "the longer, obligational relationships that are emerging between buyers and suppliers must not be confused with notions of mutual trust, partnership or alliance." Preferred suppliers are locked into relations of dependence upon oligopolistically organized retailers, while there is fierce price competition as "preferred" suppliers seek to squeeze lower-tier suppliers (Crewe and Davenport, 1992, 196) and, on occasion, as retailers pressurize even their "preferred" suppliers.

The problematic character of trust between retailers and preferred suppliers was dramatically exemplified in 1999 when Marks and Spencer abruptly canceled its contracts with William Baird, which for the preceding thirty years had been one of its major suppliers, in a way that calls into question broader claims about the significance of trust in governing interfirm relations. Severing its links with Baird was a central element in Marks and Spencer's strategy to restructure its supply chain to cut costs and revive its falling market share, reducing its main clothing suppliers from four to three. Baird had derived some 40% of its revenues from Marks and Spencer, and as a result of the latter's unilateral action Baird had been forced to announce a program of job losses and factory closures within the United Kingdom. However, in common with other suppliers, it did not have a written contract. Baird's chief executive pointed out that his company's legal advisers "have told us that a contractual relationship can exist even without a written contract."[15] In his view a written contract was never required because Marks and Spencer had always claimed to view its relationship with its suppliers as a long-term partnership based on trust. Moreover, Baird claimed that Marks and Spencer had blocked a proposed merger between Baird and Coats Viyella, another of its suppliers, because the proposed merger would not achieve Marks and Spencer's objective of restructuring its supply chain (Minton, 2000). As a consequence, Baird sued Marks and Spencer for £53.6 million in compensation, arguing that it should have been given three years' notice of the proposed change. In response, Marks and Spencer claimed that "our decision has been taken following a comprehensive review of our supply requirements for clothing. M&S has been involved in honest and frank discussions for some time with Baird and other our major suppliers" (quoted in Merchant and Voyle, 2000). Moreover, "we would strongly refute any claims that William Baird are making in terms of our disengagement from them and will be vigorously fighting any legal action. We're disappointed that they want to go down this route and we see it as a bit of an irritation" (quoted in Minton, 2000).[16]

Much of the available evidence on network relations relates to links between large firms, or between large and small firms, and is drawn from a restricted set of industries and places. Consequently, it is uncertain how widespread these types of relationships actually are (Gertler, 1995; Gertler and Di Giovanna, 1997). There is much less evidence available on links between small firms (and most of this relates to specific types of relationships within industrial districts; see below), with relatively little knowledge of the extent of formal small firm to small firm cooperation (and even less of informal networks, both national and international). Survey evidence from the United Kingdom in the 1980s reveals strong technical links between small firms and a strong pattern of quasiverticality in technical relations, however.[17] O'Doherty (1993, 142–143) notes that, while we have only a partial view of small firm–large firm links across the European Community, "there is evidence that . . . small firms appear to have a preference for linking up with firms of a similar size and where small firms have participated in European Research Programmes, informal relationships with existing or former 'formal' partners have ensued."

In conceptualizing possible forms of network relations between small firms, and between small firms and large firms, it is important to acknowledge the heterogeneity of small firms—a feature that is not surprising given that such firms remain numerically dominant in the firm-size distribution. Several commentators have generated differing classifications of small firms, with the derived categories at least partly dependent on the national context. Best (1990), for example, identifies three types of small firms in the Third Italy: first, "traditional" small firms that produce commodities only for local markets and that do not form links with other firms; second, design-dependent firms that subcontract with lead firms that shape product design and control "upstream" or "downstream" key stages in the production filière (for example, assemblers and retailers, respectively); third, design-intensive independent suppliers with the capacity to refine designs and shape products and/or markets. While such companies may not produce their own brands, they are not tied to the designs of assembly or retail firms and so can form different types of relationships with them. Hadjimichalis (1998) identifies four types of small and medium-sized firms in Greece, based upon forms of production organization, sectoral specialization, and forms of cooperation and subcontracting: first, independent small firms, that is, "traditional" firms serving local markets, "modern" ones serving national or export markets; second, vertically dependent subcontractors undertaking labor-intensive tasks for national or multinational firms and involving either "putting out" and/or "splitting in";[18] third, small- and medium-sized enterprises (SMEs) that form horizontal networks linked by nondependent subcontracting and other types of interfirm linkages; fourth, SMEs linked into industrial districts (of which there is only one example in Greece, centered on the fur processing town of Kastoria, near the Albanian border). The Greek case thus further drives home the point that most small firms are not embedded in the relatively progressive social relationships of industrial districts; most remain in subordinate positions within the supply chains of larger firms or in market niches that larger firms find unattractive and base their competitive advantage on forms of labor control and work organization that are becoming increasingly unsustainable.[19]

Moreover, different forms of network relationships develop in different cultural contexts and regulatory environments. Gertler (1997, 55) suggests that the variety of forms of interfirm relations is partly explicable via national systems of regulation. Forms of interfirm relations might be enabled (or constrained) by the character of national systems of regulation—indeed, both subnational and supranational modes of regulation could equally have a formative influence. There are significant differences in the ways in which interfirm relations are structured and regulated within the more overtly competitive market cultures of Anglo-American capitalism and the more (though very differently) cooperative cultures of German, Japanese, or Swedish capitalism.[20] For example, networks emerged in the Japanese automobile industry as parent companies (with the exception of Honda) established kyonyokukai, formal associations of cooperative parts makers (ranging from 100 to 300 in number), to advance the capabilities of suppliers. These kyonyokukai are guided in their actions by informal understandings, or "shared network norms." Imai and colleagues (1985, 273) elaborate on the character of these "informal understandings":

> Written contracts are unheard of but if the lead manufacturer delivers, a trusting relationship begins to develop. In the long-run, this kind of relationship leads the sub-contractors as a group to accept the lead manufacturer as the legitimate leader and establish a strong co-operative system in support of it. A set of "shared network norms" is established over time, laying out a basic understanding of how network business should be conducted within the network. Such a norm may tolerate an unreasonable demand made by the lead manufacturer during times of competitive crisis.

As this makes clear, while at one level the emphasis is upon trust and shared interests, there is also an at least tacit recognition of asymmetries in power between participants in the network. At the same time, most kyonyokukai members supply several automobile manufacturers, to a degree spreading risk and also lowering the dependence of any one component supplier upon any one assembler.

As individual firms come to rely more heavily upon their relations and exchanges with other firms, nonmarket forms of interaction become more important (Gertler, 1997, 47–48). As such, relationships of "trust" may become pivotal, while the concept of trust itself is open to competing interpretations. Recognition of the possible significance of trust raises questions about creating trust from mistrust and protecting trust when it is endangered by opportunism via building institutions that allow actors to have confidence in the probity of others and the conditions that allow this to happen. At the same time, there may well be recognition that "trust" can be an issue of shades of grey rather than a matter of black and white, with some forms of economic transaction allowed to take place in the "moral borderlands" of economies. In such places "normal fair dealing" is relaxed, and activity is governed by "spare rules of decency that apply, among other places, in love and war" (Sabel and Zeitlin, 1997, 23).

An emphasis upon "trust" in these relationships is more likely to arise in situations of repeated interaction in one place (Crewe, 1996; Storper, 1995; see also below). However, even if nonmarket forms of relationships of trust *are* the basis of transactions, these do not *necessarily* equate to relationships of trust among equal partners. This is particularly sharply revealed in key command and control centers of the capitalist economy (Amin and Thrift, 1992; Pryke, 1991). McDowell (1997) argues that the "old" City of London was a localized cultural and social system that served to maximize trust, characterized by "peculiar" ways of doing business that depended upon the development of face-to-face contact and talk and "a bourgeois ideal of trust between equals." As this makes clear, "trust" is not a self-evident and unproblematic concept. Different concepts of trust are relevant in different circumstances and situations, so that "trust" in the "new" City of London carries different connotations that "trust" in the "old" City (Budd and Whimster, 1992). Furthermore, in both instances it means something very different from the trust that developed among coal miners working underground in dangerous conditions. In whatever form it comes to exist, however, "trust" must be *(re)produced* and the conditions under which this happens understood rather than it being assumed that "trust" is somehow a given product of "culture," diffusing via osmosis throughout society. More generally, it has been argued that traits and attitudes commonly understood as being part and parcel of inherited culture "are *themselves produced and reproduced over time by day-to-day practices* that are strongly conditioned by surrounding social institutions and regulatory régimes" Thus, "the very practices [taken] as signifiers of distinct cultures are themselves influenced by a set of institutions constituted outside the individual firm" (Gertler, 1997, 55, original emphasis).

6.3. Boundaries of Firms and Networks: Closed and Bounded or Open and Discontinuous Spaces?

Emphasizing networks and other forms of collaborative interfirm relationships draws attention to defining the boundary of the firm and the ways in which internal structures of firms have been changed and are changing. Consequently, the intrafirm structure of large corporations may increasingly be better represented as a network structure rather than a hierarchy as firms strive for more flexible organizational structures.[22] The tendency toward flatter, more network-like structures creates scope for variety in internal organizational structures, governance mechanisms, and geographies. A corollary of focusing upon relational contracting is that firms must be conceptualized as the means to coordinate production from one center of strategic decision making and not simply as legal entities. Such centers may encompass many legal firms (Dicken and Thrift, 1992, 285). Veltz (1991, 210–212) notes "how problematic the concepts of 'interior' and 'exterior' of the firm are becoming, how integration of networks weave their web not only among firms but within a continuum that runs from 'organisation' to the 'market' or from 'production' via 'transaction' to 'consumption.' " He emphasizes the fluctuating choices that constantly confront companies as the boundary between vertical integration and disintegration shifts. Objectives concerning costs, flexibility, reliability, and product quality can be achieved through processes of integration or of disintegration. There is a "permanent dilemma," which is resolved in practice in ways that can vary a great deal, between the advantages of stabilization of interfirm relations and the advantages that derive from the existence of "significant degrees of freedom" within networks. There is evidently a considerable element of indeterminacy in the way in which the "permanent dilemma" is resolved. Asymmetries in interfirm power relations between legally defined firms within network structures influence how it is resolved in particular time-places. Consequently, not only can different network relations take different spatial forms—territorially integrated or disintegrated—but the *same* network relationships can take different spatial forms in different times and places (Leborgne and Lipietz, 1991, 38–39).

Some networks are based upon spatial propinquity, others are not. A useful distinction can be drawn between spatial propinquity and organizational proximities (Bellet et al., 1993). The former may (but does not necessarily) facilitate the latter by increasing the probabilities of encounter between agents within a system but is not necessary for interaction between individuals or groups. Organizational proximity presupposes the existence of shared knowledge and commonly held and understood representations of the environment and world within which the firm exists. Such proximity enables the synthesis of varied forms of information and knowledge via cooperative and collective learning processes between firms within the institutions of an industry. Organizational proximity is therefore both a necessary condition for, and a product of, creating innovations and resources through collective learning. However, the networks through which learning is enabled and expressed are not necessarily territorially defined and demarcated, and in some respects the growing sophistication of IT and communications technologies has weakened this link further (Miller et al., 1996). Conversely, the technological facilitation of information flows has enhanced the significance of place-specific tacit knowledge within key nodes of command and control in a global(izing) economy (Amin and Thrift, 1994).

Some networks are without doubt deeply spatially embedded. In some cases, this is because of the significance of territorially based knowledge to economic competitiveness.[23] In other cases, it is because production depends upon material interchanges between spatially adjacent processes and firms. Outputs from one become inputs to others, notably in continuous-flow industries such as bulk chemicals and steel (Hudson, 1983, 1994c).[24] In fact, corporate, sectoral, and territorial forms of collaboration often intersect to shape competitiveness. A sector can include a variety of interfirm practices and extrafirm agencies such as trade associations, sector programs, labor education facilities, joint marketing arrangements, and regulatory commissions, each of which facilitates interfirm cooperation. Consequently, sector institutions can impact upon the organization of individual firms, their strategies, and the collective competitiveness *"relative to sectors located elsewhere.* From this point of view, firms not only compete but they also cooperate to provide common services, to shape the 'rules of the market game,' and to shape complementary investment strategies" (Best, 1990, 17, emphasis added). There are, however, no rigid deterministic relationships between a particular form of sector organization, intercompany relations, and a particular geography of the supply chain. In networked just-in-time systems component supplier companies can be situated in adjacent locations or can be—

literally—located on the other side of the world (Sadler, 1994). Sometimes such companies have established one or two factories to serve the
entire global market. This is a far cry from the asserted equating of "just-
in-time" with "in one place" (Hudson, 1994b; Lung, 1992). Howells
(1993, 227) comments more generally that a "surprisingly large" number
of key suppliers are only effectively available from a highly restricted set
of locations worldwide, reducing the possibilities of establishing local
specialist subcontractor clusters.

The likely implications of new forms of high-volume production
organization involving interfirm collaboration within complex network
structures for a selective reregionalization of production may be summarized as follows. The most likely scenario is that a smaller number
of places will become the hosts to more integrated multinational corporate investments. For these favored places, the prognosis is relatively
good, as a high level of integration will yield a more diverse and qualified occupational structure. Moreover, the stability of investment, impli-
cating as it does multiple linked firms, is likely to be significantly
higher. Yet, while many local firms will be drawn into the production
complex, it is less likely that they will become core members of the
collaborative partnership, and instead will remain in a subordinate position. Moreover, as these investments become more concentrated in
particular regions, the excluded regions are likely to become more excluded. Rather than gradually incorporating progressively more territory into the productive orbit of multinational networks, the degree of
geographical differentiation in terms of investment, growth, and sectoral mix tends to increase. Commenting on the implications of "new
customer–supplier relationships" for the structure of supply networks,
and in particular the fact that for most companies there will be relatively few "preferred" first tier suppliers, Dicken and colleagues (1994,
39) point out that not every local economy can, therefore, hope to participate in these new integrated networks. The smaller the area, the less
likely it is to possess supplier firms of the necessary quality. Local
embeddedness, therefore, is double-edged: it depends both the choices
of transnational companies and the existence of appropriate firms with
which they can interact.

The rediscovery of industrial districts as territorially agglomerated
production systems is a salutary example of the way in which the organization of production and its geographies evolve in complex and nonlinear
ways. The Connecticut metalworking district developed as an industrial
district in the nineteenth century, focused on the Springfield Armory,
which lay at the center of a network of supplier firms. The armory was
not, however, simply the network coordinator, but it established stan-

dards, diffused new production methods, and facilitated the convergence of production technologies and methods. Economic linkages were underpinned by "non-market exchanges of mutual benefit," but this "spirit of co-operation did not emerge spontaneously; it was part of the social fabric" of the district. But if there was "something in the air," an "unwritten code," its presence reflected definite social processes of cooperation, collaboration, and trust (Best, 1990, 38–41). The production of "trust" through repetitive interaction within a context of a shared culture is critical to the successful reproduction of global financial centers, which have been interpreted as a particular type of industrial district (Amin and Thrift, 1992; McDowell, 1997). Gertler (1997, 55), however, cautions that much of the "celebrated collaborative culture" of firms in industrial districts might be strongly shaped by broader regulatory and institutional frameworks. Supraregional institutions may create a supportive regulatory context "to facilitate the development of trust-based open relations between firms." They may therefore help to create the necessary conditions in which collaboration and learning-by-interacting in spatially clustered interfirm networks can flourish.

Such conditions are necessary rather than sufficient, however. One reason why the Connecticut valley metalworking district failed to develop into a learning district was that "the idea of an industrial district was missing" (Best, 1990, 45). This raises two important points of more general provenance. First, recognition of a shared sense of collective purpose—"the idea of an industrial district"—is critical to the long-term success of industrial districts. Best (1990, 236, emphasis added) amplifies the point in commenting upon the culturally embedded and path-dependent character of development in successful industrial districts in the Third Italy more than a century later:

> Pursuing a particular production process alters the capabilities of resource services and the constellation of firms. *Choosing one path irrevocably closes another.* The implication is that any constellation of firms is not organic, but is contingent. . . . This implies that an industrial district in which participants do not have a concept to describe it is vulnerable to being undermined. . . . In the . . . Third Italy *common political or religious affiliations created a bedrock of community that sustained a collective identity and with it the notion of "we" as well as "I."*

Second, it is necessary to distinguish between different types of industrial district, depending upon their key organizational principles (Garofoli, 1986). Such different "logics" for agglomeration in industrial

districts are discussed by Storper (1993, 1997). "Nonprogressive" industrial districts base their competitive advantage mainly in cost savings as a
result of agglomeration economies, often with great social costs to workers because of these cost-cutting strategies (Hadjimichalis and Vaiou,
1990b). "Progressive" technology districts mainly base their competitive
advantages on product-based technological learning. This latter concept
goes beyond the "traditional" and static Marshallian concept of industrial district, however. The Marshallian notion goes "some way" toward
describing a productive system of small firms, but the source of stability
of small firms in regions such as the Third Italy is based on more than
specialization and external economies of scale (Best, 1990, 234–235).
Successful industrial districts are continuously restructuring as firms seek
to remain competitive in a world of rapid technological change and intense international competition. Firms within such districts derive their
competitive edge from a combination of high quality based on distinctive
competencies resulting from specialization by phase within the production chain and flexibility resulting from the capacity to reconstitute micro
production units along the filière as technology advances and market conditions change. To capture these opportunities an industrial district must
be collectively entrepreneurial. A static conception of such a district fails
to capture the major strengths of the Third Italy: "the institutional capacity to continuously learn, adjust and improve on economic performance."
An innovative industrial district is a dynamic constellation of mutually
adjusting firms, responding to new challenges and opportunities via continuous redefinition of interfirm relations and the external boundaries of
the district.

In summary, successful industrial districts can be thought of as
"learning regions" or "technology districts" that redefine their internal
interfirm relations and external boundaries as part of this learning process. Many former once successful industrial districts clearly have failed
to make this transformation (Sunley, 1992). Moreover, the examples
given of such successfully transforming regions and districts—Silicon Valley, the Third Italy, the Paris haute couture clothing district, and the cin-
ema district in Hollywood—"perhaps still suggest a certain cultural and
historical specificity that would be difficult to emulate elsewhere" (Perrons, 1992, 191). More generally, small firms are often rooted in their
own localities or "milieu," and this involves a range of cooperative relationships with customers, suppliers, and competitors as well as a range of
other institutions (O'Doherty, 1993; Rothwell, 1988).[25] This does not,
however, mean that such firms are embedded in the relatively progressive
social relationships of industrial districts. The clear implication is that
most agglomerations of small firms, if they are industrial districts at all,
are of the "nonprogressive" variety.

6.4. Longer-Term Strategic Collaboration: Strategic Alliances and Joint Ventures

Strategic cooperative relationships between companies can take a variety of forms. There is, for example, a long history of trade associations through which collectivities of companies promulgate common interests. These are important in establishing accepted norms and "rules of the game" within which companies conduct business. They can help regulate potentially ruinous competition between firms within a sector and enhance competitiveness in relation to firms in the same sector in other places. They are often encouraged and/or supported by national (for example, Japan) and regional (for example, in the Third Italy) governments.[26] Cartel formation is another well-established form of interfirm collaboration, a way of imposing oligopolistic regulation of markets and competition.[27] In interwar Japan, for instance, control associations, or cartels (zaibatsu), facilitated cooperation among competitors on profits, output, and investment plans, and thereby countered the tendency toward potentially "ruinous competition" without sacrificing industrial dynamism. Such cartels became illegal after the enactment of a U.S.-style legislation in 1947, but this was of little relevance due to the "flexible administration" (Best, 1990, 176) of this legislation.

More recently there has been growing emphasis on new, different, and closer forms of relationships between companies around issues that are integral to their corporate longer-term strategy (Lorange and Roos, 1993).[28] These often form an alternative to a contested—or indeed friendly—acquisition but are motivated by the same sorts of aims. Although not confined to particular types or sizes of companies, such strategic alliances are undoubtedly most common between large transnationals. As a result, they also have a distinctive geography, concentrated within and between the global triad of macroregions in North America, Europe, and Japan. Within the United States, for example, only 750 interfirm alliances were registered during the 1970s, but between 1987 and 1992 alone there were 20,000 (Giddens, 2000, 80). Equally, there has been an increase in collaborative ventures between firms across national boundaries. While not new, these too have increased greatly in number, growing at an annual rate of 20% as one response to an increasingly turbulent economic environment (Lester, 1998), and changing qualitatively in significance. Three features of this recent expansion of strategic alliances are particularly striking. First, they have become central rather than peripheral to the competitive strategies of many firms. Second, the vast majority of such alliances are between competitors. Third, many companies are forming networks of alliances rather than involving themselves in a single alliance: "relationships are increasingly polygamous rather than monogamous" (Dicken, 1998, 228). Consequently, boundaries between firms have become even more blurred and fuzzy.

To some extent the scope for such alliances is defined by the regulatory policies and practices of national (and emergent supranational) states. These may both encourage or deter such forms of cooperation.[29] Thus, in part, the recent spectacular growth in the number of strategic alliances has been linked to deregulation of national markets in sectors such as telecommunications (Mulgan, 1991). Within the limits defined by regulatory systems, such alliances are forged for a variety of purposes (Vyas, 1995). They include: market penetration and overcoming the problems of gaining access to markets—for example, via cross-distribution agreements; coping with rapid market evolution or creating such market turbulence as a competitive strategy; sharing the increasing costs, uncertainties, and risks of R&D and new joint product development, especially in technologically sophisticated sectors of production, and sharing technologies (Chesnais, 1993, 19); identifying more and less commercially promising new product areas by sharing R&D costs (Walsh and Galimberti, 1993, 187–188); joint production to realize economies of scale and scope (Lie and Santucci, 1993, 116) or to cope with problems of overcapacity; and taking advantage of coalescing product categories, especially in sectors characterized by rapid technological change and heavy reliance upon expensive technologies (Hagedoon, 1993; Mulgan, 1991). Such alliances are therefore most common between firms in sectors associated with the newest and most technologically intensive products. During the 1980s, for instance, the majority of strategic alliances were in sectors "typified by high entry costs, globalization, scale economies, rapidly changing technologies and/or substantial operating risks" (Dicken, 1998, 228, citing Morris and Hergert, 1987).

Strategic alliances typically involve long-term contracts from one company to another, based around trust and shared interests. The rationale for developing long-term collaborative relationships in areas of complex manufacturing is powerfully expressed by Best (1990, 264):

> A car assembler, which ultimately co-ordinates 20,000 parts, or a Boeing, whose planes contain some 250,000 parts, cannot possibly develop in-house the best qualified supplier, which means guessing right on technological developments in every productive activity that contributed to the final product. Instead, long-term consultative relations with suppliers in which design concepts are developed together offers the car assembler and Boeing the opportunity to specialise in design, assembly, distribution, and marketing.

Consequently, such long-term relationships may provide an alternative route for the realization of scale economies (Delapierre and Zimmerman, 1993).

Joint ventures are a form of strategic alliance specifically established to push forward collaborative projects. These often involve potentially risky projects at the boundaries of "new technologies." In Japan, for example, new products or sectors typically have been developed by joint ventures, with each of the six major keiretsu represented by a joint venture from among its constituent members. As the required scale of R&D investment rose in semiconductor production, Japanese and U.S.-based firms increasingly formed joint ventures in the 1990s to spread the costs and risks of developing new generations of integrated circuits. More generally, the decisive reason for the formation of joint ventures in sectors such as computing and communications is foreign national market penetration (Cooke and Wells, 1991). Typically, there is a significant degree of protection because of the acknowledged costs and risks of product development and the perceived strategic significance of such industries for national economic development strategies.

Joint ventures can also be used as a low-risk method of penetrating potentially high-risk territories. They have become the major organizational form through which foreign direct investment has occurred in much of eastern Europe, reflecting the preferences of foreign investors to utilize existing productive capacity and local expertise rather than embark upon more risky greenfield investments (Smith, 1998). Joint ventures provide a relatively low-risk strategy for penetrating emergent markets in eastern Europe or of establishing low-cost production bases there, with cheap but skilled labor, for export to the European Union and elsewhere. For indigenous companies, joint ventures give opportunities to increase competitiveness via access to newer production technologies, new working practices, and opportunities to upgrade product quality (Pilkington, 1999). As risks recede, however, foreign companies tend to increase their shareholding in the joint ventures. Similar processes are observable in other newly industrializing countries.

The enhanced importance of cross-national strategic alliances in various guises in the global economy represents an attempt to resolve contradictory tendencies within the new geography of global capitalism. Strategic alliances have become increasingly prevalent as one way through which companies maneuver to meet the challenges of global competition. These require both global production strategies and a strong presence in each of the "Triad" markets, recognizing the cultural and institutional specificities of these broad macroregions. Strategic alliances have become central to the competitive strategy of "virtually all large (and many smaller) corporations" (Dicken et al., 1994, 32). Such alliances represent an attempt to reconcile the limits to expansion by direct production and ownership in other Triad markets and the strategic need to be in an insider position in each of the other two regions. They do so because they allow firms to share marketing, distribution, R&D, and even production without investing directly in foreign facilities. These are at once cooperative and competitive relationships, however, often riven with tension as a result. Consequently, their successful reproduction is a crucial, often problematic, task.

6.5. Acquisitions and Mergers as Competitive Strategies

Acquisition and merger are strategies through which companies can alter the corporate anatomy of ownership and control of production. Companies can compete via acquiring other companies, often in the face of opposition from the company to be acquired, or via merging more amicably with other companies. This in turn can have perceptible impacts upon geographies of production. The extent to which companies can pursue strategies of merger and acquisition is shaped by national and supranational regulatory frameworks.[30] In some circumstances, such frameworks may prevent or discourage mergers on the grounds that these would pose a threat to competition; in other circumstances, they may encourage them to produce national or supranational "champions" that can compete internationally (Amin, 1992; Ramsay, 1992). Similarly, and related, some cultures of capitalism encourage acquisition and merger (notably the Anglo-American model), while others are or until recently have been less receptive to such corporate behavior, especially in cases in which this involves unwelcome "hostile" acquisitions (the German and Japanese models, for example).

Merger and acquisition activity displays marked temporal and spatial variability (Dickson, 1997), with peaks separated by periods of relative low levels of such activities. There was, for example, a considerable increase in merger and acquisition activity during the second half of the 1980s and the first half of the 1990s after a long period of relative quiescence. This increase was linked to global deregulation of financial markets, the creation of "macroregions" such as the European Union's Single European Market and the North American Free Trade Area, and growing competitive pressures on companies in increasingly internationalized markets (Martin, 1994). The timing of waves of acquisition and merger also varies with industry and sector, as these develop at different rates and new products, firms, and sectors emerge while existing ones decline. For example, in a period of less than two years beginning in early 1998, no less than half of the world's leading twenty-five pharmaceutical companies were engaged in merger and acquisition activity, a period of "unprecedented consolidation" in the industry (Pilling, 2000a, 2000b).[31] Most foreign direct investment during the 1980s was in the form of mergers and acquisitions rather than in the establishment of new plants (with only a minority of investment in manufacturing as opposed to services; Weiss, 1997, 6). Much of the growing international investment in producer services was via merger and acquisition and the establishment of subsidiaries in key national, although increasingly international, markets (Coe, 1997). In advertising, for instance, agencies engaged in merger and acquisition activity as a way of "going global" in response to the globalization strategies of their clients (Leslie, 1994).

The development of transnational mergers and acquisitions as the main form of foreign direct investment is linked to financial globalization, the formation of "totally internationalized" financial and monetary markets, enabled by the growth of information technologies and telecommunications and international trade agreements (Chesnais, 1993, 13). Martin (1994) links the increase in merger and acquisition activity in the 1980s and the growth of direct foreign investment to growth in the financial services that "service" this activity. This combination of factors laid the foundations for the development of industrial concentration as an international process, as distinct from a national one, and so for the onset of "world oligopoly." This has become the dominant form of supply structure in most R&D-intensive and "high-tech" industries as well as in "scale intensive" manufacturing industries.[32] Even so, as Chesnais hints, the extent to which mergers and acquisitions lead to marked centralization of capital and the emergence of truly international firms is uneven, sectorally and spatially. Despite the effects of the Single European Market and a wave of European mergers in the mid- and late 1980s, for example, there are still relatively few genuinely international companies in Europe (Townsend, 1997, 73–74). Even so, newly merged companies must define their core competencies and decide how best to integrate "local islands of knowledge" from all over the world to develop them (Amin and Cohendet, 1997, 8). They must also decide which activities are tangential and which product lines have surplus capacity and either close them down or divest them to others. Divestment and "exit" from "noncore" activities is often a key element in postmerger and postacquisition rationalizations and can have marked effects on geographies of production.

Broadly speaking, mergers fall into one of two types: (1) "Horizontal" mergers involve attempts to cut costs via combining companies in similar product markets, concentrating market share, cutting unit costs, and raising profitability; in effect, they are a form of "weak" competition. (2) Other types of mergers approximate more the form of "strong" competition, as companies seek to add qualitatively new dimensions to their activities, such as new products or organizational and management skills

(Waters and Corrigan, 1998; see Figure 6.2). There are many more specific reasons why companies acquire or merge with other companies, which often mirror the reasons for forming strategic alliances. Indeed, merger and acquisition and the formation of strategic alliances are not mutually exclusive options, and firms evaluate which can best meet their objectives in a given situation (Hamill, 1993; Naylor and Lewis, 1997; Thompson, 1999). First, big companies often take over innovative small companies in order to acquire new growth products or process technologies while avoiding the R&D costs of developing these. This is a route through which big companies can broaden their product range or acquire technological rents; conversely, small companies may be under pressure to sell out as a consequence of the way in which markets and interfirm relations are structured. In the "high-tech" electronics sector industrial districts of late-twentieth-century California, small entrepreneurs "feel that they have no time to co-ordinate among each other" (Storper, 1993, 447). There is a race to the market because others are doing what they are doing. Under these conditions, the temptations to engage in opportunistic behavior grow and with them the possibilities of business failure. The high rate of sell-out of even successful small firms is a rational response to this system of interfirm relations. A high percentage of those firms that do not exceed a certain threshold of size and product diversity in their first few years are sold to larger companies by their founders. Consequently, "market failure" is central to the logic of the market in high technology agglomerations in the United States. Markets are ordered by conventions in such a way that they fail. The sell-out process is deeply rooted in the

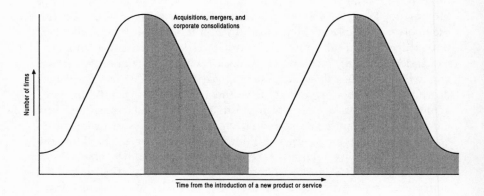

FIGURE 6.2. The cycles of innovation, acquisition, and merger.

rationalities that lead entrepreneurs to create markets in the first place. Innovation, followed by transactional failure, ultimately encourages vertical integration (Storper, 1993, 447–448). In other regional and national contexts the market is differently structured, so that there is not such pressure to sell out, buy up, and vertically integrate production. Nevertheless, even in canonical "horizontally" networked industrial districts such as those of the Third Italy, there have been growing tendencies in this direction.

Second, (large) companies often take over other large companies as a way of penetrating new markets via acquiring ready-made distribution networks. Chesnais (1993, 17) argues that market conditions are crucial in changing the emphasis within foreign direct investment to acquisition and merger. In situations of stagnant or slowly growing demand "corporate growth and multinational expansion must now take place at the expense of other firms and thus foreign direct investment occurs principally in the form of mergers and acquisitions." Third, (large) companies acquire rivals as a way of eliminating surplus capacity in a particular product range, as takeover is followed by plant closures. Acquisitions in the same product market may therefore be a prelude to rationalization and plant closure, as the geography of ownership changes and social relations are stretched over space in different patterns and as the centralization and (de)concentration of capital changes. The spatially selective impacts of acquisition can therefore be profound, especially when it is a prelude to closure. Clark (1989) defines a "geography of divestiture," with important implications for both competition and employment in sectors and areas from which companies withdraw following acquisition or merger. The potential impacts of employment loss can thus act as a barrier to mergers even in sectors characterized by considerable excess capacity (such as the automobile sector in the European Union; Simonian, 1998).

Fourth, (large) companies take over other companies as a way of creating synergies via complementarity in product ranges. Fifth, (large) companies take over others as a way of diversifying and broadening their product range and/or changing it via moving into some product areas and out of other areas. During the 1990s, for example, Imperial Chemicals Industries engaged in a series of selective acquisitions, asset swaps, and disposals of peripheral and/or weaker activities intended to transform it from its former focus on bulk commodity products to a focus on speciality chemicals. This involved hiving off its specialist chemical activities into a separate company, Zeneca, in 1993, but this proved to be simply one moment in an ongoing process of acquisition and disposal by both companies (Cleveland County Council, 1994; Edgecliffe-Johnson, 1998). Sixth, (large) companies take over other companies as a way of getting larger, increasing market share and volume of output—classic processes of concentration of production and centralization of capital. For example, in the clothing sector in the United Kingdom Crewe and Davenport (1992, 185) argue that, while organic growth was important in the creation of powerful retailers during the 1970s, this increasingly gave way to acquisition as a viable growth option during the 1980s. In another and very different part of the service sector in the United Kingdom, similar processes were at work. As a direct consequence of private firms and public agencies contracting out routine service work, leading firms in the cleaning, catering, and security industries increased their size severalfold during the 1980s through an extensive policy of acquisition. Consequently, a handful of firms now dominate each of these sectors (Allen and Henry, 1997, 197). Seventh, (large) companies merge with one another as a way of controlling markets. However, such horizontal mergers seeking to oligopolize a sector may be problematic. The economic landscape of the United States in the late nineteenth and early twentieth centuries was littered with unsuccessful attempts to control markets by horizontal merger activity, for example. Eighth, companies acquire others, or merge, as a way of spreading risks by diversifying into different products with varying business cycles, or into different spatial markets for the same products. Finally, companies may acquire other companies for no other reason than a perceived need to increase in size and not to be left behind in the face of merger and acquisition activity by their rivals. Furthermore, the same company may well be pursuing a combination of these strategies simultaneously.

Despite all the brave talk about the revival of small firms, "big is beautiful" remains the order of the day over much of production. The surge in acquisition and merger activity during the 1990s, much of it in previously nationally regulated service sector activities such as banking, suggests that this remains the case. There seems to be a continuing tendency for production in some sectors and products to become concentrated in a few giant firms via processes of centralization of capital. Size confers competitive advantage in a variety of ways, not least in terms of financial muscle and resources. These are not, however, unconditional or automatically conferred advantages, and there can be problems of "diseconomies of scale" as a result of acquisition, resulting in "conglomerates which are considered as notoriously ineffective forms of organisation" (Ramsay, 1992, 31). This is one reason why disposal often follows shortly after acquisition, as companies seek to reap the benefits without having to carry the costs of increasing size. The breakup of conglomerates such as the Hanson Group is indicative of the problems for capital and its managers of assembling unwieldy conglomerates of diverse and unrelated businesses.

Moreover, even when successful from the point of view of corporate interests and strategy, cross-national mergers can pose policy problems for national states. Globalization, especially by means of transnational mergers, acquisitions, and alliances, leads to a new concept of national interest. Because of this, some argue that governments should attract investment that can generate growth and employment irrespective of nationality of ownership. This implies a dramatic revision in the role of governments and the objectives of industrial policy in a globalizing economy (Lie and Santucci, 1993, 123). Nationality of ownership is no longer seen as a key issue in economic policy formation—a view that some would challenge. What is uncontestable, however, is that globalization emphasizes the reciprocal relationship between corporate policies, national state policy formation, and the conception of national interests in an economy that is becoming more and more complexly internationalized, if not yet globalized.[33]

6.6. Summary and Conclusions

Collaborative relationships between companies have a venerable history within industrial capitalism. There is no doubt, however, that in recent years considerable emphasis has been placed upon new forms of cooperation and collaboration between companies, such as strategic alliances, as a new element in corporate competitive strategy. There certainly has been an expansion of such relationships, and they have come to embrace a wide range of activities including R&D, product development, shared suppliers, joint manufacturing, and shared distribution systems. Major transnational companies are typically entangled in a series of such networks rather than simply being involved in one of them, so that the map of intercorporate linkages is often very complicated. These network linkages represent a considerable extension of intercorporate relations beyond the realm of the market and subcontracting on the basis of price. They typically revolve around longer-term relationships involving a strong element of mutual interdependence, albeit relationships typically characterized by considerable asymmetries of power despite a rhetorical emphasis upon equality and trust between companies locked into such networks. While they are not new, it is certainly the case that such relationships have expanded markedly, but at the same time well-established processes of acquisition and merger have continued apace. Indeed, the same major corporations that are most actively involved in acquisition and merger activity are often those most actively involved in constructing overlapping networks of strategic alliances. Despite the emphasis placed upon the alleged attractions and benefits of being small, there is abundant evidence that big continues to be seen as beautiful within worldwide contemporary capitalist production. But big is only beautiful if it is also "lean and mean" (Harrison, 1994). Consequently, the processes of centralization, of acquisition and postacquisition rationalization, disinvestment and capacity closures, as well as concentration of capital, remain of central importance to understanding geographies of production.

6.7. Notes

1. As discussed in Chapter 2.

2. The chief executive of INA, a specialized engineering company, explained the expansion of the company's workforce in the high-wage and highly regulated German labor market as follows (cited in Marsh, 1998): "We have been increasing the depth of our manufacturing, as opposed to relying on sub-contractors to do the work. This has happened as we have moved to more complex parts. . . . The skills component of what we do is increasing . . . as we move into new areas which require advanced knowledge. . . . This is why it makes sense to continue to build up our manufacturing capabilities, even in high cost places such as Germany." INA developed special manufacturing systems and tooling for use within the company. This was both cheaper and provided greater flexibility within production technologies than outsourcing these tasks. See also section 5.6.

3. While moving beyond the untenable assumptions of perfect knowledge of neoclassical theory, such transaction cost approaches nonetheless in other ways remain firmly within the confines of neoclassicism.

4. Including knowledge; see section 5.6.

5. See "Organizational Innovation" in section 5.3.

6. For example, many producers of computers, telecommunications, and other "high-tech" electronic equipment have decided that their core competencies lie in design and marketing. Consequently, an increasingly large share of their manufacturing is carried out by subcontractors, more formally known as electronic manufacturing services (EMS) companies. Such manufacturers were once part of a twilight world of price competition to which major manufacturers subcontracted labor-intensive operations such as circuit board assembly. However, they have now become companies with leading-edge business processes and advanced manufacturing capabilities, able to construct complex subsystems or even finished systems. Such EMS companies have also developed capabilities in managing the supply chain in product segments in which product life cycles and lead times have been successively reduced. Subcontracting manufacturing to them is now routine, an institutionalised part of the production strategies of major "high-tech" electronics producers. Often EMS companies have acquired their manufacturing capacity from major IT companies that have decided that in-house manufacturing is no longer part of their core competencies.

7. They add that, with the "unprecedented" scale of mergers and acquisitions in the 1980s (see section 6.5), this potential "in principle" has increasingly become "in practice."

8. Commodity chain analysis adopts a rather different and more limited di-

chotomous view of governance structures. It distinguishes between "producer driven" and "consumer driven" chains. The former constitute chains in which large vertically integrated transnational firms internalize most aspects of production, distribution, and marketing. They are typically found in capital-intensive and technology-intensive sectors characterized by economies of scale and significant barriers to entry and exit. The latter, in contrast, refer to chains typically set up by transnational retailers, marketers, and trading companies that establish and maintain arm's-length relationships with labor-intensive producers of a range of consumer goods, usually located in the Third World (Clancy, 1998; Gereffi, 1995, 2000). Such a dichotomy fails to capture the variety and subtlety of network relations and governance structures and of geographies of production.

9. See section 5.4.

10. These relationships may now also be vulnerable as a result of technical changes: "The internet, and particularly business-to-business e-commerce, looks set to rid the country [Japan] of swathes of inefficient distributors, disrupting long-established supply chains and lowering distribution costs. This could create tremendous opportunities for new entrants" (Nusbaum, 2000).

11. One consequence of this has been intensified competitive pressures upon such industries *within* Japan. The restructuring plans announced by Nissan in 1999 and "the plan to weed out weak suppliers will topple the traditional Nissan keiretsu at a stroke" (Harney, 1999).

12. This is an instructive reversal of direction in the intersectoral transfer of new methods of production. At the start of the last century, principles of continuous production were transferred from bulk continuous production industries and adapted for mass production of consumer goods. At the end of the same century, principles of just-in-time production were transferred from high-volume production of consumer goods to continuous bulk production. In both cases, the transfer involved a degree of adaptation and "hybridization" of the original production concepts.

13. British Steel (now part of Corus), for example, produced over 1,000 grades of steel at its Teesside works in northeast England, often in small batches for just-in-time delivery to customers (Hudson, 1994c).

14. The first product targeted was acrylics. Hiromara Yonekura, director of basic chemicals at Sumitomo Chemicals, commented (emphasis added): "I'm sure the new system will be extended to other plastics products. It was ridiculous. We used to make over 400 different grades of low density polyethylene and 400 different kinds of polypropylene. *It's all very well matching the customer's specifications, but because we were producing such small batches, it raised our costs horribly.* We've cut the number of grades to 300 of each and we're looking to reduce even more" (cited in Abrahams, 1994).

15. Mr. D. Suddens, quoted in Merchant and Voyle (2000).

16. While the outcome of the legal process is as yet unknown, the fact that it has been invoked calls into question claims about the significance of trust in governing interfirm relations.

17. This describes the character of linkages between innovative small and medium-sized companies and other companies: 39% contracted out R&D; 86% of subcontracting relations were with firms employing less than 200 people; 47%

were supplier firms and 18% were customers; 26% of firms engaged in some sort of collaborative R&D venture; 56% of collaborations were with firms employing less than 200 people; 47% of collaborations were with suppliers and 35% with customers; and 66% of firms contracted out some manufacturing (Rothwell, 1988).

18. As noted earlier in this section.

19. Nevertheless, small firms remain numerous and have grown in number in the recent past in the core capitalist economies. This has confounded predictions by an earlier generation of political economists of an overly mechanistic Marxian persuasion that such firms were an anachronistic form of capital organization, doomed to extinction.

20. See, for example, Lash and Urry (1987) and Albert (1993). However, there is evidence of a degree of convergence with the Anglo-American model, especially as a consequence of the globalization of certain key financial markets.

21. See also section 5.6.

22. See "Organizational Innovation" in section 5.3.

23. Discussed in section 5.6.

24. See also "Process Innovation and the New Technological Paradigms of Production" in section 5.3.

25. Rothwell (1988) provides evidence of the spatial character of linkages between innovative small and medium-sized companies and other companies in the United Kingdom, for instance. In particular: 39% contracted out their R&D, and 50% of subcontractors were located within 50 miles; 68% of firms contracted out a proportion of their manufacturing, and 66% of subcontractors were located within 40 miles of the contracting firm. This suggests strong technical links among small firms and the importance of proximity to their R&D and manufacturing partners.

26. For example, in Japan the Ministry of International Trade and Industry actively promoted trade associations as a conduit for shaping and implementing sector strategies; by 1982, 23,000 trade associations were registered with the Fair Trade Commission there, along with 77,000 small business cooperative associations.

27. See section 5.5.

28. For example, in the United States the percentage of turnover of the largest 1,000 companies generated through alliances as opposed to solely owned businesses doubled between the early 1990s and 1998 to reach 25% of turnover (cited by G. Larsen; see www.iri.com).

29. See Chapter 3.

30. See Chapter 3.

31. This included cross-national mergers between Astra and Zeneca, Hoescht and Rhône Poulenc, and Glaxo Wellcome and Smith Kline Beecham, while Pfizer was mounting a hostile bid for Warner-Lambert.

32. This is discussed in section 5.5.

33. See also Chapter 3.

7

Divisions of Labor
Cleavage Planes and Axes of Cooperation

7.1. Introduction

A central theme of Chapter 4 is that companies need workers to organize collectively to facilitate processes of recruitment, negotiation of terms and conditions of employment, and organization of the labor process. With the growth of large-scale industrial capitalism, the primary institutional form of workers' organization gradually became the trade union, as workers sought in various ways to become a class—or at least a fraction of it—"for themselves." The formation of trade unions is a contradictory process in terms of the interests of workers, however. Organizing in this way both unites groups of workers and divides them from other groups of workers. Managing the tensions inherent in this process of simultaneous unity and division constitutes a major task for trade unions. In uniting on one dimension, workers inevitably define "other" groups of workers, with whom they lack shared interests or with whom they are actively in competition. The dimensions around which workers choose to organize and unite, the formation of collective identities, the defining of "us" and "them," the construction of the underlying processes of "othering,"[1] and of the implications of this for action are all of central importance.

Just as there are tensions arising from the necessity for competition and cooperation among companies, so too are there parallel tensions in relationships among groups of workers. They must simultaneously organize to negotiate with employers and compete with other groups of workers over access to jobs, the terms and conditions on which they are offered, and so on.[2] Capital also has an interest in this process of division and fragmentation. The growth of the technical and social divisions of labor, and innovations in the organization of production and the labor process, have undoubtedly helped shape the contours of these divisions. Labor markets are often deeply and multiply segmented, in terms of industry, occupation, ethnicity, and gender. Each of these dimensions of segmentation is associated with spatial differentiation and discontinuities that divide workers from one another.

Clearly, the working class is multiply divided along several cleavage planes (as more generally are the societies of which it is a part). This raises important and difficult questions as to how these divisions interrelate—how, for example, does gender divide the working class, how does class divide gender groups? Class, gender, and divisions of labor (to which one could add other dimensions of division, such as ethnicity and place) are social structures, and it is impossible to close off one structure and observe the unambiguous effects of its operations (Sayer and Walker, 1992, 13–15). This is no more nor less than recognition of the multiple and conflicting identities that people experience and must deal with in their everyday lives, and in particular of the difficulties that confront workers seeking to find common cause around which to identify and organize; for, as Sayer and Walker go on to add, emphasizing the need to foreground the relationships between agency and structure, we "cannot expect societies to break neatly along the fault lines of class, gender and the division of labour. While the structural cleavages, like continental plates, run deep and grind mercilessly, they nevertheless turn against one another, against the wilful intransigence of human beings, and against their own internal contradictions." Class, gender, ethnicity, and divisions of labor (social, technical, and spatial) must therefore be seen as "distinct, if wholly intertwined, structures of social oppression, exploitation, and difference" (Sayer and Walker, 1992, 53). They are, however, also dimensions of identity and organization. Clearly, there are deep tensions because of these ambiguities in the organization and representation of workers' collective interests.

This chapter explores these tensions, analytically separating out these "wholly intertwined" dimensions of division and the ways in which workers are at once united and divided. However, analytically separate dimensions are cumulatively and simultaneously experienced by people. For example, a black female clothing worker and resident in Birmingham (whether in England or Alabama) experiences the totality of the interacting effects of these attributes in the labor market rather than the effects of each sequentially and separately. The chapter goes on to consider the implications of these tensions and divisions for the organization of production and its geographies, as well as for those groups of workers and their communities and places that "win" and those that "lose" in the competition for jobs.[3]

7.2. Organizing Workers, Dividing Workers: Trade Unions and the Institutions of Organized Labor

There are certainly claims about the possibilities—some would argue, necessities—of global and unitary labor organization, transcending the multiple dimensions of divisions between workers, defeating both the "merciless grinding" of deep structural cleavage planes and the "willful intransigence" of people. Consequently, there are continuing periodic exhortations for "workers of the world to unite." There are also organizations, such as the International Labor Organization, that seek to bring trade union interests together on the global stage. In practice, however, considerable divisions remain, based around varying combinations of aterritorial and territorial cleavage planes; for trade unions seek to organize people who share a common characteristic as a particular type of worker but who already have a variety of preexisting and durable characteristics and identities based on them. People come to *be* waged workers bearing these attributes and differences as constitutive of their identities. Trade unions seek to unify around people's shared attributes as wage workers but always in circumstances in which they *become* wage workers (bearing the commodity labor-power) differentiated from one another in these other ways. Therefore, short of an (idealized) world in which the workers of the world *have* united, this pattern of divisions will persist. The sorry history of various labor "Internationals" suggests that this is and *will continue to be* the case.

At least in part, these divisions are a consequence of the organizational practices of trade unions. These practices can be critical in weakening the effectiveness of individual unions and reducing the possibilities for cooperation between unions and between unions and other social forces. For example, Vanderbush (1997, 77) argues that the weakening over time of both the union at Volkswagen and UPUA-28 (the street vendors' social movement) in Pueblo, Mexico, resulted from a combination of factors, including local contexts, global developments, and a shift in national political economy. However,

> the organisational practices and decisions within the two workplace associations . . . were important parts of the explanation as well. . . . In particular, we can point to the greater concentration of power at the top of each organization and increasing reliance on more authoritarian mechanisms of control. Strategically, the unwillingness or inability to seek out allies among other groups and classes contributed to their vulnerability.

The idea of a homogeneous and unified working class is therefore greatly at variance with the practices of trade unions and workers. There is competition and division within the structurally defined working class. Moreover, it is not simply a victim of the divisive strategies of capital but rather it *divides itself*. Not least it does so via forming trade unions organized around sectional intraclass interests rather than class interests per se. The process of union organization seeks to unify some workers but simultaneously divides them from others—for example, occupationally, industrially, spatially, by gender and ethnic group (Yates, 1998). Trade unions become the institutional form of such divisions of labor, and their practices and modes of representation of shared interests often help reproduce them. Thus, the structurally defined working class helps fragment itself, in competition over jobs, wages, and working conditions and in ways that intersect with dividing the workforce according to a variety of criteria (see below). Workers are active subjects, not passive objects, in creating such divisions. They are not "cultural dopes" (Giddens, 1979, 71) but knowledgeable actors, with an understanding of the world constituted through the cultures of the places in which they live and work. Even so, they act in circumstances of imperfect and partial knowledge, unable to anticipate all the consequences of their actions. Thus, divisions between workers are actively produced, in part by workers themselves, both intentionally and unintentionally. At the same time, however, these cleavage planes of division are also dimensions of socially constructed collective identities. There is a dialectic of unity and division, and the process of labor seeking to become a class "for itself" is complex and contradictory. Workers attempt to organize themselves to further their own interests, notably through forming trade unions. However, there are inherent limits to these attempts, a result of creating distinctions and divisions between groups of workers that then offer opportunities for companies to exploit.

The existence of trade unions and other institutional forms of organizing wage labor also raises questions about the links between waged and unwaged work, and how these create and relate to social divisions along other cleavage planes, such as that of gender. Shared identities defined in terms such as place, ethnicity, or gender and those generated through social and technical divisions of labor "may act to solidify class formation" but typically do so via creating differences between "us" and "them." Consequently, it is debatable whether this is "solidifying" class formation or engendering intraclass fragmentation. For example, coal miners are "frequently the most class militant of workers, yet this [militancy] has rested in large part on severe isolation from other groups and extreme masculine identity" (Sayer and Walker, 1992, 55). This strongly suggests the ways in which shared occupational and gender identities divide coal mining unions from other sections of the working class while distinct locational identities can divide coal miners from coal miners (Beynon, 1985).

The ways in which spatial difference and territorial identity have been integral to the formation of trade unions and the ways in which workers are united and divided is of particular interest. Indeed, some argue that territorial divisions are unavoidable (Herod, 1997). The historical geography of trade unionism has often had a critical formative effect upon the tactics and strategies of trade unions (Southall, 1988), the legacies of which in many ways are still present. Trade unions typically developed from a plant or local to a national level.[4] Nevertheless, the legacies of intranational territorial division and divisions by industry and occupation have often been persistent and powerful. Even during the Fordist era, with its privileging of the national scale, marked subnational divisions continued to characterize the organizational geography of trade unions. Consequently, there were coexisting national and local variations in labor market regulation and trade union organization. In the United States, for example, "a number of industrial sectors had decentralised systems of negotiation and bargaining and states and localities retained significant powers to regulate the conditions of labour reproduction" (Jonas, 1997, 7). Thus, the power of union "locals" remained considerable (Davis, 1986). Workers developed a sense of group or class solidarity because of the experience of working in Fordized plants, associated with their status as anonymous workers. Many union locals were forged from these conditions (Yates, 1998, 139). This local variability continued in new forms of high-volume production, with spatial variations in forms of lean production and industrial relations, for example (Kim, 1995). In the United Kingdom, trade union structures in industries in which production was carried out on a non-Fordist basis, such as coal and steel, continued to be organized on "regionalized" lines, often with strong overtones of regional chauvinism and intraregional as well as interregional interplant competition (Beynon, 1985; Hudson and Sadler, 1983, 1986).

The legacy of building the national from alliances of originally autonomous local and regional organizations was not easily eradicated. Forms of labor organization, industrial relations, and trade union power are shaped more by political culture and tradition and social and institutional factors than by the imperatives of production (Martin et al., 1994; Sunley, 1990). Such cultures, institutions, and traditions are often strongly territorially based at various spatial scales.[5] For example, Warde (1989) discusses the emergence of factory régimes influenced by a variety of cultural, political, and social institutions and ideologies around which workers organize their daily lives and loyalty systems. Thus, over time each locality develops its own distinctive "politics of production" based around local patterns of production, consumption, and reproduction shaped by noneconomic as well as economic processes.[6] However, there can often be competing loyalties and attachments at different spatial scales. Consequently, there may be contradictions between the daily experience of *work*place and work*place*, as well as between these experiences and attempts to organize workers on a "class" or industry basis across places (Hudson and Sadler, 1983, 1986). Furthermore, once national institutional bases were formed and sedimented in place, they posed problems for attempts to organize labor internationally.

Labor relations are thus explicitly territorial in nature. Industries, trade unions, and labor markets are organized spatially. The question of where the locus of decision-making capacity within them should lie is fundamentally one of at which geographic scale such capabilities are located and exercised. The contested construction of such scales of representation and organization is a further potential cleavage plane dividing workers from other workers.[7] Indeed, workers' strategies do not simply reflect existing differences in spatial scales but help produce, and in some circumstances contest, different scales of organization and regulation (Herod, 1992). Such scales are produced as part of the politics and geography of labor relations. Efforts to (de)centralize decision-making processes are designed to remake labor relations and reflect the changing contexts in which employers, governments, and workers make decisions. Indeed, "geography is crucial to understanding labour relations." While local economies may be booming, national ones may be in recession. While national political conditions may favor employers, local political conditions may be more favorable to workers. "Political relations between local and national union leaderships (or between different unions) may cause each to want different scales of bargaining" (Herod, 1997, 187). Recognizing that there is also an international scale to many such intraunion and interunion disputes further complicates the potential patterns of territorial division that workers help to create between themselves.

Trade union activity is therefore unavoidably place-based and characteristically becomes "place bound" at various spatial scales (Beynon and Hudson, 1993; Wills, 1997, 1998a), whether within formal national union structures or more spatially decentralized ones. The issue is not whether such activity is place-based or place-bounded, but rather the spatial scale of that placing and/or bounding. Relations between trade union organization and the bounding and placing of "scales of organization" are, however, contingent and often contested, as both trade unions and employers may seek to negotiate at differing spatial scales, depending upon variations in labor market and other regulatory conditions. For example, national agreements may set minimum levels below which labor market standards cannot fall, but may also constrain the bargaining position of militant and powerful local or regional-level organizations. Conversely, employers with high labor costs may prefer national agreements. Moreover, there may be important relationships between scales. In the United States, for example, the process through which local unions may form is established by federal (national) labor legislation (Clark, 1988). Equally, the right of individual states to pass antiunion right-to-work laws is enshrined in federal labor legislation, the 1947 Labor-Management Relations (Taft-Hartley) Act. Furthermore, in 1984 the National Labor Relations Board created a precedent by allowing firms to relocate production from unionized to nonunionized workplaces, thereby enabling companies to outsource work to nonunion plants, lowering levels of trade union membership and dividing unionized from nonunionized workers on a workplace basis.

There has been a recent trend toward decentralization of labor relations and associated issues over much of Europe and North America, shifting the focus from central or national trade unions, employers' organizations, and government institutions to regional or local institutions and individual workplaces, even individual workers. This has been expressed in a variety of ways: the breakup of national agreements; making secondary picketing illegal to hinder national solidarity by workers; the transfer of responsibility for labor market regulation to local and/or regional state levels; and the development of collective bargaining arrangements tailored to individual plants, or of contracts customized to individual workers. Workers and their collective trade union representatives are not simply the passive victims of such changes. To varying degrees, willingly and unwillingly, people are active subjects involved in constructing them, albeit for many in circumstances and on terrain that they find unpalatable or not of their choosing (for example, against a labor market background of persistently high unemployment). In contrast, in other parts of the world that have more recently come under the sway of capitalist social relationships, the emphasis is still much more upon building national trade union structures and the national as the spatial scale at which the interests of workers are represented and pursued.

Acknowledging that workers are knowledgeable subjects with their own projects has important implications for the ways in which the production of historical geographies of labor are conceptualized. In particular, "we must think of class formation and class processes as geographical in the first rather than in the last instance. . . . Labour struggles do not simply occur *in* and *over* space. Rather *they actively shape that very space*" (Herod, 1997, 195, original emphasis). Consequently, workers' activities create labor geographies as well labor histories, historical geographies of labor. Clearly, workers have a vested interest in making space in particular ways. They seek via "labour's spatial praxis" to ensure that the landscapes of capitalism are made in ways that reflect their interests and enable them to reproduce themselves as social beings, both on an individual and day-to-day basis and on a longer-term and collective basis. They seek to make "labour's spatial fix," to create landscapes of work, or more precisely wage labor, on terms favorable to workers, in terms of employment rather than unemployment, and of trade union power rather than impotence, for example. The political practices of workers within the social relations of capitalism are thus inextricably spatial. Consequently, they are a recurrent dimension of division among them and, as such, are crucial to understanding the making of geographies of production within capitalism.

An unavoidable corollary of some workers succeeding in making space in ways that reflect *their* interests is that others will fail to do so. Recognizing that at one level capital and labor are engaged in a struggle to shape the landscapes of capitalism in their own interests, Herod (1997, 195) elaborates on this critical point. He cautions that "we should not assume that all workers have a vested interest in making space in the same way simply because they are workers in a particular class relation to capital." Trade union organization is a "messy process," in no small part because of the geographic variability that workers and union officials face in attempting to implement particular strategies. Indeed, this "messiness" may increase further because workers and their trades unions can often be in conflict over strategy and tactics (Beynon, 1985), because workers belong to different unions, and because some workers are resolutely antiunion.

7.3. Unity and Division between Groups of Workers: Dimensions of Simultaneous Unity and Division

In Chapter 2 I briefly discussed Wright's (1989) analyses of class structure and his recognition of the need to produce more finely grained and nuanced views of class than Marx's two-class model to allow for a more delicately etched map of class structures and intraclass differentiation. Thus, within the working class there are numerous dimensions of differentiation that divide workers one from another but at the same time serve as bases for the formation of (multiple) identities, both individual and collective. As such, the working class is open and subject to continuous re-formation as people with very different characteristics (of gender, ethnicity, age, and so on) are constantly brought together as the commodity labor-power. Capitalist social relations of production eradicate the differences between them in the process of creating abstract labor as they perform concrete labor. However, such differences persist within and outside the workplace, as people have identities that extend beyond their designation as labor-power.

The issue therefore is *not* one of subsequent divisions within a preformed working class. Rather, it is that capitalist production brings people as labor-power into the same time/space of capitalist social relationships. It thus classifies (increasingly across the globe) people as wage workers who enter into the wage relation with a variety of characteristics and identities based around territory, gender, ethnicity, age, and so on. People come to share the same class structural position as wage labor in relation to capital (that is, become a class in themselves) but retain these myriad differences that serve to divide them in diverse ways (so that they do not become a class for themselves). Class in this sense is conceptualized as process. It is, however a process of becoming in which commonality of class position only emerges after abstract labor links commodities produced in different locations and conjoins heterogeneous wage workers, and their concrete labors, living in different places. There are inherent tensions in this process between classes becoming "in" and "for" themselves.

Seen in this way, class is not a singularity. Far from being a "closed" domain of social relations, capitalism emerges instead as an *"inherently open system* which through abstract and concrete labour is constantly infused by putative exteriors." Differences of nationality, gender, sexuality, geographical location, and so on are constantly gathered together into the domain of concrete labor and through the abstractions of social labor and labor time "are forcibly articulated into a global system with a structured coherence" (Castree, 1999, 153, original emphasis, drawing on Postone, 1996). This forcible articulation is a contradictory process for workers seek to define and defend their interests on the basis of their "putative exteriors" as well as on the basis of differences internal to capitalist production wrought via social and technical divisions of labor (Sayer, 1995). As a result, there can be bitter conflicts between groups of workers as well as between capital and labor as the working class is torn between the contradictory pressures of homogenization (which sets it against capital) and differentiation (which sets different fractions of it against one another). These "internal" and "external" cleavage planes are discussed in turn.

Industry, Occupation, and Intraclass Differentiation

Workers are divided by industry and occupation. The growth of technical and social divisions of labor, between and within firms and sectors, has helped divide groups of workers from one another and has redefined the anatomy of these divisions.[8] Workers work in different industries and occupations, in different occupations within the same industry, and in the same occupation in different industries. This differentiation within the working class by place in divisions of labor has become more pronounced in the course of capitalist development and remains an ongoing process. One aspect of deepening technical and social divisions of labor is that specialization divides people experientially, organizationally, and ideologically. Workers work on very different terms and conditions, for variable levels of remuneration, and with varying security of employment. As a result, conflict and rupture are endemic to divisions of labor and to the working class. From this perspective, therefore, the notion of a unified working class is seen as a romantic and romanticized myth.

The growing fragmentation of work, within and between places, more or less inevitably leads to intraclass divisions by industry and occupation. This has broader implications for the conceptualization of class, of social structure, and of the defining characteristics of the contemporary capitalist economy. As a result, there are increasingly finely differentiated divisions of labor, and so not everyone has a position in the "traditional" Marxian "class structure." This does not obviate the utility of class theory in uncovering important characteristics of capitalist societies, however (Sayer and Walker, 1992, 17),[9] and indeed Wright (1989) developed a more sophisticated Marxian theory of class that takes its point of departure precisely from this insight. The division of labor in complex production processes has vastly augmented the number of workers engaged in indirectly productive activities (wrongly labeled service labor, according to Sayer and Walker, 1992, 58). Consequently, proportionately fewer workers are employed directly in the tasks of transforming materials into useful products. This represents neither more nor less than a widening and deepening of the social division of labor, part of the more general and long-established process of industrial evolution and capitalist development. New sectors have emerged with new forms of outputs, leading to a deeper and wider social division of labor as layers of intermediate goods have multiplied. The technical division of labor has likewise deepened as production processes within workplaces have become more complex and differentiated. They thus emphasize that the proliferation of so-called service sectors and occupations can be explained in terms of burgeoning social and technical divisions of labor throughout the industrial system. Consequently, "the locus of social labor has shifted over the last century . . . from production to circulation, and from direct to indirect labor, including technical and managerial work" (Sayer and Walker, 1992, 104–106). One indication of this is proliferation of people who work as problem solvers in the realms of ideas, concepts, and symbols in activities such as accountancy, advertising, design, financial and legal services, information and communications technologies, and marketing (Reich, 1991).[10]

Rather than a transition to a "postindustrial" or "service" economy, the proliferation of so-called services signifies the growing development and differentiation of a capitalist industrial economy.[11] For Sayer and Walker (1992, 50, emphasis added), "a labour service works directly on or for the consumer but does not take the form of a discrete product; typical would be theatre productions, manicures and house cleaning. A labour service is normally irreproducible and involves a unique transaction between producer and consumer. This does not mean, however, that labour services are immaterial." While this is not always an easy distinction to make, "the crux of the matter is the *discrete* product and its availability to a *particular* user."[12] As such, much of what is commonly represented as growth of service sector employment falls into one of four categories of "extended labor." Such extended labor is simply work that can be separated in time and space from the core of direct labor: preproduction, auxiliary, postproduction, repair. Circulation is a fundamental complement to production in industrial capitalism and has only a "tangential relation to the idea of a service." Moreover, wholesaling and retailing are mostly akin to postproduction labor, which simply extends production across time and space toward the point of consumption.[13] Furthermore, the growth of subcontract employment can be interpreted as further widening and deepening social and technical divisions of labor as, for employers, specialization secures more efficient and cheaper ways of doing things (Allen and Henry, 1997, 186). This differentiation within and between workforces (within the structurally defined working class) is thus linked to changing forms of corporate organization, in both private and public sectors. At its most basic, different groups of workers sell their labor-power and subsequently perform work on very different terms and conditions, between and within firms and sectors.[14] Consequently, workers are divided from one another in more finely differentiated ways.

This shifting pattern of employment can also be related to theoretical debates about changing class structures within contemporary advanced capitalism. These debates are indicative of significant changes in occupational structures and in the ways in which social structures are represented. They have far-reaching political implications and raise more immediate issues about forms of trade union organization and representation. For example, some see the decline of male manual work as heralding the "death of the working class" (Gorz, 1982). Others contest this view (Byrne, 1985). Other analysts see the working class as being restructured and differently divided, with the emergence of a new lower class composed downwardly mobile members of the (former) working class and new immigrants (Lash and Urry, 1994, 146). In addition, there is a new class fraction made up of the long-term unemployed and those permanently excluded from the wage labor force (Lipietz, 1996). Others see the growth of routine "white-collar" work as in part heralding the rise of a "new" and comparatively well resourced fraction of the working class, in part that of a re-formed middle class (Lipietz, 1996). In contrast, to others such changes are indicative of the emergence of a "new" middle or "service" class (Urry, 1981), of a class of "symbolic analysts" (Reich, 1991), of a "mass class of professional managerials" (Lash and Urry, 1994).

As the variety of terminology and concepts indicates, the "middle classes" have long proved a problem for class theorists. However, the growth of "white-collar" work and the emergence of the "new middle classes," the "modern petit bourgeoisie" (Lipietz, 1996), can be accommodated within a structural analysis of class and the economy. This can be accomplished by incorporating "a more amplified sense of social structuring than class analysis alone provides" (Sayer and Walker, 1992, 27–29).[15] This amplification can be achieved by deploying the concept of division of labor. Indeed, Sayer and Walker argue that, as soon as class theorists try to bring in more subtlety, multidimensionality, and concreteness, they begin incorporating elements of divisions of labor either explicitly or implicitly. They argue that neither Marxian nor Weberian approaches think through the division of labor before juxtaposing it to class. Thus, "the people called white collar or unproductive labour or intermediate or service classes have definite positions in industrial capitalist economies. They fall largely into three broad categories of labour—circulation, consumption and indirect." This suggests a more nuanced version of class that recognizes the overdetermined character of class formation and hints at the complexities of multiple identities. It recognizes that the two-class structure model of Marx is an analytic abstraction rather than a description of the way in which people see their class position. While they overemphasize the significance of division of labor as an autonomous causal process, the general point that they make is nonetheless well founded. Even so, there are those who still regard such a view as oversimplistic and essentialist.

Gibson-Graham (1996, 1997)[16] argues that in economic geographic discourse class is usually defined as a composite structural category denoting a specific relationship to: property ownership; power and control over the labor process; exploitation, the appropriation of surplus labor; and organizational capacity. *Taken together*, these things are seen to confer membership in a social grouping or class. By the term "structural" she denotes that classes and class position are situated within an overarching social structure or system (usually capitalism). Underlying the composite structural class definition is a vision of a unified class subject for whom the essential four relationships line up in a coherent and self-reinforcing way. In situations in which these relationships do not all line up neatly, however, analytical and political problems emerge.[17] Using a composite definition of class forces analysts, in situations where classification is not straightforward, to weight some essential class characteristics more heavily than others. Consequently, "the contradictory interaction of an individual's multiple dimensions of social and economic identity risks being understated or conceptually papered over." Undoubtedly such a risk exists, but it by no means follows that it actually materializes.

Gibson-Graham suggests that the "capital centrism" of most economic discourse has significant class effects because it leads to the privileging of capitalist class relations. Moreover, since the composite categorical definition of class rests upon the notion of a unified class subject, "subjectivity becomes a conduit by which class homogeneity rather than diversity is discursively produced. Capital centrism not only positions the capitalist economy as the principal social and economic identity (as in the term "capitalist society") *but designates the classes of capitalism as the principal form of class subjectivity.*" As an alternative, she proposes that class be defined in terms of "the production, appropriation and distribution of surplus labour" rather than in terms of power or relations of domination (though power is an important overdeterminant of relations of class). As she puts it, class "occurs wherever surplus labour is produced, appropriated or distributed" (Gibson-Graham, 1996, 52). In Gibson-Graham's conception of class "multiple class processes—capitalist, independent commodity, slave, communal, feudal, for example, can co-exist in any society, since none is associated with a systemic totality." Likewise, "class subjectivity is similarly not closed or unified around a particular class process but is structured around a variety of class experiences and positions as well as other relations: for example, of gender, ethnicity, sexuality, age or locale." As a result, "the understanding of any class subject is a theoretical project in which specific relations of power and property and particular experiences of consciousness and capacity must be theorised rather than presumed." Consequently, she argues for an "anti-essentialist" definition of class that allows "the conditions of existence of any class process . . . to assume specific importance in the formation of class societies and subjectivities *without presuming their presence or role.*" Thus, "by divorcing the concept of class from a structural or systemic totality, we are able to challenge the vision of a single axis of class antagonism and to examine the economic landscape with an eye to perceiving the heterogeneity and multiplicity of class relations" (Gibson-Graham, 1997, 91–92, emphasis added).

One way of reading this is that a capitalist society requires capitalist class relations but that in such a society other forms of class relations may be present, along with a multiplicity of nonclass relations. However, this is hardly a radical break in terms of conceptualizing class relations and the class structures of capitalist societies. From Marx onward, there has been recognition that capitalist societies encompass a variety of class relations and important social relationships that are related to but cannot be reduced to those of class. It is therefore one thing to define capitalist class generically as one of several processes through which surplus labor is extracted and redistributed. It is something else altogether to detail the *specificity* of surplus labor extraction and its redistribution in capitalist form This requires "careful and discriminating conceptual analysis of the kind Gibson-Graham seems unwilling to deliver" (Castree, 1999). Such analysis of linkages between capitalist and noncapitalist class relations is central to the meaning of combined and uneven development. Analyses of social formations and articulation of modes of production have long centered on precisely these points.[18] On the other hand, not to recognize that a capitalist society *is* capitalist precisely because of the dominance of the capitalist mode of production, and the class relations around which it is constructed, is profoundly unhelpful theoretically and disabling politically. Indeed, such complexity must not only be "theorised rather than presumed" but must be empirically investigated in a sophisticated and theoretically informed manner (Beynon, 1984). The strength of analyses such as those of Sayer and Walker and Wright is that they recognize the centrality of capitalist class relations in capitalist societies (were they not central, then society would need to be characterized in different terms) without denying that other forms of class (and nonclass) relations may be critical in some times, places, and circumstances. At the same time, they acknowledge that the very trajectory of capitalist development, with deepening and widening divisions of labor, has led to a more complicated and dynamic classification than the dichotomy of capital and labor allows or can accommodate. Equally, to recognize that people may have multiple rather than singular identities and that the formation of class subjectivities and identities is a complex process that cannot simply be read-off from objective class position (however finely differentiated) is hardly novel; were it not so, then presumably the history of trade unionism, socialist politics, and capital-versus-labor conflict would have been a very different one.

Divided by Gender

Gender constitutes a second key dimension of division within the working class (and indeed other classes). Gender divisions of waged and unwaged work are discussed below, and attention in this section is confined to gender differences in types of wage work and occupations. While patriarchal social structures predated capitalism, capital both exploited and reshaped these structures and helped underpin the marginalized and subordinate role of women in labor markets (Hartmann, 1978). Even so, there is a recognition that men and women supply their labor on different terms, with implications for gender divisions between industries and occupations. Many industries and occupations are stereotypically seen as male, others as female. Consequently, occupational, industrial, and gender divisions can become powerfully intertwined. Sometimes such differentiation results from regulatory limitations (for example, prohibiting the employment of women as underground coal miners in the United Kingdom). There are certainly industries and occupations in which the physical nature of work makes it more suitable for men than women, and vice versa. Growing emphasis on mental rather than manual work, and increasing mechanization and automation of much formerly strenuous manual work, have reduced the areas in which differences in physical strength and stamina are a legitimate cause of differentiation between men and women in the allocation of work. That said, it is important not to overemphasize the extent to which physically strenuous work has disappeared as a corollary of new methods of production.[19]

Some occupations were and are preserved by men for men by more subtle means. McDowell (1997, 122–123), for example, refers to the "old" City of London as "a set of class-based masculinist institutions . . . an elitist and masculinist environment [in which] an extreme gendered division of labour separated men from women." Even so, there are more complex processes involved than simply those of constructing male and female divisions, for the changing culture of work in the City also involves a struggle between different forms of masculinity. As the "new" working practices of the City challenged the "old," and a faster, more overtly aggressive, and open style of working emerged that was clearly different from the older, slower, and rather more staid and collusive ways of work of "gentlemanly capitalism," two rather different groups emerged that drew much of their cultural identity from contrasting versions of "entrepreneurial masculinity." The first of these was anchored in a set of meanings around paternalism and "gentlemanly" conduct, while the second was locked into a more macho, aggressive masculinity (McDowell and Court, 1994a, 1994b).

There have long been claims—without any solid foundation—that some jobs are naturally "women's work." For example, in the advanced capitalist world there have been numerous claims that women are disproportionately concentrated in certain industries and occupations because particular jobs need "nimble fingers" (such as sewing, assembly of electronic components, or secretarial work). In the clothing industry, for example, men often did the cutting while women did the sewing, although men could equally as well have sewed and women cut. Moreover, when men and women are employed within the mass production plants of industries such as automobiles, women tend to work in specific occupations and areas of the plant "off the line," usually on the basis of gender stereotypes about female capabilities and skills (Yates, 1998, 142). In other cases there is a disproportionate concentration of women because they are supposedly inherently suited to certain sorts of service sector jobs involving personal care (as in health or social work, or as domestic servants or nannies; Gregson and Lowe, 1994) or selling in shops or other retail establishments (Townsend et al., 1995; Walsh, 1990). One of the goals of restructuring the retail banking sector in the United Kingdom in the 1980s was to increase the "openness" of bank branches. "This cultural shift has clearly gendered concomitants highlighting the 'feminine' qualities of accessibility in place of the distant authoritarian image associated with the male bank manager." Consequently, Sellbank tried to put women in visible positions in the bank to encourage people to come into the banking hall and increase sales of new services (Halford and Savage, 1997, 114). Indeed, there is a preference for physically attractive young women employees in these positions.[20]

In fact, such gender divisions of wage labor reflect dominant patriarchal views as to male and female roles, and the power and authority structures prevalent in particular times and places. They are socially specific and socially produced rather than "natural" divisions of labor. Trade unions, often dominated by male leaderships, have on occasion helped legitimate such views as to a natural division between male and female jobs. As both a cause and a consequence of being classified as "women's work," such jobs are typically defined as "unskilled" and as requiring little skill: "jobs are regarded as unskilled because they are feminised, not feminised because they are unskilled" (Craig et al., 1982, 77). In turn, the predominance in particular occupations of women workers who have been ascribed a low social status also devalues the skill and social status of the jobs they do. They are poorly paid as a consequence. Much of the selective industrialization of parts of the Third World has focused upon sectors and activities in search of cheap, malleable female labor (Elson and Pearson, 1981; Eraydin and Erendil, 1999; Fröbel et al., 1980; Mitter, 1986; Ong, 1987). In extreme but by no means rare cases girls and young women provide such labor as age and gender combine to their disadvantage. For example, twelve-year-old rural-born girls work as sewing machinists in Bangkok, sewing seven days a week from 8:00 A.M. to 11:00 P.M. and sleeping eight to a room (Phizacklea, 1990, 44–46). Over 90% of people employed in export processing zones are women (International Labor Organization, 1998). Within the labor markets of the First World, gender often combines with ethnicity doubly to disadvantage women in the labor market. For example, electronics companies in Silicon Valley made growing use of immigrant female labor within increasingly segmented labor markets (Saxenian, 1984). Within the United Kingdom, West Indian women are disproportionately concentrated in occupations such as cleaning and catering within the public health services (Hudson and Williams, 1995).

Such gender divisions of labor are not immutably fixed, however. They are socially (re)constructed. They can be—and have been—contested and challenged. Allen and colleagues (1998, 101) describe the way in which, as men have entered contract cleaning—a "traditionally" female occupation—within the United Kingdom, a sexual division of labor is being "*invented*," replete with skills that accrue largely to men rather than women. For example, certain tasks associated with the use of cleaning and other large machines are increasingly allocated to men. Conversely, as social skills have increasingly been emphasized in occupations such as security guards, with an aggressive and physical masculinity replaced by the construction of a more interactive, responsive, and alert masculinity, there is "less that defines women *out* of security work" (Allen et al., 1998, 104). Indeed, increasingly it is only the "long hours" that may create problems for women seeking to juggle the responsibilities of waged and unwaged domestic labor that exclude them from such work. Male workers formerly employed in mass production industries are not constrained in this way and so tend to fill such jobs.

Divided by Ethnicity

Ethnicity is the third main dimension along which intraclass divisions are structured. Ethnicity, especially when it involves different skin color, has often been a powerful dimension of division within the working class, with ethnic difference transformed into racist discriminatory practices in the labor market and workplaces. In its extreme forms, this was institutionalized by the national state, as in the South African apartheid system. While now typically formally illegal in the countries of the advanced capitalist world, ethnic and racial discrimination in the labor market (and elsewhere) certainly continues to be a powerful dimension of division in determining who gets what sorts of jobs. While ethnic divisions within workforces and in the allocation of people to jobs remain widespread, the precise dimensions of ethnic segregation vary between places and spatially demarcated labor markets.

There are often strong ethnic divisions in labor markets linked to migration histories, both of permanent migrants and temporary migrant workers, perhaps most markedly when they involve temporary migrant workers who lack citizenship rights (all the more so, when they are illegal migrants; Brunettta and Ceci, 1998; Pugliese, 1991). Indeed, in some circumstances state regulation may help reproduce rather than restrict illegal working by migrants and help maintain a marginalized fraction of the labor force compelled to work for low wages outside of the employment protection and social insurance and welfare provisions of the state. As a result, those involved are in a very insecure position in the labor market (Cochrane and Jonas, 1999, 157–158). There have been strong links between migration and ethnic divisions in labor markets linked to the legacies of colonial and imperial histories (Yates, 1998). For example, in former colonial countries such as Australia, Canada, and the United States, a history of immigration from the late nineteenth century led to ethnically diverse workforces and the institutionalization of ethnic differences via labor market practices of skill recognition, types of employment, and pay.

Following the end of the Second World War, ethnic labor market segmentation deepened and ethnic division often intertwined with gender divisions as women and people of color in the workforce grew in number (Edwards, 1979; Gordon et al., 1982). In many instances ethnic and racial groups were concentrated in particular jobs and physical areas of workplaces—the least desirable jobs and working places. For example, in the contemporary California labor market Mexican and other Latino immigrants are heavily concentrated in seasonal agricultural jobs such as fruit picking and in the clothing sweatshops of Los Angeles. Chinese immigrants, many of them children working illegally, work in the totally unregulated clothing sweatshops of New York, 12 hours a day for less than $2 per hour in very poor working environments (Harvey, 1996, 287).[21] These divides were often perpetuated by kinship and managerial strategies that encouraged the development of ethnic and racial cleavages. Moreover, to a degree such divisions were reproduced via workers' actions and trade union practices. Sometimes these took on a perverse character. For example, during the nineteenth century in the United States there were numerous cases of white coal miners striking against the hiring of black miners (Corbin, 1981). For many years automobile unions in Australia, Canada, and the United States used a paternalistic strategy that looked after ethnic minority workers but failed to include them in the union. In the U.S. automobile industry, cooption became the dominant union strategy for addressing questions of organization and representation (Yates, 1998, 122–123).

There are also strong ethnic divisions in former centers of empire, one legacy of their imperial heritage. During the 1950s, for example, there was an influx of West Indian immigrants to work in public services, filling jobs such as hospital porters and cleaners, and working on public transport as cleaners, ticket collectors, and drivers within the United Kingdom. They continue to be overrepresented in such occupations but are almost entirely absent from senior managerial positions. There are continuing ethnic divisions within labor forces across a range of other sectors. In automobile manufacturing, for example, there are very few black workers in well-paid manual jobs in the Ford Motor Company despite the fact that they constitute some 40% of its U.K. workforce. Such black people are also virtually absent from managerial positions (Hudson and Williams, 1995, 182–192). In private sector services, Halford and Savage (1997, 115) argue that Sellbank employs very few Asian workers, and even fewer Afro-Caribbean staff, especially in "front office" positions. Ethnic divisions in the labor market are particularly sharp in the City of London. The vast majority of middle- and upper-tier managerial posts are held by white (male) Anglo-Saxons. Members of ethnic minorities occupy only a tiny fraction of such jobs. In contrast, at the other end of the City's labor markets, there is a bewildering array of ethnic groups—black British and New Commonwealth migrants, migrants from Mediterranean origins such as Portugal and Spain, as well as more distant locations such as Colombia and the Philippines. The presence of these groups at the bottom end of such labor markets primarily reflects their ethnic grouping rather than their inherent potential or skills.

As well as this major white/nonwhite cleavage plane, marginalized ethnic groups also occupy distinctive labor market niches. Differences in the characteristics of ethnic groups, such as qualifications, occupational predispositions, the extent and form of their involvement in informal ethnic networks, and other endowments, as well as the extent of discrimination, combine to channel groups into particular occupations (Cross and Waldinger, 1993). Furthermore, within particular occupations, a combination of these processes and managerial selection practices leads to different ethnic groups dominating particular workplaces. For example, in contract cleaning, "particular sites tend to have a disproportionate number of one ethnic grouping. In a real sense, an ethnic division of labour within cleaning work has sprung up in central London" (Allen et al., 1998, 106). Similar processes are observable in other global cities and major metropolitan areas (Sassen, 1991). Again, trade unions have until recently often been implicated in reproducing ethnic divisions within labor markets. Within the United Kingdom, for instance, workers from ethnic minorities tended to support trade unions and to be more heavily unionized than their white counterparts, but unions characteristically failed to address their needs or support the causes they espoused. It was not until the 1980s, after a number of hard-fought and highly publicized disputes, that the situation began to be redressed, in part because black people rose to prominence in some unions. For example, Bill Morris became General Secretary of the Transport and General Workers Union (Hudson and Williams, 1995, 190–191).

Deep ethnic divides are also much in evidence elsewhere in the European Union. For example, there are deep ethnic divisions within the German labor market. In some respects, they closely parallel those in the United Kingdom but in other respects are significantly different. Whereas most ethnic minorities in the United Kingdom are U.K. citizens, in Germany most are temporary migrant workers without citizenship status and employed on specific fixed-term contracts. This group of gastarbeiter ("guest workers") grew particularly sharply during the 1960s—to over 10% of the German labor force—becoming structurally embedded in occupations that ethnic Germans were reluctant to fill. Southern European and north African gastarbeiter are heavily concentrated in "dirty" jobs in the coke works and steelworks, in spot-welding, in foundries and paint shops in auto plants, and in low-level service jobs.[22] This process of occupational segregation strongly resembles the way in which blacks in the United States and new immigrants in Australia were also assigned to work in the least desirable and most hazardous jobs (Yates, 1998, 122). In addition, however, immigrant workers are pushed into unskilled and undesirable jobs because they have largely been excluded from the apprenticeships that are the entry route to skilled jobs in manufacturing. In Italy, a source of many migrant workers for Germany and other northwest European countries, foreign workers are heavily concentrated in agriculture, construction, and household services, for example (Brunetta and Ceci, 1998).

Not all ethnic divisions in labor markets are of such recent origin, however. Others have a longer history, although again often linked into migration histories. For example, Storper (1993, 443) describes the division of labor in the haute couture clothing industry of Paris. This is a long-established and "classic" system of subcontract cutting and sewing, in which ethnic solidarity characterizes each level of the system: design houses and better boutiques (French); cutters (Middle Eastern or Jewish); sewers (Turkish, north African); and knock-off (degriffe) outlets (Middle Eastern or Jewish). The structure of the labor market revolves around ethnic selection. Allocation of places in the technical division of labor is based on ethnic identities. Furthermore, in some circumstances ethnic divisions can generate deeply exploitative relationships *within* ethnic minority groups. In the United States, for example, several isolated ethnic communities (lacking language access to mainstream society, legal status, civil rights, and social integration) provide "docile bodies for the innumerable sweatshops [for example in New York and Los Angeles] run by the same ethnically distinct capitalist class." Community solidarities promoted by that class, strongly supported by ideologies of religious and ethnic solidarity, are an "assured vehicle for capital accumulation founded on the worst forms of exploitation" (Harvey, 1996, 312).

In summary, there is a strong dimension of ethnic division within the working class, with ethnic minorities in general occupying the lowest echelons of the labor market, especially if they are visibly different from majority social groups. The particular character of the process of allocating positions within social and technical divisions of labor depends, however, upon interactions between general processes of ethnic segregation and the specificities of local labor markets, their particular cultures and institutional forms, and the ways in which ethnic difference is translated into racial discrimination and exclusion in different places. The character and consequences of ethnic segregation in the labor markets of Birmingham, England, Birmingham, Alabama, and Birmingham, Michigan, display significant variations (Peck, 1995, 266–267).

Divided by Security and Precariousness of Employment

A further dimension of division between workers revolves around the degree of certainty or precariousness of their employment. Initially in the mid-1980s, drawing on earlier distinctions between core primary and peripheral secondary sector companies, labor market segmentation was conceptualized as a simple "core–periphery" dualism within large companies (Atkinson, 1984; Mayer, 1992). A contrast was drawn between workers with permanent, privileged, usually full-time "core" jobs "for life" and those in marginalized, precarious, usually casual or part-time "peripheral" jobs or "training" positions (see Figure 7.1). For the former group, the dominant form of flexibility was functional, linked with ideas of multiskilling or multitasking, whereas for the latter group flexibility was predominantly experienced as numerical, as individuals moved in and out of work depending upon the fluctuating level of demand for labor. Increasingly, though, it was recognized that patterns and processes of labor market segmentation, and indeed divisions of labor within companies, and the processes whereby particular types of people get particular types of jobs, was much more complex than the core-periphery dichotomy suggests. Capital deploys "divide-and-rule" strategies and uses segmentation to contain the contradictions of de-skilling and homogenization of workforces (Peck, 1994, 149). Thus, "considerable labour flexibility segments and deeply divides the labour market," with the costs of flexibility to employees experienced as burdens and risks that fall disproportionately on particular groups. For example, in Italy as over much of the advanced capitalist world, they have fallen heavily upon younger workers (Garonna, 1998, 231–233).

To a degree, however, the definition of "core" and "peripheral" depends upon subjective definitions by workers themselves, a way of creating differentiation and hierarchy within workforces, while trade unions

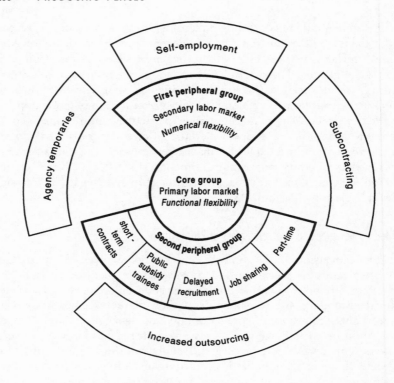

FIGURE 7.1. Flexible firm and flexible forms of employment.

seek to secure the "best" jobs for their members. Workers cannot be mal-
leably molded by capital, since they consciously reflect upon their own
activities and positions. Echoing the ways in which "skilled" workers
were often insistent on maintaining wage differentials between themselves
and "unskilled" workers, "core" workers may—and often do—consciously differentiate themselves from "peripheral," part-time, and casual
workers. This process can be particularly acute in (increasingly frequent)
situations of subcontracting. Furthermore, Standing (1989) argues that
there has been a close link between the increasingly individualistic
reregulation of labor and the growth of "contractualization" of employment, with a growing number of people employed on different contractual conditions in relation to hours, benefits, and entitlements. In their
analysis of the growth of subcontracting in segments of the service sector,
Allen and Henry (1997, 189, original emphasis) argue that it is not un-
common for a social distance to open up between the client's workforce
and the subcontract workforce. The contract relationship gives the cli-

ent's workforce "the power to define itself as central and others as marginal or subordinate to its activities." For many contract workers, this relationship defines a clear separation from those who work around them and a "real distance" from those who employ them. The nature of routine service work signifies a subordinate status, "but it becomes reified when it becomes *contract* cleaning, *contract* catering and *contract* security." If the same functions were performed "in-house," the cleaners, kitchen porters, waiters, and security guards would share the same corporate identity as the rest of the firm's workforce and thus very likely the same employment rights and benefits.

During the 1980s, labor market and workforce "flexibility" was increasingly emphasized as a means to achieving corporate competitive success across the entire spectrum of the formal capitalist economy. As noted above, such flexibility could take various forms. Subcontracting was and is a central element of the growth of "flexibility." While such "flexibility" was seen as new, in many ways it represented a return to practices that had first helped define the introduction of new ways of work as industrial capitalism initially took root in parts of the United Kingdom in the eighteenth century (Thompson, 1969). An integral part of the process was the growth of "flexibility" via homeworking and outworking subcontracting systems (and such forms of work organization remain prevalent in some industries and places; see below). Associated with the recent increase in "flexibility," there has been growing individualization of contracts and working conditions in much of the advanced capitalist world. From the perspective of labor, in significant respects this represents a regression to conditions prior to the rise of trade unionism, with important implications for the collective organization of labor and union practices as well as the terms and conditions of work of individual workers.[23] For individual workers, flexibility is likely to mean continuous entries into and exits from peripheral segments of labor markets and lack of bargaining power over the terms and conditions of such employment. Moreover, while "flexibility" is the language of the employer, "risk" is the language of the employee (Allen and Henry, 1997, 183), as this becomes one specific labor market manifestation of the wider transition to a "risk society" (Beck, 1992).

Beck (1992) argues that the norm of the "Fordist" era of lifelong full-time work (at least for white men in the core countries of capitalism) has become "de-standardised." The essential characteristic of employment over much of the advanced capitalist world in the postwar period, namely, standard contracts covered by collective bargaining, has begun to shatter.[24] It is, allegedly, becoming replaced by a new employment régime based upon less secure and individualized contracts, geographical dispersal, and organizational fragmentation of the workplace, and greater flexibility both in hours worked and length of employment. The reworking of work has involved a reregulation of labor along more individualistic lines (Standing, 1989). Consequently, the expansion of this sort of employment has posed major challenges to trade union organization.[25] Nonetheless, there are limits to such forms of employment and practice and contracts, although for many workers in particular sectors and occupations work has indubitably been reworked along these lines of greater "flexibility." Equally, in some industries and occupations these forms of employment contract and relationships have been well established for a considerable period of time.

Furthermore, there are clear relationships between ethnic and gender divisions in labor markets and the distribution of jobs within deeply and multiply segmented labor markets. At the risk of some oversimplification, within the advanced capitalist world women and people from ethnic minorities are much more likely to be in marginal, precarious, part-time jobs. Most of these are concentrated within the service sector (the main, or only, recent source of net employment growth there). For example, in retail banks in the United Kingdom in the 1980s, the pattern of demand for labor changed as workforces became increasingly segmented, with use of casual and part-time female clerical staff both in regional service centers and High Street branches (Halford and Savage, 1997, 112). Women are also disproportionately concentrated in part-time and precarious employment in catering, contract cleaning, and hotels (Rees and Fielder, 1992; Walsh, 1990).

The introduction of new forms of production and work organization has undeniably led to more complex patterns of divisions between workers. For example, it has led to divisions on the basis of age, health and physical fitness, degree of commitment to the employer, and shifts worked. Few of these divisions have the enduring structural roots of the primary dimensions of cleavage around class, skill, gender, or race/ethnicity. Nonetheless, they have the capacity to fracture existing solidarities built around workplace and union experience. Moreover, "these secondary cleavages overlay the primary ones, often re-articulating and augmenting expressions of conflict around the dimensions of skill, gender, and race/ethnicity. This multiplication of fissures among workers poses particular challenges to unions" (Yates, 1998, 120). The complexity of these fissures and the resultant challenge to trade unions increases still further once due recognition is given to a further crucial cleavage plane—that of territory.

Divided by Territory

The fifth dimension of division between workers to be considered here is that of territory. Workers are chronically divided on a territorial basis, at varying spatial scales, as a product of the interaction of their collective strategies with those of capital and states. The activities of workers in forming trade unions and the attachments that people form to places in which they live and learn as well as work are important constitutive moments of territorial division (as discussed above in section 7.2.). Processes of class formation are inextricably tied up with processes of territorial identity, as attachments to place and class are worked out at a variety of spatial scales.

There are numerous examples of these processes. For example, supranationally the interests of workers in the core territories of capitalism in the First World are seen as threatened by those in industrializing peripheries of the Third World, with this conflict often expressed through trade disputes and calls for import controls to protect "our" jobs or conflicts over (dis)investment decisions and associated job creation or destruction. Similarly, the interests of workers in the European Union are pitted against those of workers in the United States or Japan. Workers within the Euro-currency zone of the EU and those in the countries of the EU that are not Euro-zone members are engaged in similar processes of competition. National states often encourage nationalistic and often only thinly disguised racist politics as they seek to gain the support of workers in struggles over the location of investment and production via appeals to "the national interest." Companies too have a vested interest in playing off national states and groups of workers on a national basis, as they compete for investment and employment. There are undoubtedly often deep divides between workers in different parts of the world.

However, the international expansion and integration of capitalist social relations does not *necessarily* undermine working-class political organization at lower spatial scales. It may well be that in an international economy "looking for comradeship abroad may be the only possible strategy for fighting successfully at home" (Wills, 1997, 12). Indeed, there are suggestions of a tendency toward the superconcentration and/or "translocalization" of some elements of labor relations (Herod, 1997, 186). There is, for example, growing evidence of cross-national border workers' organizations, of the implementation of internationally imposed labor and workplace standards by entities such as the EU, via the Social Chapter and European Works Council directives, although some of the initial optimism associated with such initiatives is waning (Wills, 1999). There is also evidence of efforts to develop coordinated transnational bargaining strategies and practices in response to globalization and of growth in the international activities of trade unions in helping to reconstruct the union movements of eastern Europe. Despite these efforts to transcend national boundaries, however, workers tend to remain deeply divided from one another at the national scale, in part because of differences in national regulatory and "factory régimes" and terms and conditions of work (Burawoy, 1985). Workers in more affluent parts of the world seek to protect their employment positions, while those on the peripheries of the global economy seek to improve their position.

Below the national scale, there are often strong regional and local divisions within unions, typically grounded in the historical-geographical processes of trade union formation.[26] Over much of the capitalist world these divisions are becoming increasingly linked to campaigns for investment and jobs and the competitive activities of "pro-active" localities and regions engaging in "boosterism" and "place marketing." This emphasizes the ways in which organized labor engages in place-specific interclass alliances in defense or pursuit of jobs. Cox (1997, 178) emphasizes that the rhetoric of cooperation with employers in confronting competition "elsewhere" underlines the "significance of the meaning systems that workers subscribe to and the importance of an independent organizational base for the construction of those meanings." All too often workers have been persuaded by a discourse of globalization, whereas "a deeper understanding of capital, and the pressures and temptations to which firms are subject, might have led to a better bargain for labour." Cox thus points to critical relationships between the material processes of the political economy of capitalism and the cultural and discursive contexts in which these are formed and understood.[27]

The growth of outsourcing has also divided workers territorially from one another in new ways. For example, within systems of mass production in the automobile industry male and female workers tended to be occupationally and spatially segregated within the same plant. The growth of outsourcing as one part of new high-volume production strategies has tended to reinforce and redefine such segregation. It is precisely the off-line jobs that women occupied within mass production plants that are the most susceptible to subcontracting to independent parts suppliers. Many of these suppliers operate in peripheral and marginalized segments of the labor market in which wages are lower and working conditions and health and safety provision are poorer, often associated with the use of more rudimentary production technologies. This both reinforces women's position in peripheral segments of the labor market and reinforces their physical and occupational segregation from men whose work remains within the assembly plants (Yates, 1998, 142).

Finally, there is a very important difference between those who work in specifically designated workplaces (be they factories, offices, or someone else's house) and those who work for a wage in their own home.[28] For homeworkers, their home becomes part of the forces of production and not simply a focal point for the reproduction of labor-power and a place in which to escape from waged work. Homeworkers are spatially divided from other workers in distinctive and significant ways. There has been a resurgence in homeworking, which has become a global phenomenon. In countries such as Bangladesh homeworkers assemble electrical components, roll cigarettes, and make cane furniture (Allen and Wolkowitz, 1987). Often the growth of homeworking is directly linked to the subcontracting and outsourcing strategies of multinational companies. The use of homeworkers (and sweatshops) has become a routine element in their repertoire of tactics to ensure low cost routine production. Much of this work is performed by women, young and old, often outside the boundaries of the formal economy (Portes et al., 1988). In Mediterranean Europe, many farms are very small and incapable of providing an adequate income for those who farm them. As a result, homeworking has expanded rapidly in many such areas, often linked to the growth of subcontracting and outworking in "mature" consumer goods industries, such as clothing and textiles. Furthermore, homeworking in manufacturing is often prominent in urban areas in Mediterranean Europe, involving male as well as female workers (Leontidou, 1993, 64). In countries such as the United Kingdom or United States, women work for a wage in their homes, producing a wide range of commodities: clothing, shoes, windshield wipers, transmission belts, or carrying out tasks such as copyediting books and other publications. In the United Kingdom homeworkers in the clothing industry in the West Midlands had cloth delivered at 8:00 A.M. and the product collected at 6:00 P.M. on the same day by drivers who would pay the women in cash (at an hourly rate of £1.08 in 1984: Phizacklea, 1990, 96–99). Usually the women did not know the name of the contractor for whom they were working. Often homeworkers in the cities of the core capitalist economies are migrant women (with illegal migrants in particularly vulnerable labor market positions, especially if they have dependent children) as labor market conditions from the periphery of global capitalism have been transposed into the cities of the core (Mitter, 1986).

Since homeworkers produce diverse commodities, homework can involve the deployment of a wide range of production technologies, from the very simple using traditional craft skills to those incorporating sophisticated computer technologies. While a global phenomenon, there are, however, marked local differences in the cultural contexts and consequences of homeworking. As a result, homeworking can take on varied connotations, depending upon variations in labor market conditions and the cultures in which homeworkers are embedded. For example, there are significant differences between migrant homeworkers in Los Angeles and those in Miami (Fernandez Kelly and Garcia, 1989). In the former, female (often illegal) immigrants from Mexico resorted to homeworking as a strategy of last resort, given their particularly vulnerable labor market position. In contrast, in Miami Cuban refugees were able to become homeworkers as a way of reconciling cultural and economic pressures. The presence there of a Cuban entrepreneurial class allowed women to work within their own homes and ethnic community, albeit one marked by strong patriarchal organization. One consequence of this is that often middle-class immigrant women to Miami from Cuba and Vietnam would accept menial homeworking jobs in order to preserve the family unit (Portes and Jensen, 1989).

From the point of view of employers, homeworking lowers fixed capital costs, reduces wage costs, and allows intensification of the labor process (especially when homeworkers are illegal migrants; Fernandez Kelly and Martinez, 1989). A corollary of this is that unpaid family labor absorbs a range of functions that might otherwise fall upon the state. While there has been much discussion of the emergence of new electronic cottages and enriching forms of homework (Toffler, 1981), very little of the recent expansion of homeworking can be described in these terms, although there are undeniably a few professionals for whom homeworking is advantageous and desirable. In general, however, homeworkers are confined to their homes for a variety of reasons—by domestic responsibilities, to evade taxation, to avoid employment or health and safety at work legislation, because of their status as illegal migrants or because they are illegal child workers. In short, homework tends to inhabit the shadowy margins of the formal economy, and as a result homeworkers are isolated and divided both from one another and from other workers.

Unity and Division across Different Forms of Production and Work

Capitalist societies are constituted under the dominant sway of capitalist relations of production, but there is a much greater variety of social relationships than simply the class relations of capitalism woven through them. Noncapitalist class relations may continue to have an important influence, even if only in relict form. More generally, capitalist societies depend upon a complicated interplay between the class relations of capitalism and a variety of nonclass relationships. It is important to appreciate these relations between different forms of production and work within capitalist societies. They encompass links between various forms of waged and unwaged work and between different nonwage forms of labor and production to those of wage labor and the production of surplus-value. It is salutary to recall that coal miners, perhaps most commonly seen as the archetypical proletarians, typically engaged in a variety of forms of self-provisioning via production of a proportion of their foodstuffs (Beynon and Austrin, 1993; Corbin, 1981). These varied relationships are set out schematically in Figure 7.2.

Consider first of all paid work or employment. Perhaps the most fundamental division is between work that is legal and work that is illegal (acknowledging that the boundary between legality and illegality varies with cultures of governance and regulatory structures). Often illegal work is performed by illegal workers—such as illegal migrants or children below the minimum age of legal labor market participation. Estimating the numbers of illegal child laborers is by definition problematic. The International Labor Organization estimates that there are "hundreds of millions" of child workers, though 90% of them work in agriculture and linked activities in rural areas, and most work within the family rather than for outside employers as wage laborers. Even so, there is substantial evidence that, in many cases, young children are employed in industrial production, both within factories and as outworkers, making commodities such as clothing, footwear, toys, sporting goods, and artificial flowers. Furthermore, "their wages are a pittance and their working conditions often abysmal" (Dicken, 1998, 464).[29] In China, for example, children employed making toys often work between 12 and 16 hours a day for less than 10 pence (14¢ U.S.) per hour, and in El Salvador children making clothes are paid even less (Brooks, 1999).

While the extent of illegal employment is difficult to estimate empirically, the conceptual distinction is fundamental. Within the legal sector of employment and work there is a significant division between formal and informal sector employment and so important links between different types of wage labor in the formal and informal sectors. The informal economy denotes those income-generating activities that lie beyond state

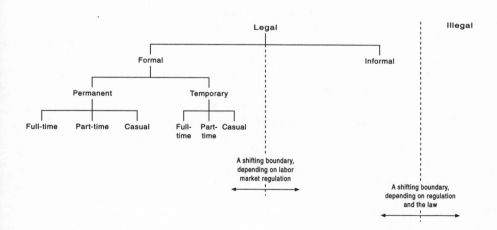

FIGURE 7.2. A typology of terms of employment and work.

regulation in contexts in which similar activities are state-regulated (Roberts, 1994; Williams and Windebank, 1998). Such activities are not illegal per se but are performed in settings beyond "normal" (for that time and place) state regulation; thus, the boundary between formal and informal is flexible rather than fixed. Hadjimichalis (1998) suggests that the relationship between the formal and informal is perhaps most appropriately thought of as a continuum between two poles rather than distinct dichotomous categories. The informal sector provides waged employment but on very different terms and conditions than the formal sector. As Brunetta and Ceci (1998, 280) put it, "Underground labour [results from] a desire to reduce business costs." The sort of work that is—and indeed can be—done "informally" is clearly limited to relatively simple tasks that do not require complex production technologies. Such tasks include agricultural harvesting, relatively simple manufacturing tasks performed by homeworkers (discussed above), retail selling, shoe shining, and manual labor on construction sites (Mingione, 1985, 1995). Such informal activities are often concentrated in urban areas, although in some parts of the world—for example, over much of Mediterranean Europe—informal activities in manufacturing are concentrated in rural areas (Leontidou, 1993, 44).

In addition to some women working for a wage as homeworkers, the vast majority of women perform unpaid domestic labor in the home (Mackenzie and Rose, 1983). Salleh (1994, 110) asserts that "a housewife in the 'developed' world often puts in at least 70 unsalaried hours a week," so that housework can be estimated to be equivalent to 35–40% of GNP. While the estimates are open to dispute, there can be no doubt about the significance of the boundaries and links between unpaid domestic labor and wage labor and the formal economy. They clearly relate to gender divisions of labor,[30] domestic labor and the reproduction of labor-power, and the role of the state in taking on responsibilities for the reproduction of labor-power. The distribution of such responsibilities is contested and variable, the boundaries between family, market, and state varying with regulatory régime. For example, welfare service functions offloaded to the market in liberal régimes and to the state in social-democratic régimes are carried out in the family in corporatist régimes (Lash and Urry, 1994, 181). Labor market structures do not simply reflect the interests of capital. As arenas of struggle, compromise, and accommodation, they also bear the imprint of supply-side influences. In addition to modes of collective action in the workplace, the organization of domestic labor and the role of the family both exert an influence upon supply-side structure.

There are three specific roles for the family in the reproduction of labor-power (Garnsey et al., 1985). First, along with the formal education system and wider community structures, it socializes and educates the young. This is particularly significant, for it shapes the expectations that individuals come to have of the world of work via processes of occupational socialization (Willis, 1977). Second, it provides care and support for other workers in the labor market as well as for other dependents (such as the sick or the old). Who is allocated these domestic responsibilities—women or men—is a critical issue in this context. Socially constructed gender divisions of labor built around notions of men working for a wage and women undertaking domestic and child-rearing roles have a powerful influence. Third, the sharing of income within the household, allied to dominant ideas of male waged and female unwaged work, impinges on both male and female roles in the labor market, as well as the distinctive functions fulfilled by younger and older workers. A consequence of this is that women are more likely to become trapped in the unstable segments of the labor market, in precarious forms of employment. Thus, "women swell the ranks of the part-time, contract, and seasonal positions, without security, advancement opportunities, or retirement benefits" (Salleh, 1994, 117). Moreover, although certainly strongly conditioned by demand, these supply-side structures are relatively autonomous in relation to the specific nature and requirements of technical and social divisions of labor.[31]

There are examples of successful urban and regional economies—such as that of Emilia–Romagna—that have been represented as "socially inclusive" and egalitarian (Cooke, 1995). Others, however, have put a different interpretation upon the bases of their market success (Hadji-michalis and Papamichos, 1990). In their view, competitive advantage in Emilia–Romagna was grounded in systems of "flexible production" that were heavily dependent upon exploitative systems of both domestic and wage labor, which seriously disadvantaged women. As such, this system was divisive and exclusionary. The social basis for producing in this way began to break down in the 1980s, however, as a direct consequence of the enhanced integration of the regional and global economies. There was an increasing reluctance to accept irregular and "semilegal" employment, for two reasons. First, the cultural values of agrarian society began to be eroded by the lures of modern consumerism. Second, "traditional" family structures were weakened as women increasingly rebelled against their subordinate role both as unwaged and waged laborers. As a result, the basis of competitive success of the Emilian economy began to be undermined because of its advancing integration into a global economy.[32]

The reproduction of labor, and the regulation of the reproduction of labor, is typically heavily "locally embedded" because labor itself—due to the social character of its production and reproduction—is the most place-bound of the factors of production (Beynon and Hudson, 1993). The production and reproduction of labor-power is dependent upon the

supportive effects of certain key social institutions (such as family structures, schools, recreational organizations, and the like) and, as a consequence, requires a substantial degree of stability. The result of this is a
"fabric of distinctive 'communities' and 'cultures' woven into the landscapes of labour" (Storper and Walker, 1983, 7). As the Emilian example
shows, this can become a problem for capital if established systems of reproducing particular types of labor-power in place break down. In recognition of this, capital, often with the express cooperation of national
states, has sought to find ways of turning this "place boundedness" to its
own advantage, playing on the aspirations of individuals and communities to improve their lot. It has done so by extending its search for labor-
power beyond the places in which it produces to other places in which labor supply outstrips demand. The reproduction of labor-power and the
links between waged and unwaged work can thus be related to issues of
international or national labor migration in a variety of time-space contexts.

Migration allows the costs of reproducing labor-power to be displaced to another location within the same country or across international borders. Such a sociospatial displacement of the costs of reproducing labor-power separates the locations of commodity production and
labor-power reproduction (Kearney, 1991, 58–59). National states have
often been involved in regulating migration streams, both within and between national territories (King, 1993). Despite the increasing involvement of the state in issues of reproduction in much of the advanced capitalist world, the family remains a crucial site for the reproduction of labor
there, and in many parts of the world the (extended) family assumes
responsibility for this task virtually unaided. One expression of this is a
predominance of family labor in subsistence agriculture, and even in locations where capitalism has taken a stronger hold such forms of agriculture remain important (for example, over much of Mediterranean Europe; Hadjimichalis, 1987). Areas such as these are often the origin points
of intranational migrants to urban labor markets in which capitalist social relationships are more fully developed and of international migrants
to the predominantly urban and industrial labor markets of the core
countries of the capitalist world. People become wrenched from their
home places and communities and become, for a while, constituted as
commodified placeless labor—and often feel this acutely (Berger and
Möhr, 1975; King et al., 1995).

The links between the formal economy and labor market and the
performance of other sorts of socially necessary but unremunerated work
beyond the realm of the family have recently attracted considerable attention. There has been a growing theoretical and practical concern with
concepts such as those of "intermediate labor markets," "third-sector

economic activities," and the "social economy" within much of the advanced capitalist world as unemployment has risen and, in particular, the numbers of long-term unemployed have reached record levels (Commission of the European Communities, 1996). From the perspective of intermediate labor markets, the critical issue is how to build a bridge between unemployment and formal employment. Emphasis is placed upon institutional innovation and new ways of empowering and re-skilling individuals via a variety of capacity-building and training programs to enable them successfully to compete in the labor market. The emphases within discussions of an emerging "third sector" of socially useful work in the "social economy" are rather different, focusing upon ways in which work that currently remains undone because "normal" effective demand is lacking in the market might be carried out. Such socially useful work could, for instance, be in the field of environmental valorization, enhancing conditions in the local environment by cleaning polluted land, for example (Altvater, 1993; Lipietz, 1992, 1995). It could also involve creation of credit unions or nonmonetized exchange metrics such as Local Exchange Trading Systems (LETS), which challenge the hegemony of conventional currencies as the monetary expression of social power in capitalist societies (Lee, 1996, 1998; Williams, 1996a, 1996b) or involve personal care and service provision beyond that currently provided by the state and markets (Gough, 1979). The emphasis here is upon institutional innovation and creating new ways of facilitating and encouraging the emergence of such forms of service provision. Clearly the extent to which such "third-sector" employment simply displaces existing formal sector employment in similar activities, or forces down wage rates in them, is a critical issue. So too is the extent to which it complements existing unwaged work in families and communities and cuts the costs of reproducing labor-power within the formal sector. Third-sector initiatives are seen as a way of increasing social inclusion, and in that sense narrowing divisions between workers and, more widely, citizens in a given territory. They in part can also be related to strategies to shift to more environmentally sustainable production systems.[33] Nonetheless, such approaches may themselves be problematic, in certain respects reproducing rather than eliminating social and economic inequality within the formal economy and labor market and transposing them into "third-sector" activities (Bowring, 1999).

The emphasis upon encouraging new forms of "intermediate" employment has specifically arisen as a response to perceptions of deepening divisions between the employed and unemployed, the nonemployed and nonemployable, in the core territories of late capitalism. The circumstances under which nonparticipation in the labor market is permitted and sanctioned and the balance between the waged and unwaged fractions of the population are critical political and regulatory issues (Offe and Lenhardt, 1984). Where the line is drawn is therefore historically and geographically contingent, depending upon the balance of social forces in a particular time-place. There was a time when unemployment in core capitalist economies was simply seen as a temporary problem, part of the necessary friction of ongoing adjustment in a full employment economy. Welfare systems focused on the needs of the frictionally unemployed, those too young yet to have reached the labor market or those excluded from the labor market because of age or ill health. Such a view of simply "frictional" unemployment is no longer tenable there, if indeed it ever really was, and in much of the capitalist economy it clearly never has been.

A major division has opened up between the long-term structurally unemployed and those in work, especially those still in full-time permanent core jobs, particularly when the former are concentrated into clearly defined places (because of the collapse of the economic basis of mono-industrial settlements, for example). In many ways, this echoes an earlier distinction and division drawn between the "respectable" working class and the "undeserving poor," confined to the workhouse. Rather than awaiting a return to the formal labor market, the long-term unemployed are often de facto expelled from the economically active population and are more appropriately conceptualized as part of a surplus population—surplus, that is, to any foreseeable labor-power demands from capital or the state. There are nonetheless often formidable pressures articulated through national states to push such people back into employment, in part because of the costs to public expenditure of persistently high unemployment. In addition to fears of fiscal crisis, growing fears of social disorder generated by this disaffected "underclass" (as it is sometimes called; Morris, 1994) concentrated in "dangerous places" (Campbell, 1992) have stimulated numerous state initiatives to devise routes back to the formal labor market. These encompass a variety of individual and community "capacity building" programs to provide steps onto the labor market ladder. Alternatively, such initiatives can be seen to provide socially useful work for such people, recognizing that they will not find employment in the formal economy. This is registered most strongly in the transition from welfare to workfare in national states (Peck, 2000) in which economic policy has taken on a distinctly neoliberal hue.

In summary, then, there are alternative conceptions of such "third-sector" employment initiatives. From one perspective, they can be seen as simply constituting intermediate labor markets that form a bridge back into employment in the formal economy (assuming that such employment exists). The alternative and more radical conception envisages such initiatives differently. From this perspective, they could be seen as building blocks in an alternative social economy that challenges and presents a meaningful alternative to the orthodoxies of the market and formally waged employment. Admittedly, it is currently difficult to conceive of such alternatives doing anything other than exist on the fringes and in the interstices of the mainstream capitalist economy. Nevertheless, they could perform an important role in opening up conceptual and political space in which different conceptions of work (as opposed to employment) and different ways of validating work (instead of market prices) might be explored and through which different economic and moral geographies might be created (Amin et al., 1999; Hudson, 1995d; Lee, 1998). These could explore ideas of a moral economy of collective provision and responsibility rather than those of the distributive relationships of a political economy of profitable production and of the possible geographies that such economies might entail.

7.4. Summary and Conclusions

In summary, workers seek to unite in various ways but in doing so also create divisions on a variety of dimensions that separate their interests from those of other groups of workers, waged and unwaged. In seeking to unify around shared characteristics as wage workers, people cannot avoid the different characteristics and identities they already have and continue to have, which intertwine in complex ways with attempts to create a degree of unity, typically via forming trade unions. Often they experience the effects of these divisions in complex, multiple, and cumulative ways, with important impacts upon their perceptions of their identities. In part intentionally, in part unintentionally, the formation of trade unions has helped create and reproduce divisions around a variety of cleavage planes. These include those between workers in different industries and occupations, between workers of different genders and ethnic groups, and between workers in different places, at a range of spatial scales. While seeking to organize to emphasize commonalities of work experience, labor market location, and identity, stressing commonalities at the same time means defining differences from "others." Such divisions are not simply imposed upon workers by employers, on labor by capital, but also reflect the ways in which workers have come to identify and represent their interests. Thus, there can be a coalescence between capital's wishes to divide labor in certain ways and workers' interests in seeking to unite around certain dimensions of common identity—be they those of occupation, industry, ethnicity, gender, location, or any combination of these.

In addition to waged work, however, capitalist societies incorporate a range of other sorts of work, organized and validated on differing bases to those of production for profit. Exploration of them, especially in the context of permanent unemployment and economic marginalization, could create spaces in which alternatives to the mainstream economic orthodoxies could be explored. While, for the foreseeable future, these would in all probability remain at the margins of the mainstream capitalist economy, they could nonetheless play an important role in demonstrating that there *are* alternatives informed by different moralities, ethics, and values to those of capitalist production. This would be particularly so in circumstances in which concerns for social justice and a more equitable distribution of work and its rewards became conjoined with concerns over environmental justice and ecological sustainability, issues explored in Chapter 9.

7.5. Notes

1. The notion of "othering," was introduced by Said (1979) in his analysis of orientalism but has subsequently come to be applied more widely in the analysis of identities and social divisions. The construction of "others" is a way of differentiating "us" from "them" and at the same time of creating a shared sense of identity.

2. Sometimes, workers compete with other workers by forming alliances (typically territorially based) with employers to defend the interests of "their place." The construction of "place" is discussed in Chapter 8.

3. A theme also explored more fully in Chapter 8.

4. See section 4.2.

5. See section 8.3.

6. These issues are discussed further in Chapter 8.

7. Location can be and often is a powerful dimension of division between groups of workers, at a variety of spatial scales; see "Divided By Territory" and "Unity and Division across Different Forms of Production and Work," both in the next section.

8. See sections 4.4 and 5.3.

9. Sayer and Walker adopt a realist position that attributes causal powers to the division of labor. But "this does not mean that it abolishes or transcends class, race or gender, but rather that it contributes actively to their making and remaking in time and space. . . . The question before us is how to *blend* theories of class, gender and other forms of social domination into an even more powerful alternative vision. This cannot be done unless the division of labour is included in the equation of social power" (Sayer and Walker, 1992, 9, emphasis added). While there is much of merit in their position, an emphasis on intraclass divisions is preferable to one on divisions of labor endowed with causal powers per se.

10. Relationships between knowledge and production are discussed more fully in section 5.6.

11. An issue taken up further in Chapter 10.

12. For a contrary view of the relationships between manufacturing and services, see Lash and Urry (1994).

13. One consequence of this "interpenetration of circulation and production" in a complex social division of labor is that it elides any hard-and-fast distinction between productive and unproductive labor, a well-established bone of contention within Marxian political economy and between Marxists and their critics. In claiming this, though, Sayer and Walker (1992, 84) may be open to the charge that they blur the sharp conceptual edges rather than clarifying the relationships, and boundaries, between productive and unproductive labor.

14. For a discussion of the U.K. case, see Hudson and Williams (1995, Chap. 3).

15. See also Wright (1989, 1997).

16. See also section 2.3.

17. Although this point is well known; for example, see Wright (1977).

18. This is discussed in section 2.3.

19. As section 4.4 makes clear.

20. Recognizing that "attractive" is a cultural construction and as such further discriminates between employees judged as suitable for such positions.

21. For further copious and detailed information on such issues in the clothing industry, see Clean Clothes Campaign at www.cleanclothes.org

22. Following reunification of eastern and western Germany, the pressures resulting from the growth of unemployment have disproportionately fallen upon migrant workers of various ethnic origins. There have been calls for their repatriation, presumably to create employment opportunities for residents of the former East Germany, since the rationale for the presence of gastarbeiter was to fill jobs that West Germans would not take.

23. See section 4.3 and "Organizing and Controlling Work at the Point of Production" in section 4.4.

24. It is important to recall that many jobs never fitted such a description, however.

25. See Chapter 4.

26. Discussed above in section 7.2.

27. Issues that are explored further in Chapter 8.

28. This distinction blurs in the case of those who live in someone else's home as their workplace, for example, domestic servants or nannies (Gregson and Lowe, 1994).

29. Seeking to ameliorate such conditions can provoke charges from governments in countries in the capitalist periphery that pressure groups in core countries use labor standards as a disguised form of protectionism. This protects commercial interests in the core while holding back the periphery's industrial development, arguments that were aired at the World Trade Organization talks in Seattle in 1999.

30. Salleh (1994, 117) argues that "the treatment of women becomes abusive when, in the analysis of capitalism, the complex of distinctively feminine la-

bours is seen as somehow auxiliary and sidelined in favour of a male historically privileged proletariat."

31. As a result, the labor market cannot be self-regulating but must be constituted and governed via, among other things, state involvement; see Chapter 3.

32. Other successful regional economies such as Baden Württemburg depend upon structurally subordinated migrant labor, but these too have encountered limits to continuing success (Herrigel, 1996).

33. A theme taken up in Chapter 9.

8
Production, Place, and Space

8.1. Introduction: Place and Space

Contrary to those who proclaim "the end of geography" (O'Brien, 1992) and argue that location, space, and place no longer matter in the "borderless world" (Ohmae, 1990) of contemporary capitalism, a recurrent theme running through the preceding chapters is that where production occurs is becoming more rather than less important. Differences between places have acquired enhanced significance as processes of time-space compression (Harvey, 1989) have restructured geographies of capitalism. Revolutionary advances in transport, communications, and computing technologies may have eradicated the tyranny of distance, but accelerated time-space compression and the creation of cyberspace has further highlighted the significance of the specificities of places (Mitchell, 1999).

Places are complex entities: they are ensembles of material objects, workers and firms, and systems of social relations embodying distinct cultures and multiple meanings, identities, and practices. They offer a setting in which production can occur and a way of organizing production systems and the circulation of capital. Capital needs workers to be in their places in the social, technical, and spatial divisions of labor. Workers and their dependents need capital to be in *their* places to provide waged labor. National states seek to keep both capital and labor satisfied. Capital, labor, states, and places thus exist in complex relationships. Where production occurs is to a degree amenable to influence by state policies that seek directly to influence corporate decisions. But people in their places make demands for the provision of facilities and services that have no direct bearing upon, or are not materially necessary for, profitable production. The processes of production of places and of social space are thus contested as different social groups seek to shape the geographies and landscapes of capitalism to reflect and further their particular interests.[1] As a result, location has become one of the competitive cleavage planes of capitalist society as places compete for both private and public sector investment.

As Merrifield (1993, 520) observes, "The global capitalist system . . . has to ground itself and be acted out in specific places." Production therefore unavoidably occurs in and through the *work*place of the factory, office, or home, set within the work*places* of cities, regions, and national territories (Peck, 1996). The requirements of production are precisely matched with the characteristics of locations at varying spatial scales. Consequently, geographies of production and spatial divisions of labor have become increasingly complex and sophisticated in response to the ways that capital seeks to use spatial differences. However, capitalist production generates and results in, as well as uses, spatial differentiation. In this chapter I want to reflect more generally upon the necessary spatiality of production, the production of places and spaces, and spatial formations more generally, and consider some of their implications in terms of identities, politics, and state spatial policies.

8.2. Conceptualizing Places within the Spaces and Structures of Capitalism

The conceptualization of place long been a matter of debate within geography.[2] For many years places tended to be seen as bounded and closed territories, perhaps internally homogeneous in respect to some characteristics, perhaps internally differentiated (for instance, by residential segregation within urban areas). There was, however, recognition that boundaries are defined in relation to specific purposes: as such, there are no "essential" places. In recent years, however, there has been a growing and reinvigorated debate as to the most appropriate ways of conceptualizing place and space and the relationships between them within human geography (Johnston et al., 1990; Thrift, 1994a).

Two principles have informed this rethinking of place and space and the relationships between them (Allen et al., 1998, 1–4).[3] First, it presumes a strongly relational approach. Both space and place are seen as constituted out of spatialized social relations—and narratives about them—that not only lay down ever new geographies but also work to reshape social and cultural identities and how they are represented. Production occurs in spaces that are socially produced rather than natural and pre-given. Thus, "processes do not operate *in* but *actively construct* space and time and in doing so define distinctive scales for their development" (Harvey, 1996, 53, original emphasis). Nevertheless, while socially produced, geographical space is manifestly material; it is the physical space of cities, roads, and factories and workplaces (Smith, 1984, 75). Socially produced space can thus be conceptualized as a product of social relationships "stretched out" over space and materialized in various forms.

Second, places only exist in relation to particular criteria. They are not "out there" waiting to be discovered; they are both material and social constructions. The spatiality of the dynamics of capitalism, the mechanisms of growth and decline and their uneven geographies, represent one way of conceptualizing the processes underlying the (re)production of places. This therefore provides a different way of thinking about place and space than those more "traditional" in geography. It provides an approach that reveals a place that is by no means necessarily a "whole," with all the characteristics of coherence which that term implies; nor is this place necessarily a bounded and closed entity. Thinking about a place in terms of stretched-out or "distanciated" (Giddens, 1984) social relationships reveals a complex and unbounded lattice of articulations constructed through and around internal relations of power and inequality. It is a discontinuous lattice, punctured by structured exclusions. Thus, in addition to places being unbounded and perhaps spatially discontinuous, there will also be intraplace variation "because of the uneven nature of the overlay of different [defining] criteria" (Allen et al., 1998, 55–56). Each relational network has its own spatial reach, and the spatial reaches may not be coincident, although they may mutually influence one another. Intraplace heterogeneity and discontinuity imply that, metaphorically, the fabric of places is "torn" or "ragged" (Painter, 1998, 11–24). Conceptualizing places as open, discontinuous, linked in various ways to social relationships "stretched out" over, and defining, space "is a general argument for how we should conceptualise any place" (Allen et al., 1998, 65). As such, the issue is not how and whether to draw lines around places—the regional geographer's traditional preoccupation—but to seek to understand the processes through which places are (re)produced—though this cannot be divorced from questions of how the variable geometry of places is conceptualized. The concept of the "aterritorial place" (Painter, 1998) emphasizes that the diverse elements that constitute places are parts of networks of social relations that are not confined within the place. It therefore challenges the assumption that places have any *necessary* territorial integrity.[4]

Indeed, Allen and colleagues (1998, 143, emphasis added) argue that an adequate understanding of place can "*only*" come through a conception of places as open, discontinuous, relational, and internally diverse. While many places may be now more open, less bounded, and more interconnected than they once were, they have always had these characteristics to some degree, and "maybe those notions of a coherent settled place were always inaccurate. This means that *in principle* the conception of places as bounded and undisturbed is incorrect" (Massey, 1995b, 64, original emphasis).[5] All places are to a degree open (Harvey, 1996, 310). There have always been connections in various ways to a wider world, as places have *never* been entirely closed, especially since the onset of industrial capitalism. However, on average, the frequency, intensity, and spatial reach of such connections have tended to increase as the social relationships of capitalism have become more stretched and redefined spaces in new ways, especially with the intensification of time-space compression in recent years. Nevertheless, the density and geography of linkages can decline as well as increase in particular places—for example, as a result of disinvestment decisions by transnational companies or political decisions to seek a greater degree of closure within a place.

While there is therefore great advantage in conceptualizing places as open, discontinuous, and permeable, to claim that it is the only way is to overstate the case. It is one possible approach but not the only one. In some circumstances conceptualizing places as closed, continuous, and internally homogeneous may offer greater analytic and/or political advantage (a point explored below). The degree to which places are closed, continuous and bounded or open, discontinuous and permeable, is best regarded as a matter to be resolved ex post facto and empirically rather than a priori and theoretically.[6] There may well be a continuum of places, exhibiting varying degrees of openness and closure, continuity and discontinuity, internal homogeneity and heterogeneity. Irrespective of how their geometry is conceptualized, places must not only be defined in terms of their spatial location and attributes but also in terms of their location in time. They must be seen as time-space envelopes (Hudson, 1990). Any settlement of social relations into a spatial form will be temporary. However, some of these settlements last longer than others, forming relative permanences in a world of dynamic and fluid processes. Consequently, adequate understanding can "only" come through conceptualizing places as constructions in space-time. To see them as anything less "is to settle for an inadequate understanding" (Allen et al., 1998, 143).

In the specific context of the production of profits through the production of things, places must be conceptualized in relation to the dynamics of capital accumulation and economic growth. As Harvey (1996, 295) puts it, "Places arise, constituted as fixed capital in the land and configurations of organisations, social relations, institutions etc. on the land." Noncapitalist social relationships may help shape these places—and routinely do (see below)—but capitalist social relationships routinely have a decisive, although not inevitable, shaping influence. Places must therefore be envisioned in the context of capitalist relations of production "stretched out" in various ways over space. Places grow economically as a consequence of their relationship to various "growth mechanisms." Some places do not relate at all to dominant growth mechanism(s) at a particular time, while others relate directly not to processes of growth but to processes of decline

The relationships between the fate of places and mechanisms of growth and decline are most evident where there is only one dominant mechanism, producing a "one industry" place. Although such places are comparatively rare in the historical geographies of capitalism, "mono-industrial" or "single occupational communities" (Dennis et al., 1957).[7] represent an illuminating limit case at one end of a continuum. Even in these particular cases, claims about social homogeneity and bounded closure need to be treated with caution. There was often marked social differentiation within such places, reflected in distinctive intraplace social geographies. Steel towns were marked by social distinction that flowed from the occupational hierarchy within the works, for example (Bell, 1985). Even in the archetypical coal-mining village, social differences translated from the division of labor in the mines into the social geography of the place. "Office Street," the housing for mine managers, typically contained houses that were larger than those in the terraces for the miners, often with individual gardens and adjacent to the colliery. The coal owner typically lived in a large residence beyond, or on the fringes of, the colliery village. Moreover such places were only ever *relatively* closed. There were ongoing and continued links with the wider world via trade and migration.[8]

If more than one growth mechanism intersect in a place, the result is a more complex economy and place. Such places of multiply intersecting growth mechanisms can be thought of as "hot spots" within a particular phase of accumulation and growth. Processes of (re)production are more complex in places that are caught up in a maelstrom of several strands of growth mechanisms, especially when these became cumulative over a long period of time. Different growth mechanisms might, where their distributions overlap, produce emergent, interactive, and cumulative effects at certain scales, further increasing the virtuous circle of growth (Allen et al., 1998, 50). Such places are characterized by much greater complexity, and this can arise in several ways. In part, it relates directly to the more varied character of capitalist economies within bigger and more complicated urban environments. Such environments are characterized by greater differentiation of the social relationships of capitalism, a wider range of industries and occupations, and more finely grained divisions of labor, with a larger range of occupations in technical and social divisions of labor. Moreover, such metropolitan and major urban environments are the recipients of more varied and recurrent but changing flows of immigrants. This is associated with more differentiated patterns of intraurban residential geographies and sociospatial divisions (Hamnett, 1994).

Greater complexity can also arise because of the incorporation of precapitalist legacies, both in the built environment and social relationships (Massey and Catalano, 1978). In many places the built environment predates the rise of industrial capitalism, and the relict and residual forms of precapitalist social relationships are still evident in the contemporary built environment and socioeconomic patterning. For instance, in the early phases of capitalist development, the new production spaces in areas such as northeast England, south Wales, Lorraine and the Nord in France, and the Ruhrgebiet in Germany did not simply obliterate those of the preceding era. Capitalist industrialization entailed not simply the creation of previously nonexistent new places but also the insertion of capitalist relations of production into existing places.[9] In such places the issue was and is more one of adopting and adapting existing built forms and socioeconomic relationships as capitalist social relationships became dominant. The built form of many European cities and towns continues to show strong continuities with their precapitalist pasts as well as the footprint of earlier phases of capitalist development.[10] The new forms of economic activity were, to a degree, absorbed into, contained within, and entwined with the places and built forms of that precapitalist era.

Furthermore, contemporary nonclass social relations can significantly impact on the structuring of places and their patterns of internal sociospatial differentiation. Ethnic and gender divisions, while they may be related to those of class, are not reducible to them (Massey, 1992) and can have relatively autonomous effects in shaping places. So, too, can a variety of different groups within civil society. To some extent, therefore, pre- and/or noncapitalist social relations continue to underlie the formation of the built environment and the character of places. As a consequence of these cumulative, interactive, and emergent effects, such complex places are different in principle to simpler monoindustrial places.[11]

The complexity of processes of place (re)production is amplified when mechanisms of decline and growth overlap in a specific time-place. In practice, this is perhaps the most common occurrence, given the fluidity and unpredictability of the accumulation and circulation of capital. The growing complexity of places reflected the fact that, as capitalist production developed, it increasingly widened the choices open to companies in terms of their (dis)investment decisions. As a result, different forms of organization and geographies of production relate to one another and to the character of places to create a complex sociospatial mosaic of ever evolving spatial divisions of labor, helping reshape places and their links to a wider world. As such, patterns of connections between places have changed. The changing mix of flows through a place can have important implications for its fate, for, as the social spaces of production are re-shaped, the opportunities and threats that this poses for particular places change. New opportunities may be created, but existing places can be endangered, threatened by crisis (see Hudson, 1988, 1989b).[12]

On the other hand, the character of capitalist development at the same time seems to offer a degree of certainty and security to at least some places, for, while the development of the forces of production has apparently led to capital becoming more emancipated from the constraints of distance (and nature),[13] the social production of space and places has imposed growing constraints on the location of production. After all, capitalist production encapsulates contradictory processes, expressed in tensions between place and space: "it takes a specific organization of space to try and annihilate space, and it takes capital a long turnover time to facilitate the more rapid turnover of the rest" (Harvey, 1996, 246). Both private sector companies and national states have had to invest to create the material preconditions for places. Capital fixed in various built forms cannot simply be moved from one place to another. Nor can it be prematurely devalorized without endangering capitalist interests. Once produced, such built environments constrain the locational choices of capital. In this sense, they produce a certain inertia, a limit on the pace at which places can be changed. They can also provide a material basis in place around which the interests of capital, labor, and other social forces can coalesce. Nevertheless, while this may offer a degree of certainty to many places, the dangers inherent to places can only be placed in suspended animation, not abolished.

While there are constraints on the premature devalorization of capital, as Harvey (1982, 425–431) stresses, the brutal truth remains that devalorization is an integral feature of the way in which capitalists seek to resolve crises of profitability. Indeed, one can think of devalorization as genetically encoded within the structural relationships of capital. Precisely because production has to be placed, devalorization is always—necessarily and unavoidably—time- and place-specific. Allen and colleagues (1998) deploy the metaphor of the doily to capture this uneven and discontinuous character of capitalist growth and decline, with the holes representing those places that do not relate to dominant growth mechanisms. Such places could be a particular town, or they could be a region or country. It is important to develop the analogy further and to stress that the distribution of holes in the fabric of the doily is not fixed. Indeed, the doily itself is a malleable and flexible material, one that can be folded and which shifts its geometry of presences and absences and peaks and troughs as an integral part of the processes of capital accumulation.

In summary, places can be conceptualized as complex condensations of social relationships, of varying density and variety. Places take a material form in the built environment of workplaces, residential areas, communication and transport routes, and so on, as these social relationships are stretched over and produce spaces. Such relationships come together contingently in specific time-space combinations to produce what are, in the last analysis, "unique places" (Massey, 1995b). The complexity, density, variety, and degree of copresence of different types of social relationships, of moments of the social process, can be thought of as defining different types of places—a village is characterized by a very different density and mix of social relationships than is a global city, for example. The simultaneous development of particular locations as elements of social spaces and as places, and the evolution of patterns of spatially uneven development, reflects their shifting engagement with mechanisms of growth and decline in the flux of real historical time. Such mechanisms can relate to all phases of the production process. This defines places in relation to the totality of capitalist relations of production—not just those of production in the narrow sense but those of circulation and consumption as these are stretched over space. It unambiguously emphasizes that capital-versus-labor relations are and must be reproduced in place; similarly, relations of cooperation and competition between capitals—which are reshaped as part of a shifting social division of labor that is central to the course of capitalist development—and between groups of workers or people as consumers occupying different segments of markets are embedded in place.[14] Indeed, more generally places are not embedded in markets but markets are embedded in and constituted through places (Sayer and Walker, 1992, 147). Such relations of production, exchange, and consumption are undoubtedly an important source of individual and collective identities, which may be intertwined in complex ways with the identities of places (a point developed in the next section).

8.3. Producing Identities and Senses of and Attachments to Places

Sense of place refers to the feelings that people have for places and their attachments to them. Places become inscribed with socially produced meanings. As such, places have histories, which make them what they are. Places are sites of constructed and disputed historicities, of displacement, interference, and interaction. The identities of places are, in part, relationally defined and constructed through relationships to "other" places. Not only are places themselves provided with identities but they can also provide a basis through which people form *their own* identities.[15] People and places may thus become linked in complex ways. Places only take shape in specific contexts defined in relation to particular perspectives, purposes, and projects. There is therefore no "essential place" existing in its real authenticity and waiting to be discovered (Allen et al., 1998, 10–34).[16]

Not least, there is no essential place because (among other things), capital and labor have very different and largely mutually exclusive interests in and commitments to places. In general, capital is more mobile than labor. Not all capital is equally mobile, and not all labor is equally immobile—occupationally, industrially, or geographically, however.[17] Locations that are, for capital, merely temporary resting places—albeit, by definition, ones more attractive financially than others—become for workers, their families, and friends (hopefully) permanent places in which to live. For people do not simply exist to create their identities in terms of the social relationships of commodity production and consumption. To borrow a phrase made memorable by the striking steelworkers of Longwy, in northeast France, in the late 1970s as they fought to preserve their communities: "people live and learn, as well as work, in places" (and not all work is waged work). This highlights the importance of social relationships other than those of capitalist production. Relations of ethnicity, gender, household, family and friendship, and indeed noncapitalist social relations of production and work all may be central to the constitution of place. After all, places become imbued with meaning in a variety of ways (Beynon and Hudson, 1993). Places created "from scratch" as "new industrial spaces," with capitalist relations of production established there "for the first time," eventually can become transformed into "*meaningful places*" in which people live and learn as well as work (Hudson, 1993, emphasis added).[18] People may make considerable individual and collective cultural investment in such places and may become deeply attached to them. In return, the places may create powerful emotional ties and symbolic meanings among those resident in them, although the impact may vary significantly from person to person. There will always be multiple coexisting characterizations of particular spaces or places. Different social groups within a place may have different—even highly contested—readings of its character and different stakes or interests in the place. Consequently, attachments to and feelings about place become caught up in "the power relations which structure all our lives" (Rose, 1995, 89).[19] Furthermore, different groups also have differential powers and resources to promote their vision of the place. Nonetheless, despite these differences, such attachments are strongly indicative of the ways in which people live their lives as socialized human beings with ties of community, friends, and family and not merely as the abstract commodity labor-power.

Thus, while capital creates spaces and evaluates locations within them in a predominantly one-dimensional way—focusing on their capacity to yield profits—people who live in them evaluate them on a multidimensional basis, in short, as places rather than merely as spaces of production. Certainly for most people these locations must yield a monetary reward to pay the costs of living there, and this entails successfully selling their labor-power to holders of capital or, perhaps, the state. In this sense, workers, their families, and capitalists—both those who buy their labor-power and those with whom they spend the resultant wage income—share an interest in that location as a successful space for producing profits. This partial shared interest of capital and labor in the same location also suggests that while the qualitative distinction between place and space is clear in principle, in practice it is less so. Often it may seem one of degree rather than kind. For, while the interest of capital qua capital is profit—neither more nor less—the interests of capital are of necessity pursued by its owners and managers. As people they are involved, to varying degrees, in social relationships other than those of the workplace in those locations in which they, as the agents of capital, are seeking to make profits.

The degree to which such agents engage with a location as place rather than simply as space in turn varies with the type of organization of production, the extent and character of relationship between capital, and the form of capital-versus-labor relations. For example, "sociable production" (Amin and Thrift, 1992) in industrial districts, with successful production dependent upon relations of trust and cooperation between companies and between them and their workers, is more conducive to a necessary blurring of the distinction between place and space than is production organized through a disarticulated branch plant located primarily to exploit cheap labor. Furthermore, one of the attractions to capital of the great postwar growth of temporary international labor migration is that migrant workers whose true place remains elsewhere have a much more restricted basis of attachment to their workplace location as only a location in which to work for a wage. This situation often reflected their lack of citizenship rights—especially so in the case of illegal migrant workers. It is, therefore, also important to recognize that the form in which capital-versus-labor relations are constituted in a particular location may have important implications for the ways in which people become attached to their classes and their places. Such relationships can take a variety of forms both within the workplace (for example, along a continuum from direct control to responsible autonomy)[20] and more widely within civil society outside the workplace (for example, in the form of paternalist social relationships). These variations may have important effects on the ways in which working people become attached to their place that go beyond earning a wage in their workplace.

Allen and colleagues (1998) have suggested that places *must* be conceptualized as open and unbounded. Yet, people who live in particular places have often thought of and spoken about them as closed, bounded, and clearly territorially identified. In the process they have conferred identity upon people who live there. And they have done so even though it is acknowledged that such "bounding" can only be partial by virtue of the socioecological processes through which places are constituted. Places acquire much of their distinctive character and permanence from the collective activities of people who live there, who build distinctive institutions, forms of organization and social relations *"within, around or focused on a bounded domain"* (Harvey, 1996, 310, emphasis added). Harvey goes on to add that the "practical and discursive practices of 'bounding' space and creating the permanences of particular places . . . is a collective affair." These viewpoints are not necessarily incompatible, however. Places that came to be seen as closed communities, associated with a strong sense of place and deep attachments to them on the part of their residents, often developed in that way out of necessity. This was one way of coping with the fact that they were created "from scratch," discursively and materially, with people often thrown together from a wide variety of locations. As the local indigenous population typically was unable to meet the burgeoning demands for labor-power, labor had to be imported from other locations. From the outset, therefore, they were in part constituted via their relations with other areas, as open, porous, and hybrid places.

The issue is not whether places were objectively bounded and closed but rather why people living *in* them constructed images *of* them as such. The subsequent development of place-specific institutions and identities, and a sense of community by their residents, was a way of surviving and dealing with the risks and uncertainties of their precarious existence, especially in monoindustrial places (such as colliery villages and steel towns). This was particularly the case as these were places in which access to wage incomes could depend upon the decisions, whims, and prejudices of a single employer. People who lived and/or worked there sought to come to terms with the exigencies of daily life via creating placed identities that both defined a shared interest in the place and differentiated them from other people in other places. People developed placed identities in what they experienced as placeless times, identities that they sought to make bounded, centered, and coherent as a coping strategy in a shifting and uncertain environment. It was precisely this perception and experience of changes beyond individual and embryonic community control that stimulated the need for the discursive construction of places as secure and stable.[21] While capitalist expansion creates tendencies toward placelessness, people seek to create and preserve places (Relph, 1975). Thus, there is a constant tension between deterritorializing forces as a consequence of the consti-

tution of places through fluid and shifting networks of social relationships and political pressures to reterritorialize places, both institution-
ally and discursively (Painter, 1998, 25).

Accepting the qualification that these were risky places in which to
live and never more than relatively closed communities, the key point
nevertheless remains that for workers, their families, and friends their
place is never just (or, for many, even) a space in which to work for a
wage. There is much more to it than that. This collective attachment to
place did not emerge overnight. On the contrary, it typically emerged
slowly and haltingly. There were often deep divisions among populations
thrown together via migration from a variety of origin areas into the
same location for no other reason than to try to survive by meeting the
labor-power requirements of capital. Gradually, unevenly, usually
through a process of bitter struggle with capital, such differences became
more muted as the working class sought to form itself as a class "for itself" in its emerging places. This often led, in due course, to the creation
of a certain "structured coherence" (Harvey, 1985) and "sense of place"
in relatively closed and bounded communities. People thrown together—
to supply the commodity labor-power—in circumstances not of their own
choosing sought to create a working class "in place." They sought to discover ways of "getting by," of identifying and protecting their interests
not just as workers but as people living in their place. In short, they strove
to establish the right to live and learn, as well as work for a wage, in
places that, to them, were (and invariably still are) more than simply centers of profit creation.

Consequently, institutions and organizations were created to represent the interests of working people and an embryonic working class in
their places. The most important of these, typically, were trade unions
and formal political parties, and in this way place-specific and more general national class interests became interlinked. This came to be the case
especially in the major capitalist states with the creation of various forms
of welfare state during the second half of the twentieth century (Lash and
Urry, 1987). This in turn created a potential for tension between attachment to place and class that remains problematic for the representation of
class and territorial interests (Hudson and Sadler, 1983; 1986). More immediately and locally, the sense of social order that organizations such as
trade unions and political parties conferred diffused more widely within
the institutions of local civil society. In this way, a social fabric of community evolved, with its constitutive institutional tissue, through which people could learn to become part of their place. Their place is the location in
which they were born, or perhaps to which they migrated, in which they
grew up, went to school, have networks of friends, relatives, and acquain-
tances. Thus, it is the location through which they learned about life, a

place where they are socialized human beings rather than just bearers of the commodity labor-power and, as a result, a place to which they have often become profoundly attached. In this sense, one can talk of a place-specific culture, a continuously fashioned mélange of meanings, values, and relationships that are effected by shared and ongoing social practices. These practices construct, sustain, and transform the context in which economic, social, and political life is produced and reproduced on a daily basis and into which new members are socialized. Such a culture is born of a lived unity of experience that generated particular "structures of feeling" (Williams, 1989b). Place denotes a complex intersecting grid of social practices but with no presumption that any single component of these is necessarily granted causal explanatory primacy. Place thus becomes the imbrication of cultural processes in particular environments (Griffiths and Johnston, 1991).

It is important to reiterate that, while there is clearly a progressive side to this creation of place-based institutions and identity with place, there is often also a darker side expressed in intraclass division and particular patterns of ethnic and gender relations.[22] Intraclass differences within such places were by no means automatically eradicated and often persisted. Many traditional working-class communities became constructed around regressive and patriarchal patterns of gender relations and a strongly gendered division of labor between waged and unwaged work. There were often also deep divisions along ethnic cleavage planes within such communities. Clearly such divisions could lead to clashes between identities constructed around shared territorial interests and those reflecting aterritorial communities of interest. Despite this darker side, they nonetheless are places that have come to have socially endowed and shared meanings for people that touch on all aspects of their lives and that help shape who they are, what they do, and how they do it by virtue of *where* they are.

Finally, the processes of social differentiation, identity formation, and attachment to place are typically more complex than those of the archetypically monoindustrial working-class place. Many towns and cities are constituted as places with much more complex economic and social structures. The greater complexity of external linkages and internal socioeconomic structure and spatial patterning is also connected to more complicated characterizations and senses of places. Complex urban environments are seen as composed of mosaics of socially distant—if not wholly discrete—social worlds in the "same" place. This proliferation of local social worlds is linked to more subtle and nuanced processes of multiple identity formation and of representation of interests. Places are thus seen to be marked by more complex divisions, as alternative social worlds coexist within larger social worlds (Meegan, 1995).

8.4. Defending and (Re-)Presenting Places

Places may develop a "structured coherence," generating a sense of shared identity and interest in the place by a range of social groups and forces that are expressed via a particular "structure of feeling" but typically predicated upon capital's having an interest in continuing to produce in them. This convergence of interests between capital and people in place can thus be ruptured and the "coherence" of places threatened if the economic rationale for production there is eroded. This is one aspect of the destructive character of capitalism as an ongoing process of creative destruction. Consequently, such places and their constitutive cultures may often lead a precarious existence, vulnerable to the disinvestment decisions of companies and the policies of national (and emergent supranational) states. This can lead to a variety of attempts to "defend places" and seek to ensure their successful reproduction, involving complex processes, material, social and discursive. These can range from the development of a politically progressive place-based "militant particularism" (Williams, 1989a) to regressive campaigns that pit place against place in a divisive struggle. For example, an instrumental attachment to a location as source of wage income may lead workers and their families who reside there to engage in competition with other workers and their families in their places to keep existing jobs or gain new ones.

Such campaigns to defend and promote places involve modes of place re-presentation and processes of identity re-formation as well as material changes there. This involves representations of shared interests in place, centered around particular social groups that discursively construct these place-specific interests. In this way, echoing an old idea from Marxian class analysis, places are transformed from being "in themselves" to being "for themselves" (Lipietz, 1993). For some, this involves places becoming agents (Cooke, 1989, 1990; Cox and Mair, 1991). Places as such do not become "proactive," however. Rather, it is the case that some social groups foster the construction of a shared place-based interest that becomes a basis for action in campaigns to defend places or promote their interests in other ways. Such a "territorial social bloc, a place sensitive alliance of social forces," acquires a legitimate capacity to act on behalf of a place via political and social struggle (MacLeod, 1998, 7). Places thus are not coherent, integrated wholes, but the image of the place as such can be mobilized rhetorically. Places as apparently coherent entities can be (re)produced discursively, as when local political leaders "speak for" the place "as a whole" and claim to represent "its interests." But such discursive constructions are always contestable and are often contested, although inequalities in power may result in one such construction becoming dominant or even hegemonic.

Campaigns to defend places can either involve seeking to preserve their existing economic bases or seeking to create a new one. Often, disinvestment is grudgingly accepted, without challenge, as the focus comes to be on attracting new jobs and activities. Sometimes, however, disinvestment is vigorously resisted. One option is to mount a political campaign rooted within democratic processes to restructure the territorial organization of the state, devolving more powers for economic development to local and regional levels. Demands for devolution can become particularly powerful when issues of economic development become interlinked with those of culture and identity (Anderson, 1995). Such pressures can also coincide with national states wishing, or needing, to draw in the scope of their activities as they seek to become "hollowed-out" institutions.[23] Sometimes the possibilities of democratic channels seem to be exhausted or to have failed. Another option therefore is to move beyond normal democratic forms of protest and adopt the tactics of direct action, challenging the power of the state head-on as people in threatened places resort to nondemocratic methods of defending their place. This threat to place can be especially stark in monoindustrial settlements. As a result, it can lead to campaigns to defend place based on a resurgence of place-based class conflict. This is particularly so in circumstances in which the state is seen to be directly involved in the processes of economic decline via sectoral or industrial polices, such as those of nationalization and public ownership giving way to privatization, particularly in monoindustrial places (Hudson and Sadler, 1983).[24] This can involve strikes and industrial disputes in which workers take over and occupy their workplaces (see, for example, Thompson and Hart, 1972). It can also involve workers, their friends, and families taking their concerns beyond the boundaries of the workplace and into the streets of their place and beyond. For example, during the late 1970s and 1980s steelworkers in northeast France engaged in a series of direct actions, including protesting violently in the streets of Paris (Hudson and Sadler, 1983).

In other times and places, the defense of place is pursued not through class conflict but via the emergence of place-based cross-class alliances, which in turn may be linked to intraclass territorial divisions.[25] Workers, their families, and friends may form alliances with small companies, such as those involved in retailing and the provision of personal services, that are tied to that location and see their future threatened by the loss of jobs and working-class incomes. There are, then, situations in which capitalists or their representatives, such as plant managers, enter into the social relations of place, rather than just those of space, in a location as a necessary requirement of reproducing the conditions needed for the production of profits there. Once this requirement no longer holds, the bonds of the social relations of place for them may dissolve, though for some forms of capital and capitalists this is more difficult than for others. The actual or potential threat may thus provide the catalyst that stimulates campaigns that can encompass some capitalist interests within more broadly based social movements to defend places against the dangers posed by job loss and workplace closure.

Such campaigns to defend places, however prosecuted, both draw on and reproduce, sometimes in modified form, the culture in which they are grounded and the understandings of the world and what is possible within it that this provides. In this sense, "militant particularisms" are always in some sense profoundly conservative because they seek to perpetuate patterns of social relations and community solidarities—loyalties—achieved under a certain sort of oppressive and uncaring industrial order (Harvey, 1996, 40). But, partly because attachment to place is grounded in more than just access to profits and wages, it does not necessarily follow that such a "conservative" defense of place is divisive or socially regressive, setting places in competition with one another. Place-based campaigns need not necessarily be place-bound and can be a basis from which to try progressively to overcome, rather than reinforce, the negative social impacts of spatial differentiation while respecting the specificities of people in their places. They can be grounded in a radical politics that seeks to forge wider connections and affiliations in the best traditions of socialism. The 1984–1985 British coal miners' strike is one, albeit unsuccessful, example of this process (Beynon, 1985; Beynon and Hudson, 1993). Indeed, this strike in defense of mining jobs and communities can only be understood in terms of its being grounded in a deep, place-based communal solidarity that sought to challenge the political-economic project of Thatcherism, albeit in the end in vain (Hudson and Williams, 1995).

As such, that strike's failure powerfully illustrates the immanent dangers involved in seeking to move from one level of abstraction grounded in a place-based militant particularism to broader campaigns that seek to link a variety of places and issues. For "in the act of translating, something important gets lost, leaving behind a bitter residue of always unresolved tension" (Harvey, 1996, 359). A combination of an unprecedented (ab)use of state power, brutality, and violence, the extent of which only became revealed in subsequent court cases, a bitter interunion dispute between the National Union of Mineworkers and the nascent Union of Democratic Mineworkers, which was also expressed as a territorial conflict between Nottingham and the other coalfields, and a particular, often partisan and selective representation of the struggle in the media, led to the miners' attempts to defend their communities failing. As such, it generated powerful intraclass conflicts as workers in one place competed with workers in other places to preserve their jobs. Class solidarity was subordinated to more immediate concerns with life and work in territorially delimited communities[26] as the dialectic of class and region (Mandel, 1963), the tensions between commitment to class and place, came to be worked out in particular ways. The continuing interunion and interregional disputes do indeed constitute a "bitter residue of unresolved tension."

The failure of such campaigns to preserve the existing economic rationale of places often leads territorial social blocs to lobby to attract fresh public and private sector investment to such places. Their failure often triggers fresh attempts to re-present these places as attractive locations for alternative economic activities. Successfully attracting public sector investment, usually from national governments, can directly underpin places by providing jobs, services, local facilities, and so on, and in doing so also help create conditions attractive to private sector investment. Such attempts to attract public sector resources to places usually are conducted through "normal" parliamentary channels but can sometimes include peaceful demonstrations in support of places (Hudson and Sadler, 1983). Sometimes, however, the existing policies and organizational structures of national states are seen as insufficient to guarantee the future of places.

The production of goods and services cannot take place *everywhere*, but it must take place somewhere. It is precisely because of the spatiality of production that there can be intense competition between places for a variety of activities to underpin "local" economies (Ward, 1998).[27] Increasingly such competition is international. Such activities can range from new manufacturing branch plants or small and medium-sized enterprises, to new forms of service sector activity as diverse as call centers and tourism, to new centers of consumption and gentrified residential areas (Hudson, 1994). Thus, places increasingly seek to forge a distinct images and to create an atmosphere of place, nature, and tradition that may prove enticing to particular sorts of potential investors, residents, and visitors of various sorts (Lash and Urry, 1994, 303). For example, seeking to sell places to tourists and visitors requires the commodification of leisure space, giving powerful meanings to "place products" via association with popular novels or television programs (Shaw and Williams, 1994, 224). Tourism companies seek to cultivate particular types of "tourist gaze" in order to sell places as holiday destinations (Urry, 1990). Seeking to create such images of place involves diverse social groups resident within them signing on to a shared image of "their place" that is distinct and different from that of other places. Enhanced interplace competition in a burgeoning and increasingly global place market has been intimately associated with the withdrawal of the state from established forms of territorial development policies as part of a resurgence of neoliberal regulatory régimes at the national and international levels.[28] The re-presentation of place typically involves various "boosterism" campaigns. People seek to accentuate the positive, projecting their place as a good place to "do business" or "take a break" via a selective presentation of its attributes in competition with other places that face similar threats to their future (see, for example, Bennett et al., 2000). Attempts to present a more attractive image to the outside world often involve local authorities and other organizations in significant expenditures. Sometimes such boosterism campaigns reflect particular sectional interests, but on other occasions they can reflect the existence of a broad alliance—or partnership—of social groups with a shared interest in "their place." Re-presenting the place in particular ways unavoidably marginalizes the interests of some groups, while attempts to project a particular sense of place unavoidably involves erasing alternative interpretations and senses of the place.

As with private sector companies, however, competition can also involve cooperation. There are strategic alliances and coalitions of strong growth regions and of the economically weak and disadvantaged. For example, within the European Union there is the "Four Motors" coalition of the strong (Catalonia, Lombardy, Baden Württemburg, and Rhône-Alpes, to which Wales and Ontario were subsequently added as it became a transatlantic as well as intra-European alliance) and also coalitions of disadvantaged peripheral regions. Such coalitions seek not only to compete for public and private sector investment but also to shape the conception of spatial policy to suit their interests. For them, the ideal situation is for their view to become hegemonic and for their interests to be indistinguishable from the national or European Union interest. Coalitions of the strong seek to preserve success, coalitions of the weak to engender it, often by trying to emulate the performance of the strong, to learn from the success of the "winners."[29]

8.5. Reconciling the Tensions of Meaningful Place versus Profitable Space: State Policies, Social Cohesion, and Spatial Integration

Why did national states come to see it as necessary to devise spatial policies as spatially uneven development ceased to be just an unremarked feature of industrial capitalism and became a potential political problem to which the state "had" to respond? In part, the answer to this question lies in more general arguments about the necessities for state involvement in economy and society and the varied pressures shaping these.[30] In part, the answer also lies in the variety of social groups with an interest in wishing to reproduce places "as they are" or wishing to change them. As a consequence there are varying coalitions of state institutions, corporate interests, employees, and residents seeking to define and promote their conception of how a place ought to be—a normative conception of "structured coherence" grounded in shared identities developed in and through "their place."

The root of the problem for state spatial policies and policies for places lies in the conflict between a location as a socially produced place to which its inhabitants are attached and as part of a socially produced space in which capital can make profits. In contrast to capital's one-dimensional concern with spaces of production and profit, places have multipally dimensional meanings for a variety of people, organizations, and institutions. Thus, places are constructed and experienced as material ecological artifacts and networks of social relations, a product of an "intricate and confusing" dialectical interplay of different moments of the social process. However, it is "precisely the way in which all these moments are caught up in the common flow of social process that in the end determines the conflictual (and oftentimes internally contradictory) processes of place construction, sustenance and deconstruction" (Harvey, 1996, 316). Put another way, places are in the realm of use values while space is in the realm of exchange values, in which money and capital connect places, generating unavoidable tensions and latent conflicts as a result.

For much of the time, this conflict remains latent, submerged, at worst simmering but certainly not boiling over as the tension between place and space remains within tolerable limits. But the tendency toward boiling over and erupting into crisis never disappears; it always is (and must be) immanent in the social relations of capital. Capitalist states play a decisive role in containing these tensions within socially acceptable, or at least politically justifiable, limits. From the earliest stages, capitalist development and the social order it represents have been underpinned by national state policies.[31] Thus, the space in which the economic laws of capitalism can operate is politically determined; in this sense, to invert a familiar Marxian aphorism, the political, not the economic, is determinate in the last instance. But at a certain point in the process of capitalist development within the territorial boundaries of national states, intranational spatial differentiation and inequality may cease to be seen simply as an unavoidable, if undesirable, aspect of such development and come to be seen as a political problem. As such, spatially uneven development may pose serious problems and threaten the legitimacy of the state and, beyond this, the hegemony of capitalist social relations.

For such states, the question of whether locations within the national territory are meaningful places in which people live their lives or simply part of spaces in which capital produces profits is a complicated one, however. For them, the same location may simultaneously need to be treated as a place and as part of a space in central state policy formation and implementation. As Taylor (1999) puts it, states impose spaces on places. Spaces are the outcome of top-down political processes while places can be a site for bottom-up opposition. Such states must therefore grapple with and try to resolve the competing demands of people defending their places (often articulating these through locally based parts of the state apparatus) and capital demanding the creation or maintenance of profitable spaces. Both these demands make claims, often substantial, on public expenditure as contradictory social relationships are transposed into the internal functioning of the state, emerging as conflicts between central state departments and between the central and locally based parts of the state apparatus. Neither the interests of capital nor those of labor can be safely ignored, though for different reasons.

On the one hand, a national state is subject to pressures from its citizens, not least via the electoral process in parliamentary democratic states. Ignoring the demands of people seeking to defend their place could trigger a legitimation crisis. In most places in a capitalist economy their relationships to the ebb and flow of the accumulation process, their conjunction with particular mechanisms of growth and decline, is critical to their (re)production *as* places. This can raise an acute problem when they cease to be within the ambit of growth mechanisms and suffer economic decline, perhaps even cataclysmic collapse. While people may cease to be in demand as the commodity labor-power, they still may have a variety of other deep, powerful, and long-lasting attachments to their place. Such places could simply be left to decline and rot, and in particular time/space phases of capitalist development this is precisely what has happened. Increasingly within the advanced capitalist world, however, it came to be seen as illegitimate simply to stand back and allow places to decline. Political pressures emerged for the state to become actively involved in ensuring the reproduction of places. On the other hand, for a state to ignore the demands of capital for profitable production spaces could precipitate capital flight and threaten its source of revenues in taxes on profits and wages. Capitalist states characteristically attempt to meet varying demands in the same location by asserting that differing interests are complementary. This allows them to be addressed via intranational (and within the EU, intra-European Union) regional, urban, and other territorially targeted policies that seek to influence the location of economic activity and the map of prosperity.

Thus, the content, form, and mode of implementation of state spatial policies partly depends on the relative strengths of capital, labor, and other social actors, such as environmental groups. One can envisage, therefore, a range of possibilities as to agreement and consensus or disagreement and conflict as the latent tension between place and space becomes actualized in particular locations. While the capacity to pursue competing interests is structurally loaded in the direction of capital, it does not follow that the particular trajectory of stasis or change in a location is always the one that capital would prefer. There is, nonetheless, a crucial qualitative difference between situations in which there is a consensus between the major social actors and the state as to the desirability or otherwise of locational change and change in a location and those in which there is disagreement or conflict over these matters. There are numerous examples of cases in which there has been a broad measure of agreement as to the desirability of either preserving the specificity of particular places or patterns of spatial differentiation or of changing them in agreed directions (for example, via corporatist regional modernization programs). The fact that the trajectory of changes often diverges from that intended raises important questions about its determinants and the limits to state policies, but this is of less significance here than the emergence of a consensus on an agreed program of changes.

Those situations in which there is conflict as to the desirability or otherwise of locationally specific changes are in general still more complicated. For example, the relationships between class interests and commitment to place/space can become more convoluted and class and spatial attachments can pull in opposite directions. In these situations, the asymmetry of power relations, especially between capital and labor and, to a lesser degree, between different forms of capital, becomes crucial. Capital is generally in a more powerful position to pursue its interests than is labor, while transnational companies are in a much more powerful position than small, locationally tied companies. Moreover, the growing globalization of production has altered the balance of power between capital and many national states (to say nothing of emergent supranational ones). In this sense, managing the tensions generated by the different connotations of place and space in the same location is becoming still more problematic for many capitalist states.

However, even in situations of consensus and agreement, spatial policies and attempts to re-create places may have unintended consequences. For example, the growing mobility of people, sometimes allied to state policies toward the provision of public sector (social) housing, has led to localized systems of representation and ties of people to their places becoming disrupted or destroyed. A failure to appreciate this social construction of attachment to place underlay many attempts at sociospatial engineering, informed by the best of social democratic reformist intentions. These are perhaps best typified by the bleak tower blocks of many inner and outer urban areas or by new towns and other settlement policies such as those pursued in the United Kingdom (Hudson, 1989b) or France (Rubenstein, 1978), intended to improve working-class housing and living environments. For a long time, such policies naively assumed that attachment to place could be transferred from one built environment to another; the subsequent emergence of individual, community, and social problems, of alienated populations, sometimes culminating in violence and riots, dramatically revealed that this is not the case.

8.6. Varieties of Capitalist State Spatial Policies

The transformation of spatially uneven development from being simply an integral feature of capitalism to a political problem can be quite precisely dated. In 1928 the United Kingdom government first invented embryonic and tentative forms of regional policy. Subsequently, such territorial development policies evolved in a variety of ways—in form, content, target territorial unit, and the balance between centralized and decentralized policy delivery—and diffused outward to virtually all capitalist states. Consequently, a complex mix of spatial policies has emerged.

Their initial form was of "top down" centrally directed central government regional policies *for* regions, informed by a mixture of social welfare and economic efficiency and growth motives. Later, the emphasis shifted from regional to urban—a move that roughly coincided within the ending of the long postwar boom in the 1960s and 1970s in the advanced capitalist world. Such policies revolved around very well known attempts to influence geographies of production via a variety of carrots and sticks. These encompassed infrastructure provision, grants and loans to private sector companies to induce them to locate in some areas, financial penalties and taxes as the price of locating in other areas, and a prohibition on certain activities locating in other types of area (Aldridge, 1979). On occasion, such policies were allied to others that relocated public sector industries or parts of governmental activities to peripheral regions. As constraints on public expenditure tightened and unemployment problems stubbornly persisted, there was a shift from automatic payment of fixed levels of grants to a more selective approach, with lower amounts of grants tied to employment creation targets.

While the administration of such policies was typically devolved to the regional level within the structures of central government ministries, decisions about their content and the criteria to be used in administering them remained firmly at the central level within national states. Such policies often seem more concerned with reshaping the contours of profitable production spaces or addressing national economic policy objectives than with meeting the developmental needs and concerns of particular places. Furthermore, implementation of such policies was often seen as creating vulnerable urban and regional economies and ensembles of "global outposts" at the extremities of corporate command and control chains (Austrin and Beynon, 1979), as well as a dependence upon decisions within national political capitals and the offices of transnational corporations (Firn, 1975). Despite claims as to the emergence of new forms of qualitatively different embedded branch plants, such fears remain (Hudson, 1994a, 1995a).[32]

As Keynesianism reached its limits and neoliberalism became the dominant political-economic philosophy over much of the capitalist world, national states withdrew somewhat from an engagement with problems of uneven development within their national territory. Not least this retreat reflected their increasing concern with national economic performance in the context of fierce international competition for investment and jobs. There was a shift from central state to local policies, from centralization to decentralization and in some respects to recentralization, as part of the restructuring of states. Insofar as central governments retained a concern with territorial development policies, this increasingly centered on initiatives targeted at small areas, often involving institutional innovation—for example, via enterprise zone policies (Anderson, 1983, 1990) or urban development corporations (Imrie and Thomas, 1993). Perhaps the most dramatic manifestation of this tendency is the export-processing zones found in many parts of the periphery of the capitalist economy. They are de facto "offshore states" in which the "usual" regulatory procedures are greatly weakened or wholly absent. Increasingly, in the core territories of capitalism, small area policies became linked to the promotion of small and medium-sized enterprises (SMEs) as large plants and companies became identified as a source of job losses and a cause of urban and regional problems. With more general changes in economic structures there has been a growing focus upon seeking to influence the location of private service sector rather than manufacturing activities. The end result, however, was often to again create fragile economies. These were composed of vulnerable SMEs locked into dependent relationships with larger companies elsewhere, occupying niches that larger companies found unattractive, or dependent upon people spending incomes earned elsewhere, and the service sector analogues to the global outposts of manufacturing branch plants (Hudson, 1994a; Hudson and Townsend, 1992)

Central government disengagement led to responsibility for economic development issues and policies being increasingly decanted to subnational levels. Consequently, cities and regions were pitched into intensified competition in pursuit of all manner of economic activities and employment, both within and between national territories. This often entailed a variety of institutional innovations at the subnational level. Enhanced competition between places spawned a new service industry of "place promoters" and organizers of "boosterism" campaigns. This spans both the growth of private producer services and the restructuring of the state as local planning officers became converted to local economic development officers, tourism development officers, or, in the European Union, European liaison officers seeking EU funding. In some circumstances, decentralization involved meaningful transfer of power and resources from central to local and regional levels of the state, enabling new forms of policies to promote places to emerge (Dunford and Hudson, 1996). This allowed greater sensitivity in responding to the requirements of particular places in policy formation. In other circumstances, however, there was little transfer of such powers or resources, resulting in limited capacities to act at the local and regional levels. In these circumstances, it was largely *responsibility* for local and regional conditions that was devolved (Hudson and Plum, 1986), sometimes with an enhanced centralization of power and resources within central government (Hudson and Williams, 1995).

Local and regional authorities have sought to construct economic development strategies around varying economic activities, depending upon their location and the characteristics of their areas. Such strategies revolve around notions of place-marketing, maintaining or adapting existing users of the place or expanding and diversifying into new categories of users (Ashworth and Voogd, 1990). The choice of strategy often reflects the character and location of the place. For example, within the United Kingdom it was feasible to seek to redevelop the London Docklands around high-order financial and business services and to regenerate inner city waterside locations in other deindustrialized conurbations as consumption, residential, and recreational places for the new middle and service classes. In contrast, in peripheral places the focus of regeneration policies is more likely to be on manufacturing branch plants, Taylorized "back-office" service activities, or forms of tourism (Hudson, 1994a). Competition between cities and regions allocates private and public sector resources between places and sorts "winners" from "losers." As competition has intensified, the mechanisms for projecting images of place have become more varied and technologically sophisticated. While sober statistical reports depict places in competition for public sector funding as deeply problematic, a range of media from newspaper advertisements and glossy brochures to videos and web sites in cyberspace are simultaneously used to promote the attractions of these places to private capital (see Figure 8.1). The aspects of local environments that are emphasized and valued vary with the substantive focus of development polices—strategies centered around tourism tend to stress different environmental aspects than do those centered on encouraging new forms of manufacturing activity, for example (see Figure 8.2).

Enhanced competition between places led to increased interest in

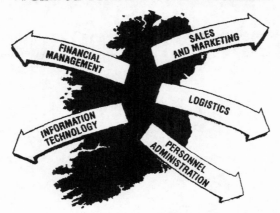

A Shared Services Centre in Ireland

FINANCIAL MANAGEMENT

SALES AND MARKETING

LOGISTICS

INFORMATION TECHNOLOGY

PERSONNEL ADMINISTRATION

reduces cost and improves quality

Ireland provides a competitive solution to companies seeking to rationalise traditional networks of national administrative centres. Ireland offers a highly skilled and flexible workforce with an extensive supply of business and language skills and a telecommunications network which is one of the most advanced in Europe.

Companies who have already availed of Ireland's unique opportunities as a shared services centre include Andersen Consulting, Bertelsmann DFS, Black & Decker, Citibank, Continental AG, DER, Lafferty Publications, MSAS, Sea-Land and Whirlpool.

IDA IRELAND
INDUSTRIAL DEVELOPMENT AGENCY

For further information contact IDA Ireland at
United Kingdom: Ireland House, 150 New Bond St., London W1Y 9FE.
Tel: +44 171 629 5941 Fax: +44 171 629 4270
Germany: Tel: +49 211 51 89 99-0 Fax: +49 211 43 36 54
Netherlands: Tel: +31 20 679 8666 Fax: +31 20 679 1321
France: Tel: +33 1 53 43 12 00   Fax: +33 1 47 42 84 76
Ireland: Wilton Place, Dublin 2. Tel: + 353 1 603 4000 Fax: + 353 1 603 4040
e-mail: idaireland@ida.ie Web http://www.idaireland.com

FIGURE 8.1. Selling places: Service centers in Ireland.

links between local policies and institutions and economic success and in the possibilities for transferring recipes for success from more to less successful places. Claims about the basis of the success of the economically successful regions and the importance of place for successful production[33] focused attention on the characteristics of the places within which firms operate as a key—perhaps *the* key—to such success. Competitive economic performance is seen to relate to cultural and social variables: intense levels of interfirm collaboration and cooperation; trust; a strong shared sense of common industrial purpose; extensive institutional sup-

FIGURE 8.2. Promoting "high-tech" growth in Arizona.

port for local businesses; and institutional forms that encourage innovation, diffusion of new ideas, and skill formation. Economically successful places seemingly have numerous local institutions within civil society and spanning the boundaries of civil society, economy, and state, in which the cooperative relationships of success are grounded.[34] This has significantly impacted on the conception and practice of local economic development policies, offering alternatives that draw upon particular sociocultural explanations of success to other more problematic policies and territorial development models.[35] Such places are seen to possess appropriate institutional formations.[36] As such, economically successful spaces for profitable production are culturally constructed, constituted via instituted processes, and necessarily embedded in socially cohesive "places." Local institutional capacities and distinctive forms of local regulation and governance are therefore seen as necessary conditions for economic success. Supportive institutions and collaborative forms of behavior thus seem to be key features of local regulatory systems in those places that are "winners" in the global economy. Furthermore, they may enable them to become intelligent "learning places," able to move smoothly along existing development trajectories and, more importantly, to anticipate the impending limits of existing trajectories and move to new ones. Consequently, the task of local economic development policies in the places that are "losers" is to try to ensure that the necessary conditions are satisfied to enable them to change trajectories and become "winners."

In short, such approaches tend to assume that territories, not firms, are the relevant competitive units and that these "soft" attributes of territories are the key to competitive success (rather than, say, agglomeration economies). Such assumptions may be valid in some times, places, and circumstances, but certainly are not generally so (Hudson, 1999). First, successful places tend to be in successful national economies, often with strong and enabling national states. Just as discourses of globalization underplay the continuing significance of national states, so too do many of those that emphasize the local bases of economic success in global markets.[37] At a minimum, it is necessary to analyze relationships between local and national regulation in underpinning local economic success. Second, there are critical questions about the links between place-based learning and corporate learning, especially learning within the structures of major transnational companies. It is important not to conflate local with tacit as major corporations base their competitive strategies on knowledge that is company-specific. Transnationals are often in a dominant position to capture and use locally based learning for *their* corporate goals.[38] There is no guarantee that the interests of such companies will coincide with those of the majority of the population of the places in which they choose to invest. Despite claims about the emergence of "embedded performance plants" within such corporations, they remain capitalist enterprises, constrained by the structural logic of capitalist production. This raises difficult questions about the most appropriate form of local developmental trajectories and *whose* interests they serve. Third, local economic structures can change so that institutional arrangements that were formerly an advantageous source of support become a barrier to future success. Places can be left with relict institutional formations that inhibit constructive change (Grabher, 1993; Hudson, 1994a). Fourth, if appropriate local institutional formations are necessary to underpin economic success, then unless they are transferable between localities—

which is a highly dubious claim[39]—the vast majority of places are doomed to exclusion from the benefits of economic success. Certainly there have been attempts by places that have "lost" to mimic the structures of those that have "won"—but without conspicuous success (Dunford and Hudson, 1996).

8.7. Summary and Conclusions

Space can be thought of as a product of stretched-out social relationships, place as the condensation of intersecting social relationships in a specific time-space context. Places may be thought of as closed, homogeneous, and bounded or as open, heterogeneous, and permeable. Production must take place somewhere, and the process of production helps form both social spaces and places. Within the confines of capitalist social relations, the production of space is closely linked to the imperatives of commodity production. Capital seeks to shape space in its interests, informed by the demands of profitable production. In contrast, people seek to construct meaningful places, which have a much wider range of meanings for them than capital's one-dimensional concern with profitable spaces of production. People require capital to produce in order to sell their labor-power for a wage and as such develop a material base for their places. However, capital's endless quest for profits may mean that it devalorizes in situ, destroying the economic rationale and structured coherence of places. Devalorization is always necessarily place-specific. Nonetheless, devalorized places remain meaningful for people who live and learn there, embedded in social networks of family, friends, and relations. There is an ongoing tension arising from the attempts of people to develop coherent and meaningful places and capital's ceaseless search for profits that lead it to flow in and out of places (within the limits imposed by the need to ensure that capital invested is amortized). As a result, people often seek to defend their place against the threat of capital flight, workplace closure, and employment loss.

This tension between space and place poses particular problems for national states seeking to maintain social and spatial cohesion in the territories over which they have jurisdiction. This is especially so when they are seen to have been directly involved in creating local economic crises via closures of state industries. In these circumstances, local campaigns may emerge that challenge the authority and legitimacy of the state via direct action, outside "normal" democratic channels of protest. These further intensify pressures on states to find ways of making locations attractive to companies while preserving people in their places as they compete in various ways for both private and public sector investment to help construct alternative economic bases for their places. They have sought to tackle this difficult task in a variety of ways. Recently, the emphasis has shifted from central government regional and urban policies for places to decentralization to local and regional levels, with responsibility (though seldom adequate resources and powers) for local and regional economic well-being devolved to those levels as one component of more complicated systems of multilevel governance. As a result, increasing attention has been given to the specific features and unique attributes of places as a source of competitive advantage. This has intensified the competition between places for investment and jobs and has sharpened the map of regional and local inequality between "winners" and "losers."

8.8. Notes

1. Historically the attempt to replace capitalism with socialism sought to define those large-scale landscapes and geographies by different social ordering principles. Within contemporary capitalist societies there are social forces that seek to create spaces of resistance and more localized geographies around different rationales to those of the dominant capitalist social relationships.

2. This was perhaps most typically so in relation to conceptualizing the region; for a while, it seemed that in some schools of thought it was the *only* conceptual issue of concern.

3. This debate has extended beyond human geography into the social sciences, a consequence of growing recognition of the importance of the spatiality of economic, political, and social life; see Gregory and Urry (1985); Giddens (1979, 1981, 1984); Lash and Urry (1987, 1994).

4. On the other hand, to claim, as does Castells (for example, 1983, 1996), that space is dissolved into flows and places are emptied of their local meanings is to go too far. Social life may to a degree have been "aterritorialized" and disembedded from place, but in important ways it remains territorially embedded, and necessarily so.

5. For a fuller theoretical critique of the notion of places as bounded, settled, and stable that is grounded in feminism, see Massey (1994).

6. There is certainly evidence that places have displayed a considerable degree of closure at particular times (Carney and Hudson, 1978; Hudson, 1989b).

7. Monoindustrial places were by no means unique to capitalism, however. Indeed, they were at least as equally prevalent within the state-directed industrialization strategies of state socialism. As eastern Europe and China began to undergo transitions to capitalism from the 1990s onward, such places were particularly vulnerable to economic restructuring and social dislocation (see, for example, Shen and Hudson, 1999; Smith, 1998; Stenning, 2000).

8. The latter often forced via compulsory military service.

9. In addition, spatial differences in natural conditions and raw material locations were very influential in shaping geographies of production.

10. Indeed, such historical geographies are often central to their attempts to attract tourists as part of local economic development strategies (see below).

11. In a similar fashion, Smith (1984, 83) refers to cities and regions as "composite commodities," arguing that spatial relations help determine their particular form. Harvey (1996, 417) refers to the contemporary city as a "palimpsest," a composite landscape made up of many different built forms superimposed on each other with the passing of time. In fact, all places could be conceptualized in this way (cf. Massey, 1995a).

12. See also section 8.4.

13. The extent to which production can be divorced from the constraints of nature has been revealed to much more limited than had once seemed the case, however. Production involves more than simply subjugating an untamed nature to the forces of production (a theme explored in Chapter 9).

14. These issues are discussed in Chapters 4–7.

15. Wider discourses—political, cultural, or economic—may yield yet other identities, raising questions as to how various territorially and aterritorially defined identities relate to one another.

16. This does not mean that claims to the contrary may not be made, especially when invoking places as part of wider political projects such as those of nationalism.

17. The history of migrations, both international and intranational, provides evidence of the extent to which people will move often massive distances in search of work (King, 1993).

18. See also section 8.4.

19. See also Bagguley and colleagues (1990).

20. See Chapter 4.

21. Analysts such as Harvey (1989) and Robins (1991) have argued that the recent intensification of globalization processes has enhanced such a perceived need for settled places. Indeed, the phrase "placed identities for placeless times" is borrowed from Robins. The point to emphasize here is that this need to counter the pressures of placelessness has existed from the earliest phases of industrial capitalism, as the stability of precapitalist places was rudely disturbed by that phenomenon.

22. See also "Divided by Gender" and "Divided by Ethnicity" in section 7.3.

23. This is discussed in section 3.6.

24. As formerly socialist states underwent the processes of transition to capitalism, leading to draconian restructuring of industries and monoindustrial places, similar pressures reflecting opposition began to emerge. In China, for example, plans to cut tens of thousands of jobs in the steel industry were "raising the prospect of strong opposition from local authorities and one industry towns" (Kynge, 2000).

25. See "Divided by Territory" in section 7.3.

26. In such ways the working class actively and simultaneously both forms and divides itself territorially; see also section 7.3.

27. As Ward makes clear, however, such competition is not new. It has a venerable history, although recently it has intensified.

28. See section 3.7.

29. A point amplified in section 8.6.

30. See Chapter 3.

31. An issue discussed fully in Chapter 3.

32. For example, in 1998 Fujitsu and Siemens closed brand-new state-of-the-art integrated circuit plants in northeast England as world market prices for these products collapsed.

33. See section 5.6.

34. For instance, Storper (1995) describes these as "systems of untraded interdependencies," while Putnam (1993) emphasizes the importance of "social capital" to urban and regional economic success.

35. See sections 2.4, 5.6, 6.2, and 6.3.

36. Amin and Thrift (1994) emphasize the importance of "institutional thickness," Storper (1997) focuses on "conventions," while Peck and Tickell (1992) draw attention to "appropriate local modes of regulation" in underpinning successful regional economies. In essence, however, different analysts are using different terminology to refer, broadly, to the same things.

37. See section 3.6.

38. See section 5.6.

39. In the language of critical realism, even if it were possible to transfer institutional structures with their inherent causal powers intact, there is no guarantee that these would produce the desired transformatory effects. Indeed, the exigencies of local circumstances interacting with them would most probably lead to unintended and unwanted effects; see also Chapter 1.

9

Materials Transformations

Production and Nature

9.1. Introduction

This Chapter explores some implications of seeing production as a process of materials transformation. Production transforms materials and the energy embedded in them and is ultimately grounded in the autonomous and material world of nature. In seeking to understand the implications of the materiality of nature for production, it investigates relations between production, places, and the environment, both generally and specifically in the context of capitalist production transforming elements of the natural world into commodities with use and exchange values. Such transformations have environmental as well as social consequences, some intended and others accidental, some deep and irreversible, others minor and transient. But many have the potential to produce social conflicts, generating "winners" and "losers," and to raise concerns about how such antagonisms are to be resolved. Industrial production, growth, and transformation are the primary proximate causes of these impacts. In turn, externalities such as environmental degradation and pollution feed back into the costs and cultural and social acceptability of economic activities.

Furthermore, there are growing concerns over the socioeconomic uncertainties and environmental risks associated with genetically engineering new forms of plants and animals. Such genetically modified organisms (GMOs) graphically illustrate the pressures to push back natural limits on production. While seen as a way of ultimately "outflanking nature" and apparently evading many "natural" limits, they are likely to have significant feedback effects upon the organization of production of organic materials. While avoiding crude environmental determinism, or Malthusianism, it is important to recognize that there are natural limits to production and may well be social limits to the unnaturalness of production. These natural limits are not, in principle, absolute (although in practice some of them may seem to be so, given current levels of knowledge and technology) but specific to particular societies, times, and places. Equally, the social limits may vary with time, place, and circumstance. As Benton (1989, 97) puts it, "The ecological problems of any form of social and economic life . . . have to be theorised as the outcome of [its] specific structure of natural/social articulations." Despite these close connections, the articulations between the dynamics of the economy and those of the environment are only poorly and partially known and understood (M. J. Taylor, 1994, 1995).

9.2. Production as a Process of Materials Transformation: Thermodynamics, the Laws of Conservation, and the Natural Limits to Production

A first step in enhancing understanding of economy–environment links is to consider the industrial economy as analogous to a simple closed natural ecosystem. Although this analogy clearly cannot be pushed too far, it nonetheless provides a useful starting point in understanding the limits that nature imposes on production. Eco-systems consist of flows of energy and matter, which tend toward a steady state because of the effects of natural regulatory processes. Viewed from such a perspective, production can be conceptualized as involving flows of energy and chemical and physical transformations of elements of nature. In understanding production as a process of materials transformation, the laws of thermodynamics (the theory of the movement or flow of heat) and the conservation laws provide key insights. The limits that these laws unavoidably impose on any form of production are critical.[1] Perhaps *the* key point is that thermodynamics characterizes *any* material transformation as dissipative of energy and conservative of materials. Consequently *any* form of production, transport, and consumption unavoidably impacts on the environment (Jackson, 1995).

   Each industrial process and economic activity involves the *transformation* of materials and energy from one form to another. Thermodynamics provides very specific rules and limits that govern these transformations; except in very specific circumstances (see below) they cannot be altered or suspended by human intervention and in that sense set natural limits on social production and its relationships to nature. The first law of thermodynamics is also the first conservation law (the law of conservation of energy). Energy exists in various forms and is constantly being transformed from one type to another. These energy transformations allow people to carry out useful (to individuals and societies) work and provide goods and services. The first law states that energy is neither created nor destroyed during these transformations although it may change in physical form (for example, from kinetic energy to heat). The second conservation law is the law of conservation of mass during materials transformations. It states that the total mass of inputs to a transformation process is equal to the total mass of outputs. If inputs do not emerge as desired products, they must therefore appear as unwanted by-products or wastes. This is a critical insight in understanding relationships between production, consumption, and nature. The third conservation law governs the total quantity of each individual atomic element during (nonnuclear) materials transformations.[2] So, for example, the total amount of carbon contained in a quantity of fossil fuel and that released during its combustion are equal. This in principle allows precise accounting of the environmental impacts of materials transformations during processes of production and consumption (and provides the conceptual basis for the methodology of life cycle analysis and industrial metabolism, discussed below). It also makes clear that every step in the totality of the production process "is more or less a transient event, a temporary (possibly long-lived but temporary) use of some set of atoms and energy" (Frosch, 1997, 159).[3]

There is, however, a further complication. If energy is conserved, why extract more fossil fuels? If matter is conserved, why worry about exhausting supplies of metallic minerals? The key to understanding these seemingly paradoxical questions is contained in the second law of thermodynamics and in concepts such as those of entropy. This second law has been described as the basis of the economy of life, at all levels (Georgescu-Roegen, !971). The first law addresses the quantity of energy during transformation, the second addresses its *availability*. While the first law explains that the total quantity of energy is conserved, the second law addresses its *loss of availability*. As the same quantity of energy passes through successive transformations, it becomes progressively less available. Thus, this second law makes clear the impossibility of converting all the energy from an energy reservoir into useful work and ensures that some energy from a production process will always be dissipated into the environment as waste (Frosch, 1997, 158). Thus, energy is conserved but it becomes more dissipated and so less "useful" for production and human use. The link between these aspects of energy transformation and those of materials transformation is forged via the concept of entropy.[4] Entropy measures randomness or disorder in a physical system—

the greater the degree of entropy, the greater the degree of randomness or disorder. As entropy increases, energy available to do useful work decreases. As an isolated system undergoes successive transformations in real time, so less energy becomes available and entropy increases.[5] Thus, the general effect of the second law is that energy and material transformations occur in such a way as to reduce the available energy in and increase the dissipation of material through a system, assuming for the moment a simple closed eco-system.

Complex industrial societies are, however, more appropriately thought of as open systems. This difference is significant. In contrast to a closed system, in an open system the tendency toward disorder and randomness can be countered by external inputs of energy. In the case of the earth, these are provided via solar power and processes such as those of the carbon cycle, capturing solar energy during photosynthesis via green plants and thereby trapping carbon. More significantly, in complex human societies, energy is "imported" to subsidize industrial production and consumption processes, both individually and in the aggregate, from the stock of carbon fossil fuels, and to a much smaller degree from flow resources (such as solar energy and hydroelectric, wave, or wind power). These low-entropy fossil fuel reserves provide high-quality thermal energy through combustion, which can then be transformed into other forms. This energy can be used, among other things, to access resources that are unavailable to nonhuman species and can be deployed in the production of goods and services. But in developing in this way, the "natural" self-regulatory mechanisms of simple closed eco-systems, whereby the dissipation of material is limited to the degradation of nutrients and minerals that subsequently return to natural material cycles powered by solar radiation, cease to be effective. Only a small fraction of the materials extracted from nature and mobilized in production are recovered and used. Nevertheless, human society and industrial production cannot escape the constraints of thermodynamics. Perhaps the key long-term issue is whether *any* form of economy, *any* set of social relations of production, can develop analogous and effective regulatory mechanisms to contain the consequences of human intervention into the cycles of natural processes. However, while production (and the economy in general) cannot avoid the limits set by the laws of thermodynamics, "it is quite another thing to treat them [these laws] as sufficient conditions for the understanding of human history" (Harvey, 1996, 140). In succeeding sections, the implications of capitalist industrialization and the relationship between structures of governance and regulation, capitalist relations of production, and the impacts of commodity production on the natural environment are considered.

9.3. Production as a Process of Materials Transformation: The Materials Balance Principle, Industrial Metabolism, and the Social Limits to Thinking about Production in This Way

Industrial ecology and industrial metabolism[6] provide ways of considering production as a process of materials transformation and allow powerful insights into relations between economy and environment. Industrial metabolism (Ayres, 1989; Ayres and Simonis, 1994) is an approach that involves constructing a balance sheet of physical and chemical inputs to and outputs (intended and unintended) from production. A "life cycle analysis" is a cradle-to-grave mapping of the material inputs and outputs associated with producing goods and services (recognizing that many services have a high material content). Such an approach centers on the notion of mass balance—that is, that the sum total of a particular chemical within a production process remains constant as it passes from production to consumption to disposal, with human activity providing the stabilizing controls. A simplified life cycle of pulp and paper is shown in Figure 9.1. Figure 9.2 depicts a more complex example of a composite process chain for a specific product, bleached sulphate (kraft) pulp.[7] The production process is represented as flows of energy and physical matter. Pivotal points at which key chemical and physical transformations (for example, of wood to charcoal or coal to coke) occur are identified. So too are the moments at which flows cross from the realm of social processes of production and consumption to that of the natural world.[8]

The methodology of industrial metabolism offers a way of describing the trajectory of flows of chemicals through an industrial economy and tracing the discharge to and accumulation within the natural environment of the resultant pollutants. By tracing the ecological impacts of particular methods and forms of organization of production, in terms of inputs from and outputs to the natural environment, the implications of varying choices of production technologies can be clarified. By tracing the ecological impacts of varying combinations of the production and consumption of different levels and compositions of output, the macroscale implications of microscale choices can be better understood. This therefore provides a base point from which to review the ecological implications of the repertoire of possible social choices about how and what to produce. Moreover, it could in principle be extended to consider where production occurs, for example, in terms of companies' attempts to find "spatial fixes" for pollutant and environmentally noxious and hazardous production.

There are, therefore, considerable potential benefits in conceptualizing production in terms of industrial metabolism. For example, acknowledging that by-products are unavoidable suggests that, in designing meth-

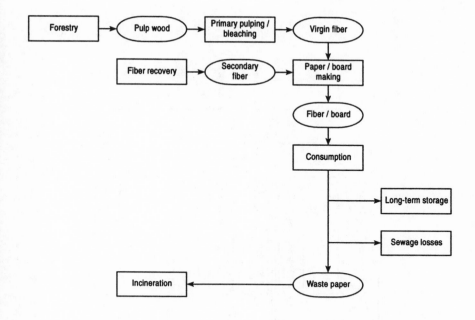

FIGURE 9.1. Simplified life cycle of pulp and paper.

ods of producing desired end-products, wastes to that process might be planned to be useful by-products and inputs to other production processes (Frosch, 1997, 158). It is also important to be aware of the limits to such an approach, however. First, the distinction between "production pollution" and "consumption pollution" is left implicit, despite its significance analytically and in terms of exploring appropriate policy options (M. J. Taylor, 1995). Dissipative pollution as a result of consumption is a more pervasive, extensive, and generalized source of environmental pollution than that arising from production per se, not least because it has typically been less subject to restrictive regulation. The ubiquity of dissipative pollution takes on added significance because the industrial metabolism approach places sole reliance upon the market as a regulatory mechanism rather than upon physical limits and minimum standards set by the state. Second, the "cradle-to-grave" metaphor of life cycle analysis suggests that a production activity can be considered in isolation and that its most important features are endogenous to the process. Furthermore, it implies that the environmental impacts of a production process can be modeled in a continuous, uninterrupted, and linear fashion and that the "cycle" itself is a linear path. Yet, the repetitive character of production

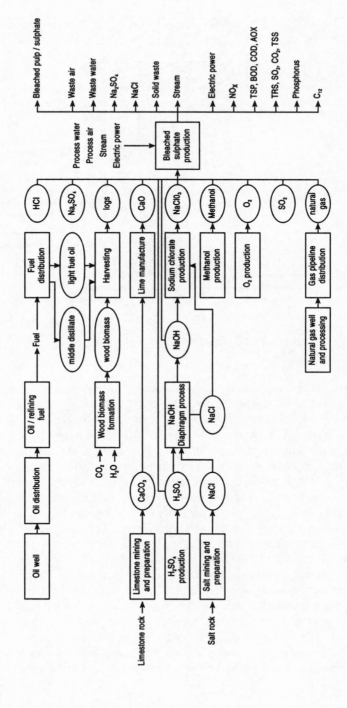

FIGURE 9.2. Example of a composite process chain for bleached sulphate (kraft) pulp.

292

processes, their divergent impacts on different human groups and ecologies, and the concurrent costs and benefits of interrelated production processes and systems are cyclical and nonlinear events integral to the production of goods and services (Doig et al., 1994, 2–3).

This leads into a third and more serious limitation. Seeing production only as a process of materials flows is at best a one-dimensional perspective, abstracted from its sociospatial context and the specific socially produced imperatives that generate particular configurations of the what, how, and where of production. The industrial metabolism approach is grounded in an undersocialized conception of production based on biological analogy and a naturalistic view of markets, a reflection of its links with the orthodoxies of neoclassical economics (Ayres, 1989; Frosch, 1997). Insofar as industrial metabolism does incorporate a consideration of social processes, it is in a partial and emaciated form, with market prices seen as the only regulatory metabolic mechanism. Furthermore, it incorporates a simplistic view of the mechanisms of price formation. Consequently, it fails to give due recognition to the environmental costs of economic activities that are not reflected in market prices but that appear as externalities[9] and provides a systematic incentive to firms to lower their production costs by causing pollution.

The industrial metabolism approach also implies that the causes of environmental problems lie in market failure, leading to inefficient resource allocation because of the existence of externalities and common property resources, such as the atmosphere. As such, solutions to these problems are seen as requiring the correction of market failure via pricing formerly free environmental goods or by taxing pollution. There is scant recognition of the possible role of state regulatory mechanisms that do not rely upon manipulating market pricing and little recognition that such forms of nonmarket regulation may be necessary in relation to at least some aspects of the natural world (for example, via imposing maximum legally permissible limits or outright prohibition, or by regulatory approaches that compel companies to produce in less polluting ways). At the same time, however, as recognition of the socially constructed character of markets makes clear, it is important to avoid simplistic dualisms that posit market and state as dichotomous alternatives for environmental regulation. Just as states are deeply implicated in the construction of markets, so too are they inextricably bound into the societies of which they are a part.

In summary, while the industrial metabolism approach gives useful insights into the organizational dynamics of capitalist production and the ways in which relations between the economy and the environment are regulated within capitalism, these are partial and incomplete. As a result, it also provides at best a restricted view of the links between the economy and the environment and the dynamics of human-induced environmental change. The specific implications of capitalist relations of production for the ways in which environment–economy links are shaped must be examined explicitly.

9.4. Capitalist Relations of Production and the Production of Nature

The "mastery of nature" has been a centuries-long process that predates the rise of industrial capitalism. It was not planned or designed but has come about as the outcome of millions of small changes and tiny advances that, in a nondeterministic way, have resulted in massive transformations of relationships between people and nature (Lash and Urry, 1994, 241). Marx specifically identified human labor, the labor process, as the critical moment of metabolic interaction through which society and nature mediate one another: "nature is humanised while men are naturalised" (Schmidt, 1971, 77). The character of the labor process has, however, been strongly influenced by developments in technology and the forces of production. Since the emergence of industrial capitalism there have been spectacular developments in these forces, and the process of the transformation of nature has assumed qualitatively new dimensions. Science and technology have not simply been systematically applied in production, but the development of science and technology has been increasingly and explicitly focused on production for profit. The production of scientific knowledge is increasingly shaped by the demands of producing profits while the production of such knowledge becomes in part commodified.[10]

Relations between people and nature have therefore been progressively mediated and structured via socioeconomic and socioecological institutions specific to capitalist production. The character of capitalist class relations defines a specific form of relationship with the natural world. The abstract logic that attaches to the creation of value and accumulation of capital structures the form of relations with nature. Abstract determinations at the level of value are continually translated into concrete social activity involving interactions between people and nature (Burkett, 1997). This produces a very complex determination of relationships between people and nature. While there are strong strands in Marx's writing that emphasize people "conquering," "dominating," and "mastering" nature, there is equally evidence of an extraordinary understanding of and sensitivity toward the ecological costs of capitalism and of nature as a source of use values (Merchant, 1995). As such, nature and society are seen to be indissolubly linked within capitalist societies in specific ways. Capital circulation and ecological processes intertwine to create complex forms of environmental transformation (Harvey, 1996, 59) as the drive for profits and, moreover, for increasing profits in successive accounting periods shapes the appropriation of nature. As a result, there is a strong tendency to remove entities from their eco-systemic contexts. No part of the earth's natural environment—its surface, the atmosphere, the oceans and their floor, the geological substratum, or the biological populations that inhabitant air, land, and water—is immune from dislocation and transformation by capital in search of profits. There are certainly technological limits to the extent to which the effects of capitalist social relations can in practice penetrate beneath, say, the earth's surface in search of minerals at any given point in time. Such limits are, however, constantly being pushed back.

As capitalist relations have penetrated increasingly deeply, widely, and spatially, connections between nature and society have been more and more shaped by them, both directly and indirectly. An important distinction can be drawn between "first" and "second" natures. While historically predating the emergence of capitalist production, this was central to the development of forms of social organization based on production for exchange and in turn was increasingly eroded by it. Capitalist production increasingly produces nature "from within," continuously redefining relationships between "first nature" and "second nature," expanding the scope of the latter at the expense of the former. In part this involves processes of "capitalising nature," designating as valuable stocks of erstwhile "uncapitalised" aspects of nature, enabling capital to delineate clear property rights over natural domains and so facilitate their "highest and best" use, as defined by the logic of capital (M. O'Connor, 1994c, 144). For example, patenting plants and seeds that previously were part of the commons of indigenous societies transforms them from first to second nature, to private property with economic rights. More generally, with the transition from first to second nature (J. O'Connor, 1994, 158, emphasis added), "we enter a world in which capital does not merely appropriate nature then turn it into commodities . . . but rather a world in which *capital remakes nature* and it products biologically and physically (and politically and ideologically) in its own image. *A pre-capitalist nature is transformed into a specifically capitalist nature.*" Moreover, the residual first nature is increasingly humanized, even if its components remain "wild," as their use and management may be subject to detailed human control—for example, in forests, grouse moors, or "big game" parks.

As first nature is increasingly produced from within and as a part of second nature, these natures are themselves redefined. With production for exchange, the difference between them becomes simply the difference between nonhuman and humanly created worlds. Once first nature be-

comes produced by people, however, this distinction ceases to have substantive meaning. The significant distinction now becomes that between a
first nature that is concrete and material and a second nature that is abstract and derivative of the abstraction from use value that is inherent in
exchange value. The same piece of matter thus exists simultaneously in
both natures. As a physical entity, it exists in first nature and is subject to
the laws of physics and chemistry, the laws of thermodynamics.[11] As a
commodity, it exists in second nature, subject to the law of value and
market movements. Material nature is thus produced via socially organized human labor, which is subject to the determination of the imperatives of second nature, the incessant drive for profits that defines capitalist relations of production. Thus, "human labour produces first nature,
human relations produces the second" (Smith, 1984, 55). More specifically, the social relations of capital produce second nature, as natural, cultural, and social impediments to the circulation of capital are progressively removed. This "usurpation" of space is intended to remove barriers
to the acceleration of production and transportation activity. This usurpation is simultaneously "the production of space"[12] and the construction of a "second nature" (Altvater, 1994, 77).

This social production of nature has important implications for the
way in which nature is treated in the economy and the process of capital
accumulation is regarded (M. O'Connor, 1994c, 126):

> Through the capitalization of nature, the modus operandi of capital as
> an abstract system undergoes a logical mutation. What formerly was
> treated as an external and exploitable domain is now re-defined as a
> stock of capital. Correspondingly, the primary dynamic of capitalism
> changes from accumulation and growth feeding on an external domain,
> to ostensible self-management and conservation of the system of capi-
> talised nature closed back on itself.

Indeed, he goes on to emphasize that the modus operandi of modern capital in its "ecological phase" is not profit as such but "semiotic domination. What matters is to *institute socially* the commodity form" so as to
represent all nature (including human nature) as capital, ipso facto in the
service of capitalism as a legitimate social form. Looked at systemically,
the pricing of a good, the successful capitalization of an element of nature, or the successful repulsing of a shifted cost signals a "semiotic con-
quest," namely, "the insertion of the elements and effects in question
within the *dominant representation* of the overall capitalist system activity." This has "an undoubted 'use value' for the project of the reproduction of capital as a *form of social relations*" (M. O'Connor, 1994c, 144,
original emphasis).

Consequently, the distinction between first and second natures is increasingly rendered obsolete by the development of capitalist forces and relations of production and by the discursive strategies of capital. As such, second nature increasingly encompasses both the material world (the built environment, forces of production, and so on), the social world of the institutional formations that makes production possible, and the discourses propagated about both. Because of the expansion of production for exchange, more elements of nature, previously unaltered by human activity, were transformed via the labor process to become elements of a socially produced second nature. The production of first nature from within capitalist social relations and as part of second nature results in the production of nature per se, rather than of first or second nature in themselves, becoming the dominant reality.[13] Clearly the production of nature in this way requires the development of particular sorts of "scientific" knowledge, which provide a cognitive basis for the appropriation and transformation of nature into socially useful products.[14] People construct natural laws—that is, laws about nature—based on scientific discovery and investigation that can subsequently be applied in production. By implication at least, the production of such laws also means recognition of their limits and so of the natural limits upon production, irrespective of the particular forms of social relationships within which it is organized.

No matter how efficiently (in terms of energy and materials transformations) the production process is organized and human society is seemingly emancipated from the constraints of nature, people and their societies and artifacts continue to be subject to the limits imposed by "natural" laws and processes. This is an unavoidable aspect of the human condition, irrespective of which particular social relationships of production happen to be dominant in a particular time and space. It is important to recall that a defining feature of capitalist relations of production is that they tend to undercut the conditions that make production possible, both in the worlds of first and second nature. As such, capitalist production threatens its own future viability via its rapacious appetite for natural resources and its incessant pressures to treat the natural environment as a free waste dump for pollutants. As Smith (1984, 62, original emphasis) stresses, "The production of nature should not be confused with *control* over nature." Significant elements of first nature remain beyond human influence and control and pose risks to people. For example, earthquakes, floods, and hurricanes continue to wreak havoc on human societies, with no foreseeable prospect of their becoming internalized as part of second nature due to technological advances. Equally, prediction should not be confused with control over nature, even when it can be achieved. While predictive power is one criterion against which the adequacy of natural laws is judged, successful prediction depends upon a series of side conditions being satisfied. They may not be, but even if they are, prediction does not necessarily translate into control.

Relationships between production and nature are prone to generate unintended consequences, reflecting the complexity of interrelationships between natural and social systems.[15] Pollutants are not the immediate goal of production but are nonetheless an integral part of it. Equally, the production of nature is not the immediate goal of production but an unintended by-product of it. The focus of production is quite precise—the production of profits, not the production of nature. Much of the production of nature (like that of pollution) is therefore an unintended and uncontrolled by-product of processes of capitalist production. The next two sections explore the character of intended and unintended transformations of nature in greater detail.

9.5. Capitalist Production as a Process of Deliberate Environmental Transformation

A useful way to conceptualize relationships between capitalist production as a process of deliberate environmental transformation and the natural environment draws upon analyses of food production. Goodman and colleagues (1987) focus on the ways in which attempts to "outflank nature" via industrializing agriculture are shaped by capitalist relations of production, although the relevance of this approach is not limited to such production.[16] Processes of production, to varying extents depending upon the nature of the product, are shaped by the biological, chemical, and physical properties of raw material inputs and outputs. As such, both the scale and predictability of agricultural production—and the profits to be made from it—are prey to the vagaries of nature. Capital has therefore sought to overcome these barriers and constraints via technical and other innovations. However, such attempts are limited in their effectiveness by the distinctive character of the labor process in capitalist agriculture.[17] In agricultural labor processes, human labor is deployed to sustain or regulate environmental conditions under which seed or stock animals grow and develop. There *is* a transformative moment in these labor processes, but transformation is brought about by naturally given mechanisms and processes, not by the application of human labor. Such labor is applied primarily to optimize the *conditions for* transformations that themselves are organic processes, relatively impervious to intentional human modification and in some cases absolutely nonmanipulable. For example, the incidence of solar radiant energy is such a process, and labor processes in agriculture are thus confined to optimizing the efficiency of its "capture" by photosynthesizing crop plants or complementing it with artificial energy sources. Despite efforts to "industrialize agriculture" production involves seeking to optimize natural conditions in relation to the growing requirements of particular species (Benton, 1989, 67–69).[18]

Therefore, within agriculture people seek "localized" adaptive solutions to problems posed by the natural environment for predictable and profitable production.[19] For example, capitalist development of food production has sought to outflank biological processes such as ripening and rotting via refrigeration and air transport. Other technological innovations allow production in a wide range of locations through creating appropriate environmental conditions via techniques such as irrigation and hydroponics (replacing natural soils with a variety of growing media) and the creation of the artificial environments of glass and plastic houses, sometimes with atmospheres enriched with carbon dioxide to enhance growth, and fish farms and so on (Murdoch et al., 1998). Such intensification of agriculture substitutes energy for cultivatable area, fossil fuels for solar energy. Often the creation of such environments is accompanied by use of a range of biological and/or chemical fertilizers (Grübler, 1992). It may also involve the deployment of other techniques (such as the use of mass-produced bumble bees to pollinate tomatoes grown in glass houses, in this case seeking to adapt nature to the requirements of production rather than conquer nature)[20] to stimulate growth. Typically, pesticides are used to ensure that the crop is not eaten by unauthorized consumers before it can be sold in the marketplace. In these ways, as a result of innovations in communications, transport, and production technologies and the ready availability of large masses of cheap labor-power in many locations in the Third World, links between the locations of natural resources and economic activities have been loosened.

There are therefore strong systemic pressures to bring the diverse times needed by natural entities to survive and reproduce more into line with the time/space imperatives of capitalist production, resulting in often massive time/space dislocations for the former. Production of animals and plants becomes possible "out of time" and often "out of place," and agricultural production becomes increasingly globalized (Friedland, 1994; Goodman and Watts, 1997).[21] One consequence of this is that "exotic" tropical fruits and vegetables constantly appear on the shelves of supermarkets in affluent areas of Europe, southeast Asia, and North America. Another is that seasonality is increasingly rendered irrelevant, and supermarket shelves become filled with the same fresh products throughout the year. Rather than attempt to dominate nature in some overarching sense, the aim is to find localized solutions that allow particular sorts of production to be possible.[22]

Such forms of localized environmental modification have increasingly been combined with computing and information technology control systems to allow more precise manipulation of growing conditions in artificially created growing places and of the times at which crops are harvested within them. In some cases this extends to allowing total traceability of individual items of fruit or vegetables, to a level of detail that includes the employee harvesting a particular item and the precise time and location—the individual plant—at which (s)he does so. Such electronic control systems can also allow greater closure of energy flows within the production environment. Other technological changes seek more than just local adaptation, however. Genetic engineering seeks a more profound and global domination, seeking to alter the character of food products so as to improve various desired characteristics (such as color, size, shape, taste, and longevity) and at the same time push back further the natural constraints on production. It can involve simply the modification of existing species. For instance, genetically altered ragweed plants have been developed that clean soil contaminated by lead and other metals. Beyond agriculture, microorganisms have been developed to "eat" toxic wasted generated in semiconductor production (J. O'Connor, 1994, 157–158). More dramatically, genetic engineering can involve the creation of new species.[23] However, such attempts at genetic modification may be problematic, with side effects that are both unintended and unwanted.[24]

Another approach linking capitalist production to deliberate transformation of the natural environment centers on the ways in which capital has regarded, and in many ways still regards, the natural environment as a source of raw materials, of renewable flow and nonrenewable stock resources. Conquering nature is seen as one overarching route to profitable production and emancipating society from natural constraints.[25] There have been massive demands upon the natural resource base, especially the finite stock of nonrenewable resources such as metallic minerals but especially carbon fossil fuels. In the last analysis, this growing demand for materials from nature will constitute a threat to production, economy and society as *all* production depends on and is grounded in the natural environment. This prospect of resource exhaustion raises a related and familiar, but nonetheless quite critical, question: what converts natural materials into natural resources? Harvey (1996, 147) offers a "relational definition" of a natural resource as a "cultural, technological and economic appraisal of elements and processes in nature that can be applied to fulfil social objectives or goals through material practices." Thus, natural resources are not naturally resources. Natural materials become or cease to become resources under specific combinations of social and technical conditions. At least three conditions must be met simultaneously for natural materials to "become" resources: first, the existence of a need or, more generally in a capitalist economy, effective demand that will generate profits from production; second, the existence of appropriate enabling technology and relevant knowledge—both know-where and know-how.[26] However, there is an interdependence between technology and the degree of concentration of resources—as measured by ecology or geology—as this strongly influences the quantity of labor and nonhuman energy needed for their transformation from raw material in nature to natural resource (Deléage, 1994, 39). Third, there must be political control and the guarantee of property rights to exploit resources. If any of these conditions ceases to hold, resources could "unbecome" and revert to being "neutral stuff," simply naturally occurring materials or conditions, a common occurrence with severe localized socioeconomic impacts (Beynon et al., 1986, 1991).

At various times in the past, there have been (neo)Malthusian fears expressed about the apocalyptic consequences of finite stock resources, especially metallic minerals and fossil fuels, becoming exhausted, imposing limits to growth and leading to economic decline (Meadows et al., 1972; Paley, 1952). While in the long run such resources will certainly be exhausted, these fears have yet to be realized. This is primarily because of the emergence of successive technological fixes, allied to changing prices and market conditions, that have delayed stock resource exhaustion. Regular improvements in "exploitative technology" have allowed expanding production at declining prices, despite exhaustion of the richest ore deposits (Young, 1992) and the most accessible deposits of fossil fuels. There are several dimensions to these changes. First, there have been significant improvements in methods of exploration, notably remote sensing based on satellite data, allowing exploitation of previously unexplored areas of land and the generation of maps that identify geological structures likely to contain significant mineral resources (Andrews, 1992). There have been equally dramatic improvements in methods of exploring the ocean floors, revealing the existence of manganese nodules, a hitherto untapped source of mineral wealth (Hoagland, 1993).[27] On the other hand, as mineral ores become leaner, with a smaller ratio of the desired mineral(s) to waste material, or only available in less accessible locations, there are countervailing pressures that increase the energy requirements and environmental consequences of raw material acquisition.

Second, both mining and processing technologies have become more efficient. For example, more effective ways of extracting oil and natural gas reserves led to revisions in the estimated life of existing oil and gas fields, though this is only delaying the inevitable (Hargreaves, 1992). At the same time, processing technologies have become more efficient in their conversion of natural resources into finished product: the energy inputs to smelt and refine metals have fallen markedly (Young, 1992).

Third, there has been a considerable increase in recycling, with around 25–30% of materials previously fabricated into commodities or produced as waste by-products being recycled in the advanced capitalist world. The extent of recycling typically depends, among other things, upon the relative prices of recycled and virgin materials. The reasons for the limited extent of recycling "appear to be not so much physical as economic" (Wernick et al., 1997, 146). As such, there is considerable scope for further recycling. Some companies and industries already achieve much higher levels. Steel produced by the electric arc route can be produced entirely from scrap. Furthermore, complex products such as automobiles could be designed from the outset (via design for disassembly principles) to facilitate total recycling once they reach the end of their useful lives. The closure of material loops through reuse of materials complements the reduction in the quantity of materials used per unit output in a range of products from aircraft to cars to cans (Wernick et al., 1997, 143–145). For example, in the 1990s glass factories used as much as 90% recycled materials, while 85% of cars produced by Honda and Toyota were recyclable. Carbon fossil fuels cannot be so recycled, however, and this may pose a major constraint on future patterns of production, directly and indirectly. Moreover, while recycling is generally less energy intensive than production from virgin raw materials, it is not necessarily so and may also have other undesirable environmental impacts via pollution (for example, in the case of paper; Weaver, 1994).

Fourth, there may be possibilities to substitute a ubiquitous, or more widely available, material for another that is less widely available. For instance, aluminum can be substituted for copper in electrical applications, but it is a less conductive metal and so cannot be safely used in underground ducts or in other confined spaces in which there is a risk of overheating. Another option is to substitute a different and environmentally more benign material for a more hazardous one. Ceramics based on widely available clays can be substituted for metals (for example, in automobile engines) and sand for copper (as in fiber optics, the use of which has grown enormously in telecommunications because of fiber's greater information-carrying capacity), for example. Such changes are often linked to process innovations and changes in the way in which products are designed and produced. More problematic is the substitution of plastics for metals (for instance, for lead or copper pipes or for metal parts in automobiles). While these may be commercially attractive, they are typically produced from oil and in addition may be difficult to recycle (Griffiths, 1993). In some circumstances, it may be possible to create synthetic substitutes or to replace naturally occurring materials with new products that do not naturally occur as part of creating a "second nature." Finally, there is the possibility of replacing naturally occurring finite stock resources with renewable flow resources. For example, coal, oil, and gas could in principle be replaced as sources of primary energy generation by biomass, hydroelectric, solar, wave, or wind power. Perhaps in the longer term fossil fuels could be replaced by environmentally benign forms of nuclear power based upon hydrogen and nuclear fusion rather than fission, although disasters such as Chernobyl (see Marples, 1987) have hardened popular resistance to nuclear power in much of the world.

9.6. Capitalist Production as a Process of Unintended Environmental Transformation and Pollution

Capitalist production therefore involves deliberate and intentional transformation of elements of nature in search of profits. However, material practices are always transformative activities engaged in by people operating in a variety of modes, with unintended as well as intended consequences (Harvey, 1996, 146). As such, production unavoidably generates unforeseen—and often unwanted—effects as well. This is for two reasons: first, as a result of the nonmanipulability of the materials balance principle; second, because production always occurs in circumstances in which the agents involved lack full knowledge of the circumstances in which they act and of the consequences of the processes that they set into motion. Cast in the terms of critical realism, the point may be stated more precisely as follows: production involves agents identifying the relevant properties (causal powers, liabilities, and tendencies) of natural materials and processes required to achieve their intended purposes. For any given production process, however, these will only form a subset of the properties of its elements. The remaining properties constitute an indefinitely large "residual" category that, from the standpoint of the calculations of the agents involved in the process, may be known or unknown, or seen as relevant or irrelevant to the achievement of the immediate purposes of production. Insofar as this class of properties does not enter into these calculations, the practices of agents—that is, the processes of production—will have unforeseen and/or unintended consequences in addition to those intended. These may counteract, exceed, or otherwise modify the intended outcomes. These unintended consequences are typically characterized in terms of pollutants of various sorts. As such, causal mechanisms set in motion by production processes *that are extrinsic to the achievement of their purposes* may undermine the future sustainability of such production (Benton, 1989, 73–79).

Capitalist production regards the natural environment as a source of natural resources to be exploited efficiently in search of profits. All commodity production ultimately can be traced back to appropriation of elements of nature as a prelude to further transformative processes. While at times fears have been expressed that some key natural resources (notably hydrocarbons and metallic minerals) would become exhausted and pose "limits to growth," Young (1992, 5) has remarked that "in retrospect . . . the question of scarcity may never have been the most important one. Far more urgent is another question: can the world afford the human and ecological price of satisfying its present appetite for minerals?" Such resources undoubtedly are absolutely limited in supply, but a variety of technical and social innovations have for the moment kept this issue relatively low on the agenda. However, the way in which the natural environment continues to be regarded as a sink of infinite capacity for deposition of unwanted wastes, the unpriced by-products of production, poses more serious problems.[28] Yearley (1995a, 161) argues that "the vast majority of pollution arises from economic activities themselves, from power generation, from the operation of chemical plants, from mining operations, from travelling to and from work and from agricultural enterprises." While the reference to commuting hints at dissipative pollution as a consequence of products being consumed, it fails to give sufficient weight to this latter form of pollution. In addition, once such products are sold, consumers of them treat the environment as a waste dump for the unwanted by-products of consumption. There is abundant evidence of such impacts (Jackson, 1995). Limits to this waste dumping can be set by national states placing a total prohibition on particular types of waste discharged, by setting maximum permissible limits, by creating prices for them via taxation systems, or by creating trading systems in pollution permits. A consequence of this is that pollution standards vary among countries, with important implications for the location of pollutant industries and for patterns of trade in wastes (which are examined below).

Although many economic activities have considerable locational room for maneuver, others such as mining remain unavoidably tied to the location of natural materials because of historical geology. As a result, mining and often processing generate a range of localized environmental impacts that impinge upon the health and living conditions of local residents. This can be experienced as noise, visual intrusion, and pollution of the atmosphere, land, and water bodies by a wide range of hazardous and noxious materials (Beynon et al., 2000). More generally, the unwanted environmental consequences of industrialization have been and continue to be heavily localized, both between and within countries. The harsh reality of pollution is time-and-space-specific. Industrial production has varied impacts upon places in which people live and work, on their health, and on death rates. People live in visually blighted landscapes punctuated by the noise of mining and manufacturing, and breathing polluted air. There is, however, often a distance-related decay effect from the pollutant source, resulting in an externality gradient relating intensity of impacts to distance from source.

There is an enormous weight of evidence that points to such impacts throughout the course of industrial capitalism, often graphically described by contemporary commentators. Consider the following three passages. The first is from James Naysmith, inventor of the steam hammer, commenting upon the impacts of ironworking at Coalbrookdale, one of the birthplaces of industrial capitalism in the late-eighteenth century (cited in Springett, 1999): "The grasses had been parched and killed by the vapors of sulphureous acid thrown out by the chimneys. And every herbaceous object was a ghastly grey—the emblem of vegetable death in its saddest respect. Vulcan had driven out Ceres." The second passage (written by the wife of a Teesside iron master) forcefully points out that such fallout also impacts upon people, and refers to the environment in and around the ironworks of nineteenth-century Teesside, England (Bell, 1985, 30):

> Besides the fumes and the gases, every breath of wind at the ironworks carries dust with it, whirling through the air in a wind, dropping through it in a calm, covering the ground, filling the cabins, settling on the clothes of those who are in reach, filling their eyes and their mouths, covering their hands and their faces. The calcined limestone sends forth red dust, the smoke from the chimneys and furnaces is deposited as white dust, the smoke from the steel rolling mills falls as black dust; and, most constant difficulty of all, the gases escaping from the furnaces are charged with a fine, impalpable brownish dust, which is shed everywhere, on everything.

The third passage describes the environment in the coal mining village of Shotton in east Durham (England) in the 1930s, in the shadow of the colliery spoil heap (Priestley, 1934, 336–337):

> Imagine then a village . . . at the base of what looked at first like an active volcano. This volcano was the notorious Shotton "tip." The "tip" itself towered to the sky and its vast dark bulk, steaming and smoking at various levels, blotted out all the landscape at the back of the village. Its lower slope was only a few yards from the miserable cluster of houses. One seemed to be looking at a Gibraltar made of coal dust and slag. But it was not merely a matter of sight. The monster was not smoking for nothing. The atmosphere was thickened with ashes and sulphuric fumes, like that of Pompeii, as we are told, on the eve of its destruction. I do not mean that by standing in any one particular place you could find traces of ash in the air and could detect a whiff of sul-

phur. I mean the whole village and everybody in it was buried in this thick reek, was smothered in ashes and sulphuric fumes. Wherever I stood they made me gasp and cough.

Environmental costs on this scale were interpreted and accepted as a necessary price of employment. Attempts to preserve or protect the natural environment often provoked powerful alliances (of companies, trade unions, and local political organizations, for example) seeking to prioritize employment, production, and profits over environmental concerns (Beynon et al., 1994; Blowers, 1984).

Such conditions have certainly been ameliorated by state regulation in much of the advanced capitalist world, although they have by no means been eliminated there (Beynon et. al., 2000; Blunden, 1995). For example, Chicago's southeast side contains 50 commercial hazardous waste landfills, 100 factories (including seven chemical plants and five steel mills), and over 100 abandoned toxic waste dumps. Consequently, it has one of the highest rates of incidence of cancer in the United States (Bullard, 1994, 14–15, 279–280). Another grim example of this is Times Beach, a small town in Missouri irreparably contaminated by dioxin. Dioxin had accumulated in factory sludge as a by-product of manufacturing antiseptic hexachlorophene. When the factory closed at the start of the 1970s, the sludge was combined with waste oil and sprayed as a dust-settling mixture on the streets of the town. Subsequent health complaints eventually led the Environmental Protection Agency (EPA) to identify dioxin as the cause of the problems. A winter flood then spread the contaminated dust and silt throughout the town, across the river floodplain. The town was subsequently evacuated as a result of a mass buyout of its inhabitants by the EPA. Access was barred by fences and armed guards, with huge signs proclaiming "Hazardous Waste Site." Entry was possible only after signing a "general release of liability" under which all risks and perils were assumed by the visitor (Calton, 1989).

While rare but not unknown in the core territories of capitalism, such events are only too common over much of the industrializing world in the peripheries, in places in which the imperatives of economic growth and employment unashamedly take precedence over those of the natural environment and human living conditions. Disasters such as that at Bhopal (India) are painful reminders of this. On December 2, 1984, five tons of poisonous methyl isocyanate gas leaked from the Union Carbide of India Ltd. pesticides plant there. More than 3,000 people were killed immediately and tens of thousands injured. Recent (1999) estimates put the longer-term death toll at over 6,000, while people exposed to the leak continue to live lives blighted by a range of physical and psychological illnesses. There is still substantial and in some locations severe pollution of land and drinking water supplies from heavy metals and organic contaminants, with residents of these areas exposed to the risks of hazardous chemicals on a daily basis.[29]

Modern "industrial" agricultural practices, especially those involving the wholesale destruction of natural environments (for example, clearing rain forests to create cattle ranches) can lead to marked reductions in genetic variety and biodiversity (Yearley, 1995a). In addition, such practices can have other impacts such as increased soil erosion and silting of rivers and fertilizer pollution of inland waters. For example, use of artificial fertilizers can have unintended pollutant consequences; nitrates that can no longer be held down by the colloids of the vegetal soil are carried away by running water to accumulate in coastal waters and lakes (Deléage, 1994, 40). Mining and industry continue to have a range of localized impacts on natural environments. Consider, for example, the impacts generated simply via minerals' extraction. First, excavation and ore removal lead to destruction of natural habitats, increased erosion and silting, waste generation in the form of overburden, acid drainage if the ore or overburden contains sulphur compounds, and metal contamination of lakes, rivers, and groundwater. Second, ore concentration generates wastes in the form of tailings, organic chemical contamination (as tailings often contain residues of chemicals used in concentrating processes), and acid drainage and metal contamination of water bodies. Third, smelting and refining produce atmospheric pollution (via toxic emissions that include arsenic, cadmium, lead, and sulphur dioxide), solid waste (in the form of slag), and the impacts of producing energy needed for smelting and refining. The list, even in relation to this limited stage of the process of converting elements of nature to consumable commodities, is formidable (Young, 1992). Despite improvements in mining and processing technologies, these impacts have often become more pronounced as lower-grade minerals, requiring a higher ratio of overburden to desired minerals and located in more difficult and remote locations, have been worked.

While such activities and their impacts are localized, the frequency of their occurrence around the world leads to their becoming, in a sense, global phenomena. Moreover, some impacts of industrial production have become widespread in other ways (for example, diffusion of sulphur dioxide in the atmosphere, leading to acid rain and destruction of vegetation). Others have even become truly global in their effects, as in the case of enhanced global warming attributable to emissions of carbon dioxide and other greenhouse gases such as methane, leading Wernick and colleagues (1997, 138) to argue that "decarbonization of the economy is thus clearly of paramount importance." Another major global environmental problem is the thinning of the ozone layer owing to emissions of chlorofluorocarbons (CFCs). The example of CFCs is a particularly instructive and sobering one. In themselves CFCs are harmless to human and animal life and so were widely used following their development in the middle of the twentieth century. In due course, but in a relatively short period of time, they migrated to and accumulated in the upper atmosphere where, because of unanticipated chemical reactions, they destroy the ozone layer that filters out ultraviolet radiation. These processes of unintended environmental change undoubtedly reflect the production and consumption trajectories of the worlds of advanced capitalism and late modernity and the fact that these develop in circumstances in which people have at best only partial understanding of their implications for nature.

National states have become increasingly involved with environmental regulation. The initial state policy response to the environmental impacts of industrial production in the national territories of advanced capitalism was to seek to manage and contain them. This was attempted via land use planning, segregating incompatible land uses, along with public health legislation and some weak environmental regulation to limit the worst excesses of such impacts. Environmental pollution was seen essentially as a *localized* problem. However, industrial activities continue to have environmental impacts, some unavoidable if these activities and the jobs they provide are to continue. They could certainly be reduced via use of more appropriate technologies, but they could not be removed entirely.[30] As jobless and then job-shedding growth emerged and it became clear that production no longer guaranteed a given level of employment, protests grew against the impacts of polluting production in the surrounding localities. Increasingly, existing forms of state regulation were seen as inadequate by an emerging "green" politics and growing environmental concern, leading to pressures to tighten environmental standards. People living in places built around environmentally polluting industries such as coal mining, chemicals manufacturing, and steel production were increasingly resistant to their adverse effects on "their place." It was no longer generally accepted that a tradeoff between employment and the environment was inevitable, that industrial pollution was an unavoidable condition of everyday life, especially as industrial employment declined or totally disappeared in many such areas. However, such environmentally based politics and concerns were themselves unevenly developed, and environmentalist movements to curb industrial pollution were often fiercely resisted (Beynon et al., 1994, 2000).[31]

One corporate response to mounting environmental opposition and regulation that no longer permitted the environment to be treated as a cost-free waste disposal unit in some places was to relocate to others in which such constraints were weaker or nonexistent. The production of pollutants can thus *to a degree* be spatially adjusted, shifted to places where their localized impacts are more tolerated. There are several aspects to this. First, "dirty" industries can be relocated to avoid regulatory control. Historically, in the precapitalist era and in the early phases of the industrial revolution, the location of industry was closely tied to the locations of heavy, weight-losing raw materials and energy sources (such as coal and iron ore). This reflected technically inefficient—and heavily environmentally polluting—methods of production and transport.[32] As a result, there was a powerful spatial concentration of the new industries around such materials and/or in rapidly growing urban areas. This locational concentration continued into the first half of the twentieth century, with new consumer goods industries such as cars also concentrated in large but different urban areas—though more for reasons of available labor and markets than access to natural resources. From around the 1960s onward, there was growing concern, especially in densely populated urban areas, about the environmental effects of certain sorts of industrial production—specifically, that involving asbestos, arsenic trioxide, benzidine-based dyes, certain pesticides and some other carcinogenic chemicals, chemicals such as polyvinyl chloride (PVC), and some basic mineral processing activities relating to copper, lead, and zinc, for example (Leonard, 1988). As a result, enabled by advances in transport and communication technologies, companies began to relocate hazardous and polluting production activities. Initially this involved moving to peripheral regions within their home national territories but increasingly to parts of peripheral countries within the global economy, thereby constituting a formative moment in the creation of the (so-called) newly industrializing countries. Companies were often encouraged in this by financial inducements and low (or no) levels of environmental regulation as national governments there were eager to encourage the perceived benefits of modernization via industrial growth and employment, for "the state in underdeveloped capitalist countries is frequently drawn into pursuing the pursuit of accumulation at any social or political cost." As a result, "the expansion of state capitalism to Third World areas has, throughout the 'post-colonial' period, . . . extended the commodification of nature and . . . greatly exacerbated local causes and levels of environmental degradation" (Fitzsimmons et al., 1994, 209–211). Thus, there has been an increasing dispersal of the localized impacts, both positive and negative, of industrial growth. This added a rather different range of environmental impacts in the industrializing parts of the periphery of the global economy, as compared to those generated there by primary sector production and mining of raw materials.

The significance of lower environmental standards in the wholesale relocation of certain types of production to parts of the Third World should not be overestimated, however. Environmental regulation has certainly tightened considerably in many advanced capitalist states since the early 1980s, and this has acted as a push factor. For example, much of the heavily-pollutant Japanese aluminum and copper smelting industries were re-located to poorer parts of south and east Asia (such as the Philippines) to avoid Japan's more rigorous environmental regulations. However, the importance of being able to dump wastes free of charge into the environment varies among industries. For many industries favorable labor market conditions or market penetration are more potent attractions (Michalowski and Kramer, 1987). In fact, relocation is not a common corporate response to more stringent environmental standards. While there are examples of production processes in which the response has been to relocate, "these are the exceptions to the norm" (Leonard, 1988, 111). Most industries have responded to heightened environmental enforcement and standards via technological innovations, changes in raw materials, or more efficient process controls. Even when such adaptations have failed to reduce regulatory concern, the environmental problems and the costs of responding to them have generally been insufficient to offset the attractions of locating production within major markets. Even companies manufacturing polyvinyl chloride and acrylonitrile largely responded to intense environmental regulatory pressures and adverse publicity in the United States by undertaking accelerated technological innovation within the most rapidly growing market rather than relocation of production to a more lax regulatory environment. In contrast, in countries such as Federal Republic of Germany, there was a greater relocation of productive capacity in these industries, both to peripheral regions in countries such as the United Kingdom (Beynon et al., 1994) and to parts of peripheral countries such as Brazil.[33]

An alternative to exporting polluting industries is to export their pollutants. For example, environmental pollutants from coal-fired power stations can be effectively exported in molecular form via emissions from high chimney stacks and fall as acid rain hundreds of miles away. In other cases, waste products are exported in different forms, with a more deliberate targeting of destination locations. The international trade in pollutants is complex, with locations such as Sellafield in the United Kingdom importing nuclear waste from other parts of the world for reprocessing there. More often, though, such locations are in countries on the periphery of the global economy. For example, Kassa Island, off the coast of the former French African colony of Guinea, became the recipient of 15,000 tons of highly polluted incinerator ash (pollutants included dioxins and heavy metals) from power stations in Philadelphia (Yearley, 1995a). Some countries are so poor, and in such desperate need of foreign currency earnings (to buy imports or repay foreign debt) that ruling élites will consider any trade likely to generate such earnings. Risks to the environment and the health of their populations are readily discounted. As people in more economically developed countries came to understand the dangers posed by noxious pollutants, and environmental standards were increased, pressures increased to find ways of dealing with such pollutants. Exporting them to other areas desperate for foreign currency often was cheaper than dealing with them at home. That option was made easier when the recipient countries were misled about the nature of the wastes and/or had authoritarian nonelected governments who neither knew nor cared. Dealing with such wastes within their own home territory could involve not only considerable financial costs but also, perhaps more significantly, political costs—particularly in the face of widespread NIMBYism ("not in my back yard") and opposition by local communities to such wastes being treated in "their place." However, not all local communities had an equal capacity to resist either their own pollution or dumping, such that "one of the best predictors of the location of toxic waste dumps in the United States is a geographical concentration of people of low income and color" (Harvey, 1996, 368). Indeed, poorer communities within the advanced capitalist world and peripheral states within the global economy have engaged in bidding wars, seeking to act as destinations for hazardous wastes in return for monetary payments and additional income.[34]

Increasing environmental standards have also led to new forms of trade in wastes. In Germany, for example, stringent regulations on recycling were introduced in the 1990s. Picking through waste to sort and recycle it is a labor-intensive enterprise, poorly paid and of low social esteem. As such, it is exported to parts of the periphery of the global economy—and is justified as creating employment there! Although there have been international agreements aimed at regulating and limiting trade in noxious wastes that have halted the worst excesses of the trade,[35] they have stopped short of trying to eliminate it entirely. Consequently, the core territories of capitalism still offload their wastes onto those of the periphery (Yearley, 1995a). This does not entirely result in a free pass for waste exporters, however, for the impacts of pollution can still return to blight the areas of origin. For example, factories relocated from the United States into the maquiladora border zone in Mexico in response, among other things, to less stringent environmental regulations there (South, 1990). Unfortunately, they subsequently ended up exporting air pollution (via prevailing wind patterns), sewage, and contaminated food back to the United States. Thus, "ecological havoc recognises no boundaries, as is becoming increasingly clear in the U.S. states bordering on Mexico" (George, 1992, 6).

Thus, as the locational choices of economic actors and activities widened, allowing for the possibility of seeking "spatial fixes" to deal with localized problems of pollution, there was also a growing realization that the impacts of industrial mass production and consumption were not simply spatially concentrated and confinable. Indeed, they were having global impacts, with potentially disastrous implications. As Dryzek (1994, 187) notes, to the extent that states cannot simply displace ecological problems, environmental concerns become firmly established on political agendas. The critical insights provided by the materials transformation perspective (based on the chemistry and physics of production) help us to understand why this is so. Accelerated global warming attributable to the release of carbon dioxide from power stations, internal combustion engines, and so on, as well as the release of other greenhouse gases such as methane, threatens the sustainability of existing patterns of economic activity, production, and consumption. In more apocalyptic visions, it endangers the future of the planet itself.[36] From the perspective of companies and national states in the affluent core territories of advanced capitalism, this meant that there were serious limits to their attempts to deal with problems of industrial pollution via strict environmental regulation "at home" and "spatial fixes" to relocate pollution problems, for in the final analysis much of the pollutant effects of industrial production are not simply local and localizable but have global impacts and implications. They cannot be contained via spatial fixes but rather can only be displaced to other locations from which they continue to impact upon the global environment.

As a consequence of growing worldwide awareness of the problem, there have been attempts to construct global régimes of environmental regulation through most national states agreeing to limit emissions of greenhouse gases, notably carbon dioxide (as at the Rio de Janeiro and Kyoto earth summits in the 1990s). At the same time, the creation of pollution trading régimes has sought to make global limits compatible with the legacies of uneven development and contemporary differences in levels of pollution production. In this way pollutants themselves are commodified and global markets created for them via tradeable pollution permits. As Fitzsimmons and colleagues (1994, 203) put it, in this way "business and environmental groups have agreed to extend the market to resolve . . . arenas of environmental struggle through devices such as marketable pollution permits." As they note, however, this uneasy compromise is only an apparent resolution, displacing environmental struggles into the mechanisms of markets and the realm of economic contradictions, from whence they will be further displaced into the political arena as crises of state involvement.[37] Nevertheless, such global environmental changes will impact differentially because of variations in natural environments, topography, and the variable capacity to implement technological solutions to ameliorate their effects, differences that are in part a product of past uneven development. They will impact back upon the countries of the advanced capitalist world that generate the vast majority of such pollutants, but their national states also have greater financial and technological resources to cope with them.

The capitalist economic system provides no "natural" regulatory mechanisms and little or no social regulatory mechanisms to control materials dispersion.[38] Industrial production and consumption frenetically disgorge a wide array of chemicals, some of which do not exist in nature and many of which exceed natural flows by several orders of magnitude (Jackson, 1995, 7–20). The extent to which the stock of carbon-based fuels and other minerals is being depleted and dissipated, with a range of unwanted environmental impacts, is clearly of critical importance. Economic activity is essentially and unavoidably dissipative. It is conceivable that a shift to a decarbonized economy would be possible within capitalist relations of production, provided that the activities associated with it satisfied the normal profitability criteria and fell within socially and politically acceptable limits. Then again, it may not be; for "the second contradiction [of capitalism] states that when capitals attempt to defend or restore profits by cutting or externalising costs, the unintended effect is to reduce the 'productivity' of the conditions of production, and hence raise average costs" (J. O'Connor, 1994, 165). Thus, a second critical issue relates to the extent to which this second contradiction can be held in check and systems of social and political regulation and governance can be constructed to ensure that production and consumption move to more environmentally—and socially—sustainable trajectories.

9.7. Sustainable Capitalist Production: But in What Sense Sustainable?

The vision of capital accumulation as a coherent and internally self-sustaining process is clearly untenable, for such accumulation is constituted via vast numbers of commodity networks that mix people, technology, and nature at varying spatial scales and in diverse ways in pursuit of profitability, with intended and unintended consequences (Murdoch, 1997). These effects may well redefine relations between capital and nature. As such, this raises questions about the sustainability of both. Not so long ago, the rise of environmentalism as a political force was interpreted as "an expression of the interests of those whose class position in the nonproductive sector locates them on the periphery of the institutions and processes of industrial capitalist societies" (Cotgrove and Duff, 1980, 341). Thus, environmentalism's rise was linked not just with middle-class concerns but specifically with those of a fraction of the service class (Urry,

1981). Such a view now looks odd, overtaken by events and the rise of more socially and spatially generalized concerns with issues of environmental quality and sustainability.

Contemporary culture is said to be characterized by reflexive awareness of the long-term relationships between people, other animals, and the rest of nature within an almost geological notion of time. These relations are seen as very long-term and evolutionary, and there has been growing recognition that they must be kept within sustainable limits and evolve along sustainable trajectories. Current demands must be made compatible with sustainable futures in a context of considerable risk, uncertainty, and ignorance about the potential for and limits to substitutability among elements of both the natural world and the human world. Consequently, there has been a fundamental reevaluation of nature. Nature is increasingly seen as less disposable than even very recently thought and people are increasingly seen as having overarching responsibility for its preservation. This entails taking a long-term view, far beyond the lifetime of the current inhabitants of the earth, so that sustainability takes on both intragenerational and intergenerational dimensions. It redefines "progress" from "human domination of nature" to "transformation of relationships between people and nature"—that is, the adoption of more complex conceptions of people–nature relationships that acknowledge people as indissolubly *part* of nature rather than apart from it (Lash and Urry, 1994, 243–249, 293).

Sustainable development is certainly a strongly contested concept. McManus (1996), for instance, identifies no less than nine different discourses relevant to this concept. Recognition of contestation focuses attention on the necessarily political character of the issues at stake. Politically, such contestation has shifted the agenda significantly. Environmental quality is no longer seen as a luxurious positional good that only the rich can take time to consider. Rather, environmental quality is now regarded as necessary for ecological survival and further economic development. Economic growth and environmental quality are no longer perceived as competitive and incompatible but as *complementary* objectives. Thus, sustainable development is grounded in a discourse of ecological modernization, in claims that capital accumulation, profitable production, and ecological sustainability can and must be made to be *compatible* goals (Hajer, 1995). As such, ecological modernization theses conjoin doctrines of efficiency in production with those of efficient and equitable workings of ecological systems. The growing concern to discover sustainable forms of development can thus be seen in part as an attempt to bridge the divide between ecocentric and anthropocentric views of the environment (as identified by O'Riordan, 1981) or between technocratic/reductionist and ecocentric/holistic paradigms of development (Springett,

1999). This concern also increasingly reflects a desire to avoid the dangers (amounting to a "pox on all houses") of a prolonged standoff between advocates of economic growth and those of no growth, between optimistic cornucopians and pessimists for whom ecological disaster is "just around the corner."

Indeed, emphasizing the importance of devising ecologically and environmentally sustainable forms of production has become increasingly popular, often in seemingly unlikely quarters.[39] The World Bank (1994, 42), for example, argued that achieving environmentally sustainable development is a "major challenge of the 1990s." This may well be correct, but part of the problem of evaluating competing claims as to what needs to be done to achieve sustainable development is the absence of consensus as to exactly what it means in practice. There are, for example, significant differences within the ecological movement between advocates of "strong" and "weak" sustainability, between "deep" and "shallow" environmentalists and between various shades of "green politics" as to what "sustainable production" would entail (Baker et al., 1997). Implementation of some "deep green" positions would require significant reductions in material living standards and radical changes in the dominant social relations of production (Goodin, 1992). Such changes would be powerfully contested. Not least, it is unclear whether a strong ecocentric concern would be associated with a progressive politics of radical social change or reactionary conservatism designed to preserve the status quo and protect the interests of the powerful (Pepper, 1984). The politics of some "dark" green positions are unambiguously eco-fascist, with scant regard for the degraded living conditions and lifestyles of the majority of the world's population. Implementation of such views would condemn the vast majority of people to a miserable future, at best on the margins of the bare minimum of physical existence.[40] Ceasing to produce *all* toxins, hazardous wastes, and radioactive materials would have disastrous consequences for the public health and well-being of millions of people, many of them poor already (Harvey, 1996, 400). In contrast, "paler green" perspectives are conceived much more in technicist terms within current relations of production, essentially trading off economic against environmental objectives (Pearce et al., 1989). Indeed, such pale blue-green perspectives slide into nongreen "grey" views that see economic considerations as preeminent over ecological ones and take little notice of existing environmental or social inequalities.

Perhaps the most frequently quoted definition of sustainable development is that the United Nations World Commission on the Environment and Development (1987, 43), namely, meeting "the needs of the present, without compromising the ability of future generations to meet their own needs." Thus defined, sustainability encompasses relations between environment and economy and a commitment to equity intragenerationally, intergenerationally, and spatially. It encompasses a vision of development that extends beyond quantitative growth in material output and incomes to include consideration of qualitative improvements in living and working conditions. Nonetheless, in seeking to remove the developmental gap between core and peripheral states of the capitalist economy, it advocated increasing manufacturing output fivefold or tenfold in the peripheral states. While the report emphasized the need for qualitative changes in the character of growth, it was conspicuously silent on how this could be achieved. As such, it remains open to the charge that it failed to take full account of the ecological consequences of this expansion in industrial output. In broad terms, then, the so-called Brundtland Report accepts and seeks to work within the grain of, rather than radically challenge, the dominant logic of capitalist production.[41] The implications of this are considered more fully below.

A more precise identification of the ecologically damaging aspects of current methods of production, levels of consumption, and lifestyles invites consideration of more sensitive approaches. One such approach centers on notions of "eco-restructuring" (Weaver, 1993). In broad terms, this encapsulates the process of transforming modern capitalist industrial society from one characterized by highly inefficient use of virgin materials and fossil fuels, high levels of material consumption, and high emissions of wastes to one that is environmentally more benign. This would entail considerable dematerialization of the economy. There is evidence that this is already occurring. For example, "an assessment of consumption per unit of activity in the USA shows a dematerialization in physical material of about one third since 1970" (Wernick et al., 1997, 139). Others argue that this is inadequate but that current technologies could permit an increase in efficiency of natural resource use by a factor of four. This is also seen as insufficient, however, with suggestions that there needs to be an increase by a factor of ten over the next fifty years (Wuppertal Institute for Climate, Environment and Energy, 1994; von Weizsacker et al., 1998). The impetus for such changes once came from fears of exhausting nonrenewable resources, of reaching and then breaching "the limits to growth." More recently it has been motivated by recognition that there are limits to the capacity of the natural environment to absorb wastes, of reaching and then breaching the limits to pollution, as there are limits to the robustness and reproducibility of natural processes as the variety and volumes of pollutants rises. There may also be a cultural dimension, tied to medical ethics, namely, that technological advance has, for the moment at least, gone far enough, at least in the most developed areas of capitalism, in creating artificial extensions to more or less everything.[42]

One possible way forward is to examine the technical possibilities of—and economic, political, and social conditions necessary for—enhanced ecological closure in production and consumption (Ayres et al., 1988; Weaver, 1994), a transition to systems of "clean production" (Allaert, 1994). This would require process innovations and the production of "cleaner" and materially more efficient ways of producing. There are well-known limits to "end of pipe" technologies to ameliorate inherently "dirty" production processes. Moving from "end of pipe" cleaning up of inherently dirty processes and engineering in "cleanness" from the start, minimising use of virgin nonrenewable resources, and maximizing recycling and seeking to minimize use of ecologically damaging materials are all eminently desirable. It is necessary to move toward "complete 'life cycle analysis' if the transition to clean, sustainable production is to be successfully brought about" (Wernick et al., 1997, 143). The central tenet of ecological modernization theses is that such a transition is compatible with capital accumulation. "Clean technologies" can be a source of competitive advantage, subject to the existence and enforcement of regulatory régimes that set stringent environmental standards. Corporate advertising campaigns emphasize the environmental benefits of "green" production technologies and products. Companies may therefore seek the imposition of higher environmental standards as part of their competitive strategies. Within the European Union, for example, companies have been very active in seeking uniform environmental standards across the Union so that they can sell straightforwardly in the markets of all member states. Enhancing environmental standards can be a very effective way of excluding cheaper but less "green" potential competitors from markets, politically a far more palatable alternative than trade sanctions. There may therefore be strong pressures for rigorous national and international environmental regulatory régimes *precisely because* they favor some corporate interests over others.

Consequently, production can be described in politically correct environmental imagery and language, and environmental concern thereby inadvertently becomes a medium for legitimating capitalist relations of production. The possibilities for profits that this creates can lead to radical corporate restructuring. It is ironic that many dominant firms in environmental technology industries competing to clean up hazardous wastes, control pollution, and repair environmental damage were the same companies that previously *generated* these wastes, pollutants, and damage. As Pratt and Montgomery (1997) put it: "pollution, penitence, profits." This can lead some to see sustainable development as a dangerous liaison between environmentalists and capital—a potential recipe for "business as usual." There are, additionally, dangers in seeking "technological fixes" in circumstances characterized by risk, uncertainty, and partial knowledge (Beck, 1992). One has only to think of such examples as the unan-

ticipated environmental impact of chlorofluorocarbons on the strato-
spheric ozone layer, the substitution of diesel for high-octane (petrol)
combustion engines leading to increased emissions of fine particulates, or
the recycling of paper leading to increased chlorine emissions. Such cases
are painful reminders of the unintended and unwanted harmful environmental impacts that sometimes result from well-intentioned efforts to
ameliorate other environmentally harmful effects.

These examples of unintended consequences raise critical questions
about the human capacity to understand complexity and the behavior of
complex systems, in which small incremental changes in the values of one
variable may trigger major systemic change. The complexity of a system
can be thought of as a consequence of the degree of indeterminacy associated with the behavior of its elements, a product of the latent creativity
and instability of its elements and organization. Apparently small changes
in environmental conditions can radically alter the modes of activity displayed by systems and their subsequent interactions with their surround-
ings; and vice versa. As a result (M. O'Connor, 1994b, 66, emphasis
added):

> Indeterminacy of the time path of a complex system—that is, concern-
> ing the "outputs" that will obtain from some given initial state, inputs
> and environmental conditions—implies the impossibility of predicting
> in advance, and perhaps in any way controlling, the "inputs" that this
> system will provide to others co-dependent upon it. *Autonomy and
> openness are inherently linked to indeterminacy and incomplete con-
> trol.*

This is a critical insight, with clear implications for policy choices
and modes of policy implementation, for, as Dryzek (1994, 181) observes, "administrative rationalty cannot cope with truly complex
problems."[43]

There is clearly a link between state regulation and the forms in
which, and the extent to which, patterns of production and consumption
have been and could further be restructured onto more sustainable and
environmentally less damaging trajectories. There are numerous ways in
which states can change their regulatory régimes, ranging from direct
prohibition to encouragement and discouragement via financial incentives and disincentives, and facilitate the transition to more materials-
efficient and environmentally less damaging economies (Young, 1992).
Ameliorating environmental damage and pollution from activities such as
mining could be funded via taxes on virgin mineral consumption, with
the added benefit of encouraging recycling. Recycling could be encouraged in other ways via legal requirements, for example, compelling manu-

facturers to accept return of products at the end of their useful lives and recycle them, or by financial incentives. Consumers can be encouraged to return products as diverse as automobiles and beverage containers for re-use via various deposit and refund schemes. Nevertheless, there may be limits to the scope for recycling because of the materials inefficiencies of current production processes. For example, 30% of industrial minerals consumed in the United States in 1990 "dissipated into the environment and were rendered practically unrecoverable" (Wernick et al., 1997, 138). The same point applies to materials dissipated because of consumption and use of final products.

Taxation structures can be changed to penalize environmentally damaging products and production methods and encourage environmentally friendly methods and commodities produced in more sustainable ways, engineering in "clean production" and environmentally less demanding and recycleable products from the outset. Carbon taxes can be used to penalize use of fossil fuels, while incentives can be provided to switch to renewable energy sources (such as biomass, wind, wave, hydroelectric, and solar power, via photo-voltaic cells). Taxation structures can likewise be altered to encourage more efficient energy use and conservation—for example, by meeting part of the costs of insulation schemes. Environmental pollution can be reduced via imposing maximum permissible limits for discharges in the atmosphere, land, and water. Land use policies could be introduced to reduce distances and minimize transport costs between residences, workplaces, and leisure facilities and produce built environments that are more energy-efficient. Built environments could also be constructed to minimize the amounts and mixes of natural materials required. Undoubtedly, "prevention is better than cure. . . . The greatest environmental benefits are usually yielded by basic alterations to production processes and consumption patterns rather than through 'pollution control' " (Young, 1992, 53).

The economic and social consequences of policies to dematerialize production and enhance environmental sustainability beyond the realms of intercorporate competition must be considered, however. This is particularly so in relation to attempts to shift countries still seeking to industrialize onto more materials-efficient trajectories in circumstances in which there are powerful pressures to meet basic human needs and enhance human welfare. There is a critical question of how their industrial development could be financed using "state-of-the-art" technologies. Alternatively, and even more challengingly, the question could be posed as to how such countries could be helped to devise routes to improve human welfare that would not involve large-scale industrialization. These issues are particularly pressing inasmuch as many peripheral countries have been forced into massive foreign debt and structural financial dependence by international organizations such as the World Bank and International Monetary Fund. Consequently, these countries must entice transnational mining and manufacturing companies via financial inducements (unrestricted profits repatriation, for example) in an attempt to repay debt interest, leading to less stringent regulatory standards and more permissive attitudes toward the pollutant effects of mining activities (Goodin, 1992). There are grave dangers in examining possible changes to more ecologically sustainable forms of production without full consideration of either the social conditions that this presupposes or the implications of this for economic and social sustainability.[44] It is vital to consider possible moves toward ecological sustainability in terms of *their* economic and social sustainability. It would be profoundly dangerous to ignore such issues. For example, would the level, composition, and distribution of output under an eco-restructuring program be seen as socially acceptable and/or politically legitimate within the parameters of a democratic state form (as opposed to those enforceable within a dictatorial régime)? If not, what would be the ecological implications of what would be socially and politically acceptable? There is a clear need to broaden the idea of "sustainability" beyond the natural environment to encompass dimensions of economic, political, and social sustainability.

The definition of sustainable relationships between production, the environment, and places is a normative issue involving political choices and prioritization between competing, perhaps even incompatible, objectives. In many ways, it is easier to specify what to avoid than to specify what ought to be. This is easily seen by recalling certain aspects of the crises of mass production and consumption that prevailed over the industrialized world (both the western capitalist and eastern state socialist variants) for much of the postwar period. In both cases a unifying tacit assumption was that of a linear economy (Jackson, 1995). An environmentally more sustainable post–mass production successor that envisions the economy "nonlinearly" would need to preserve important material benefits from industrialization that have improved human living conditions while acknowledging that there are ecological consequences that must be respected, limits that should not be breached in humanity's self-interest. This could involve deployment of the precautionary principle in cases that, on the basis of existing knowledge, would create environmental hazards. For example, many environmentally problematic chemical compounds include chlorine; application of the precautionary principle would lead to a cautious approach to any risk of releasing chlorine into the environment. There have been several attempts to generate new "post–mass production" approaches to production and economic management at both microscale and macroscale.[45] These confirm that the mix of products and production processes would need to change radically, with distributional consequences even if total output were to continue to rise. If output was stabilized or fell, these consequences would be even more marked. Would, then, an ecologically sustainable production system be socially and politically sustainable? What sort of sustainability might be possible? How might it be achieved? What sort of regulatory régime would it imply? These are large and difficult questions not amenable to being answered easily.

9.8. Is Sustainable Production Possible within the Structural Limits Defined by Capitalist Social Relations?

Whether " 'sustainable capitalism [is] possible' is in the last, as well as in the first, instance, a political question" (J. O'Connor, 1994, 170). This emphasizes that sustainability is a multidimensional conception encompassing, at a minimum, three aspects (Hudson, 1995b): first and preeminently, an economy that yields sufficient profits to ensure continuing commodity production; second, an economy that generates enough paid employment, suitably distributed, to ensure social stability and the reproduction of labor-power. The formal and informal sectors of the labor market linked to circuits of capital are unlikely to provide enough paid employment to absorb all those capable of and seeking work. Therefore, maintaining social stability may also necessarily involve developing a "third sector" of community projects and initiatives. The third aspect of sustainability would require an economy that has moved onto technological trajectories that are sustainable in terms of the pressures that they exert upon the natural environment. Meeting all three objectives simultaneously is clearly tricky, not least in terms of demands placed upon mechanisms and processes of governance and regulation.

Eco-Keynesianism offers one possible option for seeking to reconcile these competing pressures and specifying the anatomy and physiology of a sustainable eco-capitalism (Hudson and Weaver, 1997). It represents a radically reformist attempt to combine environmental and social sustainability while respecting the profitability imperatives of a capitalist economy. Keynesianism incorporated a commitment to a degree of equity and social justice that was predicated on a regulatory régime that equated mass production and consumption—but with little regard for their environmental consequences. Its demise heralded a neoliberal growth and regulatory model predicated on increasing inequality, high unemployment, and continuing environmental destruction, albeit with some adjustments at the margin. Eco-Keynesianism aims to make environmental sustainability and fuller employment compatible goals in a more just society. Indeed, it actively pursues the search for environmental sustainability as *the* mechanism through which to pursue fuller employment and greater social justice—this, in fact, constitutes its key defining characteristic. There is certainly scope for employment creation via introducing environmentally less damaging ways of producing, moving, and consuming. Resolving environmental and unemployment problems simultaneously would, however, require more radical changes in the methods of production, modes of consumption, lifestyles, mobility patterns, and no doubt much more besides.

This eco-Keynesianism model presupposes, as a necessary condition, a new and radically different regulatory régime incorporating at least the following five key features. First, a loosening of the link between monetary rewards from work in the formal economy and individuals' living conditions and life chances. Second, measures to strengthen and legitimize the "grey economy" of the "third sector" to help create a vibrant social economy and ensure that environmentally enhancing work is carried out. Third, gradual but comprehensive revision of the tax and benefits system to one ultimately based on taxation of environmental resources used, with the revenues raised forming the basis for citizens' income and public expenditure; this is perhaps the single most important change. Fourth, an environmentally lean, mean formal sector economy based on "clean" technologies and "environmentally friendly" methods of producing and delivering services through markets. Finally, conceptualizing the economy as providing services to be delivered in part via material commodities, and taking account of the social and environmental costs and consequences of their provision. This is, clearly, simply another in a long line of reformist models, but such reformism is as much as is currently possible. Furthermore, it is a model developed in the context of the territories of advanced capitalism. Its implementation might be more problematic in the peripheries of the global capitalist economy. A shift to eco-Keynesianism in affluent core territories while much of the poor peripheries strove to embark on the path of mass production and mass consumption industrialization would create powerful tensions and add further dimensions to uneven development at the global scale.[46]

However, there may be a more fundamental problem since "the ecological contradictions of capitalism make sustainable or 'green' capitalism an impossible dream" (Pepper, 1993, 95). As such, discovering sustainable forms of production organization via technological change and innovations in national state regulation and international interstate agreements may be problematic. State regulation may fail to guarantee nonproblematic resolution of ecological problems generated by industrial production. Indeed, there is much empirical evidence that supports such a conclusion and persuasive theoretical evidence that suggests that, with respect to a capitalist economy,[47] this is *unavoidably* so, as state involvement cannot abolish its inherent economic crisis tendencies. These are simply internalized within the operations of the state in ways that must in due course undermine the viability of the mode of regulation. Hay (1994, 220, emphasis added) has this to say about the logic of crisis displacement:

> Specific manifestations of the fundamental and global environment–economic contradiction, though precipitated initially within the global economic system, become displaced to the level of the nation-state and are articulated as rationality crises of the political system—*that is, as political crises of environmental regulation.*

The best that (national) states can hope for is to "discover" modes of environmental—and other spheres of—regulation that are temporarily appropriate to particular economic growth models or régimes of accumulation. As a result, for a time conditions necessary for successful production will be more or less nonproblematically reproduced. However, contradictions displaced into the structures and operations of the state will in due course appear as crises of the state itself.[48] There is, therefore, no a priori reason to believe that state regulation will successfully resolve the problems of environmental damage and ecological destruction that arise because of the character of capitalist production. As Benton (1989, 86) puts it: "If capitalist economies have intrinsic ecological crisis-generating mechanisms, it remains to be seen whether these crises, along with more widely recognised forms of economic crisis, can be effectively managed by way of legislation and state intervention."

From a different point of departure, and using a different vocabulary, Bayliss-Smith and Owens (1994, 128) reach the same conclusion. There is, they suggest, widespread recognition that "the environmental crisis" of the First World and the poverty of the Third World are opposite sides of the same coin. Moreover, the Brandt Report, the Brundtland Report, and even the World Bank (galvanized by the threat of ecological disaster leading to debt default by Third World states) all accept the same "basic thesis" (while using different language to express broadly the same concepts), namely, that generalized poverty and other pathologies of underdevelopment in the Third World are symptomatic "of a process whereby surplus value and surplus product are extracted from people under conditions of unequal exchange." Unequal exchange (Emmanuel, 1972) is perhaps of less significance than the exploitative character of capitalist relations of production, but there is considerable validity in their argument and the conclusions that they draw. The implication is clear—and painful. The linked problems of environmental crisis, widespread poverty, and uneven development (within the core territories of a global capitalist economy and its peripheries as well as between them) cannot adequately be addressed through new forms of state policy and regulation within the confines of capitalism. Once again, the limits to capital are reached.

9.9. Summary and Conclusions

Production involves the transformation of natural materials by human labor and so has unavoidable impacts upon the natural environment. This transformation is mediated by particular forms of social relationships of production. Within capitalist social relationships the dominant influence on this mediation between people and nature is the necessity to produce profits. This has redefined relations between people and nature as the growth of scientific knowledge, and technological innovations have increasingly pushed back the boundaries of first nature and advanced those of a socially produced second nature within the logic of market resource allocation. For much of the historical geography of capitalist industrialization (and indeed state socialism from Stalin onward), this led to the natural environment being regarded both as a limitless supply of raw materials and as a waste dump of infinite capacity. The industrial footprint on the natural environment was indeed a heavy one and continues to be so. For decades the human and environmental consequences of treating the natural environment in this way were accepted as a necessary, if undesirable, cost of economic growth and employment. Rising material living standards and jobs were traded-off against polluted environments as national states sought to contain and localize these impacts via land use planning and environmental regulation.

From around the mid-1960s onward there has been a growing realization that the natural environment is neither an endless source of natural resources nor a sponge of infinite capacity that can absorb pollutants ad infinitum. Particular concerns have been expressed about the impacts of pollution upon the natural environment and the environmental sustainability of the capitalist industrial economy. Furthermore, the limits to localized solutions to pollution problems became increasingly visible with the realization that some forms of pollution could become truly global in their reach. Greenhouse gases, which are pollutants irrespective of whether they do cause increased global warming, already generate global impacts. Consequently, there has been a gradual acknowledgment that there are definite limits to relationships between people, production, and nature that arise because of the iron laws of thermodynamics, limits to economy–environment relationships that cannot, for the moment at least, be changed by human action. The theoretical questions such as these high-light practical issues of sustainable production, what sustainability would mean in this context, and the political possibilities for and difficulties of shifting production onto more sustainable trajectories. Sustainability is a slippery and contested, though powerful, concept, however. There is no consensus as to what such a transition would require or entail. It is clear, however, that sustainable production would need to encompass more than just relations between the economy and the environment and natural environmental sustainability. It would also need to include issues of equity and social and environmental justice and political legitimacy. Whether this can be achieved within the social relations of capitalist production remains at best an uncertain prospect.

9.10. Notes

1. Benton (1989, 58) correctly argues that recognition of such limits is a progressive move: "In the face of realities which are genuinely invulnerable to human intentionality, adaptation by modifying or even abandoning our initial aspirations [to control nature] is to be recognised as a form of emancipation."
2. This relationship does not hold in nuclear reactions, forming the basis for hopes of "clean" nuclear energy. However, seeking to go down this route has created significant environmental hazards and risks (Marples, 1987).
3. Frosch (1997, 159) develops this insight as follows: "We can postulate a universe of material/energy paths through the production, life, and dissolution of any product or set of products. We can also consider each path to be a sequence of transformations from one material/energy embodiment to another. We can view the whole of material industry as a network of such paths and transformations, connected at each end (extraction of materials and disposal of products) to the environment external to the process and product and at places in the middle (disposal of incidental waste)."
4. It is worth pointing out en passant that spatial interaction models draw on concepts of entropy in modeling transport flows and spatial structures (Wilson, 1971).
5. Consequently, the second law is sometimes described as the "law of increasing entropy."
6. Although these two concepts are often used synonymously, it is useful to distinguish between them. Metabolism refers to the examination of energy and materials inputs to a specific facility, industry, or sector, and the waste products—heat and materials—released from it. Ecology refers to the total process from the raw materials extraction, transportation, manufacture, use, and disposal of products and the interaction of these with the natural processes of the biosphere (Weaver, 1995a).
7. Bleached kraft pulp mills typically use chlorine or chlorine dioxide and

caustics to bleach or whiten pulp. Mills that bleach with chlorine are responsible for releasing many chlorinated organic compounds, including toxic dioxins and furans, which are persistent in the environment and biomagnify up the food chain (Gismondi and Richardson, 1994, 233).

8. Marx characterized energy and materials entering the production process but not embodied in the intended end-product as "accessory" raw materials. Since his primary focus was upon understanding the intended consequences of commodity production, he paid little attention to the "further adventures" of these materials (Benton, 1989, 73).

9. That is, costs imposed on others without consent or compensation.

10. See also sections 5.3 and 5.6.

11. These laws can be considered as simply cultural constructs, and from one point of view that is precisely what they are. However, since laws such as that of gravity continue to function with regular predictability and have a practical utility, it is reasonable to assume that they consistently relate to physical processes.

12. Altvater's views on the simultaneous production of nature and space resonate with ideas set out in Chapter 8 as to space being the product of stretched-out social relationships.

13. Thus, the development of capitalist forces of production can be seen as a process of emancipating people, to a degree, from the domination of nature; however, this relative emancipation is integrally linked to antagonistic and contradictory social relationships of production, grounded in the subordination of labor to capital. It involves the production of complex eco-systems of built environments that are central to human (and many forms of nonhuman) life.

14. See also section 5.6.

15. The reasons for this are discussed in section 1.3 in relation to critical realist accounts of knowledge.

16. More generally, Goodman and colleagues (1987) summarize how capital seeks to outflank nature via two interrelated processes: appropriationism and substitutionism. Appropriationism denotes the attempt by industrial capital to replace previously "natural" production processes with industrial activities. Substitutionism refers to the substitution of synthetic products for natural ones. In the specific context of food the synthetics comprise a strategy progressively to eradicate biological and biochemical constraints on production. In the more general context of industrial production, they represent an attempt to emancipate production from the constraints of nature via deliberately transforming natural environments as part of a process of eliminating the boundaries between first and second natures.

17. As compared to manufacturing industry; see Chapter 4.

18. Clearly, GMOs seek to circumvent these constraints via producing transgenic organisms and as such change the labor process from an agricultural to manufacturing one.

19. Adaptive technologies are constitutive of some of the most fundamental and distinctive features of human ecology: the building of shelters, of mechanized means of transport—indeed, the whole of the urban fabric and built environment

(Benton, 1989, 79). This raises important questions having to do with the purposes of production and the production of the material settings that make production possible (see also Chapter 8).

20. I am grateful to Huw Beynon, Mark Harvey, and Steve Quilley for this example. It arises from on-going work in the Center for Research into Innovation and Competition at the University of Manchester as part of a project investigating "The Tomato: Markets and Distributed Innovation Processes"; see Beynon and colleagues (1998).

21. There are simultaneous countertendencies toward localization, notably because of the growth of organic production in response to fears about the dangers of human interference in the natural processes of food chains. This involves processes of product innovation aimed at particular niche food markets; see Morgan and Murdoch (2000).

22. For example, irrigation techniques make agriculture possible in deserts and hydroponics enable production in areas devoid of suitable natural soils.

23. Such modifications relate both to the biological and material construction of the commodity and to its discursive construction and to product differentiation and marketing strategies (see section 5.4). The "traceability" of products is becoming increasingly important in relation to consumer perceptions of risk in the food chain and growing resistance to genetic modification among certain social strata and food retailers, as concerns over bovine spongiform encephalopophy and more generally genetically modified foods graphically illustrates. This in turn is impacting back on marketing strategies as food producers and retailers seek to reassure consumers that their products contain no genetically modified material.

24. As Benton (1989, 68) succinctly puts it: "The newer biological technologies have been 'sold' within a voluntaristic–Promethean discourse which has inevitably occluded or rendered marginal the limits, constraints and unintended consequences of their deployment in agricultural systems." However, there is evidence of growing consumer awareness of these consequences (see, e.g., Wrong, 1999; Wrong and Tait, 1999).

25. Within state socialism, conquering nature was an equally pressing priority, (allegedly) in the collective interests of society. It was only when it became clear that Lake Baikal was becoming an ecological disaster on a par with Lake Erie that serious questions began to be raised concerning the proper ecological perspectives that should be built into socialism (Harvey, 1996, 146).

26. See also section 5.6.

27. Establishing international legal frameworks to enable the exploitation of such resources raises complex issues, however. See also section 3.6.

28. Such costs arise because capitalist "free" markets are conceptualized and regulated in ways that give companies a systematic incentive to lower their private production costs by causing environmental pollution that is experienced as an externalized social cost; see section 9.3.

29. I am grateful to Amanda Banks for this information on the current status of Bhopal.

30. For reasons outlined in sections 9.2 and 9.3, materials transformations are subject to the iron laws of thermodynamics.

31. Thus, in some circumstances campaigns to defend places took on a strong green hue, while in others there was strong opposition to environmentalist arguments; see also section 8.4.

32. This is reflected in the early industrial location theories such as that of Weber (1909).

33. Growing pressures to deal with the legacies of previous polluting technologies allowed companies and sectors to emerge and produce profits via cleaning up and restoring the environment; see section 9.7.

34. As the resurgence of controversy in 1999 over the future of the Sellafield nuclear reprocessing plant illustrated, such dirty work by no means guarantees future jobs and incomes (though the environmental consequences will remain long after the jobs boom has dissipated.

35. For example, in 1989 the United Nations promulgated an international convention concerning such trade.

36. While there is continuing political debate over whether human activity is responsible for global warming due to increased emissions of greenhouse gases, the consensus of scientists is now overwhelming that increased emissions are very largely responsible for the problem.

37. See also Chapter 2. These contradictions are intensified because such international regulatory régimes are created by national states to influence corporate behavior. But these states lack the capacity to enforce such régimes and "their translation into behavioral effects at the corporate level is problematic" (Bennett, 1999, 197, citing Vogler, 1995, 154).

38. Nor for that matter did the state socialist ones—if anything they imposed even fewer constraints.

39. Although for some the term "sustainable development" is an oxymoron (Goldsmith, 1992; Rich, 1994).

40. A large proportion of the world's population already exists on these margins, but that is an argument for seeking to change relations of production and distribution to improve their lot, not an argument for forcing still more people into a penurious existence. For Gaians (Lovelock, 1988) the human race is in any case not seen as necessary to the survival of the earth as an organic system, which has great resilience and capacity for survival.

41. As such, the Brundtland definition represents a political compromise, constrained by the lowest-common-denominator acceptance of a common position on issues that separate a wide variety of powerful political and economic interests.

42. Ian Simmons pointed this out to me, and I am grateful to him for doing so.

43. This suggests that there may be lessons to be learned in terms of the conceptualization of learning in complex corporate environments; see Chapter 5.

44. See section 9.3.

45. These are discussed in Chapters 5 and 6.

46. If peripheral states could not afford the latest eco-technologies, how could—indeed, should—they be persuaded not to embark on industrialization

when this was seen as a route to improved living conditions for their citizens? This is an important practical question with a strong moral dimension.

47. There is an equally impressive (if that is the most appropriate term) volume of evidence that ecological devastation was frequently even worse under the political economy of state socialism. There seems little doubt that propositions about agents acting in circumstances of which they have only partial knowledge of the consequences of their actions (Giddens, 1984) would equally apply in the context of state socialism as in that of industrial capitalism.

48. These issues are discussed fully in section 3.5.

10

Postscript

10.1. Introduction

In this brief final chapter I focus on three broad sets of issues. The first concerns the object of analysis and the character of contemporary capitalist production and economies—in particular, the extent to which claims about the transition to "postindustrial" or "service" economies are valid. The second set of issues recognizes the growing complexity of the economy, however theorized. It focuses on the resultant challenges that face national states, companies, trade unions, and local communities. Finally I return to the issue of the extent to which production and the economies of capitalism can be moved onto more sustainable trajectories, acknowledging the contested and problematic character of the concept of sustainability.

10.2. What Sort of Capitalist Economy, What Sort of Geographies?

There is widespread agreement that there has been significant change in the character of capitalism but disagreement as to how this should be interpreted. One effect of the influence of regulationist approaches has been claims that the historical geography of capitalist development can be understood as a series of shifts from one régime of accumulation, with its associated mode of regulation, to another. The most recent of these is seen to be that from Fordism to post-Fordism. There is an assumption that the national is the decisive organizational scale and an assumed correspondence between macroscale economic changes and microscale workplace- and firm-level changes in the organization of commodity production. For some analysts, therefore, the emergence of new forms of high-volume production and the (re)discovery of old forms of batch pro-

duction and production by small firms linked into industrial districts constitute evidence of a transition from a Fordist to post-Fordist industrial
economy. Such a perspective, however, is problematic on several counts.
It assumes a tight national scale coupling of an aggregate economic
growth model and mode of regulation but there is growing recognition
that governance systems are complex and multilevel. Furthermore, it is
clear that there is no necessary stable coupling between mode of regulation and growth model. Nor is there a necessary correspondence between
macroscale and microscale changes. As a consequence, others have taken
a different view, emphasizing the strong threads of continuity between
past and present, and interpreted observed changes as a more complex
form of organization of after-Fordist industrial production. Processes of
governance and regulation are seen as complex and, at times, contradictory rather than nonproblematically corresponding with the requirements
of a given growth model. There is also acknowledgment of variation in
microscale models of production even in the canonical Fordist period and
that this continued in heightened form into an after-Fordist phase. Consequently, changes cannot be appropriately captured in a dichotomous
transition from Fordism to post-Fordism, as the conjuncture of aggregate
growth models, microscale models of commodity production, and regulatory practices is complicated and variable through time and over space.
Moreover, it is as yet unclear what will succeed Fordism—hence the emphasis on "after-" rather than "post-" Fordism.

For others, the focal point of attention is service sector growth, seen
as one of the most marked features of recent capitalist development. As a
result, there have been strong and persistent claims that the capitalist
economy has become a "postindustrial" or "service" economy. While the
economy continues to be dominated by the imperatives of commodity
production, the character, composition, and mix of commodities produced has changed radically. Others dispute the claimed transition to a
postindustrial service economy, however. They argue that, although the
anatomy of the capitalist industrial economy has altered, material production remains of central significance to it. The rise of the services sector
and the theoretical challenges that this poses thus create problems in understanding contemporary capitalist economies on two counts: definitional and interpretative.

As companies considered the make, buy, or network choice, many
decided to contract out a variety of noncore "service" functions. This
reflected the relative disadvantages of vertical integration and producing
in-house as compared to vertical disintegration and subcontracting and
buying services in the market. Both manufacturing and service sector
companies have adopted such strategies, which have been important in
the expansion of service sector employment and output in the core capi-

talist economies. New sectors have arisen, and the division of labor has widened and deepened as layers of intermediate goods have multiplied. In many accounts, producer services are a key stratum in these intermediate layers, of central importance to contemporary capitalist economies. For some their expansion confirms the emergence of a postindustrial service economy. Others, however, argue that this is misleading, a product of conceptual confusion, since services must be consumed as they are produced. Products such as advertising copy are material commodities, not services—although the performance of services may well necessarily involve their use. For example, about 80% of all computing and IT equipment is purchased by service sector companies, striking evidence of the material basis of service production (Castells, 1989, 137).

This definitional dispute is indicative of a deeper debate as to how "services" in general and "producer services" in particular should be conceptualized and how they relate to the accumulation process. These competing claims require careful scrutiny. Some years ago, Bell (1973) asserted that the capitalist economy had become postindustrial. More recently, expansion of business and financial services has been seen as confirming the emergence of a putative post-Fordist régime of accumulation. Knowledge-creating and -managing activities and business and financial services are seen as the "leading edge" of a new post-Fordist era of "flexible" or "reflexive" accumulation. For others, this is a mutation of existing tendencies rather than a radically different departure. The alleged transition to a service economy is best characterized as a widening and deepening of social and technical divisions of labor, part of a more general and continuous process of industrial evolution and capitalist development. This is a complex evolutionary process, with too many threads of continuity between the past and the future to be adequately represented via a sharp break from Fordist to post-Fordist accumulation régimes. The division of labor in complex processes has vastly augmented the number of workers engaged in indirect productive activities—incorrectly labeled "service labor" and increasingly contracted out—leaving proportionately fewer workers engaged in the direct hands-on tasks of transforming materials into useful products. As a result, there is an *increase* in the "roundaboutness" of the production of material commodities (Walker, 1985, 1988).[1] Material commodity production has *always* involved a degree of "roundaboutness." What *is* new is the increase in its extent. As such, the change is quantitative rather than qualitative.

Seen in this light, the growth of producer (and many other) services has in fact simply been part of the trend toward firms subcontracting work within an industrial capitalist economy. Not all of such growth results from increased subcontracting, however. Less than a third of recent producer services growth can be unequivocally linked to vertical disintegration (Lentnek et al., 1994), suggesting that there are more autonomous processes leading to the growth of such activities. Does this then constitute a transition to a new model of service-based growth per se? If such services *are* at the "leading edge" of a new model of capitalist growth, how do they fit into the accumulation process? There is a well-established and unresolved debate in Marxian political economy as to whether "services" are "productive" of surplus-value. While not dismissing all such activities as parasitic vis-à-vis productive capital, it is nonetheless important to raise a couple of questions. First, *which* of the activities relate to production, circulation, and consumption of commodities and production, circulation, and realization of surplus-value? Second, *how* do they do so?

Expansion of service sector employment has also had important implications for spatial divisions of labor. There have been important shifts in the geographies of service production, echoing those in manufacturing, closely connected with technological advances in communications and transport. These enable the location of different producer service occupations to be matched to labor market conditions. While technological developments permit greater spatial dispersion of some producer service activities, overall there has been sharpened spatial differentiation *within* producers' services. The new "electronic highways" are in this way "freezing" spatial patterns, reinforcing existing tendencies rather than acting as a catalyst for the emergence of radically new ones. Time-space convergence is leading to greater *qualitative differentiation* in the geographies of producer services and, more generally, in the geographies of capitalist economies. In particular, it has reinforced the need for key decision makers to be in "information-rich" environments while allowing spatial dispersal of routine functions to a wide—though not an infinite—variety of locations as connections to electronics networks become a crucial locational determinant.

These tendencies can be observed at spatial scales from the global to the local. Key decision-making, command and control, and financial functions are concentrated in a very few global cities, a particular type of industrial district dedicated to producer services, the "switching points" of the global economy. Increasingly, the geographies of these services are being recast globally as a variety of other jobs are shifted beyond the boundaries of the core capitalist countries. Within the advanced capitalist world there are related trends with key decision functions concentrated in national capitals and "back offices" decentralized to peripheral locations within national borders. Within major cities key jobs remain concentrated in central areas while routine "back office" activities are relocated to suburban locations (Nelson, 1986). This greatly heightens intraurban sociospatial differentiation within them. Such tendencies are very visible in global cities and, in more muted form, are evident in other major metropolitan economies (Hamnett, 1994). This emphasizes the ways in which changes at different spatial scales are linked and woven together within an increasingly complex overall geography of production.

In summary, there are ongoing debates as to the extent to which more complex divisions of labor indicate a transformed industrial economy or an emergent postindustrial one and about the resultant geographies of capitalist economies. The position advocated here is that capitalist production remains just that, with material production remaining of central significance. Nevertheless, the anatomy of the capitalist industrial economy *has* changed in important ways as divisions of labor have become more finely differentiated. Geographies of production and their regulation involve an increasingly complicated mix of spatial scales and mosaics of uneven development. This complexity makes claims about the transition from one régime of accumulation and mode of regulation to another problematic.

The complexity of the contemporary capitalist economy extends beyond the scope of the formal sector; however, I will simply make four summary points, briefly. First, there is a considerable "informal" sector of activities that are legal but beyond the reach of "normal" regulatory and governance mechanisms. Second, there is a large illegal economy—activities beyond the bounds of what is defined as legal. Third, there is in many areas a burgeoning "third sector" of community economic initiatives, linked in varying ways to states and markets. Fourth, there is a considerable economy of unwaged labor, some of it for subsistence and self-provisioning, much of it performed in the home and linked to the reproduction of labor-power. Thus, the contemporary capitalist economy is constituted as a complex mosaic of different forms of production, employment, and work, complex divisions of labor in which industry, occupation, age, ethnicity, gender, place, and space are linked in complicated ways. Put another way, there is much more to the contemporary capitalist economy than capitalist social relationships and many forms of work and employment that are not validated through the market mechanisms.

10.3. Challenges for the Future

The growing complexity of capitalist economies, and their increasingly finely differentiated geographies, pose a variety of problems for national states, companies, trade unions, and local communities. Challenges arise for national states from processes of increasing globalization and international interfirm linkages that problematize the concept of national economic interest. Challenges also arise from the emergence of new modes of governance and regulation in which both supranational states and subnational state institutions are also involved in a complex multilevel architecture. National states are confronted with an increasingly demanding policy agenda in an increasingly volatile environment. Managing the crises of capitalist development and crisis management strategies have become ever more crisis prone. Part of the response to this by national states has involved withdrawal from direct involvement in seeking to shape both production and its geographies within their national territories. Power has been ceded upward to create transnational regulatory organizations and downward to cities and regions. Within their national territories, states have invented new forms of enabling actions to replace direct state provision of goods and services, but these simply transfer crisis tendencies from the state to civil society and the economy rather than resolve them. However, rather than becoming irrelevant in terms of regulation and governance, national states have become enmeshed in new ways in these processes that they have helped constitute and in some respects their significance has been enhanced.

Second, there are challenges to companies as a result of having to deal with the problems of organizing complexity, of coordinating complex technical, social, and spatial divisions of labor within and across company and national boundaries. Networking and other forms of interfirm cooperation have become of greater importance in the organization of production, redefining the nature and boundaries of firms. This poses significant challenges in managing knowledge and innovation and seeking to create Schumpeterian competitive advantage via market disturbing activities in the context of decreasing product life cycles and the increasing ephemerality of production. Indeed, the concept of product life cycle ceases to be relevant in the context of mass customization, as the process life cycle assumes central importance in competitive strategy. Many large and some small companies can often use such changes to their advantage—indeed, they deliberately manufacture them to create opportunities for technological and other rents. However, for the vast majority of small firms, locked into dependent positions within the structure of supply chains, there are different challenges. These changes make their survival more difficult, as the intensity of price and other forms of competition becomes more profound.

Third, there are challenges for organized labor and trade unions as technological change in production processes and changes in social, technical, and spatial divisions of labor increasingly outflank their established methods of operation, recruitment, and representation of their members' interests. Unions are faced with difficulties as a result of deepening labor market segmentation and fragmentation dividing workers from other workers in the context of growing global mobility for many (but by no means all) types of capital and economic activity. Some unions are seeking to transform from an industrial to a community basis, but such a transition is far from easy. At the same time, however, the introduction of new production technologies and methods of organizing production, the increasing significance of interfirm relations to intrafirm production, creates possibilities for unions to organize in new ways, although there are serious difficulties for them in realizing this potential.

Fourth, national states, capital, and labor are confronted with the threats and opportunities that arise because of the enhanced significance of finely grained spatial differentiation and divisions of labor in shaping what is produced where. This has been associated with increased competition between places and territories at all spatial scales. Place marketing, and the construction of place-based interests within this competitive struggle, has reached new heights as places compete for investment and jobs. However, the "speedup" of the economy as processes of time-space compression continue to intensify as transport and information and communication technologies have developed further (and have been given a further spurt as a result of the emergence of e-commerce) continues to pose threats to the economic rationale of places. The challenge to states to maintain their own legitimacy while balancing the competing demands of capital for expanded accumulation and people in their places who insist on a sustainable future has become more severe.

Fifth, capitalist development has become even more uneven, between firms, sectors, and territories. Advances in transport, information, and communications technologies have formed the basis on which heightened uneven development has occurred. Given the claims made as to possible "high roads" to economic development, is a future of rewarding (materially and intrinsically) work possible within the social relations of capital? If so, for whom, where, and when? What are the implications of this for those condemned to the "low road," or indeed no road at all, as they are condemned to a future of permanent unemployment and exclusion from the wage labor force? This will pose severe challenges for states and civil societies in managing a more complex map of sociospatial inequality. There are suggestions that such tensions could be contained, at least in part, via the emergence of "third sector" economic initiatives. However, for this to come about without such initiatives reproducing existing sociospatial inequalities and becoming simply a source of cheap labor that underpins accumulation poses a major challenge to states and societies.

10.4. The Final Frontier?

Increasing recognition of the unavoidable grounding of production and the economy in nature has thrust the question of sustainability center stage. This is without doubt the $64,000 question for humanity. It is essentially a normative and political question, the answer to which will have profound implications for the world's population. While radically reformist proposals for forms of eco-capitalism go far beyond what is currently being contemplated in the realms of formal politics, they do not challenge capitalist logic sufficiently strongly on fundamental economic issues to allow social justice, income and resource redistribution, and enhanced democratization to be given more than marginal consideration alongside a strong conception of ecological sustainability (cf. Mol, 1996). As J. O'Connor (1994, 154–155) puts it: "The short answer to the question 'Is sustainable capitalism possible?' is 'no,' while the longer answer is 'probably not,' " and "while the prospects for some kind of 'ecological socialism' are not bright . . . those of a 'sustainable capitalism' are even more remote." This suggest that, however difficult the transition, the future cannot lie in eco-capitalism but in eco-socialism, whatever that comes to mean as a noncapitalist alternative.

There have been several suggestions as to how to reconcile ecological and socialist concerns in restructuring production along eco-socialist lines. However, eco-socialism is a slippery concept, defying easy definition and even more so practical application. However, there clearly will need to be dramatic changes in the composition, methods, and geographies of production (and so of consumption and lifestyle) if sustainability is to be achieved. In particular, there will need to be changes in the social relations of production if relations between people and nature are to be restructured onto more sustainable trajectories. Harvey (1996) argues that a practical eco-socialist movement will have "no option" but to retain for itself a "non-co-opted and non-perverted version of the theses of ecological modernization." This would require detaching concerns for environmentally less damaging forms of production from the exigencies of capital accumulation. Thus, "alternative" modes of production, consumption, and distribution, as well as alternative modes of environmental transformation, must be explored

> if the discursive spaces of the environmental justice movement and theses of ecological modernization are to be conjoined in a program of radical political action. This is fundamentally a class project, *whether it is exactly called this or not*, because it entails a direct challenge to the circulation and accumulation of capital which currently dictates what environmental transformations occur and why. (400–401, emphasis added)

Altvater (1994, 89, original emphasis) makes the point powerfully, as follows: "We must create social and political border lines before the frontier of capitalist expansion reaches the last ecological border, which could be fatal for the survival of the human race. Once we realize that a transformation in the *social* forms is what is required, fruitful discussion about ecological reform might begin."

Whether such transformations will be possible remains an open question. But for those who wish to change the world and its systems of production progressively, "theoretical practice must be constructed as a continuous dialectic between the militant particularisms of lived lives and a struggle to achieve sufficient critical distance and detachment to formulate global ambitions. . . . Theory cannot be brought to bear upon the world of daily political practices without finding ways to embed it in the materialities of place, space and environment" (Harvey, 1996, 40). And conversely, without effective translation into everyday political practices, theory will have little if any effect upon that world. Wolf (1986, 40) suggests that there is a broad spectrum of social forces pressing for such a transition:

> A "conversion" of the material structure of agricultural and industrial production is being raised by workers struggling against plant closures, by women struggling against a sexist division of labour, by post-colonial countries struggling against material dependence built into their productive apparatus and, last but by no means least, by consumers; and conservationists' initiatives and by the peace movement's focus on the deep "deformations" in the international productive structure induced by the arms race.

While pressures from such diverse sources undoubtedly do exist, they currently do not amount to a coherent political campaign, and so it remains uncertain whether and in what ways they might be translated into the everyday practices of a radical mass political movement. Nevertheless, the struggle to effect such a translation is still worthwhile. Indeed, the future of humanity may well depend upon its outcome.

10.5. Note

1. In contrast, Lash and Urry (1994, 95) argue that manufacturing is becoming a more roundabout method of producing services. Perhaps the key point is not whether Lash and Urry or Walker are correct in their imputed direction of causality but rather to recognize that formerly useful sectoral classifications are increasingly redundant in the face of the changing character of linkages and relationships within and between companies involved in commodity production.

References

Abrahams, P. (1994). Just in time now just too much. *Financial Times*, 30 March.

Aglietta, M. (1979). *A Theory of Capitalist Regulation: The U.S. Experience.* London, New Left Books.

Aglietta, M. (1999). Capitalism at the turn of the century: Regulation theory and the challenge of social change. *New Left Review* 232: 41–96.

Albert, M. (1993). *Capitalism against Capitalism.* London, Whurr.

Aldridge, M. (1979). *The British New Towns: A Programme without a Policy.* London, Routledge and Kegan Paul.

Allaert, G. (1994). Towards a sustainable Scheldt region. *Issues in Environmental Planning.* H. Voogd (Ed.). London, Pion: 131–144.

Allen, J. (1997). Economies of power and space. *Geographies of Economies.* R. Lee and J. Wills (Eds.). London, Arnold: 59–70.

Allen, J., A. Cochrane, and D. Massey. (1998). *Re-Thinking the Region.* London, Routledge.

Allen, J., and C. Hamnett. (Eds.). (1991). *Housing and Labour Markets: Building the Connections.* London, Unwin Hyman.

Allen, J., and N. Henry. (1997). Ulrich Beck's Risk Society at work: Labour and employment in the contract service industries. *Transactions of the Institute of British Geographers,* 22(2): 180–196.

Allen, S., and C. Wolkowitz. (1987). *Homeworking: Myths and Realities.* London, Macmillan.

Althusser, L. (1977). *For Marx.* London, New Left Books.

Altvater, E. (1990, March). *Fordist and post-Fordist international division of labour and monetary régimes.* Paper presented at the Conference on Pathways to Industrialization and Regional Development in the 1990s, UCLA.

Altvater, E. (1993). *The Future of the Market: An Essay on the Regulation of Money and Nature, after the Collapse of Radically Existing Socialism.* London, Verso.

Altvater, E. (1994). Ecological and economic modalities of time and space. *Is Capitalism Sustainable? Political Economy and the Politics of Ecology.* M. O'Connor (Ed.). New York, Guilford Press: 77–90.

Amin, A. (1992). Big firms versus the regions in the single European market.

Cities and Regions in the New Europe. M. Dunford and G. Kafkalas (Eds.). London, Belhaven: 127–149.

Amin, A. (1998, July). *An institutionalist perspective on regional economic development*. Paper presented at the RGS Economic Geography Research Group Seminar, Institutions and Governance, UCL, London.

Amin, A., A. Cameron, and R. Hudson. (1999). Welfare as work? The potential of the UK social economy. *Environment and Planning A*, 31: 2033–2051.

Amin, A., and P. Cohendet. (1997, September). *Learning and adaptation in decentralised business networks*. Paper presented at the EMOT Final Conference, Stresa.

Amin, A., and J. Hausner. (Eds.). (1997). *Beyond Market and Hierarchy: Interactive Governance and Social Complexity*. Lyme, NH, Edward Elgar.

Amin, A., and N. Thrift. (1992). Neo-Marshallian nodes in global governance. *International Journal of Urban and Regional Research* 16: 571–587.

Amin, A., and N. Thrift. (Eds.). (1994). *Globalization, Institutions and Regional Development in Europe*. Oxford, Oxford University Press.

Amin, A., and J. Tomaney. (1995a). *Behind the Myths of the European Union: Prospects for Cohesion*. London, Routledge.

Amin, A., and J. Tomaney. (1995b). The regional dilemma in a neo-liberal Europe. *European Urban and Regional Studies* 2(2): 145–170.

Anderson, B. (1982). *Imagined Communities*. London, Verso.

Anderson, J. (1983). Geography as ideology and the politics of crisis: The Enterprise Zone experiment. *Redundant Spaces in Cities and Regions*. J. Anderson, S. Duncan, and R. Hudson (Eds.). London, Academic Press: 313–350.

Anderson, J. (1990). The "new right," enterprise zones and urban development corporations. *International Journal of Urban and Regional Research* 14: 468–489.

Anderson, J. (1995). The exaggerated death of the nation state. *A Global World*. J. Anderson, C. Brook, and A. Cochrane (Eds.). Oxford, Oxford University Press: 65–112.

Anderson, J. (1996). The shifting stage of politics: New medieval and postmodern territorialities. *Society and Space* 14: 133–153.

Anderson, P. (1979). *Lineages of the Absolutist State*. London, Verso.

Anderson, P. (1984). *In the Tracks of Historical Materialism*. London, Verso.

Andrews, C. B. (1992). Mineral sector technologies: Policy implications for developing countries. *Natural Resources Forum* 16(3): 221–20.

Angel, D. P. (1989). The labour market for engineers in the U.S. semi-conductor industry. *Economic Geography* 65: 99–112.

Angel, D. P. (1994). *Restructuring for Innovation: The Remaking of the U.S. Semiconductor Industry*. New York, Guilford Press.

Antonelli, C. (1999). The evolution of the industrial organisation of the production of knowledge. *Cambridge Journal of Economics*, 23: 243–260.

Arora, A., and A. Gamborella. (1994). The changing technology of technological change: General and abstract knowledge and the division of innovative labour. *Research Policy* 23: 523–532.

Arrow, K. (1962). The economic implications of learning by doing. *Review of Economic Studies* 29: 155–73.

Asheim, B. (1996, April). *Learning regions in a globalised world economy: Towards a new competitive advantage of industrial districts?* Paper presented at the European Urban and Regional Studies Conference, University of Exeter, England.

Ashworth, G. J., and H. Voogd (1990). *Selling the City.* London, Belhaven.

Athreye, S. (1998). On markets in knowledge. *ESRC Centre for Business Research, WP 83*, University of Cambridge.

Atkinson, J. (1984). *Flexibility, Uncertainty and Manpower Management.* Falmer, Institute of Manpower Studies, University of Sussex.

Austrin, T., and H. Beynon. (1979). *Global outpost: The working class experience of big business in north east England.* University of Durham, Department of Sociology. Mimeo. 4 pages.

Ayres, R. U. (1989). Industrial metabolism and global change. *International Social Science Journal* 121: 363–373.

Ayres, R. U., and U. E. Simonis. (Eds.). (1994). *Industrial Metabolism: Restructuring for Sustainable Development.* Tokyo, United Nations University Press.

Bagguley, P., M. Lawson, D. Shapiro, J. Urry, and S. L. Walby. (1990). *Restructuring: Place, Class and Gender.* London, Sage.

Bagnasco, A. (1977). *The Italie: La Problematica Territoriale dello Svilupo Italiano.* Bologna, Italy, Il Mulino.

Baker, S., M. Kousis, D. Richardson, and S. Young. (1997). Editors' introduction. *The Politics of Sustainable Development: Theory and practice within the European Union.* S. Baker, M. Kousis, D. Richardson, and S. Young (Eds.). London, Routledge: 1–40.

Baran, P., and P. Sweezy. (1968). *Monopoly Capitalism.* Harmondsworth, UK, Penguin.

Barnes, T. J. (1995). *Logics of Dislocation: Models, metaphors, and meanings of economic space.* New York, Guilford Press.

Barnes, T. J. (1998). Political economy III: Confessions of a political economist. *Progress in Human Geography* 22(1): 94–104.

Bassett, K. (1999). Is there progress in human geography? The problem of progress in the light of recent works in the philosophy and sociology of science. *Progress in Human Geography* 23(1): 27–48.

Bayliss-Smith, T., and S. Owens (1994). The environmental challenge. *Human Geography: Society, Space and Social Science.* D. Gregory, R. Martin, and D. Smith (Eds.). Basinstoke, Macmillan: 113–145.

Beck, U. (1992). *Risk Society: Towards a New Modernity.* London, Sage.

Beckouche, P. (1991). French high-tech and space: A double cleavage. *Industrial Change and Regional Development: The Transformation of New Industrial Spaces.* G. Benko and M. Dunford (Eds.). London, Belhaven: 205–225.

Bell, D. (1973). *The Coming of Post-Industrial Society.* New York, Basic Books.

Bell, F. (1985). *At the Works.* London, Virago.

Bellet, M., G. Colletis, and Y. Lung. (1993). Economie de proximites. *Revue d'Economie Regionale et Urbaine* 3, 357–361.

Bennett, K., H. Beynon, and R. Hudson. (2000). *Coalfield Regeneration: Dealing with the Consequences of Industrial Decline.* Bristol, UK, Policy Press.

Bennett, P. (1999). Governing environmental risk: Regulation, insurance and the moral economy. *Progress in Human Geography* 23(2): 189–208.

Benton, T. (1989). Marxism and natural limits: An ecological critique and reconstruction. *New Left Review* 178: 51–86.

Berger, J., and J. Möhr. (1975). *A Seventh Man*. Harmondsworth, UK, Penguin.

Berry, M. (1989). Industrialisation, deindustrialisation and uneven development: The case of the Pacific Rim. *Capitalist Development and Crisis Theory*. M. Gottdiener and N. Komninos (Eds.). London, Macmillan: 174–216.

Best, M. H. (1990). *The New Competition: Institutions of Industrial Restructuring*. Cambridge, Polity Press.

Beynon, H. (1984). *Working for Ford*. Harmondsworth, UK, Penguin.

Beynon, H. (1985). *Digging Deeper*. London, Verso.

Beynon, H. (1995). *The changing experience of work: Britain in the 1990s*. Mimeo. Available from the author, School of Social Science, Cardiff University, Wales.

Beynon, H., and T. Austrin (1993). *Masters and Servants*. London, Rivers Oram Press.

Beynon, H., A. Cox, and R. Hudson. (1990). Opencast coal mining and the politics of coal production. *Capital and Class* 40: 89–114.

Beynon, H., A. Cox, and R. Hudson. (2000). *Digging Up Trouble: The Environment, Protest and Opencast Coal Mining*. London, Rivers Oram.

Beynon, H., M. Harvey, and S. Quilley. (1998, October). *The tomato: Markets and distributed innovation process*. Paper presented at the CRIC International Scientific Panel, Manchester.

Beynon, H., and R. Hudson. (1993). Place and space in contemporary Europe: Some lessons and reflections. *Antipode* 25(3): 177–190.

Beynon, H., R. Hudson, and D. Sadler. (1986). Nationalised industry policies and the destruction of communities: Some evidence from north east England. *Capital and Class* 29: 27–57.

Beynon, H., R. Hudson, and D. Sadler. (1991). *A Tale of Two Industries: The Contraction of Coal and Steel in North East England*. Milton Keynes, UK, Open University Press.

Beynon, H., R. Hudson, and D. Sadler. (1994). *A Place Called Teesside: A Locality in a Global Economy*. Edinburgh, Edinburgh University Press.

Bhaskar, R. (1989). *Reclaiming Reality*. London, Verso.

Blackburn, R. (Ed.). (1972). *Ideology in Social Science: Readings in Critical Social Theory*. London, Fontana.

Blackwell, D., and S. Voyle. (2000). 1000 jobs to go as Dewhirst factories close. *Financial Times*, January 14.

Blanke, B., U. Juergens, and H. Kastendick. (1978). On the current Marxist discussion on the analysis of form and function of the bourgeois state. *State and Capital: A Marxist Debate*. J. Holloway and S. Picciotto (Eds.). London, Arnold: 108–147.

Blowers, A. (1984). *Something in the Air: Corporate Power and the Environment*. London, Harper & Row.

Blunden, J. (1995). Sustainable Resources? *An Overcrowded World?* P. Sarre and J. Blunden (Eds.). Oxford, Oxford University Press: 161–214.

Borzaga, C., and A. Santuari. (Eds.). (1988). *Social Enterprises and New Employment in Europe*. Trento, Régime Autonoma Trentino-Alto Adige/European Commission DG5.

Bosch, L., and A. Juska (1997). Beyond political economy: actor networks and the globalization of agriculture. *Review of International Political Economy*, 4(4): 688–708.

Boulding, K. (1985). *The World as a Total System*. London, Sage.

Boulding, P. (1988). *Re-industrialisation strategies in steel closure areas in the UK*. Ph.D. thesis. Durham University, England.

Boulton, L. (1996). Energy efficiency. *Financial Times Survey*, November 11.

Bourdieu, P. (1984). *Distinction: A Social Critique of the Judgement of Taste*. London, Routledge and Kegan Paul.

Bowley, G. (1998). The hard road from Bavaria to Birmingham. *Financial Times*, November 18: 15.

Bowring, F. (1999). LETS: An eco-socialist alternative. *New Left Review* 232: 91–111.

Boyer, R. (1990). *The Regulation School: A Critical Introduction*. New York, Columbia University Press.

Boyer, R., and D. Drache (Eds.). (1995). *States Against Markets: The Limits of Globalisation*. London, Routledge.

Braczisch, H.-J., P. Cooke, and M. Heindenreich (Eds.). (1998). *Regional Innovation Systems*. London, UCL Press.

Braverman, H. (1974). *Labor and Monopoly Capital*. New York, Monthly Review Press.

Brown, J. S., and P. Duguid. (1998). Organizational learning and communities of practice: Towards a unified view of working, learning and innovation. *Organization Science* 2: 40–57.

Brown, L. A. (1975). The market and infrastructure context of adoption: A spatial perspective on the diffusion of innovations. *Economic Geography* 51: 185–216.

Brunetta, R., and A. Ceci. (1998). Underground employment in Italy: Its causes, its extent ands the costs and benefits of regularisation. *Review of Economic Conditions in Italy* 2: 257–290.

Budd, L., and S. Whimster (1992). *Global Finance and Urban Living: The Case of London*. London, Routledge.

Bullard, R. (Ed.). (1994). *Unequal Protection: Environmental Justice and Communities of Color*. San Francisco, Sierra Club Books.

Burawoy, M. (1979). *Manufacturing Consent*. Chicago, University of Chicago Press.

Burawoy, M. (1985). *The Politics of Production*. London, Verso.

Burkett, P. (1997). Nature's "free gifts" and the ecological significance of value. *Capital and Class* 68: 89–110.

Burt, T. (1995). The West embarks on long march to a low-wage world. *Financial Times*, September 21.

Byrne, D. (1985). Just haad on a minute there: A rejection of Andre Gorz's "Farewell to the Working Class." *Capital and Class* 24: 75–98.

Callon, M. (1986). Some elements of a sociology of translation. *Power, Action and Belief: A New Sociology of Knowledge.* J. Law (Ed.). London, Routledge and Kegan Paul: 196–232.

Calton, W. R., Jr. (1989). Cargoism and technology and the relationship of these concepts to important issues such as toxic waste disposal sites. *Psychosocial Effects of Hazardous Toxic Waste Disposal on Communities.* D. Peck (Ed.). Springfield, IL, Charles C. Thomas: 99–117.

Campbell, B. (1992). *Golieth: Britain's Dangerous Places.* London, Methuen.

Cane, A. (1999). BT aims to turn a tenth of its staff into teleworkers. *Financial Times,* May 12.

Carney, J. (1980). *Regions in Crisis: New Directions in European Regional Theory.* J. Carney, R. Hudson, and J. Lewis (Eds.). London, Croom Helm.

Carney, J., and R. Hudson (1978). Capital, politics and ideology: The north east of England, 1870–1946. *Antipode* 10: 64–78.

Carney, J., R. Hudson, G. Ive, and J. Lewis. (1976). *Regional underdevelopment in the late capitalism.* London Papers in Regional Science 6. I. Masser (Ed.). London, Pion: 11–29.

Carney, J., R. Hudson, and J. Lewis. (Eds.). (1977). *Coal combines and interregional uneven development in the UK.* London Papers in Regional Sciences. London, Pion.

Carney, J., Hudson, R., & J. Lewis. (Eds.). (1980). *Regions in Crisis: New Directions in European Regional Theory.* London: Croom Helm.

Castells, M. (1983). *City and the Grassroots.* London, Arnold.

Castells, M. (1989). *The Informational City.* Oxford, Blackwell.

Castells, M. (1996). *The Rise of the Network Society.* Oxford, Blackwell.

Castree, N. (1999). Envisioning capitalism: Geography and the renewal of Marxist political economy. *Transactions of the Institute of British Geographers* NS 24(2): 137–158.

Cerny, P. (1990). *The changing architecture of politics: Structure, ageing and the future of the state.* London, Sage.

Chandler, A. D. (1977). *The Visible Hand.* Cambridge, MA, Harvard University Press.

Chesnais, F. (1993). Globalisation, world oligopoly and some of their implications. *The Impact of Globalisation on Europe's Firms and Regions.* M. Humbert (Ed.). London, Pinter: 12–21.

Chisholm, M. (1962). *Rural settlement and land use: An essay in location.* London, Hutchinson.

Clancy, M. (1998). Commodity chains, services and development: Theory and preliminary evidence from the tourism industry. *Review of International Political Economy* 5(1): 122–148.

Clark, G. L. (1988). A question of integrity: The National Labour Relations Board, collective bargaining and the relocation of work. *Political Geography Quarterly* 7: 209–227.

Clark, G. L. (1989). *Unions and communities under siege: American communities and the crisis of organised labour.* Cambridge, Cambridge University Press.

Clark, G. L. (1992). Real regulation: The administrative state. *Environment and Planning A*(24): 615–627.

Clark, G. L., and M. Dear. (1984). *State Apparatus: Structures and Language of Legitimacy*. London, Allen Unwin.

Clark, G. L., and N. Wrigley. (1995). Sunk costs: A framework for economic geography. *Transactions of the Institute of British Geographers* NS 20(2): 204–223.

Clark, G. L., and N. Wrigley. (1997). Exit, the firm and sunk costs: Reconceptualising the corporate geography of disinvestment and plant closure. *Progress in Human Geography* 21(3): 338–358.

Cleveland County Council. (1994). *Changes in the Chemical Industry and the Impact on Cleveland*. Middlesbrough, Cleveland County Council.

Cochrane, A., and A. Jonas. (1999). Reimaging Berlin: World city, national capital and ordinary place. *European Urban and Regional Studies* 6(2): 145–165.

Coe, N. (1997). U.S. transnationals and the Irish software industry: Assessing the nature, quality and stability of a new wave of foreign direct investment. *European Urban and Regional Studies* 4(3): 211–230.

Commission of the European Communities. (1996). *First Report on Economic and Social Cohesion*. Luxembourg.

Conti, S., and A. Enrietti. (1995). The Italian automobile industry and the case of Fiat: One country, one company, one market. *Towards a New Map of Automobile Manufacturing in Europe? New Production Concepts and Spatial Restructuring*. R. Hudson and E. W. Schamp (Eds.). Berlin, Springer: 117–146.

Cook, I., and P. Crang. (1996). The world on a plate: Culinary culture, displacement and geographical knowledges. *Journal of Material Culture* 1: 131–153.

Cooke, P. (Ed.). (1989). *Localities: The Changing Face of Urban Britain*. London, Unwin Hyman.

Cooke, P. (1990). *Back to the Future: Modernity, Postmodernity and Locality*. London, Unwin Hyman.

Cooke, P. (1995). Keeping to the high road: Learning, reflexivity and associative governance in regional economic development. *The Rise of the Rustbelt*. P. Cooke (Ed.). London, University of London Press: 231–246.

Cooke, P., and P. Wells. (1991). Uneasy alliances: The spatial development of computing and communication markets. *Regional Studies* 25: 345–354.

Corbin, D. (1981). *Life, Work and Rebellion in the Coal Fields: The South West Virginia Miners, 1880–1922*. Urbana, University of Illinois Press.

Coriat, B. (1991). Technical flexibility and mass production: Flexible specialisation and dynamic flexibility. *Industrial Change and Regional Development: The Transformation of New Industrial Spaces*. G. Benko and M. Dunford (Eds.). London, Belhaven: 134–158.

Cornish, S. L. (1995). "Marketing matters": The functions of markets and marketing in the growth of firms and industries. *Progress in Human Geography* 19(3): 317–337.

Cotgrove, S., and A. Duff. (1980). Environmentalism, middle class radicalism and politics. *Sociological Review* 28: 333–351.

Cox, K. R. (1997). Globalisation and geographies of workers' struggles in the late twentieth century. *Geographies of Economies*. R. Lee and J. Wills (Eds.). London, Arnold: 177–185.

Cox, K. R., and A. Mair. (1991). From localised social structure to localities as agents. *Environment and Planning A* (23): 197–213.

Craig, E. A., J. Ruberry, R. Tarling, and F. Wilkinson. (1982). *Labour Market Structures, Industrial Organisation and Low Pay*. Department of Applied Economics, Cambridge University.

Crang, P. (1994). It's showtime: On the workplace geographies of display in a restaurant in south east England. *Society and Space* 12: 675–704.

Crang, P. (1997). Introduction: Cultural Turns and the (Re)Constitution of Economic Geography. *Geographies of Economies*. R. Lee and J. Wills (Eds.). London, Arnold: 3–15.

Crewe, L. (1996). Material culture: Embedded firms, organizational networks and the local economic development of a fashion quarter. *Regional Studies* 30: 257–272.

Crewe, L., and E. Davenport. (1992). The puppet show: Changing buyer–supplier relations within clothing retailing. *Transactions of the Institute of British Geographers* 17: 183–197.

Cross, M., and R. Waldinger. (1993). Migrants, minorities, and the ethnic division of labour. *Divided Cities: New York and London in the Contemporary World*. S. Fainstein, I. Gordon, and M. Harloe (Eds.). Oxford, Blackwell.

Cumbers, A. D. (1991). *The restructuring of an employment system: The experiences of North Sea oil in the north east of England*. Unpublished doctoral dissertation, University of Durham, UK.

Curry, J. (1993). The flexibility fetish: A review essay on flexible specialisation. *Capital and Class* 50: 99–126.

Damette, F. (1980). The regional framework of monopoly exploitation. *Regions in Crisis: New Perspectives in European Regional Theory*. J. Carney, R. Hudson, and J. Lewis (Eds.). Beckenham, UK, Croom Helm: 76–92.

Davis, M. (1986). *Prisoners of the American Dream*. London, Verso.

de Lamarlière, I. G. (1991). The determinants of the location of the semiconductor industry. *Industrial Change and Regional Development: The Transformation of New Industrial Spaces*. G. Benko and M. Dunford (Eds.). London, Belhaven: 171–189.

Delapierre, M., and J. B. Zimmerman. (1993). From scale to network effects in the computer industry: Implications for an industrial policy. *The Impact of Globalisation on Europe's Firms and Industries*. M. Humbert (Ed.). London, Pinter: 76–83.

Deléage, J. P. (1994). Eco-Marxist critique of political economy. *Is Capitalism Sustainable?* M. O'Connor (Ed.). New York, Guilford Press: 37–52.

Dennis, N., F. Henriques, and C. Slaughter. (1957). *Coal Is Our Life*. London, Tavistock.

Dicken, P. (1998). *Global Shift*. London, Paul Chapman (3rd edition).

Dicken, P., M. Forsgren, and A. Malmberg. (1994). The local embeddedness of transnational corporation. *Globalization, Institutions, and Regional Devel-*

opment in Europe. A. Amin and N. Thrift. Oxford, Oxford University Press, 23–45.

Dicken, P., and N. Thrift. (1992). The organization of production and the production of organisation: Why business enterprises matter in the study of geographical industrialization. *Transactions of the Institute of British Geographers* NS 17: 270–291.

Dickson, T. (1997). Helpless infant grows into mature part of the financial framework. *Financial Times,* March 27.

Doel, C. (1996). Market development and organizational change: The case of the food industry. *Retailing, Consumption and Capital.* N. Wrigley and M. Lowe (Eds.). Harlow, UK, Longman: 48–67.

Doig, A., J. Ellison, and M. O'Brien. (1994). *Combining social science and environmental data in the development of life cycle assessment.* Paper presented at the SETAC Conference on LCA Case Studies, Brussels.

Donoghue, M. T., and R. Barff. (1990). Nike just did it: International sub-contracting, flexibility and athletic footwear production. *Regional Studies* 24(6): 537–552.

Dore, R. P. (1983). Goodwill and the spirit of market capitalism. *British Journal of Sociology* 34: 3.

Dryzek, J. S. (1994). Ecology as discursive democracy: Beyond liberal capitalism and the adminstrative state. *Is Capitalism Sustainable? Political economy and the politics of ecology.* M. O'Connor (Ed.). New York, Guilford Press: 176–197.

Dunford, M. (1988). *Capital, the State and Regional Development.* London, Pion.

Dunford, M. (1990). Theories of regulation. *Society and Space* 8: 297–321.

Dunford, M. (1991). Industrial trajectories and social relations in areas of new industrial growth. *Industrial Change and Regional Development: The Transformation of New Industrial Spaces.* G. Benko and M. Dunford (Eds.). London, Belhaven: 51–82.

Dunford, M. (1997). Divergence, instability and exclusion: Regional dynamics in Great Britain. *Geographie of Economies.* R. Lee and J. Wills (Eds.). London, Arnold: 259–277.

Dunford, M., and R. Hudson. (1996). *Successful European Regions: Northern Ireland Learning from Others.* Belfast, Northern Ireland Economic Council.

Economic Policy Institute. (2000). *Manufacturing Advantage: Why High Performance Work Systems Pay Off.* Ithaca, NY, Cornell University Press.

Edgecliff-Johnson, A. (1998). Crosfield sale points to more ICI disposable. *Financial Times,* April 3.

Edwards, R. (1979). *Contested Terrain: The Transformation of the Workplace in the Twentieth Century.* London, Heinneman.

Elson, D., and R. Pearson. (1981). Nimble fingers make cheap workers: An analysis of women's employment in Third World export manufacturing. *Feminist Review* 7.

Emmanuel, A. (1972). *Unequal Exchange.* London, New Left Books.

Eraydin, A., and A. Erendil. (1999). The role of female labour in industrial restructuring: New production processes and labour market relations in the Istanbul clothing industry. *Gender, Place and Culture* 6(3): 259–272.

Esping Anderson, G. (1990). *Three Worlds of Welfare Capitalism.* Cambridge, Cambridge University Press.

Ewen, S. (1976). *Captains of Consciousness: Advertising, the Social Roots of the Consumer Culture.* New York, McGraw Hill.

Ewen, S. (1988). *All Consuming Images.* London, Basic Books.

Fernández Kelly, M.-P., and A. M. Garcia. (1989). Hispanic women and homework: Women in the informal economy of Miami and Los Angeles. *Homework: Historical and Contemporary Perspectives on Labor at Home.* E. Borris and C. R. Daniels (Eds.). Urbana, University of Illinois Press: 165–179.

Fernández Rodríguez, F. (1985). *La España de las Autonómias.* Taravilla, Madrid, Instituto de Estudios de Administracion Local, Ministerio de Administración Territorial.

Fincher, R. (1983). The inconsistency of eclecticism. *Environment and Planning A* 15: 607–622.

Fine, B., and E. Leopold. (1993). *The World of Consumption.* London, Routledge.

Firn, J. R. (1975). External control and regional development: The case of Scotland. *Environment and Planning A* 7: 393–414.

Fitzsimmons, M., J. Glaser, R. Montemor, S. Pincett, and S. C. Rajan. (1994). Environmentalism as the liberal state. *Is Capitalism Sustainable?* M. O'Connor (Ed.). New York, Guilford Press: 198–216.

Flamm, K. (1993). Coping with strategic competition in semiconductors: The EC model as an international framework. *The Impact of Globalisation on Europe's Firms and Regions.* M. Humbert (Ed.). London, Pinter: 64–75.

Florida, R. (1995). The industrial transformation of the Great Lakes region. *The Rise of the Rustbelt.* P. Cooke (Ed.). London, University of London Press: 162–176.

Foord, J., S. Bowlby, and C. Tillsley. (1996). The changing place of retailer–supplier relations in British retailing. *Retailing, Consumption and Capital.* N. Wrigley and M. Lowe, (Eds.). Harlow, UK, Longman: 68–89.

Foray, D. (1993). Feasibility of a single régime of intellectual property rights. *The Impact of Globalisation on Europe's Firms and Regions.* M. Humbert (Ed.). London, Pinter: 85–95.

Foss, N. (1996). Introduction: The emerging competence perspective. *Towards a Competence Theory of the Firm.* N. Foss and J. Knudsen (Eds.). London, Routledge: 1–12.

Friedman, A. (1977). *Industry and Labour.* London, Macmillan.

Fröbel, F., J. Heinrichs, and O. Kreye. (1980). *The New International Division of Labour.* Cambridge, Cambridge University Press.

Frosch, R. A. (1997). Towards the end of waste: Reflections on a new ecology of industry. *Technological Trajectories and the Human Environment.* J. H. Ausubel and H. D. Langford (Eds.). Washington, DC, National Academy Press: 157–167.

Fucini, J., and S. Fucini. (1990). *Working for the Japanese: Inside Mazda's American Auto Plant.* Toronto, Free Press.

Garnsey, J. Rubery, J., and F. Wilkinson. (1985). Labour market structure and work-force divisions. *Work, Culture and Society*. R. Deem and G. Salaman (Eds.). Milton Keynes, UK, Open University Press: 40–75.

Garofoli, G. (1986). Le development peripherique en Italie. *Economie et Humanisme* 289: 30–36.

Garonna, P. (1998). The crisis of the employment system in Italy. *Review of Economic Conditions in Italy* 2: 219–256.

Garrahan, P., and P. Stewart. (1992). *The Nissan Enigma: Flexibility at Work in a Local Economy*. London, Mansell.

George, S. (1992). *The Debt Boomerang: How Third World Debt Harms Us All*. London, Pluto Press.

Georgescu-Roegen, N. (1971). *The Entropy Law and the Economic Process*. Cambridge, MA, Harvard University Press.

Gereffi, G. (1994). The organization of buyer-driven global commodity chains. *Commodity Chains and Global Capitalism*. G. Gereffi and M. Korzeniewicz (Eds.). Westport, CT, Greenwood Press.

Gereffi, G. (1995). Global production systems and Third World development. *Global Change Regional Response: The International Context of Development*. B. Stallings (Ed.). Cambridge, Cambridge University Press.

Gereffi, G. (2000). The regional dynamics of global trade: Asian, American and European models of apparel sourcing. *The Dialectics of Globalization*. M. Vellinga (Ed.). Boulder, CO, Westview: 31–64.

Gerstenberger (1978). Class conflict, competition and state function. *State and Capital*. J. Holloway and S. Picciotto (Eds.). London, Arnold: 148–159.

Gertler, M. S. (1995). "Being there": Proximity, organisation and culture in the production and adoption of advanced manufacturing technologies. *Economic Geography* 71: 1–26.

Gertler, M. S. (1997). The invention of regional culture. *Geographies of Economies*. R. Lee and J. Wills (Eds.). London, Arnold: 47–58.

Gertler, M. S., and S. Di Giovanna. (1997). In search of the new social economy: Collaborative relations between users and producers of advanced manufacturing technologies. *Environment and Planning A* 29: 1585–1602.

Ghosal, S., and C. A. Bartlett. (1997). *The Individualized Corporation*. London, Heinemann.

Gibson-Graham, J. K. (1996). *The End of Capitalism (As We Know It)*. Oxford, Blackwell.

Gibson-Graham, J. K. (1997). Re-placing class in economic geographies: Possibilities for a new class politics. *Geographies of Economies*. R. Lee and J. Wills (Eds.). London, Arnold: 87–97.

Giddens, A. (1979). *Central Problems in Social Theory*. London, Macmillan.

Giddens, A. (1981). *A Contemporary Critique of Historical Materialism*. London, Macmillan.

Giddens, A. (1984). *The Constitution of Society*. Cambridge, Polity Press.

Giddens, A. (1990). *The Consequences of Modernity*. Cambridge, Polity Press.

Giddens, A. (2000). *The Third Way and Its Critics*. Cambridge, Polity Press.

Giordano, B. (1998). *A political-economic geography of Italian regionalism: The*

Northern League (Lega Nord), 1984–96. Ph.D. thesis, University of Durham.

Gismondi, M., and M. Richardson. (1994). Discourse and power in environmental politics: Public hearings on a bleached kraft pulp mill in Alberta, Canada. *Is Capitalism Sustainable: Political economy and the politics of economy.* M. O'Connor (Ed.). New York, Guilford Press: 222–252.

Goldsmith, E. (1992). *The Way: An ecological worldview.* Athens, University of Georgia Press.

Goodin, R. (1992). *Green Political Theory.* Cambridge, Polity Press.

Goodman, D., J. Sorj, and J. Wilkinson. (1987). *From Farming to Biotechnology: A Theory of Agro-Industrial Development.* Oxford, Blackwell.

Goodwin, M., and J. Painter (1996). Local governance, the crises of Fordism and the changing geographies of regulation. *Transactions of the Institute of British Geographers* 21: 635–648.

Gordon, D. (1988). The global economy: New edifice or crumbling foundations? *New Left Review* 168: 24–65.

Gordon, D., R. C. Edwards, and M. Reich. (1982). *Segmented Work, Divided Workers: The Historical Transformation of Labour in the United States.* Cambridge, Cambridge University Press.

Gorz, A. (1982). *Farewell to the Working Class.* London, Pluto Press.

Gough, I. (1979). *The Political Economy of the Welfare State.* London, Macmillan.

Gowan, P. (1999). The NATO powers and the Balkan tragedy. *New Left Review* 284: 83–105.

Grabher, G. (1993). The weakness of strong ties: The lock-in of regional development in the Ruhr area. *The Embedded Firm: On the Socio-Economics of Industrial Networks.* G. Grabher (Ed.). London, Routledge: 255–277.

Granovetter, M. (1974). *Getting a Job: A Study of Contacts and Careers.* Cambridge, MA, Harvard University Press.

Granovetter, M. (1985). Economic action and social structure: The problem of embeddedness. *American Journal of Sociology* 91(3): 481–510.

Greco, L. (2000). *Towards an Institutionalist Approach to Unemployment.* Ph.D. thesis, University of Durham.

Gregory, D. (1978). *Science, Ideology and Human Geography.* London, Hutchinson.

Gregory, D. (1994). Social theory and human geography. *Human Geography: Society Space and Social Science.* D. Gregory, R. Martin, and D. Smith (Eds.). Basingstoke, UK, Macmillan: 78–112.

Gregory, D., R. Martin, and G. Smith. (1994). Introduction: Human geography, social change and social science. *Human Geography: Society, Space and Social Science.* D. Gregory, R. Martin, and G. Smith (Eds.). Basingstoke, UK, Macmillan: 1–18.

Gregson, N. (1986). On duality and dualism: The case of time-geography and structuralism. *Progress in Human Geography* 10: 184–205.

Gregson, N., and M. Lowe. (1994). *Servicing the middle classes: class, gender and waged domestic labour in contemporary Britain.* London, Routledge.

Griffith, V. (1998). Gillette seeks 30% of market with "Mach 3." *Financial Times*, April 15.

Griffiths, J. (1993). Energy efficiency. *Financial Times*, December 7.

Griffiths, M. J., and R. J. Johnston. (1991). What's in a place? An approach to the concept of place as illustrated by the British National Union of Mineworkers strike, 1984–1985. *Antipode* 23: 185–213.

Grübler, A. (1992). Technology and global change: Land-use, past and present. *Working Paper 92–2*. International Institute for Applied Systems Analysis, Laxenburg.

Habermas, J. (1976). *Legitimation Crisis*. London, Heinemann.

Hadjimichalis, C. (1987). *Uneven Development and Regionalism: State, Territory and Class in Southern Europe*. London, Croom Helm.

Hadjimichalis, C. (1998). *Small and medium industrial enterprises in Greece*. Thessaloniki. Mimeo. 21 pages.

Hadjimichalis, C., and N. Papamichos. (1990). "Local" development in southern Europe: Towards a new mythology. *Antipode* 22: 181–210.

Hadjimichalis, C., and D. Vaiou (1990a). Flexible labour markets and regional development in Northern Greece. *International Journal of Urban and Regional Research* 14: 1–24.

Hadjimichalis, C., and D. Vaiou. (1990b). Whose flexibility? The politics of informalisation in Southern Europe. *Capital and Class* 42: 79–106.

Hadjimichalis, C., and D. Vaiou. (1996). *Informalisation along global commodity chains: Some evidence from southern Europe*. Paper presented at the Conference on La Economia Sumergita, Alicante.

Hagedoon, J. (1993). Understanding the rationale of strategic technology partnering: Interorganizational modes of cooperation and sectoral differences. *Strategic Management Journal* 14: 371–385.

Hagerstrand, T. (1975). Space, time and human conditions. *Dynamic allocation of urban space*. A. Karlqvist, L. Lundquist, and F. Snickars (Eds.). Farnborough, UK, Saxon House: 3–14.

Haggett, P. (1965). *Locational Analysis in Human Geography*. London, Arnold.

Hajer, M. (1995). *The Politics of Environmental Discourse: Ecological Modernisation and the Policy Process*. Oxford, Clarendon Press.

Halford, S., and M. Savage. (1997). Rethinking restructuring: Embodiment, agency and identity in organisational change. *Geographies of Economies*. R. Lee and J. Wills (Eds.). London, Arnold: 108–117.

Hamill, J. (1993). Cross-border mergers, acquisitions and strategic alliances. *Multinationals and Employment: The Global Economy of the 1990s*. P. Bailey, A. Parisotto, and G. Renshaw (Eds.). Geneva, International Labor Organization: 95–123.

Hamnett, C. (1994). Social polarization in global cities: Theory and evidence. *Urban Studies* 31(3): 401–424.

Hanson, S., and G. Pratt. (1992). Dynamic dependencies: A geographic investigation of local labour markets. *Economic Geography* 68(4): 373–405.

Hanson, S., and G. Pratt. (1995). *Gender, Work and Space*. London, Routledge.

Haraway, D. (1991). *Simians, Cyborgs and Women: The Reinvention of Nature*. London, Free Association Books.

Hargreaves, D. (1992). Oil and gas industry. *Financial Times Survey*, November 5.

Harney, A. (1999). Restructuring gives Japan's workers culture shock. *Financial Times*, November 2.

Harrison, B. (1994). *Lean and Mean: The Changing Landscape of Corporate Power in the Age of Flexibility*. New York, Basic Books.

Hartmann, H. (1978). The unhappy marriage of Marxism and feminism: Towards a more progressive union. *Capital and Class* 8: 1–33.

Hartwick, E. (1998). Geographies of consumption: A commodity-chain approach. *Society and Space* 16(4): 423–437.

Harvey, D. (1969). *Explanation in Geography*. London, Arnold.

Harvey, D. (1973). *Social Justice and the City*. London, Arnold.

Harvey, D. (1982). *The Limits to Capital*. Oxford, Blackwell.

Harvey, D. (1985). The geopolitics of capitalism. *Social Relations and Spatial Structure*. D. Gregory and J. Urry (Eds.). Basingstoke, UK, Macmillan: 128–163.

Harvey, D. (1989). *The Condition of Postmodernity*. Oxford, Blackwell.

Harvey, D. (1996). *Justice, Nature and the Geography of Difference*. Oxford, Blackwell.

Hay, C. (1994). Environmental security and state legitimacy. *Is Capitalism Sustainable: Political economy and the politics of economy*. M. O'Connor (Ed.). New York, Guilford Press: 217–231.

Held, D. (Ed.). (1983). *States and Societies*. Oxford, Martin Robertson.

Held, D. (1989). *Political theory and the modern state: Essays on state, power and democracy*. Stanford, CA, Stanford University Press.

Hendry, C. (1996). Understanding and creating whole organizational change through learning theory. *Human Relations* 49(5): 621–42.

Herod, A. J. (1992). *Towards a labour geography: The production of space and the politics of scale in the east-coast longshore industry 1953–90*. Doctoral dissertation, Rutgers University, New Brunswick, NJ.

Herod, A. J. (1995). The practice of labor solidarity and the geography of FDI. *Economic Geography* 15(7): 681–93.

Herod, A. J. (1997). From a geography of labor to a labor geography: Labor's spatial fix and the geography of capitalism. *Antipode* 29(1): 1–31.

Herrigel, G. (1996). Crisis in German decentralized production: Unexpected rigidity and the challenge of an alternative form of flexible organization in Baden Württemburg. *European Urban and Regional Studies* 3(1): 33–52.

Hirsch, J. (1978). The state apparatus and social reproduction: Elements of a theory of the bourgeois state. *State and Capital: A Marxist Debate*. J. Holloway and S. E. Picciotto (Eds.). London, Arnold: 57–107.

Hirst, P., and G. Thompson. (1995). *Globalization in Question*. Cambridge, Polity Press.

Hirst, P., and G. Thompson. (1996). Globalisation: Ten frequently asked questions and some surprising answers. *Soundings* 4(Autumn): 47–66.

Hoagland, P. (1993). Manganese nodule price trends. *Resource Policy* 19(4): 287–298.

Hodge, S., and J. Howe. (1999). Can the European social model survive? *European Urban and Regional Studies* 6(2): 178–184.

Hodgson, G. (1988). *Economics and Institutions: A Manifesto for Modern Institutional Economics.* Cambridge, Polity Press.

Hodgson, G. (1993). *Economics and evolution: Bringing life back into economics.* Cambridge, Polity Press.

Holloway, J., and S. E. Picciotto. (Eds.). (1978). *State and Capital: A Marxist Debate.* London, Arnold.

Howells, J. R. (1993). Emerging global strategies in innovation management. *The Impact of Globalisation on Europe's Firms and Industries.* M. Humbert (Ed.). London, Pinter: 219–228.

Hudson, R. (1974). Images of the retailing environment: An example of the use of the repertory grid methodology. *Environment and Behaviour* 6: 470–494.

Hudson, R. (1980). Women and work: A study of Washington New Town. *Occasional Publications (New Series), No. 16.* University of Durham, Department of Geography.

Hudson, R. (1983). Capital accumulation and chemicals production in Western Europe in the postwar period. *Environment and Planning A* 15: 105–122.

Hudson, R. (1986a). Nationalised industry policies and regional policies: The role of the state in the deindustrialization and reindustrialisation of regions. *Society and Space* 4(1): 7–28.

Hudson, R. (1986b). Producing an industrial wasteland: Capital, labour and the state in north east England. *The Geography of Deindustrialization.* R. Martin and B. Rowthorne (Eds.). London, Macmillan: 169–213.

Hudson, R. (1988). Uneven development in capitalist societies: Changing spatial divisions of labour, forms of spatial organization of production and service provision, and their impact upon localities. *Transactions of the Institute of British Geographers* 13: 484–496.

Hudson, R. (1989a). Labour market changes and new forms of work industrial regions: Maybe flexibility for some but not flexible accumulation. *Society and Space* 7: 5–30.

Hudson, R. (1989b). *Wrecking a Region: State Policies, Party Politics and Regional Change in North East England.* London, Pion.

Hudson, R. (1989c). Rewriting history and reshaping geography: The nationalized industries and the political economy of Thatcherism. *The Political Geography of Contemporary Britain.* J. Mohan (Ed.). London, Macmillan.

Hudson, R. (1990). Re-thinking regions: Some preliminary considerations on regions and social change. *Regional Geography: Current Developments and Future Prospects.* R. J. Johnston, G. Hoekveld, and J. Hauer (Eds.). London, Routledge: 67–84.

Hudson, R. (1993). Spatially uneven development, and the production of spaces and places: Some preliminary considerations, and a case study of Consett. *Moving Regions.* J. Hauer and G. J. Hoekveld (Eds.). Netherlands Geographical Studies: 43–68.

Hudson, R. (1994a). Institutional change, cultural transformation and economic regeneration: Myths and realities from Europe's old industrial regions. *Globalization, Institutions and Regional Development in Europe.* A. Amin and N. Thrift (Eds.). Oxford, Oxford University Press: 331–345.

Hudson, R. (1994b). New production concepts, new production geographies? Reflections on changes in the automobile industry. *Transactions of the Institute of British Geographers* 19: 331–345.

Hudson, R. (1994c). Restructuring production in the West European Steel Industry. *Tijdschrift voor Economische en Sociale-Geografie* 85(2): 99–113.

Hudson, R. (1995a). The Japanese, the European market and the automobile industry in the United Kingdom. *Towards a New Map of Automobile Manufacturing in Europe? New Production Concepts and Spatial Restructuring.* R. Hudson and E. W. Schamp (Eds.). Berlin, Springer: 63–92.

Hudson, R. (1995b). Towards sustainable industrial production: But in what sense sustainable? *Environmental Change: Industry, Power and Policy.* M. Taylor (Ed.). Aldershot, UK, Avebury: 37–56.

Hudson, R. (1995c). The role of foreign investment. *The Northern Region Economy: Progress and Prospects.* A. Darnell, L. Evans, P. Johnson, and B. Thomas (Eds.). London, Mansell: 79–95.

Hudson, R. (1995d). Making music work? Alternative regeneration strategies in a deindustrialized locality: The case of Derwentside. *Transactions of the Institute of British Geographers* NS 20: 460–473.

Hudson, R. (1997). The end of mass production and of the mass collective worker? Experimenting with production, employment and their geographies. *Geographies of Economies.* R. Lee and J. Wills (Eds.). London, Arnold: 302–310.

Hudson, R. (1999). The learning economy, the learning firm and the learning region: A sympathetic critique of the limits to learning. *European Urban and Regional Studies* 6: 1, 69–72.

Hudson, R. (2000, January). *One Europe or many? Reflections on becoming European.* Paper presented at the Annual Conference of the Royal Geographical Society and Institute of British Geographers, University of Sussex.

Hudson, R., and J. Lewis. (Eds.). (1985). *Uneven Development in Southern Europe.* London, Methuen.

Hudson, R., and V. Plum. (1986). Deconcentration or decentralization? Local government and the possibilities for local control of local economies. *Urban Political Theory and the Management of Fiscal Stress.* M. Goldsmith and S. Villadsen (Eds.). Farnborough, UK, Gower: 137–160.

Hudson, R., and D. Sadler. (1983). Region, class and the politics of steel closures in the European Community. *Society and Space* 1: 405–428.

Hudson, R., and D. Sadler. (1986). Contesting works closures in Western Europe's old industrial regions: Defending place or betraying class. *Production, Territory, Work.* A. J. Scott and M. Storper (Eds.). London, Allen and Unwin, 172–193.

Hudson, R., and D. Sadler. (1989). *The International Steel Industry: Restructuring, State Policies and Localities.* London, Routledge.

Hudson, R., and E. W. Schamp. (1995a). Interdependent and uneven development in the spatial reorganisation of the automobile production systems in Europe. *Towards a New Map of Automobile Manufacturing in Europe? New Production Concepts and Spatial Restructuring.* R. Hudson and E. W. Schamp (Eds.). Berlin, Springer: 219–244.

Hudson, R., and E. W. Schamp. (Eds.). (1995b). *Towards a New Map of Automobile Manufacturing in Europe? New Production Concepts and Spatial Restructuring*. Berlin, Springer.

Hudson, R., and A. Townsend. (1992). Trends in tourism employment and resulting policy choices for local government. *Perspectives on Tourism Policy*. P. Johnson and B. Thomas (Eds.). London, Mansell: 49–68.

Hudson, R., and P. M. Weaver. (1997). In search of employment creation via environmental valorisation: Exploring a possible eco-Keynsian future for Europe. *Environment and Planning* 29: 1647–1661.

Hudson, R., and A. Williams. (1995). *Divided Britain*. Chichester, UK, Wiley.

Hughes, A. (1996). Forging new cultures of food retailer-manufacturer relations? *Retailing, Consumption and Capital*. N. Wrigley and M. Lowe (Eds.). Harlow, UK, Longman: 90–115.

Hyman, G. (1998). Changing trade union identities in Europe. *The Challenge of Trade Unions in Europe: Innovation or Adaptation*. P. Leisink, J. van Leempt, and J. Vilkrokx (Eds.). Cheltenham, UK, Edward Elgar: 53–73.

Imai, K., I. Nonaka, and H. Takeuchi. (1985). Managing the new product development process. *The Uneasy Alliance*. K. Clark, R. Hayes, and C. Lorenz (Eds.). Boston, Harvard Business School Press.

Imrie, R., and H. Thomas. (1993). *British Urban Policy and the Urban Development Corporations*. London, Paul Chapman.

International Labour Organisation. (1997). *Annual Labour Report*. Geneva, ILO.

Isard, W. (1956). *Location and the Space-Economy*. New York, Wiley.

Jackson, P. (1993). Towards a cultural politics of consumption. *Mapping the Futures: Local Cultures, Global Changes*. J. Bird, B. Curtis, T. Putnam, G. Robinson, and L. Tickner (Eds.). London, Routledge: 207–228.

Jackson, P., and J. Taylor. (1996). Geography and the cultural politics of advertising. *Progress in Human Geography* 20(3): 356–371.

Jackson, T. (1995). *Material Concerns*. London, Routledge.

Jameson, F. (1988). *The Ideologies of Theory*. Vol. 2. London, Routledge.

Jenson, J. (1990). Representations in crisis: The root of Canada's permeable Fordism. *Canadian Journal of Political Science* 23: 653–683.

Jessop, B. (1978). Capitalism and democracy: The best possible political shell? *Power and the State*. G. Littlejohn (Ed.). London, Croom Helm: 10–51.

Jessop, B. (1982). *The Capitalist State*. Oxford, Martin Robertson.

Jessop, B. (1990). *State Theory: Putting Capitalist States in Their Place*. Cambridge, Cambridge University Press.

Jessop, B. (1994). Post-Fordism and the state. *Post-Fordism: A Reader*. A. Amin (Ed.). Oxford, Blackwell: 251–279.

Jessop, B. (1997). Capitalism and its future: Remarks on regulation, government and governance. *Review of International Political Economy* 4: 561–581.

Jessop, B., K. Bonnet, S. Bromley, and T. Ling. (1988). *Thatcherism: A Tale of Nations*. Cambridge, Polity Press.

Johnson, B. (1992). Institutional Learning. *National Systems of Innovation: To-*

wards a Theory of Innovation and Interactive Learning. B.A. Lundvall (Ed.). London, Pinter: 23–44.

Johnson, R. (1986). The story so far: And other transformation. *Introduction to Contemporary Cultural Studies.* D. Punter (Ed.). London, Longman: 277–313.

Johnston, R. J., J. Hauer, and G. Hoekveld. (1990). *Regional Geography: Current Development and Future Prospects.* London, Routledge.

Jonas, A. E. C. (1996). Local labour control régimes: Uneven development and the social regulation of production. *Regional Studies* 30: 323–338.

Jonas, A. E. C. (1997, August). *Location and globalisation tendencies in the social control and regulation of labour.* Revised version of paper presented at the International Geographical Union Conference on Interdependent and Uneven Development, Seoul.

Jones, K. (1998). Scale as epistemology. *Political Geography* 17(1): 25–28.

Jordan, B. (1997). *Globalisation and Europe's "Social Model": What Global Role for the EU?* The Philip Morris Institute for Public Policy Research, Brussels.

Kearney, J. (1991). Borders and boundaries of state and self at the end of Empire. *Journal of Historical Sociology* 4: 52–74.

Kehoe, L. (1992). Cost constraints prompt a continental shift. *Financial Times,* August 25.

Kim, C. S. (1995). *Japanese Industry in the American South.* New York, Routledge.

King, R., (Ed.). (1993). *Mass Migration in Europe: The Legacy and the Future.* London, Belhaven.

King, R. (1995). Migrations, globalisation and place. *A Place in the World? Places, Cultures and Globalisation.* D. Massey and P. Jess (Eds.). Oxford, Oxford University Press: 5–44.

King, R., J. Connell, and P. White. (1995). *Writing across Worlds: Literature and Migration.* London, Routledge.

Kofman, E. (1985). Dependent development in Corsica. *Uneven Development in Southern Europe.* R. Hudson and J. Lewis (Eds.). London, Methuen: 163–183.

Kolinsky, M. (1981). The nation-state in western Europe: Erosion from "above" and "below"? *The Nation State.* L. Tivey (Ed.). Oxford, Martin Robertson.

Kynge, J. (2000). China plans to reduce steel plant capacity. *Financial Times,* January 10.

Lakka, S. (1994). The new international division of labour and the Indian software industry. *Modern Asian Studies* 28(2): 381–408.

Lane, C., and B. Reinhard. (Eds.). (1998). *Trust Within and Between Organisations.* Oxford, Oxford University Press.

Läpple, D., and P. van Hoogstraten. (1980). Remarks on the spatial structure of capitalist development in the case of the Netherlands. *Regions in Crisis.* J. Carney, R. Hudson, and J. Lewis (Eds.). London, Croom Helm: 117–166.

Larsson, S., and A. Malmberg. (1999). Innovations, competitiveness and local embeddedness: A study of machinery producers in Sweden. *Geografiska Annaler* 81(8): 1–18.

Lash, S., and J. Urry. (1987). *The End of Organised Capitalism*. Cambridge, Polity Press.

Lash, S., and J. Urry. (1994). *Economies of Signs and Space*. London, Sage.

Lave, J., and E. Wenger. (1990). *Situated Learning: Legitimate Peripheral Participation*. Cambridge, Cambridge University Press.

Leborgne, F., and A. Lipietz. (1988). New technologies, new models of regulation: Some spatial implications. *Society and Space* 6: 263–280.

Leborgne, D., and A. Lipietz. (1991). Two social strategies in the production of new industrial spaces. *Industrial Change and Regional Development: The Transformation of New Industrial Spaces*. G. Benko and M. Dunford (Eds.). London, Belhaven: 27–50.

Lee, J. H. (2001). *Learning, adaptation and the restructuring of Korean Chaebol*. Ph.D. thesis, University of Durham.

Lee, R. (1996). Moral money? LETS and the social construction of economic geographers in south east England. *Environment and Planning A* 28: 1377–1394.

Lee, R. (1998). *Shelter from the storm? Mutual knowledge and geographies of regard (or legendary economic geographies)*. Department of Geography, Queen Mary and Westfield College, London. Mimeo. 22 pages.

Lee, R., and J. Wills. (Eds.). (1997). *Geographies of Economies*. London, Arnold.

Leidner, R. (1993). *Fast Food and Fast Talk: Service Work and the Routinisation of Everyday Life*. Berkeley, University of California Press.

Lentnek, B., A. McPherson, and D. Philips. (1994). Optimum producer-service location. *Environment and Planning A* 26: 467–479.

Leonard, H. J. (1988). *Pollution and the Struggle for the World Product: Multinational Corporations, Environment and International Competitive Advantage*. Cambridge, Cambridge University Press.

Leontidou, L. (1993). Informal strategies of unemployment relief in Greek cities: The relevance of family, locality and housing. *European Planning Studies* 1(1): 43–68.

Leslie, D. (1995). Global scan: The globalisation of advertising agencies, concepts and campaigns. *Economic Geography* 71: 402–426.

Leslie, D., and S. Reimer. (1999). Spatializing commodity chains. *Progress in Human Geography* 23(3): 401–420.

Lester, T. (1998). Electric effect of alliances. *Financial Times*, January 15.

Levinthal, D. (1996). Learning and Schumpeterian dynamics. *Organisation and Strategy in the Evolution of the Enterprise*. G. Dosi and F. Malerba (Eds.). London, Macmillan: 27–41.

Leyshon, A., and N. Thrift. (1992). Liberalization and consolidation: The Single European Market and the remaking of European financial capital. *Environment and Planning A* 24: 49–81.

Leyshon, A., and A. Tickell. (1994). Money order? The discursive constitution of Bretton Woods and the making and breaking of regulatory space. *Environment and Planning A* 26: 1861–1890.

Lie, T. C., and G. Santucci. (1993). Seeking balanced trade and competition in the context of globalisation: The case of electronics. *The Impact of Global-*

isation on Europe's Firms and Regions. M. Humbert (Ed.). London, Pinter: 114–124.

Liedtka, J. (1999). Linking competitive advantage with communities of practice. *Journal of Management Inquiry* 8(1): 5–16.

Lipietz, A. (1980). The structuration of space, the problem of land and spatial policy. *Regions in Crisis*. J. Carney, R. Hudson, and J. Lewis (Eds.). London, Croom Helm: 60–75.

Lipietz, A. (1986). New tendencies in the international division of labour: Régimes of accumulation and modes of regulation. *Production, Territory, Work*. A. J. Scott and M. Storper (Eds.). London, Unwin Hyman: 16–40.

Lipietz, A. (1987). *Mirages and Miracles*. London, Verso.

Lipietz, A. (1992). *Towards a New Economic Order: Postfordism, Ecology and Democracy*. Cambridge, Polity Press.

Lipietz, A. (1993). The local and the global: Regional individuality or inter-regionalism? *Transactions of the Institute of British Geographers* NS, 18(1): 6–18.

Lipietz, A. (1995). *Green Hopes: The Future of Political Ecology*. Cambridge, Polity Press.

Lipietz, A. (1996). *La Sociéte en sablier: Le partage du travail coutre la déchirure sociale*. Paris, Editions les Descouvertes.

Lipietz, A. (1998). Cultural geography, political economy and ecology. *Space Inequality and Difference: From "Radical" to "Cultural" Formulations*. P. Dellatetsima, C. Hadjimichalis, V. Hastaoglou, M. Mantouvalou, and D. Vaiou (Eds.). Thessaloniki, Greece, University of Thessaloniki.

Locke, R. (1990). The resurgence of the local unions: Industrial restructuring and industrial relations in Italy. *Politics and Society* 18: 347–379.

Lorange, P., and J. Roos. (1993). *Strategic Alliances*. London, Blackwell.

Lovelock, J. (1988). *The Ages of Gaia: A Biography of Our Living Earth*. Oxford, Oxford University Press.

Lovibond, S. (1989). Feminism and postmodernism. *New Left Review* 178: 5–28.

Lundvall, B. A. (1988). Innovation as an interactive process: From user–producer interaction to the national system of innovation. *Technical Change and Economic Theory*. G. Dosi, C. Freeman, G. Siverberg, and L. Soete (Eds.). London, Pinter: 349–369.

Lundvall, B. A. (1992). *National Systems of Innovation: Towards a Theory of Innovation and Interactive Learning*. London, Pinter.

Lundvall, B. A. (1995). *The learning economy—challenges to economic theory and policy*. Revised version of a paper presented at the European Association of Evolutionary Political Economists, Copenhagen, Denmark.

Lundvall, B. A., and B. Johnson. (1994). The learning economy. *Journal of Industry Studies* 2: 23–42.

Lung, Y. (1992). Global competition and transregional strategy: Spatial reorganisation of the European car industry. *Cities and Regions in the New Europe: The global–local interplay and spatial development strategies*. M. Dunford and G. Kafkalas (Eds.). London, Belhaven: 68–85.

Lury, C. (1996). *Consumer Culture*. Cambridge, Polity Press.

Mackenzie, S., and D. Rose. (1983). Industrial change, the domestic economy and home life. *Redundant Spaces in Cities and Regions?* J. Anderson, S. Duncan, and R. Hudson (Eds.). London, Academic Press: 155–200.

MacLeod, G. (1997). Globalising Parisian thought waves: Recent advances in the study of social regulation, politics, discourse and space. *Progress in Human Geography* 21(4): 530–554.

MacLeod, G. (1998, September). *Relativising the scales of governance: Spaces of dependence territorial blocs and the political structuration of "Euro-regionalism."* Paper presented at the Second EURS Conference: Culture, Place and Space in Contemporary Europe.

MacLeod, G., and M. Jones. (1998). *Re-regulating a regional? Institutional fixes, entrepreneurial discourse, and the politics of representation.* University of Wales, Aberystwyth and Manchester. Mimeo. 59 pages.

Mandel, E. (1963). The dialectic of class and region in Belgium. *New Left Review* 20: 5–31.

Mandel, E. (1975). *Late Capitalism.* London, New Left Books.

Mann, M. (1993). Nation-states in Europe and other continents: Diversifying, developing, not dying. *Proceedings of the American Academy of Arts and Sciences* 122(3): 115–140.

Mann, M. (1999). The dark side of democracy: The modern tradition of ethnic and political cleansing. *New Left Review* 235: 18–47.

Manzagol, C. (1991). The rise of a technological complex: Some comments on the Phoenix case. *Industrial Change and Regional Development: The Transformation of New Industrial Spaces.* G. Benko and M. Dunford (Eds.). London, Belhaven: 237–249.

Mariti, P. (1993). Small and medium-sized firms in markets with substantial scale and scope economies. *The Impact of Globalisation in Europe's Firms and Regions.* M. Humbert (Ed.). London, Pinter: 191–198.

Marples, D. R. (1987). *Chernobyl and Nuclear Power in the USSR.* London, Macmillan.

Marsden, T. (1998). Creating competitive space: Exploring the social and political maintenance of natural power. *Environment and Planning A* 30: 481–498.

Marsden, T., and N. Wrigley. (1996). Retailing, the food system and the regulating state. *Retailing, Consumption and Capital.* N. Wrigley and M. Lowe (Eds.). Harlow, UK, Longman: 33–47.

Marsh, P. (1997). A shift to flexibility. *Financial Times*, February 21.

Marsh, P. (1998). The benefits of doing it yourself. *Financial Times*, April 16.

Marshall. G. (1986). The workplace culture of a licensed restaurant. *Theory, Culture and Society* 3: 33–48.

Marshall, M. (1987). *Long Waves of Regional Development.* London, Macmillan.

Marshall, N., and P. Wood. (1995). *Services and Space: Key Aspects of Urban and Regional Development.* Harlow, UK, Longman.

Marston, S. A. (2000). The social construction of scale. *Progress in Human Geography* 24(2): 219–242.

Martin, R. (1994). Stateless monies, global financial integration and national economic autonomy: The end of geography? *Money, Power, Space*. S. Corbridge, R. Martin, and N. Thrift (Eds.). Oxford, Blackwell: 253–278.

Martin, R., and P. Sunley. (1997). The post-Keynesian states and the space economy. *Geographies of Economies*. R. Lee and J. Wills (Eds.). London, Arnold: 278–288.

Martin, R., P. Sunley, and J. Wills. (1994). Unions and the politics of deindustrialisation: comments on how geography complicates class analysis. *Antipode* 26(1): 59–76.

Martinelli, F., and E. Schoenberger. (1991). Oligopoly is alive and well: Notes for a broader discussion of flexible accumulation. *Industrial Change and Regional Development: The Transformation of New Industrial Spaces*. G. Benko and M. Dunford (Eds.). London, Belhaven: 117–133.

Maskell, P., H. Eskelinen, I. Hannibalsson, A. Malmberg, and E. Vatne. (1998). *Competitiveness, Localised Learning and Regional Development*. London, Routledge.

Maskell, P., and A. Malmberg. (1995). Localised learning and industrial competitiveness. *Working Paper No. 8*. Berkeley Round Table on the International Economy, CA.

Maskell, P., and A. Malmberg. (1999). Localised learning and industrial competitiveness. *Cambridge Journal of Economics* 3: 167–185.

Massey, D. (1991). The political place of locality studies. *Environment and Planning A* 23: 267–281.

Massey, D. (1994). *Space, Place and Gender*. Cambridge, Polity Press.

Massey, D. (1995a). *Spatial Divisions of Labour: Social Structures and the Geography of Production* (2nd ed). London, Macmillan.

Massey, D. (1995b). The conceptualization of place. *A Place in the World? Place, Culture and Globalization*. D. Massey and P. Jess (Eds.). Oxford, Oxford University Press: 45–86.

Massey, D., and A. Catalano. (1978). *Capital and Land: Landownership by Capital in Britain*. London, Arnold.

Massey, D., P. Quintas, and D. Wield. (1992). *High Tech Fantasies: Science Parks in Society, Science and Space*. London, Routledge.

Massey, D. B., and R. Meegan. (1982). *The Anatomy of Job Loss*. London, Methuen.

Mata, J. (1991). Sunk costs and entry by small and large plants. *Entry and Market Contestability: An International Comparison*. P. A. Geroski and J. Schwalbach (Eds.). Oxford, Blackwell: 49–62.

Mattick, P. (1971). *Marx and Keynes: The Limits of the Mixed Economy*. London, Merlin.

Mayer, M. (1992). The shifting local political systems in European cities. *Cities and Regions in the New Europe*. M. Dunford and G. Kafkalas (Eds.). London, Belhaven: 255–274.

McDowell, L. (1994). The Transformation of Cultural Geography. *Human Geography: Society, Space and Social Science*. D. Gregory, R. Martin, and D. Smith (Eds.). Basingstoke, UK, Macmillan: 146–173.

McDowell, L. (1997). A tale of two cities? Embedded organisations and embodied workers in the City of London. *Geographies of Economies.* R. Lee and J. Wills (Eds.). London, Arnold: 118–129.

McDowell, L., and G. Court. (1994a). Missing subjects: Gender, power and sexuality in merchant banking. *Economic Geography* 70: 229–251.

McDowell, L., and G. Court. (1994b). Performing work: Bodily representations in merchant banks. *Society and Space* 12: 727–750.

McDowell, L., and D. Massey. (1984). A woman's place? *Geography Matters.* D. Massey and J. Allen (Eds.). Cambridge, Cambridge University Press.

McGrath-Champ, S. (1990). Strategy and industrial restructuring. *Progress in Human Geography* 23(2): 236–252.

McGrew, A. (1997). Globalisation and territorial democracy: An introduction. *The Transformation of Democracy.* A. McGrew (Ed.). Cambridge, Polity Press: 1–24.

McManus, P. (1996). Contested terrains: politics, stories and discourses of sustainability. *Environmental Politics* 5(1): 48–73.

McRae, H. (1997). My Office? No, it's a white collar factory. *Independent on Sunday,* December 7.

McRobbie, A. (1997). Bridging the gap: Feminism, fashion and consumption. *Feminist Review* 55: 73–89.

Meadows, D. H., D. L. Meadows, and J. Randers. (1972). *The Limits to Growth: A Report for the Club of Rome's Project on the Predicament of Mankind.* London, Earth Island.

Meegan, R. (1995). Local worlds. *Geographical Worlds.* J. Allen and D. Massey (Eds.). Oxford, Oxford University Press: 53–104.

Merchant, C. (1983). *The Death of Nature: Women, Ecology and the Scientific Revolution.* San Francisco, Harper & Row.

Merchant, C., and S. Voyle. (2000). William Baird to cut its financial dividend. *Financial Times,* January 12.

Merrifield, A. (1993). Place and space: A Lebebvrian reconciliation. *Transactions of the Institute of British Geographers* NS 18: 516–531.

Metcalfe, J. S. (1996). Technology system and technology policy in an evolutionary framework. *Cambridge Journal of Economics* 19, 1.

Metcalfe, J. S. (1998a). *Evolutionary Economics and Creative Restruction.* London, Routledge.

Metcalfe, J. S. (1998b). *Evolutionary concepts in relation to evolutionary economics.* Working Paper No. 4. University of Manchester, Centre for Research on Innovation and Competition.

Metcalfe, J. S., and M. Calderini. (1997). *Compound learning, neutral nets and competitive process.* Working Paper No. 1. Centre for Research on Innovation and Competition, University of Manchester.

Michalowski, R. J., and R. C. Kramer. (1987). The space between laws: The problem of corporate crime in a transnational context. *Social Problems* 34(1): 34–53.

Miliband, R. (1969). *The State in Capitalist Society.* London, Weidenfeld and Nicolson.

Miller, P., J. N. Pons, and P. Naude. (1996). Global teams. *Financial Times*, June 14.

Mingione, E. (1985). Social reproduction and the labour force: The case of Southern Italy. *Beyond Employment: Household, Gender and Subsistence*. N. Redclift and E. Mingione (Eds.). Oxford, Blackwell.

Mingione, E. (1995). Labour market segmentation and informal work in southern Europe. *European Urban and Regional Studies* 2(2): 121–143.

Minton, A. (2000). Suppliers sue M&S for £53.6m. *Financial Times*, January 11.

Mitchell, P. (1998). Innovation in the right place. *Financial Times*, April 17.

Mitchell, W. J. (1999). *E-topia: Urban life, Jim—but not as we know it*. London, MIT Press.

Mitter, S. (1986). Industrial restructuring and manufacturing homework: Immigrant women in the UK clothing industry. *Capital and Class* 27: 37–80.

Mitter, S., and S. Rowbotham. (Eds.). (1995). *Women encounter technology: Changing patterns of employment in the Third World*. London, Routledge.

Mol, A. (1996). Ecological modernisation and institutional reflexity: Environmental reform in the late modern age. *Environmental Politics* 5(2): 302–23.

Moody, K. (1997). Towards an international social-movement unionism. *New Left Review* 225: 52–72.

Morgan, K. (1995). The learning region: Institutions, innovation and regional renewal. *Papers in Planning Research No. 15*. Department of City and Regional Planning, Cardiff University.

Morgan, K., and J. Murdock. (2000). Organic versus conventional agriculture: Knowledge, power and innovation in the food chain. *Geoforum* 31: 159–173.

Morris, D., and M. Hergert. (1987). Trends in international collaborative agreements. *Columbia Journal of World Business* 22: 15–21.

Morris, L. (1994). Is there a British underclass. *International Journal of Urban and Regional Research* 17: 404–411.

Mort, F. (1997). Paths to mass consumption: Britain and the USA since 1945. *Buy This Book: Studies in Advertising and Consumption*. M. Nava (Ed.). London, Routledge: 15–33.

Mowery, D. (1993). Does Airbus Industries yield lessons for EC collaborative research programmes? *The Impact of Globalisation on Europe's Firms and Regions*. M. Humbert (Ed.). London, Pinter: 45–55.

Mulberg, J. (1995). *Social Limits to Economic Theory*. London, Routledge.

Mulgan, G. (1991). *Communication and Control: Networks and New Economics of Communication*. Cambridge, Polity Press.

Murdoch, J. (1995). Actor-networks and the evolution of economic forms. *Environment and Planning A* 27: 731–757.

Murdoch, J. (1997). Towards a geography of heterogeneous associations. *Progress in Human Geography* 21(3): 321–337.

Murdoch, J., J. Banks, and T. Marsden. (1998, July). *An economy of conventions? Some thoughts on conventions theory and its application to the agro-food sector*. Paper presented at the Royal Geographical Society Ecnomic Geography Research Group Conference Geographies of Commodities, University of Manchester, UK.

Murphy, C. (1994). *International Organisations and Industrial Change*. Cambridge, Polity Press.

Mytelka, L. K. (1993). Strengthening the relevance of European science and technology programmes to industrial competitiveness: The case of ESPRIT. *The Impact of Globalisation on Europe's Firms and Regions*. M. Humbert (Ed.). London, Pinter: 56–63.

Naylor, J., and M. Lewis. (1997). Internal alliances: Using joint ventures in a diversified company. *Long Range Planning* 30(5): 678–688.

Nelson, K. (1986). Labour demand, labour supply and the suburbanization of low-wage office work. *Production, Territory, Work*. A. Scott and M. Storper (Eds.). London, Allen and Unwin: 149–171.

Nelson, R. R., and S. G. Winter. (1982). *An Evolutionary Theory of Economic Change*. Cambridge, MA, Harvard University Press.

Neumann, F. (1944). *Behemoth: the Structure and Practice of National Socialism, 1933–1944*, rev. ed. New York, Octagon

Nichols, T., and H. Beynon. (1977). *Living with Capitalism: Class Relations and the Modern Factory*. London, Routledge and Kegan Paul.

Nonaka, I., and J. Takeuchi. (1995). *The Knowledge-Creating Company: How Japanese Companies Create the Dynamics of Innovation*. New York, Oxford University Press.

Nooteboom, B. (1999). Innovation, learning and industrial organisations. *Cambridge Journal of Economics* 23: 127–150.

Nusbaum, A. (2000). Web cuts out entire order of middlemen. *Financial Times*, January 11.

O'Brien, R. (1992). *Global Financial Integration: The End of Geography*. London, Pinter.

O'Connor, J. (1973). *The Fiscal Crisis of the State*. New York, St. Martin's Press.

O'Connor, J. (1994). Is sustainable capitalism possible? *Is Capitalism Sustainable? Political economy and the politics of economy*. M. O'Connor (Ed.). New York, Guilford Press: 152–175.

O'Connor, M. (1994a). Copendency and indeterminacy: A critique of the theory of production. *Is Capitalism Sustainable? Political economy and the politics of economy*. M. O'Connor (Ed.). New York, Guilford Press: 51–75.

O'Connor, M. (1994b). Introduction: Liberate, accumulate and bust? *Is Capitalism Sustainable? Political economy and the politics of economy*. M. O'Connor (Ed.). New York, Guilford Press: 1–21.

O'Connor, M. (1994c). On the misadventures of capitalist nature. *Is Capitalism Sustainable? Political economy and the politics of economy*. M. O'Connor (Ed.). New York, Guilford Press.

Odgaard, M., and R. Hudson. (1998). *The misplacement of learning in economic geography*. University of Durham, Department of Geography. Mimeo. 27 pages.

O'Doherty, D. P. (1993). Globalisation and performance of small firms within the smaller European economies. *The Impact of Globalisation on Europe's Firms and Regions*. M. Humbert (Ed.). London, Pinter: 141–151.

Offe, C. (1975a). The theory of the capitalist state and the problem of policy formation. *Stress and Contradiction in Modern Capitalism*. L. N. Lindberg, R. Alford, C. Crouch, and C. Offe (Eds.). Lexington, KY, DC Heath: 125–144.

Offe, C. (1975b). Introduction to Part II. *Stress and Contradiction in Modern Capitalism*. L. N. Lindberg, R. F. Alford, and C. Offe (Eds.). Boston, DC Heath: 245–259.

Offe, C. (1976). Political authority and class structures: An analysis of late capitalist societies. *Critical Sociology*. P. Connerton, (Ed.). Harmondsworth, UK, Penguin: 388–421.

Offe, C. (Ed.). (1984). *Contradictions of the Welfare State*. London, Hutchinson.

Offe, C., and Lenhardt. (1984). Social policy and the theory of the state. *Contradictions of the Welfare State*. C. Offe (Ed.). London, Hutchinson: 88–118.

Ohmae, K. (1990). *The Borderless World: Power and strategy in the interlinked economy*. New York, HarperBusiness.

Ohmae, K. (1995). *The End of the Nation State*. New York, Free Press.

Okamura, C., and H. Kawahito. (1990). *Karoshi*. Tokyo, Mado Sha.

O'Neill, P. (1997). Bringing the qualitative state into economic geography. *Geographies of Economies*. R. Lee and J. Wills (Eds.). London, Arnold: 290–301.

Ong, A. (1987). *Spirits of Resistance and Capitalist Discipline: Factory Women in Malaysia*. Albany, University of New York Press.

Organization for Economic Cooperation and Development. (1992). *Globalisation of Industrial Activities: Four case studies—auto parts, chemicals, construction and semi-conductors*. Paris, OECD.

O'Riordan, T. (1981). *Environmentalism*. London, Pion.

Painter, J. (1998). *The aterritorial city: Diversity, spatiality, democritisation*. Department of Geography, University of Durham. Mimeo. 47 pages.

Painter, J., and M. Goodwin. (1995). Local governance and concrete research: Investigating the uneven development of regulation. *Economy and Society* 24: 334–356.

Paley, W. S. (Ed.). (1952). *Resources for Freedom*. A Report to the President by the Provident's Materials Policy Commission, U.S. Government Printing Office, Washington DC.

Palloix, C. (1975). *L'Internationalisation du Capital: Eléments Critiques*. Paris, Maspero.

Palloix, C. (1976). The labour process from Fordism to Neo-Fordism. *Conference of Socialist Economists, The Labour Process and Class Strategies*. London, Conference of Socialist Economics: 46–67.

Palloix, C. (1977). The self-expansion of capital on a world scale. *Review of Radical Political Economics* 9: 1–28.

Panitch, L. (1996). Re-thinking the role of the state. *Globalization: Critical Reflections*. J. H. Mittleman (Ed.). Boulder, CO, Rienner: 83–113.

Pasternack, B. A., and A. J. Viscio. (1998). *The Centerless Corporation: A New Model for Transforming Your Organisation for Growth and Prosperity*. New York, Simon & Schuster.

Pearce, D., A. Markandya, and E. Barbier. (1989). *Blueprint for a Green Economy*. London, Earthscan.

Pearson, R., and S. Mitter. (1994). Employment and working conditions of low-skilled information-processing workers in less developed countries. *International Labour Review* 132(1): 49–64.

Peck, J. (1989). Reconceptualising the local labour market: Space, segmentation and the state. *Progress in Human Geography* 13: 42–61.

Peck, J. (1994). Regulating labour: The social regulation and reproduction of local labour markets. *Globalization, Institutions and Regional Development in Europe*. A. Amin and N. J. Thrift (Eds.). Oxford, Oxford University Press: 147–176.

Peck, J. (1996). *Workplace: The Social Regulation of Labor Markets*. New York, Guilford Press.

Peck, J. (2000). *Workfare States*. New York, Guilford Press.

Peck, J., and N. C. Theodore. (1997). *Trading warm bodies: Processing contingent labour in Chicago's temp industry*. International Centre for Labour Studies, University of Manchester. Mimeo. 24 pages.

Peck, J., and A. Tickell. (1992). Local modes of social regulation? Regulation theory, Thatcherism and uneven development. *Geoforum* 23: 347–363.

Peet, R. (1997a). *Modern Geographical Thought*. Oxford, Blackwell.

Peet, R. (1997b). The cultural production of economic forms. *Geographies of Economies*. R. Lee and J. Wills (Eds.). London, Arnold: 37–46.

Penrose, E. (1959). *The Theory of the Growth of the Firm*. Oxford, Blackwell.

Pepper, D. (1984). *Roots of Modern Environmentalism*. London, Routledge.

Pepper, D. (1993). *Eco-Socialism: From Deep Ecology to Social Justice*. London, Routledge.

Perrons, D. (1992). The regions and the single market. *Cities and Regions in the New Europe: The Global–Local Interplay and Spatial Development Strategies*. M. Dunford and G. Kafkalas (Eds.). London, Belhaven: 171–194.

Phizacklea, A. (1990). *Unpacking the Fashion Industry*. London, Routledge.

Pilkington, A. (1999). Strategic alliances and dependancy in design and manufacture. *International Journal of Operations and Production Management* 19(5/6): 460–474.

Pilling, D. (2000a). Glaxo, SB to announce deal today. *Financial Times*, January 17.

Pilling, D. (2000b). Marriage made in the lab. *Financial Times*, January 17.

Pine, B. J. (1993). *Mass Customization: The New Frontier in Business Competition*. Cambridge, MA, Harvard University Press.

Pocock, D., and R. Hudson. (1978). *Images of the Urban Environment*. London, Macmillan.

Pollert, A. (1988). Dismantling flexibility. *Capital and Class* 34: 42–75.

Polyani, K. (1957). *The Great Transformation: The Political and Economic Origins of our Time*. Boston, Beacon Press.

Polyani, M. (1967). *The Tacit Dimension*. London, Routledge and Kegan Paul.

Poon, A. (1989). Competitive strategies for a "new tourism." *Progress in Tourism, Recreation and Hospitality Management*. C. Cooper (Ed.). London, Belhaven: 91–102.

Portes, A., M. Castells, and L. A. Benton. (1988). *The Informal Economy: Studies in Advanced and Less Developed Countries*. Baltimore, John Hopkins University Press.

Portes, R., and J. Jensen. (1989). The enclave and the entrants: Patterns of ethnic enterprise in Miami before and after Mariel. *American Sociological Review* 54: 929–949.

Postone, M. (1996). *Time, Labour and Social Domination*. Cambridge, Cambridge University Press.

Poulantzas, N. (1975). *Classes in Contemporary Capitalism*. London, New Left Books.

Poulantzas, N. (1978). *State, Power, Socialism*. London, New Left Books.

Prahalad, C. K., and G. Hamal. (1990). The core competencies of the corporation. *Harvard Business Review* 68(3): 79–91.

Pratt, L., and W. Montgomery. (1997). Green imperialism: pollution, penitence, profit. *Socialist Register* 33: 75–95.

Pred, A. (1967). *Behaviour and Location*. Lund, University of Lund, Department of Human Geography.

Pred, A. (1996). Interfusions: Consumption, identity and the practices and power relations of everyday life. *Environment and Planning A* 28: 11–24.

Priestley, J. S. (1934). *English Journey*. London, Heinemann.

Pryke, M. (1991). An international city going "global": Spatial change in the City of London. *Society and Space* 9: 197–222.

Pryke, M., and R. Lee. (1995). Place your bets: Towards an understanding of socio-financial engineering and competition within a financial centre. *Urban Studies* 32: 329–44.

Pugliese, E. (1993). Restructuring the labour market and the role of Third World migrations in Europe. *Society and Space* 11(4): 513–22.

Putnam, R., A. Leonardi, and R. Nanetti. (1993). *Making Democracy Work: Tradition in Modern Italy*. Princeton, NJ, Princeton University Press.

Rainnie, A. (1993). The reorganization of large firm subcontracting. *Capital and Class* 49: 53–76.

Ramsay, H. (1992). Whose champions? Multinationals, labour and industry policy in the European community after 1992. *Capital and Class* 48: 17–40.

Rankin, S. (1987). Exploitation and the labour theory of value: A neo-Marxian reply. *Capital and Class* 32: 104–116.

Rees, G., and S. Fielder. (1992). The services economy, subcontracting and the new employment relations: Contract catering and cleaning. *Work, Employment and Society* 6(3): 347–368.

Reich, R. (1991). *The Work of Nations: Preparing Ourselves for 21st Century Capitalism*. New York, Knopf.

Reimer, S. (1999). Contract service firms in local authorities: Evolving geographies of activity. *Regional Studies* 33(2): 121–130.

Relph, E. (1975). *Place and Placelessness*. London, Pion.

Rich, D. (1994). *Mortgaging the Earth: The World Bank, Environmental Impoverishment and the Crisis of Development*. London, Earthscan.

Richardson, G. B. (1972). The organisation of industry. *The Economic Journal* 82(September): 883–896.

Roberts, B. (1987). Marx after Steedman—separating Marxism and "surplus theory." *Capital and Class* 32: 84–103.

Roberts, B. (Ed.). (1994). Informal Economy and Family Strategies [Special Issue]. *International Journal of Urban and Regional Research* 18(1).

Roberts, J. M. (1999). Marxism and critical realism: The same, similar, or just plain different. *Capital and Class* 68: 21–49.

Robins, K. (1991). Tradition and translation: National culture in its global context. *Enterprise and Heritage: Cross-Currents of National Culture*. J. Corner and S. Harvey (Eds.). London, Routledge.

Rogers, J., and W. Streeck (1995). *Works Councils: Consultation, representation and cooperation in industrial relations*. Chicago, University of Chicago Press.

Rose, G. (1995). Place and identity: a sense of place. *A Place in the World? Place, Cultures and Globalization*. D. Massey and P. Jess (Eds.). Oxford, Oxford University Press: 87–132.

Rosenberg, N. (1982). *Inside the Black Box: Technology and Economics*. Cambridge, Cambridge University Press.

Rothwell, R. (1988). SMEs, inter-firm relationships and technological change. *Entrepreneurship and Regional Development* 1: 275–291.

Rubenstein, J. M. (1978). *The French New Towns*. Baltimore, John Hopkins University Press.

Ruggie, J. G. (1993). Territoriality and beyond: Problematizing modernity in international relations. *International Organisation* 27(1): 139–174.

Rutherford, M. (1994). *Institutions in Economics: The Old and New Institutionalism*. Cambridge, Cambridge University Press.

Sabel, C., and J. Zeitlin. (1997). *Worlds of Possibilities*. Cambridge, Cambridge University Press.

Sadler, D. (1992). Industrial policy of the European Community: Strategic deficits and regional dilemmas. *Environment and Planning A* 24: 1711–1730.

Sadler, D. (1994). The geographies of "just-in-time": Japanese investment and the automotive components industry in Western Europe. *Economic Geography* 70: 41–50.

Sadler, D. (1997). The role of supply chain management strategies in the "europeanisation" of the automobile production system. *Geographies of Economies*. R. Lee and J. Wills (Eds.). London, Arnold: 311–320.

Sadler, D., and A. Amin. (1995). Europeanisation in the automotive components sector and its implications for state and locality. *Towards a New Map of Automobile Manufacturing in Europe? New Production Concepts and Spatial Restructuring*. R. Hudson and E. W. Schamp (Eds.). Berlin, Springer: 39–62.

Sadler, D., and J. Thompson. (1999, September). *In search of regional industrial culture: The role of labour organisations in old industrial regions*. Paper presented at the Seventh seminar of the Aegean, Paros.

Said, E. (1979). *Orientalism*. London, Routledge.

Salais, M., and M. Storper. (1992). The four worlds of contemporary industry. *Cambridge Journal of Economics* 16: 169–193.

Salleh, A. (1994). Nature, woman, labor, capital: Living the deepest contradiction. *Is Capitalism Sustainable? Political economy and the politics of economy*. M. O'Connor (Ed.). New York, Guilford Press: 106–124.

Sassen, S. (1991). *The Global City: New York, London, Tokyo.* Los Angeles, University of California Press.

Saxenian, A. (1984). The urban contradictions of Silicon Valley: Regional growth and the restructuring of the semi-conductor industry. *Sunbelt/Snowbelt: Urban Development and Regional Restructuring.* L. Sawers and W. K. Tabb (Eds.). New York, Oxford University Press: 163–197.

Sayer, A. (1984). *Method in Social Science.* London, Hutchinson.

Sayer, A. (1986). New developments in manufacturing: The just-in-time system. *Capital and Class* 30: 43–72.

Sayer, A. (1989). Post-Fordism is question. *International Journal of Urban and Regional Research* 13: 666–695.

Sayer, A. (1995). *Radical Political Economy: A Critique.* Oxford, Blackwell.

Sayer, A., and R. Walker. (1992). *The New Social Economy: Reworking the Division of Labour.* Oxford, Blackwell.

Schamp, E. W. (1991). Towards a spatial reorganisation of the German car industry? The implications of new production concepts. *Industrial Change and Regional Development: The Transformation of New Industrial Spaces.* G. Benko and M. Dunford (Eds.). London, Belhaven: 159–170.

Schech, S. (1988). *A Cross and Four Stripes: The Revival of Nationalism in Contemporary Scotland and Catalonia.* Doctoral dissertation, University of Durham.

Schmidt, A. (1971). *The Concept of Nature in Marx.* London, New Left Books.

Schoenberger, E. (1994). *The Cultural Crisis of the Firm.* Oxford, Blackwell.

Schoenberger, E. (1998). Pressure and practice in human geography. *Progress in Human Geography* 22(1): 1–14.

Schumpeter, J. (1919/1961). *The Theory of Economic Development.* Cambridge, MA, Harvard University Press.

Shaw, G., and A. Williams. (1994). *Critical Issues in Tourism.* Oxford, Blackwell.

Shen, L., and R. Hudson. (1999). Towards sustainable mining cities: What policies should be sought and experiences could be learnt for China? *Journal of Chinese Geography* 9(3): 207–227.

Sheppard, E., and T. Barnes. (1990). *The Capitalist Space Economy: Geographical Analysis after Ricardo, Marx and Sraffa.* London, Unwin Hyman.

Simon, H. A. (1959). Theories of decision making in economics and behavioural science. *American Economic Review* 44(3): 253–283.

Simonian, H. (1998). Motor industry learns to drive hard bargain with its workers. *Financial Times,* May 12.

Sklair, L. (1990). *Sociology of the Global System.* Hemel Hempstead, UK, Harvester.

Smith, P., and P. Brown (1993). Industrial change and Scottish nationalism since 1945. *Redundant Spaces in Cities and Regions?* J. Anderson, S. Duncan, and R. Hudson (Eds.). London, Academic Press: 241–262.

Smith, A. (1998). *Reconstructing the Regional Economy: Industrial Transformation and Regional Development in Slovakia.* Cheltenham, UK, Edward Elgar.

Smith, N. (1984). *Uneven Development: Nature, Capital and the Production of Space.* Oxford, Blackwell.

Smith, R. P. (1988). The significance of defence expenditure in the U.S. and UK national economies. *Defence Expenditure and Regional Development.* M. Brehery (Ed.). London, Mansell: 7–16.

South, R. B. (1990). Transnational "regulation" location. *Annals of the Association of American Geographers* 80: 549–570.

Southall, H. (1988). Towards a geography of unionization: The spatial organization of early British trade unions. *Transactions of the Institute of British Geographers* 13: 466–483.

Springett, D. (1999). *Sustainable development explored.* Massey University College of Business. Mimeo. 44 pages.

Stalk, G. (1988). Time—the next resource of competitive advantage. *Harvard Business Review* 66: 45–51.

Standing (1989). Labour market flexibility in Western European labour markets. *Flexibility and Labour Markets in Canada and the United States.* G. Laflamme, G. Murray, and J. Belanger (Eds.). Geneva, International Labour Organization: 37–60.

Steedman, I. (1977). *Marx after Sraffa.* London, New Left Books.

Stenning, A. (2000). Placing (post-)socialism: making and re-making of Nova Huta, Poland. *European Urban and Regional Studies* 7(2): 99–117.

Storey, D. J., and P. Johnson. (1987). *Job Generation and Labour Market Change.* London, Macmillan.

Storper, M. (1992). The limits to globalization: technology districts and international trade. *Economic Geography* 68: 60–93.

Storper, M. (1993). Regional "worlds" of production: Learning and innovation in the technology districts of France, Italy and the USA. *Regional Studies* 27(5): 433–456.

Storper, M. (1995). The resurgence of regional economies, ten years later: The region as a nexus of untraded interdependencies. *European Urban and Regional Studies* 2(3): 191–222.

Storper, M. (1997). *The Regional World: Territorial development in a global economy.* New York, Guilford Press.

Storper, M., and S. Christopherson. (1987). The city as studio; the world as back lot: The impact of vertical disintegration on the location of the motion picture industry. *Society and Space* 4: 305–320.

Storper, M., and R. Walker. (1983). The theory of labour and the theory of location. *International Journal of Urban and Regional Research* 7: 1–41.

Storper, M., and R. Walker. (1989). *The Capitalist Imperative: Territory, Technology and Industrial Growth.* Oxford, Blackwell.

Strange, S. (1988). *States and Markets.* London, Pinter.

Summers, D. (1998). Ways to a working woman's heart. *Financial Times,* March 20.

Sunley, P. (1990). Striking parallels: A comparison of the geographies of the 1926 and 1984/5 coalmining disputes. *Society and Space* 8: 35–52.

Sunley, P. (1992). Marshallian industrial districts: The case of the Lancashire cotton industry in the inter-war years. *Transactions of the Institute of British Geographers* 17(3): 306–320.

Sweezy, P. (1938). *Monopoly and Competition in the English Coal Trade 1550–1850*. Cambridge, MA, Harvard University Press.

Swyngedouw, E. (1992). The Mammon quest. "Globalisation," interspatial competition and the monetary order: The construction of new scales. *Cities and the Regions in the New Europe*. M. Dunford and G. Kafkalas (Eds.). London, Belhaven: 39–67.

Sztompka, P. (1999). *Trust: A Sociological Theory*. Cambridge, Cambridge University Press.

Taylor, M. J. (1994, August). *Industrialisation, enterprise power and environmental change: An exploration of concepts*. Paper presented at the International Geographical Union Commission on the organisation of Industrial Space, Budapest.

Taylor, M. J. (1995). Linking economy, environment and policy. *Environmental Change: Industry, Power and Policy*. M. Taylor (Ed.). Aldershot, Avebury.

Taylor, P. (1992). Changing Political Relations. *Policy and Change in Thatcher's Britain*. P. Cloke (Ed.). Oxford, Pergamon.

Taylor, P. (1995). India's software industry. *Financial Times*, December 6.

Taylor, P. J. (1999). Places, spaces and Macy's: Place-space tensions in the political geography of modernities. *Progress in Human Geography* 23(1): 7–26.

Therborn, G. (1978). *What Does the Ruling Class Do When It Rules?* London, New Left Books.

Theret, B. (1994). To have or to be: On the problem of the interaction between state and economy in its "solideristic" mode of regulation. *Economy and Society* 23: 1–46.

Thompson, E. P. (1969). *The Making of the English Working Class*. Harmondsworth, UK, Penguin.

Thompson, E. P. (1978). *The Poverty of Theory and Other Essays*. London, Merlin Press.

Thompson, S. (1999). Takeovers, joint ventures and the acquisition of resources for diversification. *Scottish Journal of Political Economy* 46(3): 303–318.

Thompson, W., and F. Hart. (1972). *The UCS Work-in*. London, Lawrence and Wishart.

Thrift, N. (1989). New times and spaces? The perils of transition models. *Society and Space* 12: 127–128.

Thrift, N. (1994a). Taking aim at the heart of the region. *Human Geography: Society, Space and Social Science*. D. Gregory and R. Martin (Eds.). Basingstoke, UK, Macmillan: 200–231.

Thrift, N. (1994b). On the social and cultural determinants of international financial centres: The case of the City of London. *Money, Space and Power*. S. Cambridge, R. Machin, and N. Thrift (Eds.). Oxford, Blackwell: 327–355.

Thrift, N. (1996a). *Spatial Formations*. London, Sage.

Thrift, N. (1996b). Shut up and dance, or, is the world economy knowable? *The Global Economy in Transition*. P. Daniels and W. Lever (Eds.). London, Longman: 11–23.

Thrift, N. (2000, June/July). *Animal spirits: Performing cultures in the new economy*. Paper presented at the Eighth Conference of the International Joseph A. Schumpeter Society, University of Manchester, UK.

Thrift, N., P. Daniels, and A. Leyshon. (1987). *Sexy Greedy: The New International Financial System, the City of London and the South East of England*. Universities of Bristol and Liverpool. Mimeo. 32 pages.

Thrift, N., and K. Olds. (1996). Refiguring the economic in economic geography. *Progress in Human Geography* 20(3): 311–337.

Tickell, A., and J. Peck. (1995). Social regulation after Fordism: Regulation theory, neo-liberalism and the global-local nexus. *Economy and Society* 24: 357–386.

Tighe, C. (1998). Nissan shows the way in the drive to boost productivity. *Financial Times*, November 24.

Toffler, A. (1981). *Future Shock*. New York, Random House.

Townsend, A. R. (1997). *Making a Living in Europe*. London, Routledge.

Townsend, A. R., D. Sadler, and R. Hudson. (1995). Geographical dimensions of UK retailing employment change. *Retailing, Consumption and Capital*. N. Wrigley and M. Lowe (Eds.). Harlow, UK, Longman: 208–218.

United Nations (1993). *World Investment Report 1993: Transnational Corporations and Integrated International Production*. United Nations Programs on Trade and Development, Program on Transnational Corporations, United Nations, New York.

United Nations World Commission on the Environment and Development. (1987). *Our Common Future*. Oxford, Oxford University Press.

Urry, J. (1981). *The Anatomy of Capitalist Societies*. London, Macmillan.

Urry, J. (1985). Social relations, space and time. *Social Relations and Spatial Structures*. D. Gregory and J. Urry (Eds.). Basingstoke, UK, Macmillan: 20–48.

Urry, J. (1990). *The Tourist Gaze*. London, Sage.

Uzzi, B. (1996). The sources and consequences of embeddedness for the economic performance of organisations: The network effect. *American Sociological Review* 61: 674–698.

Uzzi, B. (1997). Social structure and competition in inter-firm networks: The paradox of embeddedness. *Administrative Science Quarterly* 61: 674–698.

van Tulder, R., and W. Ruigrok. (1993). Regionalisation, globalisation or glocalisation: The case of the world car industry. *The Impact of Globalisation on Europe's Firms and Industries*. M. Humbert (Ed.). London, Pinter: 22–33.

Vanderbush, W. (1997). Local workplace organising in the wake of globalisation: Street vendors and autoworkers in Puebla, Mexico. *Space and Polity* 1(1): 61–81.

Vaughan, P. (1996, May). *Procurement and capital projects*. Paper presented at the Conference on Supply Chain Management—Challenges for the 21st Century, University of Durham Business School.

Veltz, P. (1991). New models of production organisation and trends in spatial development. *Industrial Change and Regional Development: The Transformation of New Industrial Spaces*. G. Benko and M. Dunford (Eds.). London, Belhaven: 193–204.

von Weizsacker, E. U. (1994). *Earth Politics*. London, Zed Books.

von Weizsacker, E. U., A. B. Lovins, and L. H. Lovins. (1998). *Factor Four*. London, Earthscan.

Vyas, N. M. (1995). An analysis of strategic alliances: Forms, function and framework. *Journal of Business and Industrial Marketing* 10(3): 47–66.

Wade, R. (1990). *Governing the Market: Economic Theory and the Role of Government in East Asian Industrialization*. Princeton, NJ, Princeton University Press.

Walker, R. (1985). Is there a service economy? The changing capitalist division of labour. *Science and Society* 49: 42–83.

Walker, R. (1988). The geographical organization of production-systems. *Environment and Planning D: Society and Space* 6: 377–408.

Walsh, M. (1990). Flexible labour utilisation in the private service sector. *Work, Employment and Society* 4(4): 517–530.

Walsh, V., and I. Galimberti. (1993). Firm strategies, globalisation and new technological paradigms: The case of biotechnology. *Impact of Globalisation on Europe's Firms and Regions*. M. Humbert (Ed.). London, Pinter: 175–190.

Ward, N., and R. Almas. (1997). Explaining change in the international agrofood system. *Review of International Political Economy* 4(4): 611–629.

Ward, S. (1998). *Selling Places: The Marketing and Promotion of Towns and Cities, 1850–2000*. London, Routledge.

Warde, A. (1988). Industrial restructuring local politics and the reproduction of labour power: Some theoretical considerations. *Society and Space* 6(1): 75–95.

Warde, A. (1989). Industrial discipline: Factory régime and politics in Lancaster. *Work, Employment and Society* 3(1): 49–63.

Warde, A. (1994). Consumption, identity-formation and uncertainty. *Sociology* 28(4): 877–898.

Watanabe, S. (1998). Searching for a global management model: The case of Japanese multinationals. *Impact of Globalisation on Europe's Firms and Regions*. M. Humbert (Ed.). London, Pinter: 229–237.

Waters, R., and C. Corrigan. (1998). The cult of gigantism. *Financial Times*, April 11–12.

Weaver, P. M. (1993). *Synergies of association: Ecorestructuring, scale, and the industrial landscape*. University of Durham, Department of Geography. Mimeo. 35 pages.

Weaver, P. M. (1994). *How life-cycle analysis and operational research methods could help clarify environmental policy: The case of fibre recycling in the pulp/paper sector*. University of Durham, Department of Geography. Mimeo. 29 pages.

Weaver, P. M. (1995a). *Implementing change: A resource paper for the factor-10 club meeting*. University of Durham, Department of Geography. Mimeo. 26 pages.

Weaver, P. M. (1995b). *Steering the eco-transition: A materials accounts based approach*. University of Durham, Department of Geography. Mimeo. 26 pages.

Weber, A. (1909). *Über den Standort der Industrien*. Tubingen, JCB Mohr.

Weiss, L. (1997). Globalisation and the myth of the powerless state. *New Left Review* 225: 3–27.

Wenger, E. (1998). *Communities of Practice: Learning, Meaning and Identity*. Cambridge, Cambridge University Press.

Wernick, I. D., R. Herman, B. Govinch, and J. H. Ausubel. (1997). Materialization and dematerialization: Measures and trends. *Technological Trajectories and the Human Environment*. J. H. Ausubel and H. D. Langford (Eds.). Washington, DC, National Academy Press: 135–156.

Williams, C. (1996a). Informal sector responses to unemployment: An evaluation of the potential of LETS. *Work, Employment and Society* 10(2): 341–359.

Williams, C. (1996b). Local purchasing and rural development: An evaluation of LETS. *Journal of Rural Studies* 12(3): 231–244.

Williams, C. C., and J. Windebank. (1998). *Informal Employment in the Advance Economics: Implications for Welfare in Work*. London, Routledge.

Williams, K., T. Cutler, J. Williams, and C. Haslam. (1987). The end of mass production. *Industrial Policy: UK and US Debates*. G. Thompson (Ed.). London, Routledge: 163–196.

Williams, R. (1980). *Problems in Materialism and Culture*. London, Verso.

Williams, R. (1983). *Key Words*. London, Fantana.

Williams, R. (1989a). *Resources of Hope*. London, Verso.

Williams, R. (1989b). *The Politics of Modernism*. London, Verso.

Williamson, O. (1975). *Markets and Hierarchies: Analysis and Antitrust Implications*. New York, Free Press.

Willis, P. (1977). *Learning to Labour: How Working Class Kids Get Working Class Jobs*. Aldershot, UK, Gower.

Willman, J. (1998). Gillette rolls out Mach 3 fighter for staving war. *Financial Times*, April 15.

Wills, J. (1997). Harbingers of a social economy in Europe? Preliminary investigations into the Operations of European Works Councils. *Working Paper No. 1. Re-Scaling Workplace Solidarity?* London, Department of Geography, Queen Mary and Westfield College.

Wills, J. (1998a, July). *Building labour institutions to shape the world order? International trade unionism and European Works Councils*. Paper presented at the Royal Geographical Society Economic Geography Research Group Seminar "Institutions and Governance," University College London, London.

Wills, J. (1998b). Taking on the CosmoCorp? Experiments in transnational labour organisation. *Economic Geography* 74: 111–130.

Wills, J. (1999). Great expectations: Three years in the life of one EWC. *Working Paper No 5. Re-Scaling Workplace Solidarity?* Department of Geography, Queen Mary and Westfield College, London.

Wilson, A. (1971). *Entropy in Urban and Regional Modelling*. London, Pion.

Winterton, J. (1985). Computerized coal: New technology in the mines. *Digging Deeper: Issues in the Miners' Strike*. H. Beynon (Ed.). London, Verso: 231–244.

Wolf, F. O. (1986). Eco-socialist transition on the threshold of the twenty first century. *New Left Review* 158: 32–42.

Womack, J. P., D. T. Jones, and D. Roos. (1990). *The Machine That Changed the World*. New York, Macmillan.

Woo Cumings, M. (Ed.). (1999). *The Development State*. London, Cornell University Press.

World Bank. (1994). *Annual Report 1994*. Washington, DC, World Bank.

Wright, E. O. (1976). Class boundaries in advanced capitalist societies. *New Left Review* 98: 3–41.

Wright, E. O. (1978). *Class, Crisis and the State*. London, New Left Books.

Wright, E. O. (1985). *Classes*. London, Verso.

Wright, E. O. (1989). Rethinking once again, the concept of class structure. *The Debate on Classes*. E. O. Wright with Becker, U., Brenner, J., Burawoy, M., Burris, V., Carchedi, G., Marshall, G., Meiksins, P. F., Rose, D., Stinchcombe, A., and van Parijs, P. London, Verso: 269–348.

Wright, E. O. (1997). *Class Counts: Comparative Studies in Class Analysis*. Cambridge, Cambridge University Press.

Wrigley, N., and M. Lowe. (Eds.). (1995). *Retailing Consumption and Capital: Towards the New Retail Geography*. London, Longman.

Wrong, M. (1999). Americans get wise to agricultural revolution. *Financial Times*, December 16.

Wrong, M., and N. Tait. (1999). U.S. lawsuit taps into a growing consumer backlash. *Financial Times*, December 15.

Wuppertal Institute for Climate, Environment and Energy. (1994). *Carnoules Declaration*, Wuppertal.

Yates, C. (1998). Defining the fault times: New divisions in the working class. *Capital and Class* 66: 119–147.

Yearley, S. (1995a). Dirty connections: Transnational pollution. *A Shrinking World?* J. Allen and D. Hamnett (Eds.). Oxford, Oxford University Press: 143–182.

Yearley, S. (1995b). The Transnational politics of the environment. *A Global World?* J., Anderson, C. Brook, and A. Cochrane (Eds.). Oxford, Oxford University Press: 209–248.

Yeung, H. (1998). Capital, state and space: Contesting the borderless world. *Transactions of the Institute of British Geographers* NS 23(3): 291–309.

Young, J. E. (1992). *Mining the Earth*. Washington, DC, Worldwatch Institute.

Zacher, M. (1992). The decaying pillars of the westphalian temple. *Governance without Government*. E. O. Gzempiel and J. Rosenau (Eds.). Cambridge, Cambridge University Press.

Zukin, S., and P. di Maggio. (1990). Introduction. *Structures of Capital: The Social Organization of the Economy*. S. Zukin and P. di Maggio (Eds.). Cambridge, Cambridge University Press: 1–36.

Zysman, J. (1993). Regional blocs, corporate strategies and government policies: The end of free trade? *The Impact of Globalisation on Europe's Firms and Regions*. M. Humbert (Ed.). London, Pinter: 105–173.

Index

acquisitions, 6, 142, 149, 180, 187, 205, 208–214
  barriers to, 168, 173
action
  collective, 23, 246, 268–270
  radical political, 337–338
actor-network theory, 32–34, 40, 47
advertising, 116, 134, 162–166, 173, 183, 192, 209, 226, 317, 327
agency, 3, 11, 16, 27, 30–34, 39, 52, 59, 218, 329
agriculture, 192, 246, 298–300, 307
alienation, 17, 133, 172, 276
analogy
  biology, 28, 293
  physical system, 44
anthropology, 28
apartheid, 61, 91, 233
Asea Brown Boveri, 127

Barnevik P, 127
Boeing, 176–206
boosterism campaigns, 242, 272, 277
Brandt Report, 323
Bretton Woods Agreement 1944, 78
British Steel Corporation, 144, 215
Brundtland Report, 323, 328

capabilities, 35, 109, 140, 148–149, 175, 186, 188, 198, 203, 214
capital, 2–4, 39–42, 50, 65, 85–88, 122, 160, 268, 273–275, 297
  accumulation, 18–22, 27, 34–37, 50, 53–59, 68–69, 72–73, 151, 236, 258–261, 294–296, 309, 313–314, 317, 332–337

centralization of, 142, 209, 211–214
circulation of, 77, 255, 260–262, 296, 337
circuits of, 18–22, 45, 70, 321
composition of
  organic, 182
  technical, 150, 182
concentration of, 211
devalorization of, 261, 282
fixed, 89, 103, 110, 135, 150, 158, 182, 193, 244, 261
flight, 102, 274, 282
hypermobile, 103
in general, 51–52
landscapes of, 39, 244, 229, 255, 283
limits to, 287–289, 297, 324–325
money, 18–19, 34, 67–69, 88
reproduction of, 21
social, 177, 285
turnover time of, 89, 135, 159
  socially necessary, 45
capital versus labor relations, 42, 51–52, 135–138, 146, 230, 262, 264
capitalism
  Aeco, 321–324, 327
  laws of, 273
    tendential, 7
  monopoly, 162
  precapitalism, 260
  second contradiction of, 313, 322–323
  spatialities, 26, 39
  structures of, 256–262
  varieties, 2, 22, 28, 36, 168, 198, 208
carbon
  cycle, 289
  fossil fuels, 302–304, 316
  decarbonization of economy, 307, 313

causal powers, 9, 38, 252, 285, 303
civil society, 37, 39, 49, 55, 66–68, 72–
        75, 85, 92, 177, 260, 264, 280,
        335–336
    national, 54–58
class, 2, 9, 66, 76, 79, 88, 112, 116–
        117, 182, 217, 226, 244, 252,
        264, 268, 271, 294
    contradictory class locations, 23
    cross-class alliances, 242, 269
    formation, 223, 228, 241
    middle, 166, 227–228, 278, 313
    noncapitalist, 4
    relations, 26
    service, 278, 313
    structure, 24, 47, 224, 227–230
    struggle, 54, 135, 269
    two class model, 223–226
    underclass, 250
    working, 102, 218–220, 275–276,
        284
        "for itself," 217–220, 225, 266
        "in itself," 225
        divisions within, 270, 324–354
clientilism, 61, 116
coal mining, 108, 144, 220, 244
Coats Viyella, 196
commodity, 25, 89, 286
    biography of, 21
    chain analysis, 45, 214–215
    production, 4, 17–18, 42, 282, 289,
        321
community, 58, 85, 102, 106–107, 118–
        120, 203, 236, 246, 265, 270,
        276, 330, 334–336
    capacity building, 250–251
    economic initiatives, 321–334
    fabric of, 123, 248, 266
    solidarity, 270
commuting, 124, 304
competencies, 35–36, 73, 111, 140,
        148, 172, 186, 188, 191, 204
    core, 35, 148–149, 175, 179, 209,
        214
competition, 21, 35, 42, 50–52, 75, 94,
        129–131, 143–215, 221, 262,
        317
    between firms, 143–215
        adaptive, 143
        creative, 143–144
        strong, 109, 144, 147–181, 186,
            209
        structure dependent, 143, 165
        structure focused, 143–144, 165
        weak, 109, 143–147, 181, 186,
            209
    between places, 271

cartels, 80, 205
    market disturbing, 80–81, 335
    price, 168, 186
    process of, 25
    ruinous, 80, 154, 167, 186, 205
    time, 148
complexity, 174–175, 230, 240, 318, 328,
        332
consumer
    unauthorized, 299
    fashion, 160
    income constraints, 168–169
    perception of risk, 327
    preferences, 162, 192, 194
    sovereignty, 164–166
    tastes, 154, 160, 167, 173
consumption, 4, 17, 19–21, 45, 60, 76,
        160, 173, 227, 262, 271, 278, 288,
        290, 304, 318–319
    mass, 154, 163, 194, 312, 320–321
contestation, 5, 39–40, 42, 90, 314
contradictions, 21–22, 52–55, 62, 65, 70,
        91, 218, 222, 229, 261, 312–313,
        322, 331
conventions, 37–38, 158, 210, 285
    territorially bounded, 177
    theory, 37
cooperation, 36, 42
    between firms, 143–215, 262, 279
    between workers, 215–254
corporatism, 61, 67, 246, 275
creative destruction, 25, 147, 268
credit, 70, 87
    unions, 249
crisis, 22, 27, 50, 54, 61–68, 92–93, 261,
        273, 335
    economic, 62, 67, 261, 323, 335,
        local, 282
    environmental, 322–324
    fiscal, 60, 63, 68, 86, 88, 250
    legitimation, 62–63, 86–87, 274
    management, 54, 58–59, 63, 67, 312–
        323, 335
    rationality, 62, 86, 323
    theories, 22–23
critical realism, 7–9, 12, 45, 285, 303
culture, 29, 32, 36, 98, 121–123, 138,
        168, 178–179, 183, 200, 208,
        220–221, 248, 255, 267,
        314
    cultural capital, 113, 163
    cultural turn, 1, 29
    of economics, 38
    of organizations, 31
    of production, 35, 130, 192
    reflexivity of, 314
    regional, 73, 184, 221

deindustrialization, 84
  of localities, 85
demand, 25, 83, 87–88, 108–111, 117–
    119, 130, 136, 152, 156, 159,
    164–169, 191, 195, 198, 211,
    237, 240, 247–249, 274, 300
democracy, 61–63, 68, 76, 84, 90, 101,
    270, 274, 282, 320
departments of production, 22, 129
Dewhirst, 145
dialectal relations, 17, 55, 220
  of class and region, 271
  socionatural, 21, 40–41, 287
  sociospatial, 21, 38–40
dictatorship, 91, 101, 320
discourse, 22, 35, 242, 265, 281, 284,
    297
  theory, 59
distanciation, 144, 211, 257, 326
divisions of labor, 5, 23, 98, 125, 160–
    162, 176, 217–254, 259, 332–
    336
  ethnic, 98, 233–237, 334
  gender, 98, 119, 230–233, 246–247,
    267, 334, 338
  industrial, 98, 225–230, 334
  occupational, 98, 119, 225–230, 334
  social, 17, 134, 142, 163, 175–177,
    192, 217–218, 225–227, 237,
    247, 255, 259
  spatial, 98, 123, 142, 240–244, 255–
    256, 260, 333–336
    intranational, 133, 333–334
    international, 78, 90–91, 102, 133,
    145
  technical, 129, 132–134, 217–218,
    225–227, 237, 332, 335
Du Pont, 126

ecology, 93
  ecological biodiversity, 307
  ecological costs, 294
  ecological modernization, 314, 317,
    337
  eco-estructuring, 320–325
  industrial, 290, 325
ecosystems, 287–289
economies
  diseconomies of scale, 212
  of scale, 153–154, 156–157, 167–
    168, 188, 206–207, 215
  of scope, 89, 156–157, 188, 206
  of time, 148, 153–4
electronic
  commerce, 215, 336
  data interchange (EDI), 195
  highways, 333

point of scale (EPOS), 136, 195
embeddedness, 29, 31, 46, 73, 103, 107,
    124, 150, 172, 177, 184, 188, 191,
    282, 286, 338
  disembeddedness, 283
  social, 36
  territorial, 177–178, 201–203, 247, 262,
    281
embodiment, 31, 112, 138–9, 172
Employees Association of Detroit, 121
employment, 238
  casual, 111, 118–119
  contingent, 134
  destandardization of , 239–240
  female, 110, 118, 153
  full, 133, 250
  full-time, 110, 119
  illegal, 233–234, 245–246, 334
  informal, 245, 321, 334
  part-time, 110, 118–119
  permanent, 111, 119
  precarious, 103, 237–244
  seasonal, 234
  shift systems, 118, 133–135, 146
  temporary, 111, 119
energy, 287–290
  fossil fuels, 288–289, 299–300, 302,
    319
  nuclear, 87, 303, 310, 325, 328
    Chernobyl, 303
  renewable, 289, 319
Enterprise Zones, 277
entropy, 288–289, 325
  maximization, 45
  spatial interaction models, 325
environment, 286, 338
  anthropocentric view of, 314
  ecocentric view of, 314
  environmental determinism, 40, 287
  environmental protest groups, 274, 308–
    309, 315
  environmental technology industries, 317
  environmental valorization, 249
  industrial footprint on, 324
  selection, 179–180
Environmental Protection Agency, 306
epistemology, 1, 6–11, 41
equilibrium, 15, 44, 181
equity, 59, 321, 325
essentialism, 24, 228–229, 256, 262–263
ethnicity, 4, 9, 12, 31, 56, 76, 106, 112,
    232–237, 240, 252, 260, 267
European Community/Union, 57, 71–73,
    80–81, 103, 197, 211, 222, 236,
    241, 272, 317
  Mediterranean, 243, 248
  western, 74, 168

evolution, 314, 332
  evolutionary approaches in social
    science, 3, 12, 28–29, 35, 147,
    170
exploitation, 11, 26, 52, 137, 218, 236,
    264
Export Processing Zones, 121, 277

factory régime, 130, 221, 241
family, 85, 115, 122, 246–248
fascism, 61, 91
  ecofascism, 315
feminism, 13, 31, 283
fetishism
  commodity, 29, 45
  spatial, 17
Fiat, 119
flexibility, 134–135, 146, 156, 194,
    239, 332
  functional, 111, 136, 237
  numerical, 111, 237
Ford Motor Company, 99–100, 108,
    113, 132, 142, 182–183, 235
Fordism, 61, 93, 101, 156, 174, 189,
    221, 330–332
  after-Fordism, 104, 331
  post-Fordism, 1, 61, 93, 330–332
formations
  institutional, 37, 177, 280–281,
    297
  social, 22–26, 29, 49, 53, 230
  sociospatial, 46
  spatial, 256
foundational concepts, 17
"Four Motors" coalition, 272
  new towns, 275–276
Friends of the Earth, 72
functionalism, 51, 59, 85

gender, 4, 9, 12–3, 31, 56, 106, 112–
    113, 116–117, 182–183, 218,
    220, 234, 240, 252, 260, 267
General Agreement on Tariffs and
    Trade, 78
General Motors, 99, 126–127, 148
genetically modified organisms (GMOs),
    286, 300, 326
geography
  behavioral, 15–16, 30, 34
  economic, 26–27
    and moral, 251
    new, 29, 94
  locational analysis in, 14–16
globalization, 42, 68–69, 71, 73–75,
    102, 106, 166–169, 187, 206,
    209, 213, 242, 275, 281, 284,
    299, 333–334

governance, 37–38, 42, 65, 68–76, 97, 167,
    179, 215, 289, 313
  mechanisms in firms, 149, 171
  multilevel, 92, 283, 331, 334–335
  theories of, 3
Greenpeace, 72

habit, 37, 47, 60, 124
Hanson Group, 212
hegemony, 58, 156, 249, 268, 272–273
Honda, 136–137, 198, 302
household, 24, 45, 64, 97, 236, 247, 263
human resource management, 104, 111,
    134, 137–138

identities, 21, 37, 104, 106, 112, 219–221,
    225, 241, 251, 262–268, 273
  and commodity consumption, 163–165
  collective, 23, 98, 217–220, 262
  formation of, 45, 90
  multiple, 31, 40, 228–230
  national, 90
  regionalist, 90
  workers, 138, 141
"imagined communities," 90, 93, 105
Imperial Chemicals Industry, 99, 116, 132,
    182, 211
imperialism, 90, 234
  neoimperialism, 71, 91
industrial districts, 131, 161, 176, 197–
    198, 202–204, 211, 264, 331–
    333
  metabolism, 288, 290–294, 325
inequality, 13, 16, 34, 249, 257, 273, 283,
    315, 336
infant industries, 84
infrastructure, 76, 89
innovation, 25, 73, 82, 120, 147, 190, 192,
    201, 218, 280, 335
  incremental, 159
  institutional, 5, 249, 277, 304
  marketing, 162–166
  management, 135
  organizational 5, 142, 148–150, 154,
    166, 170, 181
  policy, 74
  process, 5, 142, 150–159, 163, 166, 170,
    173–174, 181, 302
  product, 4, 89, 112, 131, 142, 152, 159–
    162, 166, 170, 173–174, 181, 187
  regulatory, 5
  systems of
    national, 175–176, 178
    regional, 176–178
    sectoral, 178
  technical, 88, 298–299, 304, 310, 322–
    324

institutions, 3, 15, 28, 36–38, 52, 55,
    65, 72, 81, 97–98, 101, 123–
    124, 177, 193, 199, 204, 210–
    224, 248, 265–266, 272, 280,
    285, 294–296
  instituted behavior, 36–38
  instituted processes, 41, 281
  institutional approaches in social
    science, 3, 11, 28–29, 36, 47,
    49, 94, 170
  institutional formations, 37, 177,
    280–281, 297
  institutional practices, 102
  institutional sclerosis, 177–178
  institutional thickness, 177, 285
  tissue, 266
intellectual property rights, 82, 147
  patents, 82, 172, 295
interdependencies
  international, 57
  traded, 36
  untraded, 36, 177, 285
International Business Machines (IBM),
    126
International Confederation of Free
    Trade Unions, 105
International Labor Organization, 105,
    219, 245
International Monetary Fund, 69, 72,
    78, 320
International Trades Secretariat, 105
investment 58, 77–86, 103, 110–111,
    150, 263, 271, 283
  disinvestment, 5, 87, 214, 241, 258–
    260, 268
  foreign direct, 94, 207, 209–211
  private sector, 87–90, 103, 119, 150,
    157–161, 201–202, 205–213,
    256, 272, 277
  public sector, 76, 256, 272–282

joint ventures, 171, 180, 205–208
justice
  environmental, 252, 325
  social, 58, 252, 321–322, 325, 337–
    338

Kaizen, 173, 184, 193
Kawasaki, 194
Keiretsu, 122, 167–168, 191, 193, 208,
    215
Keynesianism, 87, 277, 321
  eco-Keynesianism, 321–324
knowledge, 3, 16, 34–36, 51, 82–83,
    111, 126, 201, 252, 301, 303,
    317, 335
  codified, 82, 171–172, 176–178

  company specific, 150, 188
  creation, 161, 169–180
  diffusion, 5
  economy, 175
  embodied, 117, 172
  "know where," 144
  "know who," 175
  place specific, 172
  production, 5, 294
  scientific, 296–297, 324
  tacit, 36, 171–173, 176–178, 184, 201,
    281
Kyonyokukai, 198–199

labor, 3, 42, 51, 88, 144. *See also*
    migration; recruitment and
    retention
  abstract, 18, 45, 224–225
  aristocracy, 105–106, 136
  child, 110, 145, 245
  cost, 102–103, 108–109
  extended, 226–227
  "green," 104, 114, 136, 152
  landscapes of, 42, 248
  placeless, 248
  process, 2, 17, 41–43, 97–99, 101, 124–
    140, 148, 294, 297–298
    intensification of, 128–129, 133, 136–
    137, 148, 244
    porosity of, 128–129
  productive, 253
  time, 127
    socially necessary, 18, 133, 151, 154,
    174, 182
  unproductive, 253
Labor-Management Relations (Taft Hartley)
    Act 1947, 223
labor-power, 7, 18–20, 43, 50, 76, 82, 85,
    98–99, 110, 120, 123, 219, 224–
    225, 227, 246, 250, 263–267, 274,
    282, 299
  price of, 107–109
  reproduction of, 246–247, 321, 334
  value of, 129
learning, 3, 5, 34–36, 82, 122, 149, 160–
    161, 168–180, 201, 328
  by-doing, 170
  by-interacting, 36, 170, 203
  by-searching, 170
  by-using, 170
  double loop, 170–171
  firms, 35, 150, 281
  product-based technological, 152, 177,
    204
  regions, 35, 176–177, 203–204, 281
  single loop, 170–171
legitimation, 57–58, 60, 84, 91

life cycle
   analysis of, 288, 290–292, 317
   process, 147, 335
   product, 147, 160–161, 165, 214,
      335
limits
   natural limits to production, 41
   to growth, 301, 304, 316
   (neo)Mathusian, 301
Local Exchange Trading Systems
      (LETS), 249
localities, 84–85, 96, 102, 204, 221,
      281–282, 308
   pro-active, 242
long waves (of capitalist development),
      57, 93

management, 148
   command and control, 120, 126,
      134, 199, 201, 277, 333
   structures of, 122, 125–127
      decentralization, 126–127
      dual, 148–149, 179
      hierarchical, 126, 138, 149, 170,
         180, 188, 200
      networked. See networks
manufacturing industries
   agribusiness, 179
   aircraft, 206
   American system A, 125, 132, 153
   automobiles, 108, 114–115, 122,
      154, 188, 192–194, 198, 232
   chemicals, 108, 154, 179, 182, 194,
      201, 306–309
   clothing and textiles, 110, 136, 152–
      154, 166, 189, 195, 212, 231–
      236
   computer integrated, 157, 161
   computers, 158, 188, 191, 194, 207,
      214
   consumer goods, 154, 163, 193
   electronics, 168, 194, 210
   engineering, 116, 122
   film, 204
   food, 136, 195
   "high tech," 86, 131, 158, 191, 210
   integrated circuits, 103, 131, 188,
      285, 300
   iron and steel, 122, 144, 154, 168,
      182, 188, 194, 201, 284
   paper and pulp, 290–292, 325–326
   pharmaceuticals, 179, 208
   shipbuilding, 116, 122
   shoe, 145, 189
   telecommunications equipment, 191,
      214
   "white goods," 154, 169, 195

markets, 17–18, 25–28, 117–118, 170,
      180, 188–189, 206–207, 211–212,
      291–293, 296, 301–312
   barriers to entry, 173, 215
   creation of, 162–166, 181–183, 227
   deregulation, 208
   disturbance of, 147, 162, 171, 181, 206,
      335
   knowledge, 82–83, 172–173
   labor, 82–83, 96–97, 102, 108, 116–124,
      133, 158–159, 172, 189, 214, 222,
      254, 310
      intermediate, 248–250
      segmentation, 98, 104, 117, 218, 237,
         335
   market shaping policies, 80–81, 327
   product, 133, 157–158
      customization, 159–160, 168
      homogenization, 166–167
      segmentation, 126, 135, 159–160,
         165, 194, 327
   race to, 160–161, 210
   structures, 166–169
Marks and Spencer, 145, 196
Marxian political economy, 1–30, 38, 49,
      94, 139, 226, 253, 268, 333
mass collective worker, 101
materials transformation, 21, 286–329
   dematerialization of economy, 319–322
   materials balance principle, 290–294,
      303
   process, 2
Mazda, 122, 184
McDonalds, 134, 192
meaning, 21, 28, 46, 177, 262–263, 267,
      282
   codes of, 172
   of commodities, 163–165, 173
   multiple, 40, 255, 273
mental maps, 16
mergers, 6, 142, 149, 180, 187, 208–213
meta-narrative, 1, 7, 9
methodology, 1–3, 6–11, 41
   methodological individualism, 30
Mexico, 133, 219, 311
migration, 77, 248, 253, 259, 266, 284
   "body shopping," 123
   illegal, 233–234, 243–244, 264
   permanent, 83, 119–120, 123, 233–234,
      259
   policies, 83
   temporary labor, 83, 123, 146, 181–182,
      233–234, 236, 253–254
Ministry of International Trade and
      Industry, 216
Mitsubishi, 194
Mitsui, 194

mode of production, 17–18, 22–26, 29–
30, 49
articulation of, 29, 230
capitalist, 27–28, 55, 230
mode of regulation, 59–60, 64, 67, 74,
77, 330–335, 337–338
local, 285
monetarism, 88
money, 17–18, 69–70, 273
inflation, 63
monoindustrial settlements,. 250, 259,
267, 269, 283–284
motives, 34–36, 62, 70
multinational companies, 91, 94, 106,
109, 145, 167, 193, 198, 202,
205, 243, 258, 275, 281
embedded performance plants, 281
global outposts, 276–277

national
national interests, 90–91, 186, 213,
241
problematicization of, 334–335
nationalism, 70, 284
states, 56–58, 68–95, 184, 255, 268,
330, 334–336
hollowing out of, 42, 68–77, 86,
94, 276
reorganization of, 68–76, 277
National Labor Relations Board, 223
nationalization, 48, 62, 84, 269
NATO, 91
nature, 76, 139, 283, 286–329
capitalizing, 296–298
natural limits to production, 287–
289, 297
natural resources, 300–303
first, 295–298, 324
second, 295–298, 302, 324
outflanking, 286–287, 298–299, 326
production of, 294–298
neoclassical economics, 12, 14–16, 26,
30, 34, 44, 46, 181, 184, 214,
293
neoliberalism, 67, 75, 83, 85, 167, 271,
277, 321
networks, 179, 266, 273, 313
associational, 191
between firms, 81, 161, 175–176,
186, 200–204
friends and family, 115–116
interpersonal, 117
managerial, 127
of alliances, 205–206
partnerships, 157, 196
state, 74
within firms, 185, 200

Nike, 145
NIMBYism, 311
Nissan, 142, 215
norms, 10, 31, 37, 60, 83–85, 98, 112,
138, 151–152, 171, 175, 193, 205
North American Free Trade Area, 208

organizations, 53, 97–107
Osram, 146
othering, 217, 252
ozone layer, 307–308, 318

paternalism, 108, 121, 125, 132, 184, 231,
234, 264
neopaternalism, 104, 119–120
path dependency, 35, 170, 180, 203
patriarchy, 230–232, 244, 267
performativity, 31–32, 112–113, 138–139
Philips, 126
Pilkington, 176
place, 5, 39–40, 56, 123, 187, 220, 255–
286, 338
attachment to, 146, 241, 262–268, 270,
274–275
based, 222, 270
militant particularizms, 268–270,
338
bound, 122, 222, 247–248, 270
construction of, 252
discursive, 265–266, 268
material, 255, 258–262
defending, 268–272, 274
marketing, 90, 242, 271, 278, 336
placelessness, 265, 284
places for themselves, 268
places in themselves, 268
(re)presenting, 268–272
sense of, 120, 262–268
erasure of, 272
pollution, 56, 286, 290, 293, 297, 303–
313, 316–317, 319
chlorofluorocarbons (CFCs), 308, 318
consumption, 291
dioxin, 306, 326
dissipative, 291, 304
export of, 310–311
externalities, 293, 305–306, 327
greenhouse gases, 307–308, 312, 324,
328
methyl isocyanate, 306
production, 291
sulphur dioxide, 307, 310
trading permits, 79, 304, 312
positionality, 10, 24
postindustrial economy, 115, 330–334
postmodernization, 13, 183
poverty, 16, 88, 323

power, 11, 34, 51, 56, 58, 138, 142,
    229, 232, 263
  asymmetries, 33, 99, 188, 191–193,
    200, 213, 268, 275
  empowerment, 138, 249
  relations, 30–34
  social, 17, 70, 252
  state, 48, 55, 270
    architecture of, 68
  structural, 47
practices, 177, 200, 255, 265–267, 300
  communities of, 36, 170–171, 173,
    179, 184
  labor, 223–224
  logistics, 194
  political, 337–338
  racial discriminatory, 233–234, 237
  sociospatial, 39
  trade union, 219–220, 234, 239
prices, 22–26, 35, 189, 192, 196, 293
  setting of, 167–168, 189
product
  development, 35
  differentiation, 35, 126, 131
  symbolic, 82
production
  automation of, 199, 156, 161, 182
  batch, 169, 330–331
  clean, 317–319, 322
  continuous flowline, 153–154, 194,
    201, 215
  craft, 130–131, 169
  cycle times, 153, 156
  dynamically flexible, 154, 157
  eco-restructuring of, 316–324
  flexibly specialized, 121, 157, 166,
    174
  forces of, 261, 284, 294
  just-in-time, 104, 114, 134–137, 192–
    196, 201–202, 215
  mass, 101–104, 114, 123, 125, 132–
    134, 137, 147–148, 151–160,
    163, 168, 189, 215, 232, 312,
    320–321
  mass customization, 147, 152, 159,
    168–169, 335
  of process, 149, 152, 335
  means of, 158, 193
  new high volume, 102–103, 114–115,
    121–123, 134–137, 151–152,
    156–157, 160, 167, 169, 174,
    202, 215, 221, 330–331
  of signs, 164
  over production, 168
  politics, 124, 221
  roundaboutness of, 332, 338
  technological paradigms of, 150–159

profit, 2, 4, 18–21, 25, 39, 41, 50, 53,
    102, 124, 137, 143, 158, 252, 258,
    261–264, 269, 274, 276, 280–281,
    294–295, 298, 301, 314, 317, 320–
    321, 324, 328
  falling rate of, 53
  repatriation, 320
  super, 168
  surplus, 151
property relations, 49, 53, 301
proximity
  cultural, 184
  organizational, 201
  spatial, 162, 175, 184, 201
psychology, 16
  cognitive, 28
  psychometric tests, 114

rationality
  actor, 34–5
  bounded, 16, 44, 190
  crisis. See crisis
  varieties of, 34–35
recruitment and retention of labor, 97, 103,
    109–124, 146, 217
  recruitment criteria, 111–115
  recruitment mechanisms, 115–118
    interpersonal networks, 115–117
    market mechanisms, 117–118
    state agencies, 118
  spatial variations in, 118–124
redundancy, 136
régime of accumulation, 59–60, 64–65, 67,
    330–334
regional
  exceptionalism, 47
  regionalism, 70, 73
regulation, 48, 68–76, 97–107, 206, 222
  environmental, 308–313, 317
    global, 312–313
  international, 71, 209, 327–328
  real, 64, 79
  regulationist approaches, 47, 92–93, 330
    French, 59–60
    limits to, 61–68
  regulatory régimes, 38–39, 74, 110, 147,
    184, 198–200, 208, 241, 246, 271,
    289, 293, 313, 317–318, 321–325,
    330–338
  social, 36–38
  theories of, 3, 37
reification, 32, 239
relational
  approaches to conceptualizing space,
    256–260
  assets, 177–178
  contracting, 190–200

representation, 103, 105, 267, 296
  of class interests, 97–107
  of place, 268–272, 275
  representational practices, 68
  representational spaces, 100
  representational struggle, 60
  scales of, 222
research and development, 4, 109, 120,
      160, 167, 171, 174, 180, 186,
      192–193, 206–210, 213
  linear model of, 161, 173–174
risk, 160, 168, 206, 212, 237–239, 266,
      297, 307, 311, 314, 325, 327
  environmental, 56, 286
  precautionary principle, 320
  society, 239
rules, 31, 37, 76, 80–81, 85, 112, 131,
      171, 177, 187, 199–201, 205,
      287

semiotic domination, 296–297
services, 110–111, 134–135, 330–334
  banking, 112, 116–118, 132, 161–
      162, 212
  business, 278, 332
  call centers, 271
  catering, 212
  cleaning, 212
  conceptualization of, 226–227
  contract cleaning, 111
  design, 156, 226
  financial, 111, 132, 150, 161–162,
      226, 278, 332
  fusion with material goods, 165, 188,
      332
  occupations, 31, 112
  private, 277
  producer, 209, 278, 332
  public, 233
  retailing, 110–111, 138–139, 194–
      195, 269
  security, 212
  software, 131, 188
  tourism, 113, 138–139, 160, 271,
      284
Sloan, Alfred P., 126–127
small firms, 197–198, 269, 271, 277
  new formation of, 161
social
  cohesion, 57, 60, 247–249, 282
  economy, 249–250
  formations, 22–26, 29, 49, 53, 230
  limits to the unnaturalness of
      production, 287
  process, 14–15, 28–41
    and spatial form, 26
  reproduction, 48–95

socialism, 230, 270, 283–284
  eco–, 337–338
  state, 320, 324, 327–329
space, 5, 187, 255–285, 338
  cyber, 255, 278, 333, 336
  of resistance, 4
  of surveillance and control, 125
  production of, 296
  relational approach to, 256–257, 262
  social, 255
spatial
  cohesion, 282
  fix, 6, 102, 130, 141, 144, 290, 308–312
  formation, 256
  scale, 36, 65, 68, 99, 160, 222, 313,
      334–336
state, 22, 27, 37, 42, 118, 187, 246, 291,
      336
  basic, 74
  capitalist, 48–95
  catalytic, 74–75
  derivation theory, 23, 49–56, 91
  enabling, 75, 281, 335
  interventionist, 61, 67, 74–75, 84–86
  liberal, 61, 67, 74, 85–87
  overloaded, 66–67
  policies
    demand management, 87
    land use, 308, 319, 324
    spatial, 272, 282
    regional, 84, 89, 274–276
    urban, 89, 274, 276
    strategic industrial, 80–81, 88, 150,
        213
    welfare, 85, 250, 266
    workfare, 250
  postcolonial, 84
  theories of, 3, 42
State Monopoly Capital, 22, 51
strategic alliances, 171, 187, 205–208,
      213
strikes, 91, 100–101, 114, 122, 133, 269
  British coal miners 1984/5, 90, 270
  French steel workers 1979/80, 91, 169
  unofficial, 101
structuralism
  post-structuralism, 1, 24, 31
structure, 16–17, 30–34, 39, 52, 59, 218
  bearers of, 22, 27
  social, 26
  structural analysis, 10
  structural dependence, 319–320
  structural determination, 11
  structuration theory, 30–33
structure of feeling, 267–268
structured coherence, 225, 266, 268, 273,
      282

subcontracting, 86, 103, 124, 134, 157,
        189, 238–239, 242–243, 331–
        332, 335
    hierarchical, 191
    systemic, 191
Sumitomo, 194, 215
sunk costs, 6, 103, 109, 123–124, 149,
        159
supply, 25, 111, 129, 135, 151, 162,
        167, 209, 231, 246–248, 304,
        324, 335
    architecture of, 79–84, 177
    strategies, 187–200
supply chain, 134, 188, 192, 196–197,
        201, 214
    e-to-e business, 215, 336
    first tier suppliers, 193, 196, 202
    hybrid forms of, 196
    input/output relations, 201
    screening of suppliers, 193
    structure of, 193–194
surplus-value, 17, 41, 70, 124, 141–
        142, 160, 165, 244, 323, 333
    absolute, 128–129
    rate of, 129
    relative, 129, 142
sustainability
    ecological, 252
    of production, 41, 249, 303–325,
        330, 336–338
    strong, 315
    weak, 315
symbolism, 29, 45, 163, 173, 226, 263
    symbolic exchange, 46

take-overs, 142
taxation, 60, 63, 293, 304, 318–319,
        322
Taylorism, 101–102, 119, 123, 132–
        134, 137–138, 157–158, 160,
        173, 278
    "bloody," 133–134
    neo-Taylorism, 130
    scientific management, 132
technological
    change, 151
    conveyance, 172
    fixes, 301–302, 317–318
        recycling, 302–303, 311, 317–319
        materials substitution, 302, 314,
            326
    rents, 152, 154, 210
    technology districts, 152, 176, 204
territorial social bloc, 268, 271
theory, 1–3, 6–11, 14–47
    adequacy of, 6–7, 44, 65
    critical, 11

nonrepresentational, 10
    of structuration, 30–33
    social, 28
    theoretical practice, 338
thermodynamics
    laws of, 41, 287–289, 296, 324, 327
time-space
    compression, 160, 184, 253, 258, 333,
        336
    dislocation of agricultural production,
        299–300
    envelopes, 258
Toyota, 137, 148, 156, 182–183, 302
trade, 58, 259, 304
    associations, 205, 216
    in waste products, 310–312, 317
trade unions, 39, 46, 62, 83–84, 88, 98–
        107, 111, 114–115, 131, 135, 140,
        217–224, 230–232, 240–242, 251,
        266, 330, 335–336
    absence of, 189
    and codetermination, 83
    company, 98
    General Municipal and Boilermakers,
        105
    geographies of, 141, 221
    IG Chemie, 105
    Iron and Steel Trades Confederation, 107
    National Union of Mineworkers, 270
    single union deals, 135–136
    social movement unionism, 106–107,
        219–220, 335–336
    Transport and General Workers, 235
    Union of Democratic Mineworkers, 270
transaction costs, 149, 188–189, 214
transformation problem, 25
trust, 36, 122, 137–138, 175, 188, 191–
        192, 196, 198–199, 203, 206, 213,
        215, 264, 279

uncertainty, 36, 49, 169–170, 188, 314,
        317
unemployment, 104, 120–121, 135–136,
        250, 276
    high, 121–122, 136, 223
    permanent, 336
unequal exchange, 323–324
uneven development, 2, 16, 28, 334–338
    combined and, 71, 230
    spatial, 39, 90, 262, 272–282, 312–313,
        322–324
    territorially, 27
unintended consequences, 22, 27, 41, 220,
        275, 285, 298, 300, 302–312, 327
Union Carbide, 306
United Nations, 91, 315, 328
Urban Development Corporations, 277

value, 11, 17–18, 22–26, 70, 127–128, 294
  analysis, 28
  creation process, 243
  exchange, 18–20, 172, 273, 286, 296
  law of, 26–27, 61, 296
  use, 18–20, 41, 46, 89, 172, 273, 286, 294, 296
vertical integration, 125–127, 158–159, 188, 200, 211, 331
  vertical disintegration, 158, 200, 331
  quasi, 161
virtual enterprises, 149–150, 173–174
  concept teams, 173
Volkswagen, 115, 219
Volvo, 130

wages, 25, 50, 53, 83, 98, 145, 181, 249, 268, 274
  low, 121, 153
  methods of wage determination, 107–109
  performance related, 103, 108
  relation, 17
wastes, 41, 291, 300, 304–305, 316–317
William Baird, 196–197
workplace, 30, 50, 61, 136
  "frontier of control," 125, 130
  workplace, 98, 222, 256

work
  artisanal, 119
  conditions, 98
  control, 127–140
    responsible autonomy, 131–132, 139, 142, 264
  craft, 99, 116, 119, 125, 132, 169, 174, 243
  deskilled, 110
  homework, 107, 110–111, 118–119, 189, 239, 242–243, 246, 334
  informal, 145, 245–246
    "bloody informalization," 145
  multiskilled, 237
  multitasked, 135
  organization of, 124–140, 148
  piecework, 107
  skilled, 99, 110
  socially necessary, 248
  team work, 108, 114–115, 138, 170–172
  unskilled, 99
  unwaged, 97, 122, 220, 244–246, 249, 324
  waged, 220, 230, 244
works councils, 83, 98, 103
  European, 105, 241
World Bank, 72, 320, 323
World Federation of Trade Unions, 106
World Trade Organization, 72, 253
worlds of production, 9, 37, 47
  regional, 177

About the Author

Ray Hudson, PhD, is Professor of Geography and Chairman of the International Centre for Regional Regeneration and Development Studies at the University of Durham, England. He holds the degree of BA, PhD, and DSc from Bristol University and an Honorary DSc from Roskilde University. He is a Fellow and past vice president of the Royal Geographical Society. He is the author of numerous scientific articles and books, including *Wrecking a Region: State Policies, Party Politics and Regional Change in North East England* (1989); *Divided Europe: Society and Territory* (with Allan Williams, 1999); *Production, Places and Environment: Changing Perspectives in Economic Geography* (2000); and *Digging Up Trouble: The Environment, Protest and Opencast Coal Mining* (with Huw Beynon and Andrew Cox, 2000).